STUDIES IN THE ARAMAIC LEGAL PAPYRI FROM ELEPHANTINE

HANDBOOK OF ORIENTAL STUDIES
HANDBUCH DER ORIENTALISTIK

SECTION ONE

THE NEAR AND MIDDLE EAST

EDITED BY

H. ALTENMÜLLER · B. HROUDA · B.A. LEVINE · R.S. O'FAHEY
K.R. VEENHOF · C.H.M. VERSTEEGH

VOLUME SIXTY-SIX

STUDIES IN THE ARAMAIC LEGAL PAPYRI FROM ELEPHANTINE

BY

YOCHANAN MUFFS

with Prolegomenon by Baruch A. Levine

BRILL
LEIDEN • BOSTON
2003

This book is printed on acid-free paper.

Library of Congress Cataloging-in-Publication Data

Muffs, Yochanan.
Studies in the Aramaic legal papyri from Elephantine / by Yochanan Muffs ; with prolegomenon by Baruch A. Levine.
p. cm. -- (Studia et documenta ad iura Orientis antiqui pertinentia ; v. 8) (Handbook of Oriental studies. Section 1, Near and Middle East ; v. 66 = Handbuch der Orientalistik)
Includes bibliographical references and index.
ISBN 9004128689 (hc)
1. Law--Middle East--History--To 1500--Sources. 2. Law--Egypt--Elephantine--History--To 1500--Sources. 3. Manuscripts, Aramaic (Papyri)--Egypt--Elephantine. 4. Law, Ancient--Sources. 5. Jewish law--History--Sources. I. Levine, Baruch A. II. Title. III. Studia et documenta ad jura Orientis antiqui pertinentia ; v. 8 IV. Handbuch der Orientalistik. Erste Abteilung, Nahe und der Mittlere Osten ; 66. Bd.

KL190 .M84 2002
340.5'3--dc21

2002190844

Die Deutsche Bibliothek – CIP-Einheitsaufnahme

Studies in the Aramaic legal papyri from Elephantine / by Yochanan Muffs; with prolegomenon by Baruch A. Levine.
Leiden ; Boston : Brill, 2002
(Handbook of oriental studies: Sect. 1, The Near and Middle East; Vol. 66)
ISBN 9004 128 689

ISSN 0169-9423
ISBN 90 04 12868 9

PRINTED IN THE NETHERLANDS

TO MY PARENTS

CONTENTS

PROLEGOMENON

Baruch A. Levine
Emeritus, New York University

In 1969, E. J. Brill published the important monograph by Yohanan Muffs on the Aramaic legal papyri from Elephantine of Egypt. It represented a significantly reworked and amplified version of his Phd Dissertation, accomplished several years earlier, and at the time was hailed as a brilliant cross-cultural study. It was my privilege to be one of its reviewers (Levine 1975). New discoveries of ancient documents, and significant advances in Near Eastern scholarship during the past thirty years or so have revived interest in Aramaic law, prompting Brill to reissue Muffs' earlier work. It is an honor for me, as a colleague and friend of Yochanan Muffs for many years, and as one who shares many of his interests, to write a *Prolegomenon* to the new printing. In retrospect, Muffs' study emerges as forward-looking in its hypotheses, and remains stimulating because of the many questions it raises, some of which can now be engaged afresh with the benefit of new evidence, and the insights of intervening investigations. In the history of modern scholarship there have been certain, special works that have retained their value with the passage of time, and this can surely be said of *Studies in the Aramaic Legal Papyri from Elephantine.*

Muffs' monograph demands a great deal from the reader; it is not a systematic outline of the legal system predicated in the Aramaic papyri from Elephantine. Rather, it is a penetrating probe of a few, telling formulas, and an analysis of certain features of the documents, in the course of which Muffs engages just about every aspect of the Elephantine legal papyri, and much more. On the basis of the analysis Muffs offers, and the broad range of sources he has examined, one should be able to construct a systematic outline, but Muffs doesn't do this for us. His approach is to proceed from the specific to the general, building block by block, until the outlines of a model just begin to appear, but aren't formulated as such. Every detail contributes to the larger context, which can be generated by exploring intersections and interactions between the formulas under discussion and other components, all of which combine to give legal documents their overall form. In a word, Muffs leaves synthesis to the diligent reader, who must make the effort to dig out of this jam-packed monograph the insight and information needed for an overview.

The difference between an in-depth probe of the Elephantine legal system and an outline of it may be illustrated by contrasting Muffs' work with Reuben Yaron's earlier book, *Introduction to the Law of the Aramaic Papyri* (1961). Yaron, a historian of law, presents just such an overview of the legal system operative at Elephantine; he organizes the data in accordance with legal models. On the surface of it, Yaron's work impresses one as exceedingly useful, in that it answers basic questions of importance about the distinctive features of Elephantine law. In a deeper sense, however, Muffs' study proves to be more enlightening, because it delineates an applicable methodology for studying Aramaic law, based on the analysis of specific features. I suppose it depends on which is more valuable for scholarship, the exploration of questions, or the presentation of factual answers.

More recently, we have benefited greatly from a Phd Dissertation by Eleonora Cussini, entitled *The Aramaic Law of Sale and the Cuneiform Legal Tradition* (1993). Her work is a comparative investigation of the development of one branch of Aramaic law, the law of sale. This is considered as a legal construct, both as part of the ongoing Aramaic tradition, and against the more extensive background of cuneiform law. Cussini's study encompasses all of the major Aramaic sources, beginning with the Elephantine corpus, through the Samaria Papyri of the 4th century B.C.E., to the Judean Desert papyri of the early Roman period (Murabbaʿat and Naḥal Ḥever), and concluding with Dura Europus and Palmyra. Elephantine law comes in for extensive discussion. Drawing upon Muffs' earlier study at many points, Cussini excels at weaving his individual insights into her systematic treatment of the Elephantine materials.

After reviewing the state of current research, Cussini presents an in-depth philological and juridical commentary to the texts, including a chapter on "Aramaic Sale Transactions and the Mesopotamian Legal Tradition" (168-210), in which she deals with the sale document as a coherent genre, analyzing its formulation and provisions clause by clause, always with an eye to the Assyriological background. Rather than probing a few test cases, she takes the whole text as her point of departure, striving to arrive at broader conclusions regarding the overall relationship between Aramaic law and cuneiform law. The Dissertation concludes with a concise summary of comparative findings.

Background

It would be well to preface some information on the provenance of the corpus of Aramaic legal papyri from Elephantine, the very material Muffs has subjected to study, anticipating the more detailed discussion that will follow. A military colony of Jewish mercenaries in the service of the Persian empire lived on this small island near Syene (in Arabic, Aswan) at the first cataract of the Nile. This was a border area dividing lower (= northern) Egypt from upper (= southern) Egypt, which made it an important outpost of the Persian Empire. The Persian king, Cambyses, invaded Egypt in 525 B.C.E., and his successor, Darius, subsequently consolidated Persian rule over the country. The garrison colony at Elephantine, which included the families of the soldiers, flourished throughout most of the fifth century B.C.E., and was organized by units under the command of Persian officers. It remains uncertain as to where the Jews of Elephantine came from, but it is likely that they were settled in Elephantine pursuant to the Persian invasion. Just before Yochanan Muffs' monograph appeared, Bezalel Porten published his historical work, *Archives from Elephantine; The Life of an Ancient Jewish Military Colony* (1968), which has been followed by his other works, to be discussed as we proceed.

Rich troves of ancient papyri in several languages, and covering a period of about three thousand years, have been retrieved at Elephantine. A sense of Elephantine's cultural treasures can be gained from perusing the impressive compendium prepared by Bezalel Porten and his associates, *The Elephantine Papyri in English; Three Millennia of Cross-cultural Continuity and Change* (Leiden; E. J. Brill, 1996). In addition to the Elephantine Aramaic papyri, presented by Bezalel Porten, himself, there are very ancient hieratic texts (Gunter Vittmann); Demotic texts, dating from the very beginning of the sixth century B.C.E. to 11 C.E. (Cary J. Martin); Greek texts, dating from 310 B.C.E. to 613 C.E. (B. Porten and J. J. Farber); and Coptic texts, whose precise dates are not registered (Leslie S. B. MacCoull and Sarah J.Clackson). Two Arabic legal texts are edited by Simon Hopkins, and two Latin personnel lists from the second half of the 3rd century C.E. are presented by Ranon Katzoff.

From the fifth century B.C.E., we have a substantial corpus of Aramaic papyri produced by the Jewish residents of the Persian military colony, including letters, legal documents, copies of literary compositions, like Ahiqar, and other sorts of texts. An active Jewish temple stood in Elephantine. The specifically legal papyri, eventually numbering more than forty, relate to the personal and business affairs of Jewish families, and of the community, as a whole. Bezalel Porten began the task of re-editing this material as early as 1968, at first together with Jonas C. Greenfield, producing a collaborative effort, *Jews of Elephantine and Aramaeans of Syene (Fifth Century B.C.E.): Fifty Aramaic Texts with Hebrew and English Translations* (1974). This publication was to set the pattern for Porten's full series of editions of almost all of the Aramaic texts from Egypt, in collaboration with

Ada Yardeni, entitled: *Textbook of Aramaic Documents from Ancient Egypt* (1986-1999, Vols. I-IV; abbreviated as *TAD*). This is a Hebrew-English publication; the texts have been collated, producing valuable new readings, and have been recopied by Ada Yardeni, whose hand drawings are also included. The Aramaic texts are presented first in Hebrew script, with full apparatus and bibliography, then translated into both academic Hebrew and English, with additional information being provided in both languages. Volume II (= *TAD* II, 1989) is entitled *Contracts*, and it is this edition that will be cited here most frequently.

It merits mention that the grammatical investigation of Empire Aramaic (in French: *l'Araméen de l'Empire*, in German: *Reichsaramaïsch*), or "official Aramaic," the phase of the language employed in the Elephantine papyri, has advanced considerably since the 1960's, as has the study of Aramaic, generally. Margaretha Folmer has written a comprehensive, and penetrating grammatical work, *The Aramaic Language of the Achaemenid Period: A Study in Linguistic Variation* (1995). Folmer goes far beyond the descriptiveness so typical of grammars to discuss such subjects as etymology and the utilization of diverse spellings. Distribution as a variable factor is discussed with respect to choice of vocabulary, and there is a pronounced focus on syntactic structures. One will find detailed analyses of selected texts, and, most relevant to the present discussion, a section of the conclusions entitled: "Possible origins of the official variety of Aramaic from the Achaemenid period" (6: 7, on pages 746-750). Folmer's conclusion is that the official Aramaic of this period is of mixed derivation, exhibiting features of the official Aramaic of the Neo-Assyrian period and of the Neo-Babylonian period. Survivals of western Old Aramaic are to be found in poetic texts, and "fossilized contexts." The point to be made is that any attempted historical reconstruction of Aramaic law must take into account linguistic developments reflected in the relevant texts, and this enterprise has progressed noticeably in recent decades.

If the history of Aramaic as a language is basic to tracing the history of Aramaic law, then the valuable study by Stephen Kaufman, *The Akkadian Influences on Aramaic* (1974) has greatly clarified the extent of lexicographical interpenetration between the two languages. Kaufman has carefully investigated the proposed borrowings from Akkadian into Aramaic, questioning some, dismissing others, and pointing out that there were Aramaic borrowings into Akkadian, as well. All of this is done with attention to phonetic and dialectal factors, producing a clear overview. Kaufman is often able to pinpoint just when transfers occurred, and his study carries us into the later development of the Aramaic dialects.

In 1991, there appeared *An Aramaic Bibliography, Part I: Old, Official, and Biblical Aramaic*, edited by Joseph A. Fitzmyer, S.J., and Stephen A. Kaufman (1991). This reference work, which contains an extensive section on the Elephantine archive, is a publication of an ongoing enterprise, *The Comprehensive Aramaic Lexicon* project. It is heavily annotated, and organizes the material in several overlapping systems, including an alphabetic listing by author. To show how this Bibliography can be utilized, let us open to the entries under "Greenfield, J. C." (*References*, 242-245). We are introduced to the enormous contribution of Jonas G. Greenfield, a prolific and foremost Aramaist. His definitive publication of the Bisitun inscription of Darius I, with Bezalel Porten (Greenfield, Porten 1982), has elucidated official terminology, and his many studies in the area of Aramaic linguistics and lexicography, covering virtually all phases, dialects, and periods of the language, have greatly clarified the history of Aramaic law.

Themes, Issues and Approach

The Aramaic legal papyri, when studied together with the letters and other Aramaic texts, have proved to be of singular importance in several respects. To some, their primary value lies precisely in the somewhat curious fact that they document the life of an exceptional Jewish community, living in the Egyptian interior. To Muffs, operating within a broader perspective, they offered an unprecedented opportunity to explore the formation of Aramaic law. From them, we learn something basic about the Aramaic common law tradition, which was shared by many diverse peoples, and which eventually impacted later Jewish and Islamic law.

The present *Prolegomenon* will take up several themes and issues basic to Muffs monograph, and it might be helpful to introduce these at the outset in a general fashion. It was the main thrust of Muffs' inquiry to trace the origins of the Aramaic legal terms and formularies, of which the Elephantine documents are composed, through utilizing the extensive, comparative evidence available from cuneiform sources, applying what he calls "the Assyriological approach." This approach proceeds from the hypothesis that in large part, Aramaic law was conditioned by Syro-Mesopotamian, cuneiform legal traditions, of both east, and west-Semitic provenance, and that it exhibits many cognates, calques, and semantic equivalents of Akkadian terms and formulas. The links are not merely linguistic and formal, but substantive: Aramaic law incorporates features and principles that are characteristic of cuneiform law which preceded it. Muffs treats the Elephantine corpus as the product of a long development in the history of ancient Near

Eastern law, seeking to discover how these documents attained their form and substance; and to know where their ingredients came from.

Muffs' approach is, therefore, essentially comparative, just as it is primarily diachronic. Nevertheless, Muffs is not indifferent to features of contemporary, late Neo-Babylonian law that may have impacted the Aramaic legal system of the Persian period synchronically. Nor is Muffs indifferent to later developments in Aramaic law that preserve features operative at Elephantine. Muffs' monograph is dotted with brief discussions of the continuity of cuneiform law, often mediated by Aramaic law, and of its eventual legacy in Rabbinic literature. It is accurate to state, all the same, that Muffs' overriding interest, at this stage, is retrospective; he is enchanted by the survival of old locutions and formulas, analyzing the semantic equivalents that replaced them at various periods. In fact, the principal subject of his monograph is an Aramaic legal formula which is equivalent in meaning and function to an Akkadian cognate known in Old Babylonian documents of the early second millennium B.C.E. The formula on which Muffs focused is the 1st person Aramaic טיב לבבי (= *ṭîb libĕḇî*) "My heart is satisfied," which is cognate with the Old Babylonian, Akkadian 3rd person formula: *libbašu ṭāb* "His heart is satisfied." Aramaic טיב לבבי occurs frequently in the Aramaic legal texts from Elephantine, having several functions, most often that of a quittance formula pursuant to receipt of full payment. Of this, more is to come.

Given the fact that we are dealing with documents that were composed in Egypt, it was also important for Muffs to examine similar formulas attested in Egyptian legal documents, including those in Demotic, to determine whether there was input from Egyptian legal traditions on Aramaic law. Chapter six is accordingly entitled: "The Egyptian Analogues of Ṭyb Lbby" (Muffs, 142-172), In his Conclusion, Muffs attempts to bring the three traditions—Assyriological, Aramaic, and Demotic—to bear on each other, conceding the enormous difficulties involved. In the end, he comes down on the side of the Assyriological approach (see below, in the section entitled: *The Language of Law*).

As Muffs has written more than once over the years, there is poetry in legal formulation. He became sensitive to the subtle, semantic transactions predicated in the ostensibly cut-and-dry legalese of business documents. He understood the semiotics of legal usage, the organic integrity of language which allows for modulation, from one context to another. In the choice of his topic, Muffs was making a statement about the language of law; he was conveying his understanding that legal formulas are not artificial, although they may often sound that way, but rather symbolic, metaphorical, and figurative. It is not surprising that what Muffs was able to discern in the development of Aramaic law has actually clarified the meaning of certain legal formulas in Akkadian and Demotic, as well. Such are the rewards of the comparative method, when applied properly.

Muffs observed that emotive phrases translate into both non-volitional and volitional legal formulas. An example of a consistently volitional formula which Muffs investigates is Akkadian *ina ḫūd libbišu* "in the joy of his heart," expressing willingness, whereas Muffs discovered that Akkadian *libbašu ṭāb* "His heart is satisfied," and Aramaic טיב לבבי "My heart is satisfied" are not volitional, or simply consensual in immediate context, as most previous investigators of these formulas had concluded. Muffs' demonstrated that in discrete legal sequences, and within certain types of documents, Akkadian *libbašu ṭāb* and Aramaic טיב לבבי connote substantial "satisfaction." Now, the utilization of an emotive phrase as a legal formula expressing willingness and agreement requires less of a leap, on the face of it, than does the utilization of an emotive phrase as a non-volitional, operative statement that is needed to clinch the deal, so to speak. The formulas *libbašu ṭāb* and טיב לבבי had gone all the way!

A second variable in the language of law is, of course, function, as determined by immediate context. Muffs is very clear in explaining the difference between theme and function. What makes it possible for emotive idioms and phrases to translate into legal formulas is primarily a change in function. Interestingly, we find functional equivalents that are not, at the same time, connected to the same theme, or metaphor. And so, it is necessary to balance these two factors, theme and function, in any analysis, and Muffs excels in this effort.

Moving from thematic considerations to the history of law, the Akkadian formula *libbašu ṭāb* presented special problems. After having been current in the Old Babylonian period, it was replaced in its operative, legal functions by other terms and formulas of similar force, all of which Muffs explores. The fact that there were contemporary alternatives, such as Old Assyrian Akkadian *šebû* "to be sated," and less frequent Old Babylonian *duppur* "sated, satisfied; quit, removed" (to be discussed below) are easier to account for on the basis of regional distribution. However, one normally concludes that consecutive replacement indicates evanescence, which is to say that the earlier formula was no longer used and had given way to a different one. At the time Muffs wrote, the non-volitional, legal formula *libbašu ṭāb* was not to be found in the intervening, cuneiform legal sources, and consequently, its re-appearance in its old functions during the much later Achemenid period, and at that, in an Aramaic realization, was puzzling, and could not be accounted for fully.

Muffs' choice of the formula טיב לבבי as his focus has had far-reaching implications regarding what have become known as the "provincial," or "peripheral" cuneiform traditions of the second millennium B.C.E. Reference is to those texts deriving not from the Mesopotamian heartland of Assyria and Babylonia, proper, but from regions that range from the land of the Hittites and Mitanni, to ancient Syria (Ebla, Mari, Emar, and other sites) and to other West-Semitic spheres, including Canaan; and Egypt of the Amarna period.

Muffs answer to the question as to what had become of a legal formula such as Old Babylonian Akkadian *libbašu ṭāb* over a period of well over a thousand years was, precisely, that it might have been preserved in these very "provincial" legal traditions. This conclusion is no longer a matter of speculation, insightful as such speculation was more than thirty years ago. It can now be confirmed by the more recent discoveries at Emar on the Euphrates of the 13th century B.C.E., where this formula is regularly employed in deeds of purchase (see below, *The Origins of Aramaic Law*).

The depth exhibited by Muffs in his ostensibly "narrow" probe of a single Aramaic formula, טיב לבבי "My heart is satisfied," has actually opened windows, rather than narrowing sights! In a word, he has shown us what to look for, and where to look for it. Methodological opportunity dictated Muffs' agenda, not the immediate prospect of resolution, and this says something about his scholarly disposition. I am reminded of the objectives that guided Talmudic study in the elite academies: Primarily, one studied Gemara to unlock the dialectic, to understand the issues at play in the interpretation of law, and to decode the hermeneutic. It was not primarily a matter of finding out the final disposition of the cases under discussion, which was regarded as a fairly simple exercise in itself. Yochanan Muffs belongs in this scholarly tradition, where acumen is its own reward.

In the years following publication of his monograph, Muffs further pursued the investigation of various formulas, especially those of a volitional character. In 1975 he published a major study entitled: "Joy and Love as Metaphorical Expressions of Willingness and Spontaneity," etc. (Muffs 1975; revised in *Love and Joy*, 1992: 121-194). There he dwelled on the formula *ina ḫūd libbišu* "in the joy of his heart," and expanded on the language of law, explaining his methodology further. Muffs found that in Jewish Midrashic literature the Hebrew verb שׂמח "to rejoice," and the noun שׂמחה "joy, happiness" often appropriated legal connotations, expressing volition, even spontaneity in such transactions as the paying of tithes, for example. Here is what Muffs had to say on this subject in his Introduction to the collection of his studies, *Love and Joy* (Muffs 1992: 1):

> Law is a synthesis of form and content, yet it is formal only on the surface . . . I came to the study of law by a rather paradoxical road. I passionately disliked the proscriptive element in what was usually called law—the coercive,

> the anti-life, the limiting. Then, suddenly, I realized that ancient legal documents were telling a story, and that they told this story by a series of interrelated metaphorical clauses, clauses that had about them a poetic quality.

Beyond rhetorical sensitivity, there is a methodological insight at work here: It is important to know where to look for evidence on the language of law. This is particularly critical in the study of ancient law, where all that we possess is in written form. A scholar who seeks to understand the development of legal formulation solely from documents of a legal character, or from law codes and royal edicts, for that matter, will predictably fail in the effort. At one point, Muffs recalls that the eminent Talmudist, Saul Lieberman, used to say something to the effect that Talmudic law represents what ancient Jews were obligated to do, whereas Aggadic Midrash informs us of what ancient Jews actually thought was the right thing to do (Muffs 1975: 8). The same is undoubtedly true in literate cultures the world over.

Yochanan Muffs' monograph is, therefore, both a demonstration of insight and sensitivity and a paradigm of method, pointing the way to further inquiry into the origins and character of Aramaic law. As such, it is more valuable for the issues it raises and the problems it explores than for the answers that it offers. The same can be said regarding the value of Muffs' monograph for exploring the later development of Aramaic law, carrying us into the Greco-Roman period, and even beyond—into Talmudic law. Actually, it is by virtue of my recent work on the Aramaic legal documents from the Judean Desert of the Roman period that I was brought back to Muffs' monograph, and to his subsequent studies, finding in them brilliant anticipations of later discovery. It has already happened that terms and formulas that Muffs expected to find, based on his analysis, have actually turned up in later sources. The discussion to follow will first treat themes in linguistic, primarily semantic perspective, and then deal with historical considerations relevant to the development of Aramaic law.

The Language of Law

We often think of law as embodying abstract principles that transcend subjective preference, and are free of emotion. By submitting to the rule of such impersonal laws, by consent or by dictate, it is hoped, so the reasoning goes, that we may be able to order our affairs, resolve conflicts, and secure our just deserts. And yet, the formulation of laws, the way they are worded, often betrays their subjective matrix, indicating that supposedly abstract principles are rooted in human perceptions, relationships, and behavior. Legal terms and formulas evoke personal associations, reflecting reciprocal dispositions and responses. This is especially so in private law, so much of which is initially optional, or voluntary. We look to the law to "satisfy" our self-interest, to the extent possible; more precisely, to mediate conflicting interests.

It is only to be expected, therefore, that the language of law will express the dynamics of relationship, preference and self-interest in a wide variety of ways that are hardly abstract or impersonal, at all. In many instances such expressions will be graphic, or descriptive of physical acts and "moves," while in other cases they will reflect genuine emotion. Such formulas can be understood more fully if their etymological derivation is acknowledged, and if their semantic predications are traced. Conversely, something is lost when we are aware only of the functional meanings of legal terms and formulas, failing to react to their semantic matrix. In a sense, it is ironic that Muffs, who has pioneered the analysis of function, should be the very one to sensitize us to semantic predications.

A prime example in the Aramaic legal papyri of a set of graphic terms and formulas, to which Muffs pays considerable attention, is expressed by forms of the Aramaic root רחק "to be distant, to withdraw" (Muffs, Index, [West-Semitic Terms], s.v. *rḥq*). Figuratively, one may be declared distant, withdrawn, or disengaged from ownership, from a parcel of land, from various legal obligations; and from the other party to litigation. One pictures a person "walking away," renouncing claims. Also attested at Elephantine is a type of document known as ספר מרחק "a writ of cession" (*TAD* II, 2.2: 22, 2.3: 23, 2.8: 14, 2.10: 20, 3.6: 18). In one instance, a person who had sold land to another, and who had been paid in full, declares in such a document that the purchaser is רחיק "distant" from any future claim against his newly acquired ownership. Thus it is that at one and the same time, but in different respects, both vendor and purchaser are "distanced." The spatial perception of distance has become a metaphor for legal disengagement, for the breaking of ties.

It was Muffs who called attention to a similar connotation for Akkadian *rêqu* "to be distant." In a conveyance document from Nuzi of the mid 2nd millennium, it is stipulated that the erstwhile holders of rights to certain fields: *ana eqlēti annâti* PN *u* PN *la uqe[rre]bu ullān eqlētišunu ir-te-qú* "PN and PN shall not lay claim to (literally: 'draw near to') these fields; they have distanced themselves from their fields" (see *CAD R* 268, s.v. *rêqu*, meaning 3, and Muffs: 178). Functionally, Akkadian *qerēbu* "to draw near" means "to lay claim," and *rêqu* "to be distant" means "to relinquish claim." The semantic progression from the spatial to the relational is to be found in many legal traditions, and carries into family relationships, where a relative is said to be "near," and one outside the family is "distant." In the discussion of Egyptian legal formulas, below, it will be noted that Demotic legal texts often employ the same image of distance.

Proceeding to emotive formulas, we encounter at Elephantine the notion that gifts are perceived as tangible expressions of love and friendship, of the desire to gratify another. It was apparently insufficient merely to state that a grant was being conveyed from one person to another without reference to the favorable disposition of the giver. In Aramaic, the operative verb is רחם "to love, be friendly," yielding such terms as רחם (also רחים), which bear the meanings "lover, beloved, friend" (*DNWSI*: 1067-1068, s.v. *rḥym*; 1069-1070, s.v. *rḥm₄*). We regularly find in deeds of grant formulas such as: ברחמן . . . יהב "to give in affection/friendship," and ברחמן . . . נתן "in affection/friendship . . . to give." (*TAD* II, 2.10: 10-11, 14, 3.5: 4, 12, 3.8: 41, etc.; note the alternative feminine form: ברחמה, in *TAD* II, 3.7: 14). In a corollary manner, a deed of grant will specify the prerogatives of ownership by stating to the recipient: למן זי רחמתי תנתנן "to whomever you [fem.] feel affection/desire you may grant it" (*TAD* II, 2.3.9-10). As explained in great detail by Muffs, and as clarified in the Assyrian dictionaries that have since appeared, the Aramaic verb רחם is cognate with Akkadian *râmu* A (*raʾamu*) "to love" (*CAD R*: 128-145; *AHw* 951-952, s.v. *râmu* II). It is of particular interest that Akkadian *râmu* A "to love" figures in formulas of bequest. To cite two of the instances: cited in *CAD R*, 145, s.v. *râmu* A, 1.f) "to have a preference for-": 1) From Old Babylonian sources: *ummum warkassa ana mārīša ša i-ra-am-mu inaddin* "the mother may give her inheritance to whichever son she prefers." 2) From Neo-Babylonian sources: PN *ašar ta-ra-ma bītu t*[*anandin*] "PN m[ay give] the house to whom she likes." These provisions sound very much like those operative in the Aramaic legal papyri, expressing the cognates, Akkadian *nadānu*, Aramaic נתן "to give."

At this point, analysis becomes more complicated. An alternative formulation, expressing the prerogatives of ownership, albeit in the negative, is: לא שליט אנת לזבנה ולמנתן רחמת לאחרנן "You do not have the authority to sell (it), or to grant (it) as *rḥmt* to another" (*TAD* II, 2.4: 7). Also note a similar formula in *TAD* II, 3:12:26: וזי תנתן לה בכסף או רחמת "And to whomever you may convey (it) for silver, or *rḥmt*," and in *TAD* II, 3:12:31: ודי תנתן לה רחמת "And belonging to whomever you grant it as *rḥmt*." Now, Muffs (133, note 5) explains that the form רחמת may represent either 1) A noun, the cognate of Akkadian *rimūtu* "present, gift" (*CAD R*: 364-365). 2) An adverbial form, written defectively (we would expect רחמית = *rĕḥimāyît*) "in friendship, with affection." Functionally, it matters very little, except that both *CAD* and W. von Soden's *AHw* (951-952) make it clear that Akkadian *rimūtu* "present, gift," is not derived from the verb *râmu* A "to love," notwithstanding its meaning, which places it in the same semantic field. In the Sumerian lexical series, it is listed under a different entry, where it is grouped with two other terms that are unrelated to the notion of friendship: *kidinnu* "divine protection, divinely enforced security," a status which often entitled citizens to payments or exemptions (*CAD K*: 342-344), and *nērārūtu* (from *nārāru*) "help, aid, support," a term used in military contexts. (*CAD N* I, 346-348, s.v. *nārāru, nārārūtu*.) Akkadian *rimūtu* even generated a denominative, listed in *CAD R*: 146-147 as *râmu* B (*AHw râmu* III) (*riamu*) "to present, to grant, to deed an estate; to remit an obligation (NA only)," in other words, to convey a *rimūtu*.

In light of the above data, there are actually three choices with respect to Aramaic legal usage: 1) Aramaic רחמת is a cognate of Akkadian *rimūtu*, in which case it is not an emotive term, at all, and is unrelated to the verbal forms of the Aramaic root רחם "to love, be friendly" so prominent in these very documents. In favor of this analysis is the position of רחמת in the syntax of the formulas, strongly suggesting that it is a noun. 2) Aramaic רחמת is an adverbial form, well related to the verbal forms, and emotive in character, with the meaning "in affection, with friendship." It would represent an unusual, defective spelling, and would be syntactically somewhat abnormal. 3) Aramaic רחמת is an abstract noun, to be pointed *reḥimût* (absolute form, *reḥimû*), essentially meaning "love, friendship," but functionally connoting "(sign of) friendship; (gift of) affection." On this basis it would be unrelated to Akkadian *rimūtu*, but cognate with Akkadian *râmu* A "to love," and virtually identical in its realization with Akkadian *rā᾿imūtu* "friendship, love, affection" (*CAD R*: 82, especially meaning b)). So taken as a term for "gift," רחמת resonates with its underlying theme; it is a tangible expression of affection. One may compare Akkadian *šulmānu* "gift of greeting" (but also "health, wellbeing"), deriving from the verb *šalāmu*, and also Hebrew שלמים, שלם, which I take to have the same meaning, namely, "offering(s) of greeting" (Levine 1974). It is this third option which is preferable here, and I would consequently translate the noun רחמת in the three passages cited above as "(gift of) affection/(sign of) friendship," thereby illustrating the emotive character of formulas of gift-giving in the Aramaic legal papyri.

This brings us to a classic example of an emotive, consistently volitional formula in Akkadian: *ina ḫūd libbišu* "in the joy of his heart," and other formulas that employ forms of the verbal root *ḫadû* "to rejoice." Muffs discusses this formula at great length, both in his monograph and in his subsequent studies. It often figures in his discussion as a foil to *libbašu ṭāb* "his heart is satisfied," since it illustrates the difference between volitional and non-volitional formulas. In this way, it helps to make the case that *libbašu ṭāb* is not volitional in the way that *ina ḫūd libbišu* is, notwithstanding the closeness in their respective meanings. Then, too, Muffs saw a parallelism between the Neo-Babylonian formula *ina ḫūd libbišu iddin* "He gave in the joy of his heart," and Aramaic יהבת לך ברחמן "I have given (it) to you in affection," which was discussed earlier, and which differs in its functions from Aramaic טיב לבבי.

At the time Muffs wrote, there was no recorded Aramaic legal formula actually employing the West-Semitic cognate of *ḫadû*, namely, חדי/חדו "to rejoice," in the same way that Aramaic טיב paralleled Akkadian *ṭābu* in the parallel formulas. Actually, forms of the root חדי are attested quite frequently in Empire Aramaic (and in later phases of the language), specifically at Elephantine, in letters and literary sources, though not in legal formulas (*DNWSI* 349, s.v. *ḥdy*$_1$, v., and *ḥdy*$_3$, subst.). Recently, E. Eshel and A. Kloner (1996) published the incomplete text of an Aramaic marriage contract from Maresha, the capital of Idumaea, dated 176 B.C.E. The principals bear Edomite names. In it we read that the prospective groom addresses a second man, probably the father of the bride-to-be (or someone else legally in charge of her), to give her to him as wife. He makes this official request בחדות לבבה "in the joy of his heart," which is to say, willingly, as the law undoubtedly required. The Aramaic form חדות is best vocalized: *ḥādût*, reflecting the abstract form in Aramaic (cf. above: *rĕḥimût* "love, affection"). Conceivably, we could read this form as a Hebraism, pointed: *bĕḥedwat* "in the joy of-" (see Neh 8: 10, 1 Chron 16: 27), but this is less likely. Thus it is that recent discovery has provided a new example of an Aramaic legal formula which represents the realization of an Akkadian antecedent, once again affirming Muffs' expectations.

Both of the formulas examined thus far are consistently volitional, whereas in the relevant legal documents, the Akkadian formula *libbašu ṭāb* "His heart is satisfied," and its Aramaic reflex, טיב ללבי, are not volitional. Also attested in Aramaic legal documents of various sorts is the Haphʿel factitive-causative formulation: הוטיבת לבבי "You have caused my heart to be satisfied," plural: הוטיבתם לבבן "You have caused our heart to be satisfied." To understand the underlying semantic transactions, it is important to emphasize that there is nothing in the meaning of טיב לבבי/*libbašu ṭāb* that counter-indicates volition. To the contrary, Akkadian *ṭūb libbi* "gladness/goodness of heart" is often synonymous with *ḫūd libbi*, and in non-legal contexts normally characterizes a frame of mind or emotional disposition, such as generosity. Negatively, *la ṭūb libbi* means "badly disposed" (*AHw* 1303, s.v. *ṭūbu*, meaning 10). The same is true in Aramaic usage. Thus, we read in one of Ahiqar's proverbs: "A man whose figure is beautiful and whose 'heart is good' (ולבבה טב) is like a fortified town with water within it" (*TAD* III, 1.1.95). Similarly, in Biblical Hebrew טוב לב may describe one who is sated with drink (Prov 15: 15, Esth 1: 10), or who is otherwise happy: שמח וטוב לב (Esth 5: 9; also cf. Jud 16: 25, 19: 6, 9, 2 Sam 13: 28, 1 Kings 21: 7, Ruth 3: 7). The analysis of Akkadian *libbašu ṭāb* and Aramaic טיב לבבי is based upon immediate context, function, and position within legal documents, not on inherent meaning.

Muffs explains that the legal satisfaction formulas are also distinctive in their construction. Both Aramaic טיב לבבי and Akkadian *libbašu ṭāb* are composed of a stative verbal form טיב / *ṭāb* "is good," namely, "is satisfied," plus a declined form of "heart." Syntactically, Aramaic places the verbal element before the subject, whereas Akkadian places it after the subject. Akkadian represents the so-called "objective" formulation in the 3rd person, whereas Aramaic represents the 1st person "subjective" formulation.

It would be well to make mention of two thematic analogues of *libbašu ṭāb* in the Akkadian of the Old Babylonian period which further illustrate the semantics of legal language. One is the stative verb *šebû* (*šabāʾu, šabû*) "to become sated, satisfied" (*CAD Š* II, 251-255, cf. West-Semitic *š/ś-b-ʿ*), used in the Kultepe texts. Muffs notes the legal connotations of this verb; semantically, it parallels the route of "goodness of heart" all the way from describing satiety from food and drink, to the passive, legal sense of being repaid in full, and the active sense (expressed by the S-stem, *šubbû*), of paying another in full. This locution connotes fulfillment of mercantile obligations, and the discharging of debt and other obligations. Its theme is "fullness," so that one who is satisfied will state that he is "full," thereby indicating that no further payment is required. It is interesting that legal usage is not volitional, but rather, like *libbašu ṭāb*, is operative pursuant to performance. Thus, one might be provided with a sealed tablet confirming that the other party had been repaid in full, expressed by a form of the verb *šebû*. Another thematic analogue of *libbašu ṭāb* is Old Babylonian *duppur* "satisfied," which is attested at Susa. It is related to a rare, poetic expression *dapāru* "to slake the thirst, to become sated." D-stem *duppuru* "to satisfy" is used infrequently in the context of the division of property (*CAD D*: 104).

It remains to discuss the Egyptian analogues to Akkadian *libbašu ṭāb*, Aramaic טיב לבבי, and related forms (Muffs 142-172). The complex historical and cultural questions regarding the relation of the Egyptian "satisfaction" formulas to their Aramaic counterparts are, as Muffs states, a matter for Egyptologists to address. And yet, Muffs' treatment of the Egyptian analogues is a major contribution, in and of itself. The satisfaction clauses are most frequent in Demotic legal texts, and the likelihood is, as Muffs concludes, that it is Aramaic law which influenced Demotic law, and not *vice versa.* The slight precedence in time enjoyed by relatively few of the relevant Demotic texts does not really contradict this conclusion. As a consequence, there is little that is definitive to say relevant to the origins of Aramaic on the basis of the Demotic texts, although it is surely possible to explore actual themes that are current in Egyptian law at various periods. In doing so we can distinguish between the fairly rare hieratic legal texts from the pre-Saitic and early Saitic periods, and the larger corpus of Demotic legal texts which first begin to appear in the mid-to-late seventh century B.C.E., and continue into the early Roman period.

In the early hieratic texts, satisfaction as a legal concept is expressed by forms of the frequent Egyptian verb *ḥtp* "be at peace, pleased," which occurs in a conveyance document from IV-V dynasties of the 3rd millennium B.C.E. Muffs also cites a Middle Kingdom (XII dynasty) litigation document where we encounter the verb *hri* "be content, pleased, quiet." First, it addresses the payer: *hr.ty* "you are pleased," then, the payee states: *hr.kwy* "I am pleased," and then both parties take an oath, saying: *hr.wyn* "We are pleased." Finally, Muffs refers to Papyrus Berlin (Amenhopis IV, XVIII dynasty), where one who had sold a female slave swears by Amun that he is satisfied by the price he was paid: *mḥ.kwy grḥ.kwy.* "I am filled/sated, I am quit!" In none of these terms or formulas do we find the element "heart." Usage of the Egyptian verb *mh* "to fill, be filled" thematically recalls Akkadian *šebû* "to be sated." All of the above Egyptian formulas express substantial satisfaction, or quittance, and none are volitional, in context. And yet, all exhibit an emotive matrix.

A different situation relates to documents from the Saitic period, where there is, on the one hand, reference to the "heart," exhibiting some thematic closeness to the Akkadian and Aramaic formulas, but, on the other hand, less closeness to them in specific function. In the Stele of Euerot (950-730 B.C.E.), Muffs found the formula *n ỉb hr* "with a satisfied heart," the prototype of what is known as the "abnormal Hieratic" formula *m ỉb hr* "with a satisfied heart, willingly," which Muffs cites from two Turin papyri, from the late seventh century B.C.E. Analysis shows that these formulas are volitional, in immediate context. Consequently, Muffs concluded that they were best compared with Akkadian *ina ḫūd libbišu* "in the joy of his heart," which is consistently volitional, not with Akkadian *libbašu ṭāb*, Aramaic טיב לבבי, which are not.

In reaching this conclusion, Muffs gave precedence to function over meaning. This is his judgment call, but in the present case, meaning is quite subtle, and may have more valence than usual. The point is that the

Egyptian verb *hrỉ* may be closer in meaning to Akkadian *ṭāb*, Aramaic טיב "content, satisfied," than it is to Akkadian *ḫadû*, Aramaic חדי "to rejoice." It must also be kept in mind that the same verb can be volitional in one context and operative in another. Thus, *m ỉb hr* "with a satisfied heart": is volitional in function, whereas *hr.wyn* "We are pleased, satisfied" which employs the same verb, is not volitional in its immediate context. This illustrates the very semantic process of which we have been speaking, namely, movement from an emotive matrix to both volitional and operative legal connotations. To paraphrase Muffs, himself:—"the fact that *Formula A* and *Formula B* are based on the same root metaphor does not necessarily indicate that they fill the same identical function" (Muffs, 155).

Turning to the Demotic papyri, we once again encounter a new situation. There is precise functional equivalence between the Demotic and the Akkadian/Aramaic satisfaction formulas, but it is not clear that the Demotic formulas exhibit the same emotive matrix. Muffs cites Papyrus Berlin 13571 from Elephantine, dated 589 B.C.E., a sale document in which the vendor addresses the purchaser. We find two interactive formulas: *dy.k-mty ḥ3ty (.ỉ)* "You (namely, the purchaser) have made my heart satisfied," then: *ḥ3ty (.ỉ) mtyw* "My heart (namely, the heart of the vendor) is satisfied." This dynamic is a regular feature of later Demotic documents, and its context is decidedly operative, not volitional, as others had thought. It refers directly to full payment received, or to the performance of a requisite oath in litigation documents, for example. In effect, it was Muffs who cleared up this ambiguity in Demotic usage incisively.

Thematically, the problem is that the Demotic verb *mty* does not really connote satiety or contentment. In a long note, Muffs (150-151) reports, on good authority, that the root metaphor of *mty* is "to be straight, equivalent to." The Egyptian/Demotic formulas are best taken as follows: "You have made things 'straight' with my heart" <> "My heart is 'straight'." In other words, all obligations have been met in right measure. These formulas are normative, even quantitative, to a degree, rather than emotive in origin, but they certainly illustrate the role of metaphor in legal language.

Earlier in the discussion of the language of law, it was explained that spatial notions of "distance" had become a metaphor for legal disengagement and withdrawal, such as the cession of claims, and release from obligations. Aramaic רחק and Akkadian *rêqu* "to be distant, to withdraw" were the operative verbs. Muffs' contribution to a proper understanding of the relevant legalities has already been underscored, but there is more: Demotic litigation documents attest the formula *ỉw-y wy-k (wy) r-* "I am far from"—the person. This corresponds to the Aramaic formula: רחקת מנכם "I am far from you." Actually, the correspondence goes further, as Muffs explains.

There are even clauses in Demotic that refer to the transaction: "I am far from the person, with respect to" (Aramaic *mn*, Demotic *n*)—the house, funds, etc. Apart from demonstrating that an historical relationship exists between the Aramaic and the Demotic formulas, such statements show how interesting is the semantic transaction from spatial distance to relational distancing, on its own.

I emphasize this because Cary Martin, in his treatment of the Demotic texts from Elephantine, a section of Porten's compendium, seems to have missed the point about the figurative sense of "distancing" in Demotic legal documents. I gather this from his notes on Papyrus Berlin 13572 ("C2"), dated 492 B.C.E. (Porten 2000: 292, note 5), a receipt with guarantee. He explains that the statement "I will cause PN to be far from you," means that one party promises to "keep . . . away" an agent "from" the other party. What it really means is that the agent, in this case, no longer has any legal standing; that he has been disengaged from the transaction. The sense of "far" is no longer spatial. This instance illustrates the applicability of Muffs' method in clarifying the language of Demotic law.

The Origins of Aramaic Law

In the first part of this *Prolegomenon* it was explained that in his monograph, Yochanan Muffs had pursued an Assyriological approach to the interpretation of Aramaic law, and to the tracing of its origins. It is important to emphasize that the Assyriological approach does not negate originality in Aramaic law, nor does it maintain that Aramaic law was devoid of elements deriving from sources other than cuneiform law. What is more, Aramaic scribes were not slavish in adopting elements of cuneiform law when they did so; they generated new combinations and broke-up existing ones; they even shifted functions and restructured sequences, and often exhibited different orientations. What this approach suggests is that we can identify in Aramaic legal documents "realizations" of many terms and formulas known from cuneiform law, representing calques and other modulated and adapted forms.

Furthermore, Aramaic legal documents, with their operative clauses, embody many principles known from cuneiform law, in all of its diversity, and even their overall composition exhibits considerable affinity to cuneiform models. Given the historical relationship of the Aramaic and cuneiform cultures, and the contacts between them, as well as the cognate relationship of the two languages, Akkadian and Aramaic, we are fully warranted in concluding that cuneiform law would have lent some of its character to the younger Aramaic law. Muffs endeavored to probe these relationships through the investigation of test cases, perfecting in the process a refined method of identifying functional and semantic equivalents, a phenomenon that will be illustrated as we proceed.

The "Provincial" Traditions of the 2nd Millennium, Early and Late

Most of the cuneiform documents attesting the legal formula *libbašu ṭāb* "His heart is satisfied," which served as Muffs' principal test case, date from the Old Babylonian period, that of the First Dynasty of Babylon (19th-17th centuries B.C.E.), but this formula is considerably older, in fact. It is Muffs' view that *libbašu ṭāb* speaks for the early Akkadian legal tradition, not originally for the Sumerian. Relatively few attestations of it come from central and southern Mesopotamia, whereas many come from the northern regions, and some from fringe areas, including Alalakh, Harmal and Khafajah, even as far as Susa. There are also occasional occurrences of this formula in deeds of the Hammurapi and Ammiṣaduqa periods.

In a brief section, "The Transition from the Akkadian to the Sumerian" (73-75), Muffs discusses the interesting process by which Old Akkadian formulas were rendered into Sumerian. He cites a sale document from the reign of the Old Babylonian king, Ṣabium, in the 19th century B.C.E., which attests both an Akkadian and a Sumerian version of the formula in question: Akkadian: *lib-ba-šu-nu ṭú-ub* is rendered as Sumerian: šà.ga.ni ì-du$_{10}$ "His heart has been satisfied." William W. Hallo (2002) has now published an exemplar from Nippur (*YBS* 9839), of a genre known as "a model court case." Though itself undated, since it was preserved as a school text for training scribes, Hallo assigns the tablet on internal grounds to the Isin I period in the 20th century B.C.E. The text concerns a dispute over the division of an inheritance, and records a complaint brought at a later date by one of two brothers before the assembly of Nippur. He claims that his older brother, since deceased, had failed to pay him his share during his lifetime. The son of the deceased brother declares before that same assembly: kù.bi u$_4$.bi.ta šà.ga.ni al.du$_{10}$ "With that silver, at that time, his heart was satisfied." (Hallo notes in passing that the relevant satisfaction formula was studied by Muffs.) The same brother's son was remanded to the gate of Ninurta for an oath, and the case was finally settled by an imposed, mutual agreement. The circumstances of this record fall squarely within the range of Muffs' analysis of *libbašu ṭāb*, and indicate that the transition from Akkadian to Sumerian referred to by Muffs is now most likely attested in the 20th century B.C.E.

The upshot of Muffs' discussion is that *libbašu ṭāb* exhibits a "provincial" provenience in its earliest known attestations, and was not part of the "core" tradition of the Old Babylonian period, a distinction which Muffs discusses in depth, and which will prove to be significant. After collecting attestations of *libbašu ṭāb* in documents from the Old Babylonian period, Muffs deals with its replacements, or isoglosses; which is to say, other terms and formulas occurring in contemporary documents, usually from different regions, and also in texts from later periods. These appear in the same slots and in the same types of documents where we would have expected *libbašu ṭāb*, and have the same operative functions. Muffs developed a very precise method for authenticating such functional equivalents, which are at times also semantically equivalent. These have been noted above, in the section *The Language of Law.*

In matter of fact, it is important to recognize that legal documents vary in their formularies, so that some slots are not always filled. In certain legal traditions it was deemed sufficient to record that a transaction had been completed, and full payment had been received, with no need being felt to say anything more by way of indicating satisfaction. At that point, a sale document would proceed directly to exclude claims and suits. (This is generally the case in Neo-Assyrian sale documents, as an example.) An in-between case is represented by the inclusion, in quittance formulas, of the term *zakû* "purified, cleared, quit." In a manner somewhat different from *libbašu ṭāb*, it nevertheless records a change in the status, or condition of the party that is "cleared," going beyond merely affirming that he had received full payment.

Formulas with *zakû*, and the D-stem verb form *uzakki* "to purify, clear of obligation" began to appear during the Middle Babylonian period in the Mesopotamian heartland. Aramaic cognates of *zakû* and *uzakki* do not occur in the Elephantine legal papyri, although they crop up again in later Aramaic and Syriac documents (Goldstein 1966). Akkadian *zakû* belongs to one of the most prevalent metaphors of innocence in the Semitic languages; of release from obligation, or the fulfillment of it. It reflects the ancient synthesis of sin > crime, and of impurity > wrongdoing. Saying that one is "cleared" is akin to saying that one is "withdrawn, removed" from a previous status, a condition conveyed by forms of the Akkadian verb *rêqu*, Aramaic רחק "to be distant, withdraw" (see above). On this basis, one could regard *zakû* as a replacement for *libbašu ṭāb*, or some similar satisfaction formula.

In the light of recent discoveries, it turns out that Muffs' analysis was correct, as was his reasoning. As already mentioned, the formula *libbušu ṭāb*, plural: *libbušunu ṭāb*, is now attested in legal documents from Emar, a town on the Middle Euphrates which thrived in the 13th century B.C.E., and where cuneiform tablets in Sumerian, Akkadian, Hittite, and Hurrian have been found. The Emar texts qualify as "provincial" in every respect. The excavations at Emar (Tell Meskene) were conducted during the 1970's and early 1980's, and a collection of the Sumerian and Akkadian texts was published by Daniel Arnaud in *EMAR VI.3* (1986). These include purchase documents, and other conveyances, in which the sought after formula occurs fairly regularly in its expected slot, and bears its distinctive functions in the Old Babylonian tradition. Aspects of these highly enlightening texts have been recently studied by Gary Beckman (1988, 1996) and Aaron Skaist (1998), among others. (For a recent Bibliography of works on Emar, see D. Fleming 2000.) Three examples will serve to illustrate its functions:

1) *ša* d*Nin-urta ù* lú.meš *ši-bu-ut* [ur]u E-mar ki [*be*]-*lu-ú* a.šà.ḫi.a PN dumu PN *a-na* 1 *me-at* 5/6 *ma-na* kù.babbar [š]ám.til.la a-šà *i-ša-am* kù.babbar-*pa maḫ-rù* šà-*šu-nu ṭà-a-b.*

> From Ninurta and the elders of the [ci]ty of Emar, [ow]ners of the fields, PN, son of PN, for 100 (shekels), 5/6 of a mina of silver, (for) the total [pr]ice, has purchased the field. They have received the silver; their heart is satisfied. (Arnaud 1986: 8-9, no. 2, lines 17-26.)

2) ki ! dNin-urta ù lú.meš *ši-bu-ut* uru E-mar ki *be-lu-ú* é-*ti*-hi.a 3 PN dumu PN *a-na* 2 *me-at* kú.babbar *ṣur-pu* šám *an-ni-ta* é-*ti*.ḫi.a 3 *i-ša-am* kù.babbar *maḫ-rù lib-bu-šu-nu ṭà-ab.*

> From Ninurta and the elders of the city of Emar, PN, son of PN, for 200 (shekels) of refined silver, (for) this price, has purchased these three houses; they have received the silver; their heart is satisfied. (Arnaud 1986: 17, no. 9, lines 24-31.)

3) ki PN *be-el k*[*i-ir-ṣi-ta*$_5$] PN dumu PN *a-na* 5/6 *ma-na* [kù.babbar] *a-na* šám.ti;.[la.]bi!. éš *ki-ir-ṣi-ta*$_5$ *i-ša-am* kù.babbar *ma-ḫi-ir* šà-*šu ṭà-a-ab*

> From PN, owner of the c[abin], PN, son of PN, four 5/6 of a mina of [silver], for its total price, has purchased the cabin. He has received the silver; his heart is satisfied. (Arnaud 1986: 115, no. 110, lines 16-22).

It would carry us afield to trace all of the various ingredients of the formulary of the Emar documents so as to come up with a complete profile. Suffice it to say that the appearance of the satisfaction formula *libbušu/ libbušunu ṭāb* in documents from Emar of the 13th century B.C.E., strengthens Muffs' identification of it with Aramaic טיב לבבי. The time gap has been narrowed by about four hundred years, bringing us to the very eve of the emergence of Aramaic, and of alphabetic writing.

Another illustration of the "provincial" cuneiform lineage of a formula occurring in the Aramaic legal papyri from Elephantine was mentioned above, in the discussion of the language of law. Muffs had called attention to the functional sense of Akkadian *rêqu* "to be distant," namely, that of relinquishing claims, and of "distancing" one's self from ownership, in the same way that Aramaic רחק "to withdraw, be distant" functioned prominently at Elephantine. Reference was made to a Nuzi conveyance document, once again indicating a relationship between Aramaic law of the Achemenid period and the "provincial" traditions of ancient Syria, in this case also from the second half of the 2nd millennium B.C.E.

Thus far, we have been keeping pretty close to the specific formula *libbašu ṭāb*/טיב לבבי, and to several others which occur together with it in the Aramaic and the cuneiform texts. There is, however, much more information to be gained from Muffs' monograph that points us in the direction of the "provincial" traditions of the 2nd millennium B.C.E. Muffs' voluminous notes are a major resource in this regard, as they are in other respects. Muffs has at his recall an immense body of knowledge, both from primary and secondary sources, and one reading his monograph can sense that he scrambled to register more and more of his insights and free associations in the notes, taking the reader "all over the map." Such pieces of information, while not fully integrated in Muffs' systematic analysis, are nevertheless positioned at relevant points in his ongoing treatment, and, in some cases, they crop up again in his main discussion.

Two examples will illustrate this pattern: 1) On page 30, note 2, Muffs discusses the Aramaic phrase: מן יומה זנה עד עלם "from this day, forever," calling attention to Ras Shamra Akkadian: *ištu ūmi annî . . . ana dāriti* "from this day . . . for all generations." 2) On page 60-61, notes 2 and 3, Muffs takes up a question directly related to the formula טיב לבבי in his discussion of dowry provisions. He analyzes a provision of the Aramaic law of divorce: כל זי הנעלת בידה תהנפק מן חם ועד חוט ותהך לה אן זי צבית "All that she brought in by her hand, be it string or sandal-lace, she may take out, and she may betake herself wherever she desires" (*TAD* II, 2.6. 24-25). Compare, in Ras Shamra Akkadian, a provision from the bill of divorce of Ammishtamru, king of Ugarit, *in re* his wife, a princess of Amurru: *ša ina bīti Ammištamri ultēribu lilqīma ištu* [*bī*]*ti Ammištamri littalak* "—Whatever she brought into the house of Ammishtamru she may take out from the house of Ammishtramru, and she may depart." Both examples, studied as well by Reuben Yaron and others, take us back to Ugarit of the Late Bronze Age, a major source of the "provincial" cuneiform traditions.

To summarize our current knowledge of the "provincial" cuneiform traditions: It can now be concluded with considerable assurance that Muffs' historical tracing of *libbašu ṭāb* was correct: On the basis of the evidence from 13th century Emar, we can say that the Aramaic scribes of Elephantine knew the formula under discussion from some proximate source, in Akkadian or, as is more likely, in a West-Semitic realization, probably in Aramaic. Admittedly, we still lack the missing links in its transmission, primarily because the events of brief period between ca. 1200 B.C.E. and the beginning of the 11th century B.C.E. remain blurred. This would be the time during which the first transmissions of the "provincial" cuneiform tradition would have occurred, corresponding roughly to the introduction of alphabetic writing. Some of the transmitted features were appropriated, and surface in contemporary Middle Assyrian and Middle Babylonian sources. Others probably flowed directly into the Aramaic legal vocabulary and remained there, suggesting that an Aramaic legal tradition developed relatively early on. Significantly, these same influences help to account for the reception in Hebrew biblical texts from the 1st millennium B.C.E. of elements of the "provincial" cuneiform traditions, including those of the Ugaritic alphabetic cuneiform. As more becomes known about this all-critical period of transition, and there is great current interest in it, the routes of transfer will undoubtedly be clarified further. The alternative that I entertained in my review (Levine 1975: 44-45), namely, that the Aramaic scribes of Achemenid times reinvented Aramaic טיב לבבי by specializing idiomatic usage, and had no knowledge of its prior currency as an operative formula in the cuneiform tradition, is implausible. Aramaic טיב לבבי should no longer be labeled "An Apparent Old Babylonian Survival," as I called it in my review; its lineage has been established.

If a digression be permitted, I would like to re-examine an issue that I raised in my review of Muffs' monograph (Levine 1975: 44-45, and note 33), and which has to do specifically with the reception of "provincial" cuneiform traditions in Hebrew biblical texts. I called attention to idiomatic attestations of "goodness of heart" in Biblical Hebrew and inquired, on methodological grounds, whether, or to what degree we can infer that the operative formula, based on the same metaphor, might also have been in use. In other words, is it likely that in a culture where "goodness of heart" expresses emotive states, scribes will also employ this metaphor to express formal quittance, or substantial "satisfaction" in texts of a legal character? Muffs was fully aware of the more or less idiomatic attestations in both cuneiform and West-Semitic sources, down through the centuries, but he drew a sharp distinction between these and the precise operative formula under discussion, and did not factor such phenomena into his historical analysis. Here is what I had to say about this issue in my review:

> It was, of course, necessary for him (= Muffs) to isolate the legal terminology for a proper analysis, and failure to do so had, indeed, hampered earlier attempts to interpret this formula properly. Conversely, however, an awareness of the interaction of general and specialized idioms within a society is basic for historical inquiry" (Levine 1975: 45).

I had in mind a single biblical passage where "goodness of heart" bears a different connotation from its usual, idiomatic sense of "satiety, generosity," so well attested in classical Hebrew. Reference is to Judges 18, which relates that the Danites offered Micah's family priest a better position with them as priest of an entire tribe. The priest accepted the offer, an act reported as follows: וייטב לב הכהן "The priest's heart was satisfied." (Jud 18: 20). The immediate context allows for at least a quasi-legal, albeit volitional interpretation. In fact, Yaron (1961: 153) had considered this very statement in Jud 18: 20 to represent legal usage. Muffs, however, dismissed such an analysis on functional grounds, regarding the phrase as merely an expression of willingness, and as essentially irrelevant to tracing the history of *libbašu ṭāb*/טיב לבבי (Muffs 140, note 1).

I would now frame the question somewhat differently: Can a statement be volitional, and at the same time possess legal, or binding force? In the present case, the priest gave his word, and formally agreed to the proposition. To be sure, this was not pursuant to payment or material "satisfaction," which presumably would come when he assumed his duties; nor is there any indication that such a statement was obligatory. And, of course, this report occurs in a narrative, not in a code of law! And yet, the priest's statement was committal, and he acted on it with dispatch. It could be argued that a biblical writer who expressed formal agreement in this way would have possessed in his vocabulary something corresponding to the very non-volitional formula we are discussing. The entire question of how biblical literature fits into the transmission of the "provincial" cuneiform traditions of the late 2nd millennium, and the Aramaic factor in Biblical Hebrew, at various periods, requires extensive study.

Enter the Arameans, en masse

It would be helpful to step back before proceeding, and focus once again on the all-critical period of transition. With the beginning of the Iron Age, and after the world shaking military and political events encircling the year 1200 B.C.E., a new demographic and socio-linguistic situation begins to emerge in Assyria and Babylonia, as well as in Syria and Canaan and the eastern Mediterranean. During the period of transition from the late 13th-12th, and early 11th centuries, western Semites migrated from Syria into both Canaan and Mesopotamia. In part, these were fugitives from the collapsed Neo-Hittite kingdom, and from the fallen kingdom of Amurru. In addition, the military campaigns of Tiglat Pileser I (1114-1076) in the West, against the Mushku and the early Arameans, brought Assyrians and these peoples of the western zones into contact with each other. These engagements persisted during the reigns of his successors, into the early 9th century B.C.E., while all the while the Arameans were migrating *en masse* into Mesopotamia, settling along the lower Euphrates all the way into Babylonia. One notes, therefore, a striking counter-valence in Syria and Mesopotamia between Assyrian conquest and hegemony, on the one hand, and the growth and expansion of Aramaic culture, fueled by the presence of a large Aramean population, on the other. Here is how A. Kirk Grayson describes the advent of the Arameans in Mesopotamia, and in other areas of the Near East outside of their Syrian homeland:

> The Arameans make up the third major invasion of the Fertile Crescent by Semitic-speaking nomads, the first being that by the Akkadians and the second that by the Amorites . . . Aramaic, the language of the Arameans, eventually became the language of the Assyrians and Babylonians, thus replacing Akkadian. Indeed, Aramaic by the middle of the 1st millennium was the international language of the entire ancient Near East (Grayson 1992: 740).

The spread of the Aramaic language from its Syrian homeland resulted in large part from Aramean migration and expansion, and was abetted by the Neo-Assyrian policy of deportation operative during the 9th to the 7th centuries. These factors led to the so-called Aramaization of Assyria and Babylonia, a process that gained momentum in the latter days of the Assyrian Empire. This process was intensified during the Neo-Babylonian period, and Aramaic functioned as the administrative language of the Persian Empire in the 6th century B.C.E., and thereafter. As an alphabetic language, Aramaic had obvious advantages over the cuneiform systems to start with, since its technology was simpler.

It is important to recognize, however, that the Aramaization process of which we are speaking was not uni-directional; both languages, Akkadian and Aramaic, were affected. Nor should one conclude that Akkadian fell out of use as a written language, which was not the case. Akkadian continued to be employed as a written language for many purposes, not the least being for legal documents, and it was impacted by Aramaic more than we were accustomed to think Both Hayim Tadmor (1982) in his cultural study of western impact on Assyrian concepts, drawing on the Aramaic Sefire treaties of the 8th century B.C.E., and Stephen Kaufman, in his study of the linguistic interaction between Akkadian and Aramaic (1974), cite suggestive examples of how Aramaic terminology and formulation affected Neo-Assyrian, and later, Neo-Babylonian. For its part, Aramaic absorbed elements of Akkadian with increasing momentum as the centuries passed.

In its various dialects, Aramaic greatly expanded in the mid-to-late 1st millennium B.C.E. and thereafter and increasingly drew on the vast Akkadian vocabulary, legal and otherwise. Kaufman charts this very process in considerable detail, establishing precise criteria for tracing the routes of transfer. It turns out that many borrowings of various sorts, including calques of Akkadian in Aramaic, first appeared only in late antiquity; and yet, the overall interaction of the two languages began much earlier.

Identifying the influence of Akkadian on Aramaic written sources is one way of tracing the origins of the cuneiform factor within Aramaic law; it is at least a good way to start, because it affords a high degree of control. In so doing, we are actually working with several cultural-linguistic phenomena, which we can now illustrate by example. This is due in part to the discovery of so-called "bilingual" texts, the earliest known being the Tell Fekherye inscription of the 9th century B.C.E. (Abou-Assaf, Bordreuil, Millard 1982). Tell Fekherye is located across the Khabur river from Tell Halaf (ancient Gozan), and the inscriptions in Assyrian cuneiform and in alphabetic Aramaic appeared on a statue of a local governor, a vassal of the Assyrians. Though not a legal text, this "royal" inscription (the local ruler is called מלך "king" in the Aramaic version, but only *šakin māti* "governor" in the Assyrian!), contains official terminology. A study of its translation techniques is informative in terms of what has been called linguistic "interference," or "interpenetration." As suggested by Mario Fales (1982, 1986: 35, and note 60), and by Greenfield and Shaffer (1983), it is likely that at least a part of these inscriptions was translated from Aramaic to Akkadian, whereas other sections were conceived in Akkadian, and then rendered in Aramaic. At the time, Aramaic was the poorer language, as we would only expect, witness the fact that in several instances the same Aramaic word translates more than one Akkadian word. And yet, we have early attestations of Aramaic titles and formulas that were later to become normal and frequent. An example is the equivalence of Akkadian *bēlu* "lord, master" and Aramaic מרא.

A valuable resource for tracing Aramaization in the composition of legal documents is the assemblage of Aramaic "epigraphs," so-called of the early 7th century B.C.E., edited by Mario Fales, in his monograph: *Aramaic Epigraphs on Clay Tablets of the Neo-Assyrian Period* (1986; on dating, see S. Lieberman 1968). These epigraphs derive from the homeland cities of Nineveh, Kalhu and Assur, as well as from the province of Gozan, by the way, the very locale of the Tell Fekherye inscription. Some of the Aramaic epigraphs are appended as "dockets" to Assyrian legal texts of several typical kinds, in some instances providing partial Aramaic translations of the Assyrian texts, including legal terms and formulas. Other Aramaic epigraphs stand independently, but are also legal in character. In all, Fales (1986: 3) lists twenty-four legal epigraphs, representing known types of documents: sales of real estate and of persons (the largest category), land leases, and one text concerning the division of an inheritance. Several sections of Fales' Introduction are particularly relevant to the Aramaic-Akkadian "symbiosis," as Fales calls it. These are: 2.1—"From decipherment to interference;" 2.2—"Theoretical frameworks: 'Mesopotamian Aramaic' and the Akkadian/Aramaic Symbiosis'" (29-47), and 2.3.g-h "Lexicon: the semantic areas;" "Mechanisms of lexical interference" (91-102). Among other things, Fales is able to identify the phonetic rules governing transcription of Akkadian in Aramaic, albeit of particular dialects of Assyrian. Andre Lemaire (2001) has now updated this valuable assemblage in his monograph, *Nouvelles Tablettes Arameennes*.

In effect, these epigraphs represent the oldest known collection of Aramaic legal documents, albeit often partial in their extent, and in every case, brief and somewhat rudimentary. Nevertheless, they antedate the Elephantine Aramaic papyri by about two centuries, and are extremely informative on several levels. They afford us a glimpse of the state of "Mesopotamian" Aramaic in the early 7th century. In terms of "languages in contact" the lexicon of the epigraphs provides examples of several phenomena, including: a) Aramaic cognates of Akkadian lexemes, e.g. חצדן (cf. Akkadian *eṣēdu*, v., *ēṣidu* s.) "harvesters;" חקל (cf. Akkadian *eqlu*) "field." b) Akkadian loanwords in Aramaic, e.g. חזן (cf. Akkadian *ḫazzannu*) "mayor, magistrate;" מת (cf. Akkadian *mātu*, but cf. in the Tell Fekherye inscription, where Akkadian *ālu* "town, city" is rendered by Aramaic מת); דנת (cf. Akkadian *dannatu*) "valid tablet, document," and again see Muffs 187, note 4). c) Aramaic words that translate Akkadian, and are semantically equivalent to the Akkadian, e.g. אחז for Akkadian *leqû* "to purchase" (see Levine 1993: 136-137). d) Original Aramaic/West-Semitic words that seem not to have entered Akkadian, e.g. חתם "seal-" of a document (*DNWSI* 413). e) Probable, original Aramaic/West-Semitic loanwords in Akkadian, e.g. אגרה, const. אגרת, (cf. Akkadian *egirtu*, and see Muffs 187-189, especially 187, note 4) "letter, document;" תחם (cf. Akkadian *taḫūmu*) "boundary."

As limited as our knowledge of Old Aramaic is at the present time, the cumulative input of what is actually available allows for the conclusion that by the early 7th century B.C.E., if not earlier, a firm legal vocabulary existed in Aramaic. It was generated in large measure in the ways just suggested, with the input of the cuneiform legal tradition very much in evidence. In the succeeding centuries, contact increased between Aramaic and Neo-Babylonian. What is more, internal Aramaic development was considerable, rising to meet the increased needs of a *lingua franca*. By the time we reach the Achemenid period, the Aramaic legal vocabulary is extensive, and it continued to grow in the succeeding centuries, drawing on cuneiform legal traditions as it went along, well into the Seleucid period. We must, of course, factor in the variable of discontinuity, whereby, both in cuneiform and Aramaic legal texts, an ingredient will appear, be utilized for a time, and then be replaced.

When tracing origins in comparative perspective, what is being sought is the point in time when a particular transfer, or appropriation actually occurred. On the basis of the Assyriological approach, this can only be ascertained when we possess both the Akkadian prototype and the contemporary Aramaic counterpart, wherein the same term, or formula occurs in sources of a similar character, and when we can establish both a *terminus a quo* and *a terminus ad quem* for the element in question. In other words, we know fairly well when the element first occurred in Akkadian legal texts, and when it fell out of use. If, then, we find the same element in contemporary Aramaic texts, in recognizable form, we may conclude that the transfer from Akkadian to Aramaic must have occurred within that "window" of time, not earlier and not later. In most cases where only one *terminus* can be established, we know less. With respect to the Aramaic legal papyri of the 5th century B.C.E. we would be looking for previously unattested innovations of the Neo-Babylonian period, or, at the very least, for a sharp escalation in the utilization of certain formulas in relation to earlier periods.

To illustrate this principle, we must jump a century or so ahead in time; when we have an excellent example of how this method can be applied systematically. Reference is to the horde of Aramaic legal papyri found at Wadi Daliyeh, and known as the "Samaria Papyri." Their decipherment and interpretation were initiated by F. M. Cross Jr. (1985, 1986), and they have since been edited and published by Douglas Gropp (2001). They were discovered near Jericho, and date from the 4th century B.C.E., consisting mostly of slave sales. Gropp has studied them with the same "Assyriological approach" as was employed by Muffs, except that he was more interested in the synchronic, and near-contemporary connections between Aramaic and cuneiform law than in tracing long-term survivals, as was Muffs.

To cite one instance: In analyzing the operative clauses of these legal documents, Gropp discovered that one of the regular "receipt-quittance" clauses in use was directly traceable to a late Neo-Babylonian model. Reference is to the Aramaic formula: כספא . . . אטיר מכיר "The silver . . . is paid, received," to which compare Akkadian *maḫir eṭir*, with the same meaning and function, in transposed order. The Aramaic form אטיר is a direct loan from Neo-Babylonian, realized as an Aramaic passive participle. Usage of this abbreviated formula (cf. *apil, maḫir, eṭir* "paid, received, paid") in the late Neo-Babylonian formulary can de dated at the earliest to the Chaldean dynasty, but only becomes obligatory in the reign of Darius I, according to Gropp (2001: 59-60).

Now, at the time Muffs' monograph was published, the contents of the Samaria Papyri were little known to scholars. For his own part, Muffs had taken due note of the innovative Neo-Babylonian usage of *eṭir* "[payment] received," a nuance of its basic meaning of "returned," in quittance formulas. As an aside, it is interesting to review how this legal term had come to Muffs' attention. He found it occurring in the slot where *libbašu ṭāb* and its replacement, Akkadian *zakû* "cleared, quit" had occurred in earlier documents. Looking ahead, Muffs also notes Talmudic אִיטְרָא (also: עִיטְרָא), a term never before understood by commentators, and occurring, as a matter of fact, in the provisions of a slave sale! In its Talmudic context it bears the meaning of "receipt" (Muffs 126, note 2; *addenda*, 201, s.v. P. 126, note 2). At the time, Muffs could only speculate as to how this Neo-Babylonian term had ended up in the Babylonian Talmud, but now we can document its entry into the Aramaic legal vocabulary in the 4th century B.C.E.

In the course of commenting on the Samaria Papyri, Gropp has been able to register many similar, synchronic connections. Gropp analyzed the conventional formulary and composition of the documents step by step, ending up with a profile of their legal lineage. The same method could be applied systematically to the Elephantine legal papyri, and, in fact, Eleonora Cussini, in her Dissertation, has initiated the process with her analysis of the sale documents from Elephantine. A mixed, synchronic-diachronic approach has been applied to the legal vocabulary of these papyri by J. Oelsner (1997), revealing the coalescence of several lines of transmission.

With respect to the question of origins, we are dealing with several distinct phenomena:

1) Terms and formulas that most likely entered Aramaic from Akkadian in the Neo-Assyrian period. I say "most likely" because if such an element, first attested in cuneiform sources of the Neo-Assyrian period, continued in use into the Neo-Babylonian period, it is impossible to ascertain when it entered Aramaic. We can only estimate when it might have entered, at the earliest, which is to say, to establish its *terminus a quo*. Muffs discusses the history of the use of Aramaic in Egypt during the Saitic period, especially after the Assyrian conquests of the 7th century B.C.E. He points out that the language of international trade and administration at that time was undoubtedly Aramaic, and adds that wherever the Jewish settlers of Elephantine hailed from, they undoubtedly employed Aramaic common law, which was also known in Israel and Judah in the late 7th century B.C.E. Muffs (190-191) cites Jeremiah 32, where there is reference to the "double document," a legal instrument of cuneiform provenience.

More than thirty years ago, when there was much less to go on, Muffs was already enthusiastic about the Neo-Assyrian factor in Aramaic law, as evident in the Elephantine legal papyri. He listed as many as twelve legal expressions that recall Neo-Assyrian formulation (Muffs, 180-187). His examples include the following: Aramaic מהרה יאבד "His dowry will be lost" recalls Neo-Assyrian *kasapšu ḫaliq* "His silver is lost" [namely, "forfeit"]; Aramaic זי לא אשתאר "there does not remain" recalls Neo-Assyrian *lā rēḫe* "there does not remain;" Aramaic הנפק (causative from נפק "to go out") + ספר "to bring out a document" echoes Neo-Assyrian *e-gér-tú . . . tu-ṣa-a* "a deed . . . goes out" [= "is issued"]. The above are semantic equivalents. There are also cognate formulas: Cf. Aramaic לא אגרנך דין ודבב "I will not instigate against you a formal suit," with Neo-Assyrian *ša dēnu dabābu itti PN iggarûni* "Whoever may instigate a formal suit against PN" (see Muffs, 31, note 2). Finally, Muffs (177-178) discusses the respective histories of the cognates, Akkadian *šalāṭu*, Aramaic שלט "to have control, "once again pointing to a Neo-Assyrian symbiosis. Fales (1987) and Cussini (1993) have added important observations on the "Aramaic/Akkadian" symbiosis, and the recent publication of Neo-Assyrian legal documents by a number of scholars, including J.N., Postgate (1976) and S. Parpola and his team (Kwasman-Parpola 1991), make it possible at the present time to enhance the tracing of specific legal features.

2) Terms and formulas that entered Elephantine Aramaic from Akkadian in the Neo-Babylonian period. Here, we are searching for innovations of that later period, some of which were discussed above with respect to the Samaria Papyri of the 4th century B.C.E. Several examples are provided by Muffs, and more are suggested by Cussini. When all is said and done, the Neo-Babylonian influence on Aramaic seems more easily traceable than the Neo-Assyrian, because there is no problem at all in explaining such contemporary transfers in cultural-historical terms. There are numerous, available cuneiform exemplars for study, and at the same time, many more Aramaic legal documents in this period than are available from the Neo-Assyrian period. The Aramaic/Akkadian symbiosis was in full swing.

3) Terms and formulas native to West-Semitic/Aramaic, and not taken from Akkadian. Several examples were noted above, in the discussion of the Aramaic epigraphs. There is much more to be done in this area of inquiry, requiring the factoring-in of Hebrew (biblical) and Phoenician evidence, as well. This inquiry would be greatly advanced if more Aramaic legal, and official texts of the early periods come to light, and, alternatively, if more Punic texts become available.

Concluding Observations

Yochanan Muffs attempted to explore the transmission of legal practices and institutions in the ancient Near East that are reflected and realized in Aramaic law of the Achemenid period, as represented by the legal papyri from Elephantine. He selected as his focus a cognate Akkadian-Aramaic satisfaction clause that had a very long, albeit spotty history from Old Akkadian times, primarily in the "provincial" cuneiform legal traditions. As limited as his evidence was, Muffs was able, in the course of studying the transmission of this particular formula, to shed light on the many phases and forms of cuneiform law, itself, while at the same time revealing its legacy in Aramaic law. He carries us through the permutations of legal formulation, its new combinations and sequences, its isoglosses and replacements, and its functional and semantic equivalents. These are the indices of continuity and change, which facilitate the definition of legal principles and provisions. Muffs was trying to draw a map of legal development, much as a historian of art traces forms and motifs down through history, and within many societies and cultures. Apart from his contribution to the history of Near Eastern law, alternatively of its diffusion and its concentration, Yochanan Muffs has deepened our understanding of the language of law, in his charming inquiries that uncover the poetic side of a formalistic tradition. There is, at the present time, a significant group of scholars engaged in Aramaic studies, and more to our immediate interest, in the interpretation of the Elephantine corpus. To be sure, scholarship has been sustained by a limited, but continuing flow of ancient evidence. Perhaps more forceful is the realization that just as archeologists must show interest in private dwellings and outlying villages, not only in the monumental architecture of major capitals, so must historians venture into the distant provinces of empires, rather than remain more comfortably lodged in their homelands.

In this mix, appreciation for the role of Aramaic has grown immeasurably, alongside widespread interest in the Achemenid period, and in the pre-Hellenistic Near East, generally. Some are searching for the continuity of Mesopotamian civilization, which is the agenda of the recently established MELAMMU project. Others are focusing on the contemporary administration of the Persian Empire, and on the cross-cultural phenomena that characterized its vastly extended societies. The urge to shed light on what used to be regarded as two dark centuries, between the fall of Babylon and the conquests of Alexander, has added impetus to this quest. Thus it is that tiny, but well located Elephantine, always a vortex of cultural dynamism, has found its spot on the stage of history.

For verification of this assessment, the reader may wish to consult the proceedings of the Gröningen 1988 Achaemenid history workshop, *Achaemenid History VI: Asia and Egypt: Old Cultures in a New Empire* (Sancisi-Weerdenburg, Kurht 1991). At least two studies are of direct relevance to the subject of Muffs' monograph: By A. Lemaire, we have: "*Recherches d'Épigraphie Araméenne en Asie Mineure et en Égypte et le Probleme de l'Acculturation*" (199-206), and by J. Weisehofer: we have: "*PRTRK, RB HYL', SGN und MR': zur Verwaltung Sudägyptens in Achaemenidischer Zeit*" (305-309). Several other studies also pertain to Egypt of this period, and there is general significance to the many contributions covering the entire panoply of cultures that participated in the Persian imperial system, in broad perspective. Thus, Pierre Briant, in his study "*Des Sardes à Suse*" (67-82) provides a fascinating socio-historical tour, beginning in Asia Minor and ending east of the Tigris! No less fascinating is the contribution of C. Tuplin, "Darius' Suez Canal and Persian Imperialism" (237-283), a detailed and well documented re-examination of ancient sources on this often attempted project. Volume VI had been preceded by a series of others (*Achaemenid History*, Volumes I-V, 1987-1990), in which basic questions of methodology were raised, and the sources synthesized. Finally, Pierre Briant has given us his monumental work, *From Cyrus to Alexander* (2002), which affords a comprehensive overview of this important period of history.

More than thirty years ago, Yochanan Muffs possessed the keen vision and the scholarly acumen to subject the Aramaic legal papyri from 5th century B.C.E. Elephantine to methodic study. He was sensitive to the pivotal juncture of their time and place, looking back to their origins, and beyond them to their future effects. It has been my purpose here merely to call attention to Muffs; findings, to illustrate his method, and to show that he was ahead of his time! Subsequent discovery and study have affirmed his essential insights. Having provided us with a field theory for decoding legal formulation, Yochanan Muffs has won the right to parrot Hillel, the Elder, and declare to each of us: ואידך, זיל גמור! "And as for the rest—go and learn (for yourself)!"

REFERENCE BIBLIOGRAPHY

1. *Abbreviations*

Ahw *Akkadisches Handwörterbuch* (W. von Soden)
CAD *The Assyrian Dictionary*, University of Chicago
DNWSI *Dictionary of the North-West Semitic Languages* (J. Hoftijzer, K. Jongeling, Leiden: E. J. Brill, 1995).
Muffs Yochanan Muffs, *Studies in the Aramaic Legal Papyri from Elephantine* (*Studia et Documenta, Volumen* XIII; ed. M. David, B. Landsberger, Leiden: E. J. Brill, 1969).
TAD *Textbook of Aramaic Documents from Ancient Egypt* (B. Porten, A. Yardeni, Jerusalem: The Hebrew University, Vols. I-IV, 1986-1999 [distributed by Eisenbrauns, Winona Lake, IN]).

2. *Works Cited*

Abou-Assaf, A., Bordreuil, P., and Millard, R.
1982 *La Statue de Tell Fekherye; et son inscription bilingue assyro-araméenne* (Etudes Assyriologiques), Paris: Éditions Recherche sur les Civilisations.

Arnaud, D.
1986 *Recherches au Pays d'Aštata, Emar* VI/3: *Textes Sumériens et Accadiens, Texte.* Paris: Editions Recherches sur les Civilisations.

Beckman, G.
1988 "Three Tablets from the Vicinity of Emar," *Journal of Cuneiform Studies* 40, 61-68.
1996 *Texts from the Vicinity of Emar in the Collection of Jonathan Rosen*, Padua: Sargon.

Briant, P.
2002 *From Cyrus to Alexander; A History of the Persian Empire*, trans. Peter T. Daniels, Winona Lake, IN: Eisenbrauns.

Cross, F. M. Jr.
1985 "Samaria Papyrus I: An Aramaic Slave Conveyance of 335 B.C.E," *Eretz-Israel* 18 (Avigad Volume), 7-17.
1986 "A Report on the Samaria Papyri," *Vetus Testamentum, Supplements* 40, 17-26.

Cussini
1993 *The Aramaic Law of Sale and the Cuneiform Legal Tradition*, unpublished Phd. Dissertation, The Johns Hopkins University.

Eshel, E., Kloner, A.
1996 "An Aramaic Ostracon of an Edomite Marriage Contract from Maresha, Dated 176 B.C.E.," *Israel Exploration Journal* 46, 1-22.

Fales, F. M.
1982 *"Note di Semitico Nordoccidentale," Vicino Oriente* 5, 75-83.
1986 *Aramaic Epigraphs on Clay Tablets of the Neo-Assyrian Period* (*Studi Semitici, Nuova Serie*, 2), Roma: Universita degli Studi "La Sapienza".
1987 "*La Tradizione Assira ad Elefantina d'Egitto*," *Dialoghi d'Archeologia* 5, 63-70.

Fitzmyer, J. A., Kaufman, S.
1991 *An Aramaic Bibilography, Part I: Old. Official, and Biblical Aramaic* (Publication of *The Comprehensive Aramaic Lexicon* Project), Baltimore: The Johns Hopkins University Press.

Fleming, D. E.
2000 *Time at Emar; The Cultic Calendar and the Rituals from the Diviner's House*, Winona Lake, IN: Eisenbrauns, 312-330.

Folmer, M. L.
1995 *The Aramaic Language in the Achaemenid Period; A Study in Linguistic Variation*, Leuven: Peeters Press.

Goldstein, J.
1966 "The Syriac Bill of Sale from Dura- Europus," *Journal of Near Eastern Studies* 25, 1-16.

Grayson, A. Kirk
1992 "History and Culture of Assyria," in *Anchor Bible Dictionary*, Volume 4, 732-755.

Greenfield, J. C., Porten, B.
1982 *The Bisitun Inscription of Darius the Great: Aramaic Version*, Corpus Inscriptionum Iranicarum I/5, London: Lund Humphries.

Greenfield, J. C., Shaffer, A.
1983 "Notes on the Akkadian-Aramaic Bilingual Statue from Tell Fekherye," *Iraq* 45, 109-116.

Gropp, D.
2001 *Wadi Daliyeh II: The Samaria Papyri from Wadi Daliyeh, Qumran Cave 4, Miscellenea, Part 2*, ed. E. Schuler, *et al.* (*Discoveries in the Judaean Desert XXVIII*), Oxford. Clarendon Press.

Hallo, W. W.
2002 "A Model Court Case Concerning Inheritance," *Riches Hidden in Secret Places; Ancient Near Eastern Studies in Memory of Thorkild Jacobsen*, ed. Tzvi Abusch, Winona Lake, IN: Eisenbrauns, 141-154.

Kaufman, S. A.
1974 *The Akkadian Influences on Aramaic*, Chicago: University of Chicago Press.

Kwasman, Th., Parpola, S.
1991 *Legal Transactions of the Royal Court of Nineveh, Part I: Tiglath-Pileser III through Esarhaddon* (State Archives of Assyria VI, Helsinki University Press).

Lemaire, A.
2001 *Nouvelles Tablettes Araméennes (École Pratique dès Hautes Études)*, Genève: Librairie Droz.

Levine, B. A.
1974 *In the Presence of the Lord; A Study of Cult and Cultic Terms in Ancient Israel*, Leiden: E. J. Brill, 3-45.
1975 "On the Origins of the Aramaic Legal Formulary at Elephantine," *Christianity, Judaism, and Other Greco-Roman Cults; Studies for Morton Smith at Sixty, Part Three; Judaism before 70*, ed. J. Neusner, Leiden: E. J. Brill, 37-54.
1993 "On the Semantics of Land Tenure in Biblical Literature: The Term *ʾaḥuzzāh*," *The Tablet and the Scroll; Near Eastern Studies in Honor of William W. Hallo*, ed. Mark E. Cohen, *et al.*, Bethesda, MD: CDL Press, 134-139.

Lieberman, S. J.
1968 "The Aramaic Argillary Script in the Seventh Century," *Bulletin, American Schools of Oriental Research* 192, 25-31.

Muffs, Y.
1975 "Joy and Love as Metaphorical Expressions of Willingness and Spontaneity in Cuneiform, Ancient Hebrew, and Related Literatures," *Christianity, Judaism and*

Other Greco-Roman Cults; Studies for Morton Smith at Sixty, Part Three: Judaism before 70, ed. J. Neusner, Leiden: E. J. Brill, 1-36.

1992 *Love and Joy; Law, Language, and Religion in Ancient Israel*, New York and Jerusalem: The Jewish Theological Seminary. (Hebrew version entitled: אהבה ושמחה, etc., trans. A. Meltzer, Jerusalem: Hebrew University-Magnes Press, 2002.)

Oelsner, J.

1997 "*Neü/spätbabylonische und Aramäische Kaufverträge*," *Ana šadi Labnāni lū allik* (Festschrift W. Röllig), Neukirchen-Vluyn, 307-314.

Porten, B.

1968 *Archives from Elephantine: The Life of an Ancient Jewish Military Colony*, Berkeley and Los Angeles: University of California Press.

1996 *The Elephantine Papyri in English; Three Millennia of Cross-Cultural Continuity and Change*, with: J. Joel Farber, Cary J. Martin, Günter Vittmann, Leslie S. B. MacCoull, Sarah Clackson, and contributions by S. Hopkins, R. Katzoff, Leiden: E. J. Brill.

Porten, B., in collaboration with Greenfield, J. C.

1974 *Jews of Elephantine and Aramaeans of Syene (Fifth Century B.C.E.): Fifty Aramaic Texts with Hebrew and English Translations*, Jerusalem: Academon.

Postgate, J. N.

1976 *Fifty Neo-Assyrian Legal Documents*, Warminster: Aris & Phllips.

Sancini-Weerdenburg, H., Kuhrt, A.

1991 *Achaemenid History VI; Asia Minor and Egypt: Old Cultures in a New Empire* (Proceedings of the Groningen 1988 Achaemenid History Workshop), Leiden: Nederlands Institut voor het Nabije Oosten. (Note studies by P. Briant, A. Lemaire, C. Tuplin, and J. Weisehofer.)

Skaist, A.

1998 "The Chronology of the Legal Texts from Emar," *Zeitschrift für Assyriologie* 88, 45-71.

Tadmor, H.

1982 "The Aramaization of Assyria: Aspects of Western Impact," *Mesopotamien und seine Nachbarn* (*Berliner Beitrage zum vorderen Orient* I), ed. Nissen, H. J., Renger, J., Berlin: Reimer, 449-470.

Yaron, R.

1961 *Introduction to the Law of the Aramaic Papyri*, Oxford: Clarendon Press.

ACKNOWLEDGMENTS

I am deeply indebted to my teacher, the late E. A. Speiser, for having suggested this topic and for his encouragement and guidance from the inception of this study to its completion. I would also like to express my gratitude to the following: Professors Moshe Greenberg and S. N. Kramer who read this study in thesis form and made some helpful suggestions; Professor Richard A. Parker who was kind enough to discuss some of the Egyptian material with me.

In addition, I would like to express my thanks to the Society for Religion in Higher Education for having awarded me a Kent Fellowship and to the Philip W. Lown Institute for Advanced Judaic Studies, Brandeis University, for financial support during the writing of this study. The publication of this study was made possible by a major subvention from the Lucius N. Littauer Foundation with additional subventions provided by the Stroock Publication Fund of the Jewish Theological Seminary and the National Foundation for Jewish Culture. My deepest thanks to Harry Starr of the Littauer Foundation, Mr. Harry Barron of the National Foundation for Jewish Culture, and Professor Louis Finkelstein of the Jewish Theological Seminary, for having made the necessary funds available.

I owe a deep debt of gratitude to the Jewish Theological Seminary not only for much of my early training, but also for providing me with a year's leave of absence during which this study was completed. To Professor Finkelstein, the Chancellor of the Seminary, I am especially indebted for his abiding interest in my work. I would also like to express my warmest thanks to my teachers, H. L. Ginsberg, Thorkild Jacobsen and Saul Lieberman for their encouragement, friendship and counsel. To my parents, my first teachers, this study is gratefully dedicated.

Although the manuscript was submitted in the summer of 1964, substantial additions were made in the last chapter during the summer of 1967 and a section of addenda et corrigenda was added in the summer of 1968.

An asterisk in the body of the text indicates the presence of an addendum or a corrigendum. All these additions have been incorporated into the glossaries and indices and are marked with an asterisk (*). Thus, for example, 100 n4* means: cf. the addendum or corrigendum to p. 100, note 4.

New York — Yochanan Muffs
August, 1968

CHAPTER ONE

INTRODUCTION

1. The Discovery of the Papyri

In the first decade of this century, a series of Aramaic papyri were found on the island of Elephantine [1] on the upper Nile near the city of Assuan. [2] The deeds were written during the fifth century B.C. [3] by a group of Jewish mercenaries [4] in the employ of the Persian government. [5] The find consisted of legal documents, letters, and the Aramaic versions of the Aḥiqar romance and the Behistun inscription. The letters record the official correspondence between the leaders of the colony and the Persian governor of Judea concerning the restoration of the temple of *Yhw*, destroyed by the local Egyptian priests in an anti-Jewish riot. [6] In some respects, the discovery of these Aramaic papyri [7] did as much

---

[1]) Elephantine-Aramaic *yb*, from the Egyptian *ʿiēbew* „elephant-place." Elephantine is thus the literal Greek translation of the Egyptian name. Cf. *BP*, p. 23.*

[2]) Assuan-Aramaic *swn*, from the Egyptian *sewen* "mart/tradingpost." The name reflects the fact that there, from time immemorial, the raw materials of inner Africa and the finished products of Egypt were exchanged. The name is also recorded in the Bible: cf. Ez 30 : 6 and 1Q Isa^a 49 : 12. For a discussion of the Egyptian name and the Biblical evidence, cf. *BP*, p. 21, n. 1.

[3]) The oldest known Elephantine Aramaic papyrus is dated 495 B.C.; cf. *AP* 1. The oldest known Aramaic legal papyrus from Egypt—not from Elephantine—is dated 515 B.C.; cf. H. Bauer and B. Meissner, "Ein aramäischer Pachtvertrag aus dem 7. Jahre Darius' 1.," *SPAW*, 1936, pp. 414-424. The same text has been re-edited by A. Dupont-Sommer, "Un contrat de métayage égypto-araméen de l'an 7 de Darius Ier," *MAI*, 14^2 (1944), pp. 1 ff.

[4]) For a discussion of Jewish mercenaries in antiquity, cf. P. Korngreen, *Jewish Military Colonies* [in Hebrew] (Tel-Aviv, 1948). See also M. Greenberg, "Ezekiel 17 and the Policy of Psammetichus II," *JBL*, 76 (1957), p. 307.

[5]) The origins of the colony are still not clear. Only one fact is certain: the colony was established before the Persian conquest of Egypt. In *AP* 30: 13-14, the elders of the colony write to Bigvai, the governor of Judea, as follows, concerning the origins of the temple, recently destroyed by the priests of Khnub: "Already in the days of the kings of Egypt our fathers had built that temple in the fortress of Yeb, and when Cambyses came into Egypt, he found that temple built." Opinions concerning the origins of the Jewish colony range from the fall of Damascus in 732 to the reign of Amasis (659-626 B.C.). For a survey of the various dates that have been suggested, cf. *BP*, Chapter IV: "Nature and Origin of the Jewish Colony," pp. 41-48. Cf. now, Porten, Chapter I.

[6]) For a discussion of the temple of *Yhw*, cf. Vincent, *Religion*, pp. 312-91.

[7]) For a comprehensive survey of the history of the discoveries, and surveys of the publications, cf. the various introductions to *BP*. See also the article of Ben-Ḥayyim, *Documents*, pp. 425-439.

to change the Biblical studies of that day as the finds of Qumran and Chenoboskion [1]) did to the studies of our generation.

The first Aramaic Elephantine deed was published by J. Euting in 1903. [2]) In 1906, the archive of Mibṭaḥiah was published by Sayce and Cowley. [3]) Subsequently, more deeds were published by E. Sachau in 1907 [4]) and by O. Rubensohn in 1909/10. [5]) In 1911, Sachau re-edited all the documents which had been found by German scholars until that time. [6]) Important popular editions of the deeds were prepared by W. Staerk [7]) and A. Ungnad. [8]) All the papyri discovered in these early excavations were re-edited by A. Cowley in his *Aramaic Papyri of the Fifth Century B.C.*

Paradoxically, the papyri which were first brought to the attention of the scholarly world were not the first to be discovered. In 1893, the American archaeologist, Charles Edwin Wilbour, discovered a series of Aramaic legal documents at Elephantine. Since he did not read Aramaic, he was evidently unaware of the nature of his find. For some reason he did not announce his discovery to the world at large, and when he died in 1896, he took his secret with him to the grave. Many years later the deeds were found by his daughter, who entrusted them to the Brooklyn Museum for publication. [9]) They were edited by Emil Kraeling and appeared in 1953 as *The Brooklyn Museum Aramaic Papyri*. Kraeling provided this volume with copious notes and a series of introductory studies in which he discussed, among other things, the history of all Aramaic papyri discovered until that date, Egypt under Persian rule, and the history of the Jewish colony at Elephantine, its origins and institutions.

---

[1]) J. Doresse, *The Secret Books of the Egyptian Gnostics*, trans. P. Mariet (New York, 1960).

[2]) J. Euting, "Notice sur un papyrus égypto-araméen," *MAI*, 11 (1903), pp. 297 ff.

[3]) A. H. Sayce and A. E. Cowley, *Aramaic Papyri Discovered at Assuan* (London, 1906).

[4]) E. Sachau, *Drei aramäische Papyrusurkunden aus Elephantine*, *APAW*, 1907.

[5]) W. Honroth, O. Rubensohn, and F. Zucker, "Bericht über die Ausgrabungen auf Elephantine in den Jahren 1906-1908," *ZÄS*, 46 (1909-10), pp. 14-61.

[6]) E. Sachau, *Aramäische Papyrus und Ostraka aus einer jüdischen Militär-Kolonie zu Elephantine* ... (Leipzig, 1911), with folio of plates.

[7]) W. Staerk published three different popular editions of the Aramaic papyri: a) *Die jüdisch-aramäischen Papyri von Assuan* (Bonn, 1907). This was a popular edition of the Sayce-Cowley texts; b) *Aramäische Urkunden zur Geschichte des Judentums* ... (Bonn, 1908). This was the popular edition of the Sachau texts of 1907; c) *Alte und neue aramäische Papyri übersetzt und erklärt* (Bonn, 1912). This was the popular edition of Sachau's 1911 texts.

[8]) A. Ungnad, *Aramäische Papyrus aus Elephantine* (Leipzig, 1911).

[9]) For the history of this discovery, cf. *BP*, p. 3.

2. The Legal Documents

The information gleaned from the legal documents—the most common type of papyri discovered—was no less revolutionary than that obtained from the historical and religious papyri. Among other things, we learn that Jews with monotheistic names like Mibṭaḥiah pronounce oaths in the name of Egyptian deities without any apparent duress or compunction. [1]) Furthermore, women enjoyed such a measure of social and economic freedom that they were allowed the right of instituting divorce proceedings against their husbands [2])—a right denied not only by the Law of Moses but also by Old Babylonian practice. [3]) Moreover, even a cursory investigation of the formulary used in these documents made it quite clear that the documents were less Jewish in origin than Demotic or Near Eastern. [4])

A. *Previous Studies of the Legal Material*

Early Studies (*of the Cowley Volume*). At the turn of the century, the legal documents were overshadowed by the more dramatic historical finds: thus, the study of sale or marriage law seemed a less profitable field of investigation than the problems of religious syncretism or the correspondence between the colonists and the Persian government. In

---

[1]) Cf. *AP* 14: 4-6. Mibṭaḥiah takes an oath by the goddess Sati to clear herself of charges raised against her by her former husband, The Egyptian Piʾ.

[2]) Cf. *AP* 15: 22-23 and *BP* 7: 24-25; cf. the discussion of Yaron, *LAP*, pp. 53 ff.

[3]) According to actual Old Babylonian practice, wives who repudiated their husbands, no matter what the circumstances, were subject to severe punishment: cf., for example, Schorr, *Urkunden*, No. 2 (the woman is thrown into the river) and No. 4 (the woman is thrown from a tower). According to CH 142-143, if a woman's husband is a philanderer and she, on the other hand, has behaved in a proper manner [for an alternate interpretation of *naṣ/zrat*, cf. G. Dossin, "L'article 142/143 du code de Ḫammurabi, "*RA*, 42 (1948), pp. 113-124], she may refuse to have intercourse with him; the court upon investigation of the matter may award her a divorce. This law may be a reflection of the theoretical character of the CH (cf., for example, J. J. Finkelstein's review of Kraus, *Ammi-Ṣaduqa* in *JCS*, 15 (1961), pp. 91-104. However, even if it was a reflection of OB legal reality, it is still a far cry from the absolute and unconditional right of the Elephantine woman to institute divorce proceedings against her husband. The closest analogue of the Elephantine procedure is found at Kültepe (cf. B. Hrozný, "Über eine unveröffentlichte Urkunde von Kültepe," in *Symbolae Koschaker*, pp. 108 ff. For slightly later examples, cf. Weisman, *AT*, Nos. 92 and 94. These parallels were first pointed out by Mendelsohn in *On Marriage in Alalakh*, pp. 352 ff. Cf. also Yaron's comments in *LAP*, pp. 48 ff.*

[4]) This was seen most clearly by Lidzbarski in his review of Sayce-Cowley (*DLZ*, 1906, p. 3205 and *ibid.*, 1907, p. 3160). Cf. also the comments of Revillout, *Les origines égyptiennes*: "Supplément sur les contrats égypto-araméens d'Éléphantine," pp. 52-60.

general, that generation of orientalists and Bible scholars was more concerned with problems of religion and literature than with matters of law and sociology. [1]) This relative lack of interest in law manifested itself in the primitive state of ancient legal studies—whether Biblical, [2]) cuneiform, [3]) or Demotic [4])—at the turn of the century.

Nevertheless, it cannot be said that the legal aspect of the Elephantine find was altogether neglected. Talmudists such as Epstein, [5]) Blau, [6]) Fischer, [7]) and Freund [8]) pointed out many similarities between the Aramaic deeds and later Jewish legal literature. Spiegelberg [9]) and Revillout [10]) also noticed some significant Egyptian parallels.

At the same time, the first attempts were made to illuminate the cuneiform background of the Aramaic deeds. Nöldeke, [11]) Buhl, [12]) Cler-

---

[1]) Cf., for example, the introduction by J. Pirenne to *AHDO*, 1 (1937), pp. ix ff.

[2]) Cf. Greenberg, *Postulates*, p. 5: "The study of biblical law has been a stepchild of the historical-critical approach to the Bible. While the law had been a major preoccupation of ancient and medieval scholars, in modern times it has largely been replaced by, or made to serve, other interests. No longer studied for itself, it is now investigated for the reflexes it harbors of stages in Israel's social development, or it is analyzed by literary-historical criticism into strata, each synchronized with a given stage in the evolution of Hebrew religion and culture.... It is a remarkable fact that the last comprehensive juristic treatment of biblical law was made over a century ago."*

[3]) Cf. San Nicolò, *Beiträge*, Chapter I, pp. 1-31.

[4]) Cf. the works of E. Revillout, one of the very few scholars who occupied himself with the study of Demotic law at the turn of this century. Cf. his *Les origines égyptiennes* and his *Propriété*. The rest of Revillout's publications are cited in Pirenne, "Introduction à l'histoire du droit égyptien," *AHDO*, 2 (1938), pp. 11 ff. Revillout's work has been criticized by most modern scholars. Cf. the comments of Malinine, *Choix de textes* vi, and Seidl, *Einführung*, p. 13, n. 5.

[5]) J. N. Epstein, "Notizen zu den jüdisch-aramäischen Papyri von Assuan," *JJLG*, 6 (1908/9), pp. 359-73.

[6]) Blau, *Judaica*, pp. 207 ff. Blau also published a series of review articles on the Elephantine papyri in Hungarian in *Magyar-Zsidó Szemle*, 24 (1907), pp. 222 ff.; *ibid.*, 25 (1908), pp. 236 ff.; *ibid.*, 29 (1922), pp. 41 ff.

[7]) L. Fischer, "Glossen zu den jüdisch-aramäischen Papyri von Assuan," *JJLG*, 8 (1910/11), pp. 391 ff. Also by the same author, "Die Urkunden im Talmud," *ibid.*, 9 (1911/12), pp. 45-197.

[8]) L. Freund, "Bemerkungen zu Papyrus G. des Funds von Assuan," *WZKM*, 21 (1907), pp. 169 ff. Also, by the same author, "Zum semitischen Ehegüterrecht bei Auflösung der Ehe." *ibid.*, 30 (1917/18), pp. 163 ff., and *Zur Geschichte des Ehegüterrechtes bei den Semiten* (Wien, 1931).

[9]) Quoted in T. Nöldeke, "Die aramäischen Papyri von Assuan," *ZA*, 20 (1907), pp. 130 ff.

[10]) Revillout, *Les origines égyptiennes*, "Supplément sur les contrats égypto-araméens d'Éléphantine," pp. 52-60.

[11]) *ZA*, 20 (1907) pp. 130 ff.

[12]) F. Buhl, "Remarques sur les papyrus juifs d'Éléphantine," *Danske Videnskabernes Selskabs, Forhandlinger*, 1908, No. 2, pp. 37 ff.

mont-Ganneau, [1]) Cowley, [2]) and Pritsch [3])—to name but a few—all made significant contributions in this area. Cowley, especially, emphasized the Near Eastern background of the documents. In his introduction to the *Aramaic Papyri* he states:

> The courts over which the *rbḥyl'* and the *prtrk* presided, . . . administered no doubt the law of the Persian empire, but this law, like so much else, was evidently taken over by the conquerers from the Babylonians, or was based on their system. . . . In general the connection with Babylonian law is well worthy of a thorough study. [4])

The most important contributions in this area were made by two of the very few orientalists then actively engaged in the study of cuneiform law—Peiser [5]) and Ungnad. [6]) Peiser devoted three studies to the Aramaic papyri, especially to the cuneiform elements preserved in them. [7]) He was keenly aware that the study of the deeds was not only significant as an end in itself but also because of the light it obliquely shed on cuneiform legal history. The following comment is typical of this suggestive approach:

> Es ist eigenartig, dass dieser Terminus altbabylonischer Rechtsurkunden [i.e., the Aramaic/Akkadian term *grh/gerû* "to contest"] sich so lang gehalten hat und hier auftaucht, während er in Babylon in Abgang bekommen war. [8])

The question raised by the Aramaic documents is thus, essentially, an inner-Assyriological question which obliges the Assyriologist to make fuller use of the resources of cuneiform law in connection with apparent echoes in outside documents.

The Assyriological comments of Ungnad were incorporated in his popular edition of the needs known until 1911, namely, *Aramäische Papyrus aus Elephantine*. He noticed that the Aramaic *r'š*, literally "head," but contextually "capital," was equivalent to the common

---

[1]) C. S. Clermont-Ganneau, *Revue Critique d'Histoire*, 1906, Part II, pp. 341 ff.

[2]) In the notes and introduction to *AP*.

[3]) E. Pritsch, "Jüdische Rechtsurkunden aus Aegypten," *ZVRW*, 27 (1912), pp. 7 ff. Pritsch returned more recently to the Elephantine documents in his contribution "Die aramäischen Urkunden," in the series "Zum gegenwärtigen Stand der juristischen Papyrusforschung," *ZVRW*, 60 (1958), pp. 99-117.

[4]) *AP*, Introduction, p. xxix.

[5]) Cf. Peiser, *KB* IV. Especially noteworthy was the collaboration between Peiser and the noted legal historian, J. Kohler, which resulted in the series *Babylonischen Rechtsleben*. The same authors also edited *HG* I-V.

[6]) Kohler also collaborated with Ungnad in *ARU*.

[7]) Peiser, *OLZ*, 10 (1907), p. 622; *ibid.*, 11 (1908), pp. 24 ff. and pp. 73 ff. (reviews of Staerk, *Die jüdisch-aramäischen Papyri von Assuan* [1907]).

[8]) Peiser, *ibid.*, 10 (1907), p. 625.

Akkadian *qaqqadu* "head/capital." [1]) Other significant Aramaic-Akkadian parallels established by Ungnad are: a) *šlṭ/šalāṭu* "to be master of/own"; [2]) b) *yhk bdyn wlʾ yṣdq* "let him go to court (lit. to trial) and not win" = *ina dēnišu idabbub-ma lā ilaqqi* "may he institute a suit (lit. may he lodge a complaint in his suit) and not receive (anything)." [3]) c) *lʾntw/ana aššūti* "(to take) as a wife; lit. in wifehood." [4]) It is strange that these valuable comments of the pioneers in this field have been overlooked by more recent investigators. This is especially true of the comments of Lidzbarski—the pioneer of West Semitic epigraphy.

In a series of review articles, [5]) Lidzbarski presented what could be called a unified field theory concerning the origins and the historic role of the Aramaic documents. He was impressed by the fullness and great complexity of the formulary used in the documents. Such a fully developed formulary could not have possibly been created during the fifth century or even the one immediately preceding: it could only have emerged gradually, over a period of hundreds of years. [6]) Furthermore, the fact that the deeds were written in Aramaic suggests a Syrian rather than an Egyptian origin. According to Lidzbarski, the deeds are a clear indicator of the active role the Arameans must have played in the economic life of the Near East prior to the fifth century. The Aramaic formulary must have been created as the instrument of this widespread business activity. [7])

Lidzbarski argued that the Aramaic formulary was based on cuneiform prototypes [8]) but was strongly influenced by West Semitic legal and business terminology. [9]) The later Nabatean deeds and inscriptions, as

---

[1]) Ungnad, *Aramäische Papyrus*, p. 46, n. 6. Cf., more recently, the discussion of Kutscher, *New Aramaic Texts*, p. 243.

[2]) Ungnad, *Aramäische Papyrus*, p. 47, n. 8.

[3]) *Ibid.*, p. 47, n. 18.

[4]) *Ibid.*, p. 54, n. 5.

[5]) Lidzbarski, *Ephemeris*, Vol. II (1908), p. 210-250; Vol. III (1915), pp. 70 and 238 ff. (exegetical notes). Lidzbarski's historical comments were incorporated in his reviews of Sayce-Cowley in *DLZ*, 1906, p. 3205; in his review of Sachau, *Drei aramäische Papyrusurkunden aus Elephantine*, *ibid.*, 1907, p. 3160 ff.

[6]) "Die festen Formulen, in denen die Sprache der Dokumente sich bewegt, setzen eine lange Entwicklung dieses Schrifttums und somit ein altes ausgedehntes Handelsleben in Syrien voraus" (*DLZ*, 1906, 3207).

[7]) *Ibid.*

[8]) *Ibid.*

[9]) "Die Sprache ist . . . stark mit kanaanäischen Elementen durchsetzt, und diese Idiomismen sind über die aramäische Amtssprache der Achämeniden Zeit sogar in das religiöse Schrifttum der Perser gedrungen. In diese Papyri, die von Juden herrühren, werden die meisten kanaanäischen Wörter als Hebraismen hineingeraten sein, sonst haben sicherlich die Bewohner der blühenden phönizischen See- und Handelstäte die Amtssprache mehr beeinflusst als die Juden" (*DLZ*, 1907, p. 3162).

well as the fragments of the deeds found in the Talmud, are all natural offshoots of this early Aramaic formulary. [1]) As we shall soon see, Lidzbarski's comments are as valid today as they were sixty years ago.

Recent Studies. The publication of the *Brooklyn Museum Aramaic Papyri* in 1953 ushered in a new period in the history of Aramaic legal studies. Since almost all of the documents published by Kraeling were legal in content, [2]) all of the reviewers—Ginsberg, [3]) Kutscher, [4]) Cazelles, [5]) Volterra, [6]) Milik, [7]) Driver, [8]) and others—were forced by the very nature of the material to turn their attention to juridical matters. In most cases, however, the comments of these scholars were philological rather than legal.

Recent developments in Near Eastern studies have set the stage for a comparative investigation of the legal papyri. Because of the pioneering labors of scholars like Cuq, [9]) Peiser, [10]) and especially Koschaker, [11]) cuneiform legal studies now constitute a well-established discipline. Tens of thousands of documents from all periods and most major sites have been published. [12]) Demotic law, almost completely neglected from

[1]) *Ibid.*, 1906, p. 3207.

[2]) The only nonlegal document in the Kraeling volume is *BP* 13—a letter.

[3]) H. L. Ginsberg, "The Brooklyn Museum Aramaic Papyri," *JAOS*, 74 (1954), pp. 153 ff.

[4]) Kutscher, *New Aramaic Texts.*

[5]) H. Cazelles, "Nouveaux documents araméens d'Égypte," *Syria*, 32 (1955), pp. 75 ff.

[6]) E. Volterra, *Iura*, 6 (1955), pp. 349 ff.; cf. also Volterra's article "La affrancazione di schiavi nei documenti aramaici del V secolo a.C.," *Rivista degli Studi Orientali*, 32 (1957), pp. 675 ff. Cf. also his article "Osservazioni sul divorzio nei documenti aramaici," in *Studi orientali in onore di Giorgio Levi Della Vida* II, pp. 586 ff.

[7]) J. T. Milik, *RB*, 61 (1954), pp. 247 ff.

[8]) G. R. Driver, *PEQ*, 87 (1955), pp. 91 ff. Cf. his earlier comments on the Cowley volume, "The Aramaic *Papyri*: Notes on Obscure Passages," *JRAS*, 1932, pp. 77 ff.

[9]) Cuq, *Études.*

[10]) Peiser's main legal works are cited above, p. 5, n. 5.

[11]) Cf. especially his first major work, *Bürgschaftsrecht.*

[12]) For a comprehensive survey of the development of cuneiform law until 1930, cf. San Nicolò's *Beiträge*. For a summary of the literature until 1938, cf. G. Boyer, "Introduction bibliographique à l'histoire du droit suméro-akkadien," *AHDO*, 2 (1938), pp. 63-110. For the literature until 1955, cf. Boyer, "Introduction bibliographique à l'histoire du droit suméro-akkadien II," *RIDA*, 3 (1956), pp. 41-79. The most recent bibliographical studies are those of J. Klíma, entitled "Über neuere Studien auf dem Gebiete des Keilschriftrechtes" in *ArOr* [No. I in *ArOr*, 18 (1950), pt. 1/2, pp. 525 ff.; No. II=*ibid.*, 18 (1950), pt. 4, pp. 351 ff.;No. III=*ibid.*, 20 (1952), pp. 539 ff.: No. IV = *ibid.*, 21 (1953), pp. 604 ff.: No. V = *ibid.*, 26 (1957), pp. 224 ff.] and the series, "Bibliographisches zum Keilschriftrecht," in the *JJP* [No. I=*JJP* 6 (1952), pp. 153 ff.; No. II=*ibid.*, 7/8 (1953-54), pp. 295ff.; No. III=*ibid.*, 9/10 (1955-56), pp. 431 ff.; No. IV=*ibid.*, 11/12 (1957-58), pp. 195 ff.; No. V=*ibid.*, 13 (1961), pp. 269-290.*

the time of Revillout, has now found its devoted student in Michel Malinine. [1])

Thus, by 1953, the necessary *Vorstudien* for the comparative study of the Aramaic papyri were all at hand. Nor was the interest in such an undertaking lacking; San Nicolò, [2]) Volterra, [3]) Speiser, [4]) and others had been calling for a study of the cuneiform elements in the later legal systems of antiquity. Koschaker, in his study of the cuneiform elements in the Greek documents from Dura Europus, had presented the methodological model for just such an undertaking. [5])

a) Yehezkel Kutscher was one of the first scholars to attack the problem. In his review of *BP*, [6]) Kutscher called attention to the wide-ranging historical affinities of the Aramaic deeds. On the one hand, the Elephantine documents are quite similar to the contemporary Demotic deeds [7])—a fact which had escaped the notice of most contemporary students of Demotic law. On the other hand, the Aramaic deeds seem to be the *Vorlagen*—direct of indirect—of the Talmudic [8]) and Gaonic documents, and the Syriac deed of sale from Dura. [9])

Kutscher then suggested a theory which would account for these affinities. To do this, he borrowed the term Reichsaramäisch ("royal"

---

[1]) Especially his *Choix de textes*. See also his various articles: "Une vente d'esclave à l'époque de Psammétique Ier," *Revue d'Égyptologie*, 5 (1946), pp. 119 ff.; "Un jugement rendu à Thèbes sous la XXVe dynastie," *ibid.*, 6 (1951), pp. 157 ff.; "Un contrat de vente d'emplacements à construire de l'époque du roi Achoris," *ibid.*, 7 (1950), pp. 107-120; "Trois documents de l'époque d'Amasis relatifs au louage de terres," *ibid.*, 8 (1951), pp. 127-150; "Deux documents égyptiens relatifs au dépôt" *MDAIK*, 16 (1958), pp. 219 ff.*

[2]) Cf. his *Beiträge*, Chapter II: "Die Stellung der Keilschriftlichen Denkmäler innerhalb der vorderasiatischen Rechtsentwicklung," especially pp. 52-62.

[3]) E. Volterra, "Introduction à l'histoire du droit romain dans ses rapports avec l'Orient," *AHDO*, 4 (1949), pp. 117 ff.; see also "Les rapports entre le Droit romain et les Droits de l'Orient," *RIDA*, 2 (1955), pp. 135 ff.; *Diritto romano e diritti orientali* (Bologna, 1937).

[4]) *Proceedings of the American Philosophical Society*, 107 (1963), pp. 536 ff.

[5]) Koschaker, *GRÖG*. The Greek deeds from Dura and the Aramaic deeds from Elephantine have much in common: in both cases, older cuneiform material has been adopted to a later legal and linguistic milieu; in both cases, the limited number of documents which have survived is hardly an ideal point of departure for a legal study. Koschaker was able to learn so much from so few documents by focusing almost all of the available comparative material, whether Greek or cuneiform, upon the few Dura documents that survived. A similar approach is attempted below in the study of the Elephantine legal documents.

[6]) Kutscher, *New Aramaic Texts*, pp. 233 ff.

[7]) *Ibid.*, pp. 234-238.

[8]) *Ibid.*, pp. 244-245. Cf. his important articles "Concerning the Terminology of Legal Documents in the Talmud and in Gaonic Literature," *Tarbiẓ*, 17 (1939), pp. 125 ff. and *ibid.*, 19 (1947/8), pp. 53 ff. and pp. 125 ff.

[9]) Kutscher, *New Aramaic Texts*, p. 244.

or "standard" Aramaic) from the lexicon of the linguist and successfully applied it to the interpretation of legal history. According to Kutscher, a standard Aramaic common law formulary must have emerged at about the same time as standard Aramaic did, and under similar circumstances, and enjoying the same wide diffusion. [1]) Unfortunately, the more ancient examples of this formulary have not been preserved. But certainly, the Aramaic legal documents of Dura and the Talmud are the natural offshoots of this formulary.

Kutscher argued that since there are no known examples of Egyptian influence in the later Aramaic deeds, it seems unlikely that the older Elephantine prototypes were based on Demotic models. However, the Elephantine and Demotic deeds are remarkably similar in structure and general formulation: some historical relationship, therefore, must exist between them; they are not merely the product of parallel development. Since the Demotic legal historians have themselves suggested that the Demotic formulary may have come into being under the influence of oriental models, it would seem, argues Kutscher, that the Aramaic formulary may have been the oriental factor that scholars have been looking for. [2])

Kutscher also discusses the origins of the Aramaic formulary. According to him, the formulary was based mainly on inner-Aramaic legal resources but "it well may be assumed that the Aramaic has assimilated Phoenician, Canaanite-Hebrew, and Akkadian elements, especially during its stabilization in Syria. This process, which is quite likely, is of course rather difficult to prove because of the lack of sources, especially legal documents, in most of the languages concerned." [3]) This statement needs to be modified in the light of later studies by R. Yaron and the author. The cuneiform element is much more decisive than Kutscher assumed. In all probability, the Aramaic formulary is based, on the whole, on actual cuneiform models, many of which still have to be isolated. This is not, however, to deny the creative role of the Aramaic scribes. But before we can speak about indigenous Aramaic legal elements, we must carefully determine whether or not such elements are not actually cuneiform in origin. It is, however, only on this one point, i.e., the problem of origins, that I disagree with Kutscher. On the other hand, his theory concerning the diffusion of the Aramaic common law formulary has been a guiding principle in this study from its inception.

b) The second scholar who contributed to the legal interpretation of the documents was J. Rabinowitz. Rabinowitz devoted himself to the

---

[1]) *Ibid.*, pp. 245 ff. [2]) *Ibid.*, p. 246. [3]) *Ibid.*, p. 247.

study of Jewish law and especially to its influence on other legal systems, both ancient and modern. The results of his investigations, first published in his numerous articles, are summarized in his two books, *Jewish Law: Its Influence on the Development of Legal Institutions* (New York: Bloch Publishing Company, 1956) [1] and *Studies in Legal History* (Jerusalem: R. H. Cohen Press, 1958). The Aramaic legal papyri of Elephantine were at the very center of his studies since he considered them to be the prime example of ancient Israelite law, outside of the Bible. Thus, any alleged influence of the papyri on Demotic and Greek sources was for him *prima facie* evidence of Jewish influence. Even though I have to disagree with Rabinowitz in his historical evaluation of the texts—much of the material he calls "Jewish" is simply Near Eastern, as Yaron pointed out in a review article of *Jewish Law* [2])—it cannot be denied that he called attention to many significant parallels and was able to interpret in their light many a difficult passage. Many of his more speculative interpretations are often confirmed by further investigation. [3])

Reuven Yaron: The Law of the Aramaic Papyri. Aramaic legal studies were elevated to new levels with the appearance of Yaron's articles [4]) and finally by his book, *The Law of the Aramaic Papyri* (Oxford: Clarendon Press, 1961). [5]) A trained Romanist, Yaron has produced a descriptive

---

1) Cf. the reviews of V. Pavlovský (*Biblica*, 39 [1958], p. 388-92), D. Daube (*JSS*, 2 [1957], p. 407-08), R. Taubenschlag (*Kiryat Sefer*, 33 [1958], p. 182 and *JJP*, 11 [1958], pp. 306 ff.), J. Sedláková (*BiOr*, 16 [1959], p. 49-50), E. Volterra, *Iura*, 8 [1957], pp. 546-58.

2) R. Yaron, "Jewish Law and Other Legal Systems of Antiquity," *JSS*, 4 (1959), pp. 308 ff.

3) Examples of such cases will be pointed out in the course of this study.

4) "The Schema of the Aramaic Legal Documents," *JSS*, 2 (1957), pp. 33 ff.; "Aramaic Marriage Contracts from Elephantine," *ibid.*, 3 (1958), pp. 1 ff.; "Aramaic Marriage Contracts: Corrigenda and Addenda," *ibid.*, 5 (1960), pp. 66 ff.; "Notes on Aramaic Papyri," *RIDA*, 5 (1958), pp. 299 ff.; "Notes on Aramaic Papyri II," *JNES*, 20 (1961), pp. 127 ff.; "On Divorce in Old Testament Times," *RIDA*, 4 (1957), pp. 117 ff.; "Aramaic Deeds of Conveyance," *Biblica*, 41 (1960), pp. 248-274 and 379-394; "On Defension Clauses," *BiOr*, 15 (1958), pp. 15 ff.

5) The book appeared simultaneously in a Hebrew edition: *HaMišpāṭ BeMismᵉḵe Yēḇ [The Law of the Elephantine Papyri]* (Jerusalem, 1961). The introductory chapter describing the earlier research and the final chapters devoted to comparative matters are slightly fuller in the Hebrew version; otherwise, the Hebrew and the English versions are identical. The chapters on the schema of the documents, and the law of conveyance are essentially the same as in Yaron's earlier articles on these topics (cited in the preceding note). The chapter on marriage law is entirely reworked. The chapters on the law of inheritance, persons, and litigation are all new. The final two chapters on comparative matters are essentially a summation of all the comparative notes found throughout the book. Cf. now the review of A. Verger, *Oriens Antiquus*, 3 (1964), p. 47 ff.

study of the various types of law reflected in the papyri: the schema of the deeds, courts and procedure, the law of persons, marriage and divorce, succession, the law of property, the law of obligations, etc. In this procedure, he has admittedly followed the examples of Seidl's various introductions to Egyptian law [1]) and Steinwenter's thematic presentation of Coptic law. [2]) Comparative material is employed to a more comprehensive degree than ever before. Yaron has incorporated most of the valid insights of his predecessors into his own work. As far as the explanation of the texts is concerned, his greatest contribution is in the realm of marriage law, while his most significant comparative contribution is in the realm of property law.

Comparative considerations, however, are not Yaron's major preoccupation: his main goal is the interpretation of the deeds, the unraveling of their exegetical difficulties, and the systematic-typological presentation of the norms reflected in them. Comparative evidence is only marshaled as an aid to exegesis: what is not clear from the thirty or so Aramaic deeds may often be clarified from a comparison with parallel, even though historically unrelated, legal systems. [3])

At the end of his book, Yaron does devote two chapters to the problem of affinities and origins. He does so, on these grounds: "However great their intrinsic value as evidence of legal institutions and usage, the documents will gain in interest and importance if it is possible to establish, at least to some extent, their relationship to other systems of ancient law, within Egypt and outside of it." [4]) Furthermore, Yaron limits the scope of this comparative investigation to the proximate antecedents of the Aramaic formulary: he is not interested in using the documents as the point of departure for a diachronic study of Near Eastern legal terms and institutions.

Yaron's method is characterized by great care and reserve: he correctly stresses the dangers of confusing similarity produced by parallel development with historical dependence. Furthermore, he calls attention to the lacunae in our knowledge of the cuneiform material and the problems for the legal historian created by these gaps. [5])

Yaron comes to the following conclusions:

a) Even though Egyptian influences are common in the Aramaic

---

[1]) Cf. Seidl, *Einführung*, *ÄRg*, and *PRg*.

[2]) Steinwenter, *RKU*. In the preface to *LAP* (p. vii), Yaron notes the books of Seidl and Steinwenter as the models for his study.

[3]) *LAP*, p. 99.

[4]) *Ibid.*

[5]) *Ibid.*, pp. 100 ff.

papyri, the cuneiform legal tradition had a more decisive role in the formation of the Aramaic formulary. [1])

b) The Syrian-Canaanite branch of the cuneiform tradition had a greater influence on the Aramaic formulary than the Babylonian branch.[2])

c) There are no Neo-Babylonian analogues and only one possible Neo-Assyrian analogue in the Aramaic legal documents. [3])

B. *The Assyriological Approach*

In general, Rabinowitz and Kutscher approached the documents from the vantage point of the later Aramaic legal tradition—the Nabatean, Talmudic, Gaonic, and Dura documents. They interpreted the relatively unknown (Elephantine) on the basis of the known (the later Aramaic tradition). Yaron, on the other hand, studied the deeds as an independent and self-contained system, placing little faith in analogies from the later Rabbinic tradition, [4]) and working his way back to the cuneiform tradition only when forced to by the exigencies of interpretation. The following study will be based on a third orientation: the Assyriological. The Elephantine deeds will be studied neither as a self-contained system nor as the prototype of the later Aramaic common law formulary but rather in the light of the millennia-old cuneiform legal tradition.

Cultural and societal norms—and especially legal institutions—rarely

[1]) Cf. the final chapter: "Sources and Contacts," pp. 114-128.

[2]) *LAP*, pp. 116-117, 123, and *passim*.

[3]) For the virtual absence of Neo-Babylonian influence, cf. *LAP*, p. 120: "We may then assert that the Aramaic legal style, whether in Egypt or outside of it, had reached the phase observable in the Elephantine documents before the Neo-Babylonian influence could make itself felt. Its Eastern contacts apparently date from considerably earlier times." For the comparative absence of Neo-Assyrian influences, cf. *LAP*, p. 122: "I am unwilling to attach much importance to the Assyrian interlude . . ." [namely, the short period of Assyrian domination over Egypt]. However, as we shall see later on, the Aramaic deeds are strongly influenced by the Neo-Assyrian formulary: over twelve of the key legal terms used in the documents are derived from proximate NA models. Furthermore, this Neo-Assyrian influence was not the result of the Assyrian conquest of Egypt but of the Assyrian political and economic domination of the Near East for many centuries. Finally, it may be assumed—with all due reservations—that many older Near Eastern analogues of the Elephantine documents (Nuzi, Ugarit, Alalakh) made their way into the Aramaic formulary via a NA medium.

[4]) Cf. Yaron's scepticism concerning the relationship between Elephantine and the later Jewish deeds in *LAP*, p. 127 and more recently in his review of the legal documents from Wadi Murabbaʿat in *JJS*, 11 (1960), pp. 157-71. While Rabinoweitz's position is often overstated, I feel that Elephantine and Murabbaʿat, in spite of the real differences that Yaron has pointed out, have more in common historically and linguistically than Yaron will allow. The problem, therefore, is one of balance.

die in the Near East. [1]) In spite of its history of constant invasion, political instability, and a series of "dark ages," [2]) the ancient Near East was characterized by a remarkable cultural continuity. [3]) Norms did not die; they were simply transformed into a new linguistic garb and in their new form continued their functions as of old. Thus, as Sumerian was about to die as a spoken language, its legal and religious traditions were carefully preserved in an Akkadian garb. This early process of transmission and preservation—the very hallmark of cuneiform civilization—prefigures a series of later ones. As Akkadian was replaced by other languages and clay tablets gave way to skin and papyrus, the cuneiform legal tradition did not suddenly disappear: old terms and clauses reappear in an emerging Aramaic formulary, [4]) and, from there,

---

[1]) E. A. Speiser, "Cultural Factors in Social Dynamics in the Near East," *Middle East Journal*, 7 (1953), pp. 133-152.

[2]) For the dark ages of the third millennium, cf. Edzard, *ZZB*, pp. 1-4. For the later periods, cf. Landsberger, *Dunkles Zeitalter*, pp. 31-73 and 106-133. For the period of political confusion at the end of the second millennium, cf. Goetze, *Hethiter*, Chapter VII: "Die Völkerbewegungen des ausgehenden II. Jahrtausends," pp. 152-185. Cf. also Scharff and Moortgart, p. 392.

[3]) This remarkable continuity and stability was stressed by San Nicolò in his *Beiträge* (pp. 253 ff.) as a general characteristic of cuneiform legal history: "Ich kann diesen knappen Ueberblick über einzelne Vertragsformen aus dem Verkehrsrechte des Zweistromlandes nicht beschliessen, ohne auf einen Punkt, der mir sehr wichtig scheint, noch einmal zurückzukommen: nämlich auf die im Verhältnis zu den in Betracht kommenden Zeiträumen *überraschende Beständigkeit* [italics San Nicolò's] der hier behandelten Rechtsinstitute. Das babylonische Verkehrsrecht steht bereits am Ende der altbabylonischen Periode, also zu Beginn des 2. vorchristlichen Jahrtausends, im grossen und ganzen in den meisten seiner Geschäftsformen voll ausgebildet vor uns. Sein Wesen und auch seine Institute haben sich während der nachfolgenden fast zweitausendjährigen Entwicklungszeit, welche zwischen Ḫammurapi und dem Ausklingen der keilschriftlichen Urkundenüberlieferung liegt, nur verhältnissmässig *wenig verändert.*" Cf. also his statement: "Bei diesem Versagen der Ueberlieferung glaube ich aber, dass man in der *ehernen Stabilität* [italics San Nicolò's] des babylonischen Verkehrsrechtes und in seiner mehrtausendjährigen, in Vorderasien fest eingewurzelten Tradition ein wichtiges Moment erblicken darf, welches bei der Beurteilung der Frage nach der Möglichkeit einer Beeinflussung des spätrömischen Rechtes im Osten stark in die Wagschale fallen muss" (p. 256). The details of this stability deserve an independent study. One example, however, nicely illustrates this abstract principle. One of the most revolutionary periods in the cultural and political history of the Near East was the dark ages that separated the OB from the MB periods. (Cf., for example, O'Callaghan, *Aram Naharaim*, Chapter IV: "The Mitanni Kingdom," pp. 51-92; see also Landsberger, *Dunkles Zeitalter*. In spite of these revolutionary political changes and the introduction of a new ethnic factor into the area—the Indic-Aryan (cf. E. A. Speiser, "The Alalakh Tablets," *JAOS*, 74 (1954), p. 19; see also A. Alt, "Die Herkunft der Hyksos in neuer Sicht," *Kleine Schriften*, III, p. 81)—nevertheless, the legal formulary of Alalakh VII (OB) is remarkably similar to that of Alalakh IV (MB; fifteenth century B.C.).

[4]) For a general description of this process of transformation and translation, cf. San Nicolò, *Beiträge*, Chapter II: "Die Stellung der keilschriftlichen Rechts-

make their way to other traditions, such as the Persian [1]) and the Demotic. [2])

Thus, in a sense, the Aramaic formulary is the recipient of over two millennia of cuneiform legal experience; it is the culmination of many developments and inner-Assyriological trends, an amalgamation of various cuneiform traditions. As will be demonstrated in this study, every Aramaic term and clause is, to a very great degree, like a palimpsest: preceding stages of cuneiform legal history transpire through them. [3]) Hence, the Aramaic legal material can only be understood properly if all preceding *Vorlagen*—not merely the proximate ones [4])—are thoroughly reinvestigated, philologically, legally, and historically. [5]) In a sense,

denkmäler innerhalb der vorderasiatisch-ägyptischen Rechtsentwichlung," pp. 52-62. See also his statement: "Für den vordern Orient aber ist der Vergleich der demotischen Papyri mit den aramäischen Urkunden der jüdischen Militärkolonie von Elephantine einerseits, und mit den zeitgenössischen Tontafeln aus Babylonien anderseits, ein reizvolles und gewiss löhnendes Unternehmen. Es soll uns nämlich zeigen, inwieweit durch der Perserherrschaft auch auf dem Gebiete des Privatrechtes vorderasiatisches Rechtsgut in Aegypten eingeführt worden ist" (*Beiträge*, p. 53).

Von Soden in his review of Cardascia, *Les archives des Murašû*, in *BiOr*, 11 (1954), p. 206, also stressed the importance of comparing the Neo-Babylonian tablets with the contemporary Aramaic documents of Elephantine, for their mutual elucidation.

1) In this context, attention should be called to Ebeling, *Glossar*. Ebeling has demonstrated that the late Aramaic-Persian glossary was based on older Near Eastern antecedents such as the *ḪAR.ra=ḫubullu* and *SIG.ALAM-nabnītu*. He assumes that just as Akkadian scribes needed Akkadian books of Sumerian formulae, so later Aramaic scribes needed Aramaic books of Akkadian formulae. Such glossaries served as the proximate models of later Persian-Aramaic glossaries. The continuity between these three sets of glossaries is so great that the late Persian glossaries still contain Assyrian terms (*ibid.*, pp. 86-112).

2) Cf. Seidl, *ÄRg*,: "Das Verhältnis des ägyptischen Rechts zu dem vorderasiatischer Völker," p. 71.

3) Speiser, both in writing and orally, has compared Near Eastern culture to a palimpsest. The same holds true, more specifically, of late legal terms. Cf. Speiser's statement: "The question is how far down one must reach beneath a given stratum to arrive at the origin and gain an understanding of what is being transformed at long last. The answer will depend on the length and tenacity of historic tradition that is still a living force in the area involved. Because the Near East started the world on its historic course, no other part of the globe has been watched over by history to a comparable degree ("Cultural Factors in Social Dynamics in the Near East," *Middle East Journal*, 7 [1953], p. 134). See also: "The present, in any case, has deep roots in the Near East and these must be traced through countless paths and bypaths. The region, in short, is much like a multiple palimpsest. There may be concern only with the latest inscription; but the key to its interpretation might well be hidden in the legend at the very bottom" (*ibid.*, p. 135).

4) Contrast the method of Yaron, *LAP*, p. 99.

5) As Koschaker has shown us in his pioneering studies, these three disciplines must be combined in order to produce significant results. Furthermore, as valid as the typological-substantive treatment of legal material may be, a deeper understanding of legal processes may be elicited from the texts by the philological study

the Assyriological check of the Aramaic deeds calls for diachronic studies of all Akkadian terms, clauses, and legal categories whose analogues are found in the Aramaic deeds. In spite of the work done in editing cuneiform texts in the past generation, [1]) such typological and historical studies, based on the principles of comparative dialectology, [2]) are often antiquated or nonexistent. Without them, however, Aramaic legal studies will always remain superficial and inconclusive.

Thus, the first goal of any thorough study of the Aramaic documents —i.e., the interpretation of the deeds themselves—necessarily calls for a reinvestigation of the legal and lexical resources of cuneiform law—the second and complementary goal of such a study. The Aramaic deeds thus provide the student of cuneiform law with a new vantage point from which to survey the long history of this tradition. In a sense, Aramaic law is the late and provincial reflex of cuneiform law: it is not surprising, therefore, that new and unexpected patterns and combinations begin to emerge. The legal traditions of Susa and Nuzi, of Cappadocia and Ugarit, of the Neo-Assyrian and Arsacid periods—all seemed "atypical" from the point of view of Old Babylonian law, [3]) which had

---

of key legal terms, their history and distribution. The legal-philological sections of Kraus, *Ammi-Ṣaduqa*, are good examples of such treatment. Furthermore, history cannot be equated with mere chronology, as Yaron often does. History means the sum total of cultural-sociological and religious conditions in their ebb and flow. Any historically oriented study of the Aramaic papyri and their origins must consider the role of the Arameans in the history of the Near East and the particular symbiosis between Aramean and cuneiform civilizations. From this point of view, Kutscher's philological orientation is closer to the historical truth than the chronological orientation of Yaron.

[1]) Cf. Koschaker's *Bürgschaftsrecht*; Eilers, *Gesellschaft*; Lautner, *Streitbeendigung* and *Personenmiete*; Petschow, *Pfandrecht*. All of these studies are usually limited to but one period of cuneiform legal history. Most of the diachronic studies of a given legal genre are found in the second volume of the *RLA*. Cf., for example, "Darlehen" by San Nicolò (pp. 123-131). These entries provide excellent introductions to the diachronic study of the legal norms of the various periods. However, rarely do we find a comparative study of the schemata, clauses, and legal terminology.

[2]) For an example of comparative dialectology, cf. Moshe Held, "*mḫṣ/*mḫš* in Ugaritic and Other Semitic Languages," *JAOS*, 79 (1959), pp. 169 ff.

[3]) The legal norms reflected in these provincial documents seemed so atypical to A. L. Oppenheim that he attributed them to the indigenous peoples who inhabited the mountains surrounding the fertile crescent. Cf. *Der Eid*; *Studien*; "Ein Beitrag zum Kassitenproblem," *Analecta Orientalia*, 12 (1935), pp. 266 ff. Although Oppenheim's isolation of the phenomenon is correct, his historical interpretation is less satisfactory than the one suggested by P. Koschaker (*Randnotizen* p. 224). Koschaker noted that the provincial documents of Nuzi and Susa are formulated almost entirely in Akkadian and that Sumerian logograms, although used in these documents, are quite rare. For him, this was but another indication of the possible Old Akkadian provenience of the provincial tradition. Both Koschaker and Speiser (orally communicated) assume that Old Akkadian (Semitic) legal

assumed an almost normative-paradigmatic quality in cuneiform legal studies. However, seen through the prism of the Aramaic documents, they begin to assume a more significant quality: they represent trends and traditions which culminated in the formulary used at Elephantine.

The Assyriologist who steps out of his own field to aid the Aramaicist in the interpretation of the Aramaic deeds finds himself richly rewarded in his own field. As Peiser already realized, [1]) the Aramaic deeds raise new and unexpected questions concerning the history and the lexical resources of cuneiform law. As we all know, many new scientific breakthroughs are the result of such new approaches.

3. General Subject of this Study: Aramaic Business Law

The method described above can be applied profitably to all aspects of Aramaic law. Such a comprehensive investigation, however, is beyond the limits of any one study. Accordingly, the present investigation has focused on one of the most significant areas of all law: the law of business.[2])

A. *Definition of the Topic*

This study will be based on the evidence of those Aramaic documents which record the transfer of property and/or the confirmation of the rights thereto. Ten of the thirty extant Elephantine legal documents fall into this class. Purely from a statistical point of view, therefore, such a study needs no further justification.

---

norms were brought to the fringe areas in the wake of the Sargonic conquests and were conservatively preserved in these areas, while they succumbed to Sumerianizing influences in the heart of lower Mesopotamia, the place of their origin. During the second millennium, these archaic norms are preserved in the deeds of Nuzi, Ugarit, Alalakh, Susa, and other fringe areas. The later reflex of this formulary is the Neo-Assyrian legal tradition. As I shall attempt to demonstrate below, it was mainly from the Neo-Assyrian tradition that cuneiform legal norms made their way into the later non-cuneiform legal systems of antiquity.*

[1]) Cf., above, p. 5, n. 8.

[2]) During the past few years, comparative legal historians have been devoting a great deal of attention to the concepts of property, ownership, and business. Cf. the following studies, all of which appeared in the *ZVRW*: R. Schott, "Die Eigentumsrechte der Buschmänner in Südafrika, *ZVRW*, 61 (1959), pp. 101-223; I. Hilgers-Hesse, "Das Eigentumsrecht bei den Toba-Batak in Nord-Sumatria," *ZVRW*, 63 (1961), pp. 185-217; J. Henninger, "Das Eigentumsrecht bei den heutigen Beduinen Arabiens," *ZVRW*, 61 (1959), pp. 6-56; J. D. M. Derret, "The Development of the Concept of Property in India c. A.D. 800-1800," *ZVRW*, 64 (1962), pp. 15-130; W. Bauer, "Die Frühgeschichte des Eigentums in China," *ZVRW*, 63 (1961), pp. 118-184; H. Kelm, "Die Eigentumsrechte auf Samoa," *ZVRW*, 64 (1962), pp. 131-230.

These ten deeds may be divided into the following three sub-categories:

1) Deeds of gift (*AP* 8 and *BP* 9) which record the free-will donation of property;
2) Deeds of sale (*BP* 3 and *BP* 12) which record the relinquishment and transfer of property in return for a satisfactory consideration;
3) Deeds of *mrḥq* ("cession" or "relinquishment"). [1] Two different types of *mrḥq* can be distinguished according to function:

a) Transfer-*mrḥq* (*AP* 13 and *AP* 25): this *mrḥq* records the transfer and relinquishment of goods without specifying the reason for the transfer;

b) Litigation-*mrḥq* (*AP* 6; *AP* 14; *AP* 20; *BP* 1); here the plaintiff in a litigation renounces all claims against the defendant in return for some satisfactory performance, usually a purgatory oath.

Since these three types of business deeds all record the transfer and/or the confirmation of property rights, I feel justified in subsuming them all under the general name of "conveyance." [2] Furthermore, all Aramaic conveyances share the same over-all structure and employ similar terminology. All Aramaic conveyances may be divided into two sections:

1) The operative section, [3] which records the creation of a new legal status, the result of the "constitutive" [4] actions of the right-holders, both old and new.
2) The *Schlussklauseln* (final clauses), which insure the newly created legal status against future suits and litigations.

B. *A Problem of Method: Operative Section or* Schlussklauseln

The Problem. An important methodological problem immediately presents itself: which of these two sections lends itself most readily to

[1]) For a discussion of these terms borrowed from Demotic legal studies, cf. Pestman, p. 17, n. 6.

[2]) This term was first applied to the Aramaic legal papyri by Yaron in his study "Aramaic Deeds of Conveyance," *Biblica*, 41 (1960), p. 248. My use of the term differs somewhat from that of Yaron: he includes under this rubric sale and gift but excludes *mrḥq* (he does not make any distinction between transfer and litigation *mrḥq*). The *mrḥq* transactions are discussed by Yaron under a separate heading, cf. *LAP*, "Courts and Procedure," pp. 27-35.

[3]) This useful term was coined by Yaron (cf. "The Schema of the Aramaic Legal Documents," *JSS*, 2 [1957], p. 33).

[4]) "Constitutive" is used here in the following sense: Any element in a legal transaction or a legal deed, whether it be an inner state of mind (such as volition), or an external performance by one of the parties (such as payment of a consideration), or a formal element in the deed itself (such as the order of clauses, phrasing, or punctuation), which establishes the validity of the deed or transaction, and whose absence either weakens the transaction or makes it null and void, is called constitutive. Almost all elements in a contract, no matter how narrative, unlegal, or superfluous they may seem, usually have some constitutive function.

an investigation of the underlying principles of the Aramaic conveyance, i.e., in which section are these principles most clearly and immediately reflected? The answer to this question will determine the form and direction of the present investigation.

Since San Nicolò's book, *Die Schlussklauseln der altbabylonischen Kauf- und Tauschurkunden: Ein Beitrag des Barkaufs* (München: C. H. Beck'sche Verlagsbuchhandlung, 1922), is still the fundamental treatment of ancient Near Eastern sale law, and has, in many respects served as the model for this study, San Nicolò's point of departure should be considered carefully before one embarks on a similar investigation of the Aramaic material.

San Nicolò explicated the basic principles of Old Babylonian sale law from a study of the *Schlussklauseln*. This orientation is clearly indicated by the title of his book and by San Nicolò's statement that in order to understand the legal effects of the Old Babylonian sale document, "Wir müssen dabei von den Schlussklauseln des Vertrages als *sedes materiae* ausgehen." [1])

San Nicolò's choice of the *Schlussklauseln* as his point of departure was partially determined by the nature of the Old Babylonian sale document. It is quite possible, therefore, that the final clauses may not be the ideal starting point for the investigation of non-OB sales transactions or, for that matter, of the Elephantine conveyances, which, on the whole, seem to be closely related to the non-OB cuneiform legal tradition.

Comparison of Operative Sections. In the following discussion, the operative sections of representative OB and non-OB sale documents will be compared, in order to determine the distinctive characteristics of each tradition and as a method of determining which of the two sections—operative or final clauses—is the more suitable point of departure for a study of non-OB sale law.

a) OB sale; operative section

x sar é.dù.a ki A B in.ši.šám x mana kù.babbar šám.til.-la.ni.šè in.na.lá

"X *sar* of built (i.e., cultivated) land, from A, B bought; he weighed out x minas of silver as its full price." [2])

---

[1]) San Nicolò, *Schlussklauseln*, p. 38.

[2]) This is the formula commonly used at Larsa (cf. Jean, *Larsa*, No. 7). For the most recent study of the various OB sale formulae, their history and distribution, cf. Kraus, *Nippur und Isin*, pp. 90 ff.

The Old Babylonian operative section is characterized by its objective and impersonal quality: the names of the parties are given, the amount of the price is stated. Only one of the subjects of the transaction—the buyer- -performs any significant (or constitutive) action. Even then, the verbs of action—*išām* "he bought" and *išqul* "he weighed"—tell us very little about the underlying process of the transaction. [1])

Significantly missing are (a) the reaction of the seller to the receipt of the money; (b) the seller's renunciation of claims; (c) the transfer of property; (d) the investiture of the new right-holder. Furthermore, a temporal element is also missing: the transaction does not unfold in proper stages (in fact, in some OB deeds, *išqul* "he weighed" can appear before *išām* "he bought" without any significant change in meaning); finally, the transaction is not described in terms of action and reaction, of performance and counter-performance. The transaction simply exists: it is a static fact rather than an evolving event.

Even though such obligatory and constitutive elements are missing from the operative section of the OB sale document, they are found, to some degree, in the *Schlussklauseln*. It was probably for this reason that San Nicolò chose the *Schlussklauseln* rather than the operative section as the point of departure for his study.

b) The non-OB tradition

When we turn to the non-OB legal tradition—Susa, Kültepe, Assyria, Nuzi, Ugarit, etc.—an entirely different picture emerges.

1) Middle Assyrian Sale [2])

eqla ana šīm gamir ana x manê anāka A ana B iddinma ušappīma eqlu uppû laqi tuāru u dabābu laššu anāka šīm eqlišu A maḫir apil zakû eqla uzakka ina ašal šarri imaddad u ṭuppa dannata ana pāni šarri išaṭṭar.
"A sold permanently a field: at full price for x minas of tin to B; the field is permanently transferred (acquired); there shall be no appeal for reversal. The tin—the full price of his field—A has received; he is paid and quitted. He will clear the field (of claims), will measure (the field) with the royal measuring rope and will draw up a *ṭuppa dannata* in the royal bureau." [3])

[1]) In fact, the order of these two clauses may be reversed without changing in any way the legal meaning or the validity of the transaction (cf. Kraus, *Nippur und Isin* pp. 91-92).

[2]) All of the MA deeds of sale have been transliterated and translated by Ebeling, *Kaufurkunden*, pp. 54 ff. The law of these deeds has been studied by Koschaker in *NKRA*, Chapter II: "Veräusserung von Liegenschaften," pp. 27 ff.

[3]) Cf., *KAJ* 149. (for *ṭuppu dannatu*, cf. Koschaker, *NKRA*, p. 32.)*

2) Neo-Assyrian Sale

kaspu gammur taddin bītu šuātu ṣarip laqi [1])

"The full price has been paid; the aforesaid house is permanently transferred (acquired)."

3) Ras Shamra Akkadian Sale

A ipšur [2]) *eqlētišu ana B ina x kaspa eqlu ṣami/ad* [3]) *qadi serdīšu qadu karānīšu qadu gabbu mimmūšu* [4]) *ana B u ana mārī mārīšu ana dārīti*

"A sold (lit. "released") his fields to B for x (amount) of silver. The field—together with its olive trees, together with its vineyards, together with everything in it (lit. "all its whatever-it-is")—has become the vested/inalienable property (lit. "it is [now] yoked to") B and his children's children for [all] generations." [5])

---

[1]) Cf., for example, *ARU*, No. 173 ff. Koschaker (*NKRU*, p. 29, n. 2) has the following to say about the NA variant *uppiš ṣarip* and the MA phrase *ušappi-uppû*: "*Ušappi-uppu* entspricht dem *uppiš* der neuassyrischen Kaufverträge in der Einleitungsformel: Kaufobject *K upiš-ma ištu pan V ina libbi* Betrag *ilqi* 'hat der K(aufer) . . . von dem V(erkäufer) um (Betrag) genommen.' Vgl. auch *ARU* 509, 9, wo es ganz entspricht dem mittel-assyrischen *eqlu uppu laqi* heisst: (die verkaufte Sklavin) *uppušat ṣarpat laqiat* 'ist . . . gekauft, genommen.' Kohler-Ungnad, ARU pass. übersetzen *uppiš* 'er hat erworben' und treffen juristisch dass Richtige." This interpretation of *epēšu/uppušu* "to make/ to acquire" is confirmed by the royal confirmation of property rights recorded in *ARU* 16. The king confirms the ownership of all the property which one of his courtiers *ina ṣilliya iqnu epušū* [cf. *ARU* 15 and 16, 11. 21 and 22] "acquired and took possession of under my protection."

[2]) The verb *pašāru* lit. "to untie" is used regularly in the Akkadian deeds of sale from Ras Shamra. It is rare, however, outside of Ugarit. Cf. CH 17. In actual documents, the term is used of people selling their children for money in time of famine (cf. A. L. Oppenheim, " 'Siege-Documents' from Nippur,' " *Iraq*, 17 [1955], p. 78). See especially p. 79, n. 40.

[3]) For the legal functions of this term, see, for the time being, *CAD*, Ṣ, pp. 93-95 and O. Loretz, *Biblische Zeitschrift*, 6 (1962), pp. 269-279. There is little doubt that the biblical expression *li-ṣᵉmīṯūṯ* "(sale) beyond redemption" (Septuagint: βεβαίως), Lev. 25:30, is the reflex of the Canaanite term. For the d/t sound change, cf. M. Held, *Eretz-Israel*, 3 (1954), pp. 101-103.

[4]) The clause "with its x and with its y and with its everything" is also found in Alalakh (cf. *AT* 87: 14 ff.) and in the Bible. Cf. Gen 23: 17 "So Ephron's land in Machpela, facing Mamre—the field with its cave and all the trees anywhere within the confines of that field—passed to Abram as his possession." (*qām lᵉAbrām lᵉmiqneh*=Lev 25: 30 *wᵉqām habbayiṯ . . . laqqōnē ōṯō lᵉdōrōṯaw*). Exactly the same clause reappears in the legal documents of Wadi Murabbaʿat. In *Les grottes de Murabbaʿat*, No. 30: 18-19, a field is sold together with *htʾnym hzytym hʿṣ* (19) *hmrb[h] hrby[h] ʾlk kl šbw wšḥyw ʿlyw* "(its) fig (trees) and olive (trees), the trees (19) the vegetation (?) which grows (?) in your direction (?): (namely), everything in it [Akkadian *qadi gabbu mimmūšu*] and everything that lives on it."

[5]) This particular example is based on *PRU* III, No. 16.353 (p. 113). For a discussion of the related sale terms *ittaši ittadin*, cf. Speiser's review of the texts, "Akkadian Documents from Ras Shamra," *JAOS*, 75 (1955), pp. 157 ff.

The number of constitutive elements in these contracts—and others which have not been cited—is considerable; the difference between the Old Babylonian operative section and its non-OB counterparts is obvious. In the MA, NA, and RS deeds of sale, the movement of property from one owner to another is clearly depicted. For example, NA: *eqlu ṣarip laqi* "the field is permanently transferred"; MA: *eqlu uppû laqi* with the same meaning; RS: *eqlu ṣamid ana* . . . "the field is (now) the vested/inalienable property of . . ."; Kültepe: *amassu šūma* "she is (now) his slave-girl." [1])

Furthermore, in many of the sale transactions derived from the non-OB tradition the movement of the old owner away from his property and the movement of the new owner toward his acquisition are carefully recorded as significant (or constitutive) aspects of the transaction. In some of the Nuzi deeds of sale, the seller lifts his foot from his property and places the foot of the buyer in its place. [2]) In some of the OB deeds from the Diyala region, the seller digs up a clod of earth from his property and throws it into a nearby canal. [3]) All of these symbolic gestures magically effectuate the severing of old ties and claims and the creation of new ones. [4])

The non-OB deeds of sale have, as a rule, a greater subjective quality about them. This expresses itself in several ways: a) first of all, the

[1]) Cf. the Old Assyrian text published by J. Lewy in *AHDO*, 1 (1937), p. 99, line 11. See also B. Hrozný, "Un nouveau texte juridique du Kultépé," *AHDO*, 1 (1937), p. 88, line 11. This formulation is almost identical with the Aramaic version of the transfer clause—*zylk hw*—"it (the house) is yours." The only difference between the two formulations is that the Akkadian is formulated in the third person ("The slave girl is [now] his"), while the Aramaic is in the second person ("The [house] is [now] yours").*

[2]) Cf. Cassin, *Symboles de cession*, especially pp. 120-124.

[3]) *Ibid.*, pp. 108 ff.

[4]) Similar symbolic actions accompanied the sale of land in old Germanic and Anglo-Saxon law. Cf. Heubner, *Germanic Private Law*, pp. 185 ff. For Anglo-Saxon law, cf. Pollock and Maitland, Vol. II, pp. 84-85: "Really and truly the feoffor must quit possession; really and truly the feoffe must acquire possession." Or: "The two men each with his witnesses appear upon the land. A knife is produced, a sod of turf is cut, the twig of a tree is broken off; the turf and the twig are handed by the donor to the donee; they are the land in miniature, and thus the land passes from hand to hand. Along with them the knife may also be delivered [cf. the Akkadian *bukannu šūtuq*!], and it may be kept by the donee as material evidence of the transaction; . . . Even this is not enough; the donor must solemnly forsake the land. May be he is expected to leap over the encircling hedge" (*ibid.*, p. 85).

It is interesting to note that when the actual gestures gradually went out of use, they are still vaguely reflected in the terms which took their place. Originally, the seller upon receipt of the price actually left his property; he went away. It is, therefore, no coincidence that in a later generation when the seller (or any other right-holder) no longer actually left the property, the regular term for "quitted" in the Susa documents is *duppur* "departed, far away."

reaction of the seller to the receipt of the sale price is usually recorded (cf. Nuzi *elteqīmi aplākumi* "I have received and I am paid off"; Old Assyrian *šabû* "he is satisfied"; MA *apil maḫir zakû* "he is paid off, he has received (the price), is quitted"; [1]) b) there are now two active subjects to the transaction; the seller's performance and reactions are now described in some detail. In general, the transaction is constructed in terms of action and reaction. Thus, the seller gives his field for a price, the price is paid by the buyer, the seller is satisfied and quitted, the land is transferred, etc.; c) the temporal element is now of greater significance: the transaction is now a many-staged event rather than a static fact.

Above all, it should be noted that, at least in the Nuzi documents, the objective formulation so well known from the Babylonian tradition, is replaced, at times, by the subjective first-person narration of the *lišānšu* document. (Cf. the declaration of the seller *elteqīmi aplākumi* "I have received (the price) and I am paid off.") [2])

C. *The Meaning of the Contrast*

To sum up: the operative section of OB sale is objective (i.e., the reactions are not described), static (i.e., there is little or no movement of property or persons), and one-sided (only the actions of the buyer are recorded). On the other hand, the non-OB tradition is subjective (i.e., reactions are recorded and first-person formulations are common), dialogic (the seller as well as the buyer plays an active role in the transaction), and the movement of property and persons is constitutive.

The contrast pointed out between Babylonian and non-Babylonian operative sections is paralleled by a more fundamental contrast between the grammatical orientations of East and West Semitic language groups. According to both Landsberger [3]) and Speiser, [4]) Akkadian places greater

---

[1]) All of these quittance terms will be discussed in the chapters devoted to the isoglosses of the OB *libbašu ṭāb*. Cf. below Chapter V.

[2]) For the time being, see Koschaker's study of the *lišānšu* documents in *NKRA*, pp. 21-23. Since the publication of Koschaker's study, *lišānšu*-type documents have appeared in the Old Akkadian documents published by Gelb, in the Old Assyrian deeds of Kültepe, sporadically in the OB deeds of Susa, and quite frequently in the Akkadian deeds of Ras Shamra. All of this new material relating to subjective formulations in cuneiform legal documents will be discussed in an excursus to the section on *libbašu ṭāb*. Cf. Chapter VII of this study, p. 175.

[3]) Landsberger, *Eigenbegrifflichkeit*, pp. 360 ff.

[4]) Speiser, "Pitfalls of Polarity," *Language*, 14 (1938), pp. 187 ff. "There are two traceable types of primitive Semitic sentence: the verbal, which employed the actor-action form **ta-q(a)ti/ul-* 'thou-st' (pronominal element + verbal theme), and the nominal, expressed by the equational scheme **qati/ul-ta* 'x (art) thou' (noun + implied verbal copula + pronominal element)." Landsberger differs from Speiser in that he denies the existence (or at least minimizes the importance) of

emphasis on the objective-static aspects of language, while West Semitic is characterized by its relatively greater subjective-active orientation. It seems likely that the contrast in legal traditions is—at least to some degree—a reflection of two very different linguistic and cultural orientations.

As we shall see in the following section, the Aramaic operative section, with its emphasis on subjective formulation, reactions, and movements of persons and transfer of property, is clearly rooted in the non-OB legal and linguistic tradition. Therefore, the operative part of the Aramaic conveyance rather than its *Schlussklauseln* is the ideal *sedes materiae* for a study of the underlying principles of the Elephantine conveyance.

"proto-Semitic." (Cf. *Eigenbegrifflichkeit*, pp. 364 ff.) According to him, East Semitic was based on the noun and the objective stative, while West Semitic was based on the verbal orientation. According to Speiser, however, both types existed in both groups even though the nominal-stative orientation was the dominant one in Akkadian, while the verbal-subjective was dominant in West Semitic. As a rule, the Aramaic of the East (whether "Kurdo-Mesopotamian" or "official"), under the influence of Akkadian, is stative-objective in orientation, the verb usually placed at the end of the sentence (cf. H. L. Ginsberg, "Aramaic Dialect Problems. II," *AJSL*, 52 [Jan., 1936], pp. 97-99). Western or "Levantine" Aramaic [for the term, cf. Ginsberg, "Aramaic Dialect Problems," *AJSL*, 50 (Oct., 1933), pp. 6 ff.], resembles West Semitic, with the verb placed at the beginning of the sentence.

Kutscher has pointed out in his study, "Is Biblical Aramaic Eastern or Western Aramaic? [in Hebrew]," *Lešōnēnu*, 17 (1951), pp. 119-122, that both grammatical orientations are to be found in Elephantine Aramaic. Syntactically, the language of the legal documents is to be distinguished from the nonlegal material. The language of the legal documents is West Semitic in orientation, while the more modern language of the nonlegal documents is East Semitic in orientation (the verb, for example, is at the end of the sentence and passive formulations are more common). Cf. also Kutscher's comments in his review of Driver, *Aramaic Documents*, in *JBL*, 76 (1957), p. 338.

Kutscher's general statement can be supported by specific legal examples. In the Akkadian *Schlussklauseln*, the seller promises not to raise claims in the future by saying: "The field was not sold/given" (*eqlu lā nadin*). The parallel Elephantine clause is formulated in the active-subjective voice: *hn mḥr ʾw ywm ʾḥrn ʾršnky dyn wdbb wʾmr lʾ yhbt lky* "If tomorrow or some other day, I institute against you a formal suit and say: 'I did not give (it) to you'" (*AP* 8: 20). [Notice also that the formulation is not *bytʾ lʾ yhbt* nor is it *bytʾ lʾ yhyb*.] Conversely, almost all of the Akkadian transfer clauses are objectively formulated: for example, Assyrian *eqlu uppû/ṣarip* "The house is transferred." Note that the formulation is so objective that the personal indirect object—*ana* the buyer—is also missing. The Ras Shamra Akkadian clause of transfer—*eqlu ṣamid ana* the buyer—is also objectively-statively formulated but now the indirect object is also mentioned: the formulation is becoming more subjective. Furthermore, the stative *ṣamid ana* rapidly develops into an active West Semitic perfect *ṣamad*. The change from the Eastern to the Western orientation is seen most clearly in the Aramaic transfer clause: *ʾnt šlyṭ bbytʾ*—not: "The house is owned by you" but "You are now the owner/master of the house."*

D. *Analysis of the Aramaic Operative Section*

The Terms. The most common terms used in the operative section of the Aramaic conveyance document are the following:

1) *hwṭbt lbby/ṭyb lbby* "You have satisfied my heart/my heart is satisfied with (the performance)."
2) *rḥqt mnk/h* "I have removed myself from you/it."
3) An investiture [1])/transfer clause consisting of the following (variable) elements:

   a) *zylk hw* "It (the property) is yours."
   b) *'nt šlyṭ b* "You are (now) in control/owner (of the property)."
   c) *lmn zy rḥmt/ṣbyt tntnnh* "You may give it to whomever you wish."
   d) *bny wtb bgw* [2]) "Build (on the land) and settle thereon."

---

[1]) The term is borrowed from Anglo-Saxon and Germanic law (cf. Pollock and Maitland, p. 85). In old Germanic sale transactions, the seller would "invest" the buyer with his garment to effectuate the transfer of ownership. Exactly the same practice is recorded in the oldest Sumerian sale documents. For a discussion of these documents, cf. Koschaker, *Eheschliessung* pp. 253-254, n. 47. Cf. also his comments in *Begriff des Kaufs*, pp. 89 ff. The later Akkadian and Aramaic transfer is the formulaic metamorphosis of these earlier magical investitures. It should be mentioned at this point that German and Anglo-Saxon law have much in common with cuneiform law, especially in its early stages. From the point of view of sociological development, early cuneiform law and medieval German law were much on the same level. This is especially true in respect to the alienation of real estate—one of the most primitive and "magical" aspects of ancient law. In both societies, the land was almost mystically bound to the family. One would as easily sell one's children as one's land. Furthermore, the land was often held in common: one could not alienate without the consent of relatives and even neighbors. All sorts of magical-symbolic actions were needed to sever the old ties and create new ones. As we have seen above, many of these actions were the same in both societies. (For a study of the most ancient cuneiform sale law, cf. Boyer, *Formation de vente* and Koschaker, *Begriff des Kaufs*.) Much of the material in this study is taken from atypical-archaic legal practices (i.e., non-Old Babylonian). I have been greatly aided methodologically by the studies of Heubner and Pollock and Maitland, which deal with material which is structurally similar to the non-OB legal tradition. Therefore, I have often borrowed Germanic legal terms rather than Roman ones because the former are in greater harmony with the cuneiform tradition than the latter. The importance of Anglo-Saxon law for the study of cuneiform legal tradition was suggested to me by J. J. Finkelstein.

[2]) Cf. the Ras Shamra expression, "the donee *uraṣṣipšunu ušēšibšunu* rebuilt and resettled them (the properties transfered to him); cf. *PRU* III, 15.147: 12'-13' (p. 125). Or, the recipient "shall rebuild" (*iraṣṣap*) the property (*PRU* III, 15.114: 9 (p. 112) and *PRU* III, 15.168: 9 (p. 137). The exact juridical force of these clause has yet to be explained. Cf. for the time being, J. Nougayrol, "Guerre et paix à Ugarit," *Iraq*, 25 (1963), p. 113. It is quite possible that the transfer of ownership was effectively established only after the new owner had asserted his ownership in an act, creative or destructive, such as walking into the property (cf. *MDP* XXII 155: 17 *ana eqlim urrad*), breaking a branch, or by settling and building the property. This concrete act of taking possession is known as *Seisin*

Less common are the following clauses, which are found only in gifts:

1) *bḥyy wbmwty* "In my lifetime and after my death."
2) *yhbt lk brḥmn* "I have given (it) to you in affection."
3) *ʿšt lk* "I have turned my thoughts to you."
4) A combination of the preceding clauses: *ʿšt lk bḥyy wyhbt lk brḥmn bmwty* "I have turned my thoughts to you during my lifetime and have transferred (the property) to you in affection in the event of my death."

The Distribution Pattern. Each of these three types of conveyance —gift, sale, and *mrḥq*—employs these constitutive terms in its own unique manner. The following chart presents the distribution of the terms within the various types of conveyance:

Gift	*Sale* (*BP* 12)	*Sale* (*BP* 3)	*Litigation-mrḥq* [1]	*Transfer-mrḥq* [2]
ʿšt lk bḥyy	*ṭyb lbby b*	*ṭyb lbby b*	*hwṭbt lbby b*	0000000
yhbt lk bmwty brḥmn	*ṭyb lbby b*	*rḥqt mnh*	*rḥqt mnk*	*rḥqt mnk/h*
zylk hw	*zylk hw*	*zylk hw*	000000	*zylk hw*

The Explication of the Distribution. Several significant patterns emerge:

a) Sale and *mrḥq* overlap to a remarkable degree. All three terms— *ṭyb lbby* "my heart is satisfied," *rḥqt mnk* "I have removed myself from you," and *zylk hw* "it is yours"—used in sale are found in one or the other of the *mrḥq* transactions. Conversely, all terms used in *mrḥq* are found in sale. Furthermore, even though *ṭyb lbby* is missing from transfer-*mrḥq* and *zylk hw* is missing from litigation-*mrḥq*, no alternate terms take their places: the slots are simply left blank. This remarkable degree of overlap between the operative terminology of sale and *mrḥq* would seem to indicate some underlying affinity between these two subcategories of conveyance. [3]

---

in Germanic and Anglo-Saxon law (cf. Pollock and Maitland, Vol. II, p. 30) and as *ḥazaqah* in Rabbinic law (cf. Gulak, *Jewish Law*, Vol. I, pp. 111 ff.). It is interesting to note that the term *Seisin* is related to the German *sitzen* "to sit (on the land)." It would thus be parallel to the Aramaic *bny wtb* and the Akkadian *uraṣṣip ušēšib*.

[1]) *AP* 14 and *AP* 20; the litigation-*mrḥq*, *AP* 6, uses only the term *hwṭbt lbby*; this phenomenon will be discussed below in the chapter on the relationship between *ṭyb lbby* and *rḥqt*, pp. 48 ff.

[2]) *AP* 13 and *AP* 25.

[3]) The close relationship between sale and litigation was noticed by San Nicolò. In his *Schlussklauseln* (p. 39), he points out that OB deeds of sale and the *ṭuppi lā ragāmim*, the Old Babylonian equivalent of the later Aramaic *spr mrḥq*, both

b) Gift, on the other hand, contrasts with both sale and *mrḥq*; its typical set of terms—*'šst lk bḥyy wyhbt lk brḥmn bmwty* "I have turned my thoughts to you during my lifetime and have transferred (the property) to you in affection upon the event of my death"—is found neither in sale nor in *mrḥq*. Gift stresses the personal affection (*rḥmn*) and thoughts of the donor for the donee (*'šst lk*); sale and *mrḥq*, on the other hand, stress the "satisfaction" the old right-holder enjoys from the performance tendered to him by the new owner. Sale and *mrḥq* also stress the aspect of relinquishment (*rḥq* "to be far") not found in gift. One has to assume, therefore, that contrasting sets of terms reflect underlying contrasts in legal principles and psychologies.

c) Gift and sale, however, do have one clause in common: the transfer/investiture clause; the same clause is also found in the transfer-*mrḥq*. It is the common possession of all transactions which record the transfer of property. It is not found in the litigation-*mrḥq* because this type of deed records the confirmation of contested rights rather than the transfer of property and the rights pertaining thereto. [1])

---

employ the same clauses of no-contest. Commenting on this significant phenomenon, he says: "Auch scheint der Ausgangspunkt der Verzichtsklausel überhaupt nicht im Vertragsrechte, sondern im Prozesse gelegen zu sein. Von den Prozessurkunden aus ist sie dann auf die rechtsgeschäftlichen Verfügungen, darunter auch auf die Kauf- und Tauschverträge, übertragen worden" (*ibid.*, pp. 39-40).

[1]) There is one other deed that should be mentioned in this context—*AP* 5 (471 B.C.). It is not actually a conveyance and its use of the operative/constitutive terminology does not fall into any of the patterns outlined above. Nevertheless, it has marked affinities with regular conveyances. The content of the deed is the following: Maḥseiah allowed Ḳoniyah to build on his property. In this deed, Ḳoniyah declares that the property belongs to Maḥseiah. Since the deed neither transfers rights nor reconfirms contested ones, it does not fall into any of the categories of conveyance listed below. It simply reassures the owner that the property is his. Only one clause is used in the deed: the transfer/investiture clause, "the gate is yours; I will not be able to stop you from building on it" (lines 11 f.).

The legal function of the deed seems to be the following: If use (*ḥazaqa*) is necessary to establish ownership (cf. above, p. 24 n. 2), then it is quite possible that use gives at least a weak or putative claim to ownership, even when the object being used has not been formally transferred to the user, but is simply lent as a favor. Thus, when Maḥseiah allowed Ḳoniyah to use his property, there was always the danger that Ḳoniyah or his children (who may have been unaware of this friendly agreement) would claim that the property actually belonged to Ḳoniyah, since he had been exercising uncontested dominion over the property for such a long time. In order to prevent such a contingency, Ḳoniyah draws up a deed which insures the property from all such litigation. As far as I can tell, the only real analogue to the Aramaic documents is a late Demotic deed published by A. F. Shore and H. S. Smith, "Two Unpublished Demotic Documents from the Asyūṭ Archive," *JEA*, 45 (1959), pp. 52 ff. (However, a more exhaustive comparative study of these deeds in the light of the material discussed by Lautner in his *Rechtsverhältnisse* may well uncover the cuneiform models of both the Aramaic and the late Demotic transactions.)

4. Specific Object of this Study: Investigation of *ṭyb lbby*

The three terms *ṭyb lbby*, *rḥqt*, and *zylk hw* reflect a legal chain reaction; *zylk hw* depends on *rḥqt* as *rḥqt* depends on *ṭyb lbby*. This would explain the rigid positional order of the terms. Ideally, therefore, the terms should be studied together as an organic unit. Since an adequate treatment of the whole complex would exceed the limits of a monograph, the first term—*ṭyb lbby*—has been selected as the subject of further investigation because it seems to initiate the constitutive process which continues in *rḥqt* and culminates in *zylk hw*.

The term *ṭyb lbby* has been given precedence also because, of all three phrases, it is probably the best suited for a comparative legal analysis. It has recognized analogues in the Old Babylonian *libbašu ṭāb* "his heart (the seller's) is satisfied" and the Demotic *dj.k-mtj ḥ3tj(.i)* "You (the buyer) have satisfied my heart." [1]) Although the relationship between the Aramaic and the Demotic terms is not altogether clear, almost all are agreed that these later terms are ultimately derived from the older cuneiform model. [2])

A. *Suggested Meanings: Previous Studies*

Although terms of satisfaction are common in Aramaic, Demotic, and cuneiform sources, relatively little attention has been paid to the meaning and especially to the legal function involved. Yaron considers the Aramaic term to be a stylistic flourish devoid of any specific legal function. His opinion of the Akkadian *libbašu ṭāb* seems to be the same. [3])

---

[1]) Pritsch, "Jüdische Rechtsurkunden aus Ägypten," *ZVRW*, 27 (1912), p. 14, n. 3, pointed out both the Akkadian and the Demotic analogues. The relationship between *libbašu ṭāb* and *ṭyb lbby* was pointed out by many of the early interpreters. Cf., for example, *AP*, p. xxix; Epstein, *JJLG*, 6 (1908), p. 366, n. 5; the Demotic analogues have been discussed more recently by Seidl in *ÄRg*, pp. 40-53.

[2]) Seidl assumes that the Demotic term is derived from the Akkadian *libbašu ṭāb* (*ibid.*, pp. 40-43 and 71); however, he denies the possibility that the Demotic may have received the cuneiform term through an Aramaic medium (*ibid.*, pp. 72-73). For the ultimate cuneiform origins of the Aramaic, cf. *LAP*, pp. 105-107.

[3]) Cf. the Hebrew version of *LAP*, p. 107: "In these documents, the payment of the price (and the concomitant satisfaction) is treated more as a part of the factual narration than as a clause with specific legal functions." Even though this statement does not reappear in the English version of *LAP*, it seems that Yaron has not changed his mind concerning the nonlegal nature of the expression. Although he has gathered much relevant material in connection with *libbašu ṭāb*/*ṭyb lbby*, nowhere does he discuss its legal implications.

Another point should be made in this context. Yaron considers *ṭyb lbby* to be a nonessential element in the deed because of its nontechnical, narrative quality. However, it is just such a nontechnical, narrative quality which is characteristic of so many cuneiform legal terms. For example, the Nuzi terms *iptaṭar* and *uṣṣi* "he goes out/away" are technical terms describing the cessation of some servile

The parallel Demotic term has fared somewhat better. Seidl, especially, has devoted much effort to its elucidation. According to him, the term expresses volition and consent. [1] Furthermore, the use of the term in early Demotic deeds of sale seems to indicate that volition had taken the place of *Entgeltlichkeit* as the constitutive element of the Demotic sale transaction. [2] Seidl also applies this volitional interpretation to the Akkadian term *libbašu ṭāb* which he considers to be the prototype of the Demotic term. [3]

Boyer, one of the latest Assyriologists to have investigated *libbašu ṭāb*, is in substantial agreement with Seidl's volitional interpretation. According to Boyer, the term *libbašu ṭāb* is to be interpreted in the light of the etymologically related term *ina ṭūb libbi* "in the joy of heart/willingly." Thus, *libbašu ṭāb* is understood as a term of volition and consent. [4]

B. *A New Interpretation*

The present reinvestigation of all the available material—Aramaic, Akkadian, and Demotic—does not support any of the interpretations suggested so far. Yaron is certainly not correct in denying the terminological function of *ṭyb lbby/libbašu ṭāb*. The frequency and care with which these terms are used is a clear indicator of their constitutive character. Moreover, any expression used in a legal document, no matter how narrative or untechnical it may seem, usually plays some clearly defined role within the structure of the transaction. The Akkadian and the Demotic terms of satisfaction are no exceptions to this rule.

Accordingly, Boyer and Seidl are on the right track when they stress the terminological function of these expressions. I cannot, however, agree with their volitional interpretations, plausible as they may seem at first sight. In the following study, the thesis will be presented that the term *ṭyb lbby/libbašu ṭāb* does not express volition and transcendence of the compensation (*Entgelt*) principle, but that, on the contrary, it is the terminological expression of *Entgeltlichkeit* par excellence!

Nevertheless, whether the term expresses volition or *Entgeltlichkeit*,

---

relationship, such as slavery, personal antichresis, or apprenticeship. The Nuzi-Middle Assyrian term *ul iqerreb* "he shall not approach, encroach on" may seem sufficiently "narrative" not to merit attention, but in reality it expresses the clearly defined legal concept "he shall have no claim." There are very few elements in legal contracts which do not have some specific juridical-constitutive role to fill within the structure of the transaction, no matter how untechnical or narrative they may seem.

[1]) Seidl, ÄRg, pp. 40-43.

[2]) *Ibid.*

[3]) *Ibid.*

[4]) Cf. Boyer, *ARM* VIII, p. 189.

its frequent use in three systems of ancient law indicates its high constitutive significance; furthermore, if the term had not been important in its original application, it would hardly have been borrowed by outsiders. The goal of this study, therefore, will be the inductive-contextual definition of the Aramaic term, and the establishment of its cuneiform and Demotic analogues. To do this, it will be necessary to isolate the particular cuneiform tradition that may have served as the prototype of the Aramaic term, to define this tradition on the basis of comparative dialectology, and to determine the historical conditions in which the cuneiform term(s) were translated into an Aramaic garb.

The study will consist of three sections: the first will be devoted to the Aramaic term, the second to the definition of the Akkadian *libbašu ṭāb*, and the third to a discussion of the Egyptian terms, especially the Demotic *dj.k-mtj ḥ3tj(.i)*. The results of these three sections will be coordinated in a concluding section.

CHAPTER TWO

TERMS OF SATISFACTION IN CONVEYANCE

1. The Texts

A. *The Term* ṭyb lbby *in Litigation*-mrḥq [1])

1) *AP* 20 (420 B.C.)

Menaḥem and Ananiah, sons of Meshullam, sued Yedoniah and Maḥseiah, sons of Asḥor and Mibṭaḥiah, concerning goods which had been deposited—either as a pledge or as a loan—with Asḥor by Shelomem, their grandfather. The plaintiffs declared that the goods were not returned. The defendants then satisfied the hearts of the plaintiffs with/concerning the goods. The plaintiffs thereupon relinquished all further claims to the goods.

(8) . . . *w'nt ydnyh wmḥsyh bny 'sḥwr hwṭbtm lbbn b'lk nksy'* (9) *wṭyb lbbn bgw mn* [*ywm*]*' znh ʿd ʿlm 'nh mnḥm wʿnnyh rḥyqn 'nḥnh mnk* (10) *mn ywm' znh ʿd ʿlm l*[*'*] *nkhl 'nḥnh wbnyn* . . . (11) . . . *l' ykhlwn yršw*[*nk*]*m* . . . *dyn wdbb*

(8) . . . "And you Yedoniah and Maḥseiah, sons of Asḥor, have satisfied our hearts with/concerning) these goods (9) and our heart is satisfied therewith from this [day] forever. [2]) I, Menaḥem and Ananiah—we are

---

[1]) The term *hwṭbt/ṭyb lbby* is not used in the transfer-*mrḥq* deed; cf. above, p. 25.

[2]) The position of the clause "from this day forever" is subject to some disagreement. Cowley divided the clauses in the following manner: "From this day forever, I, Menaḥem and Ananiah—we renounce all claim on you. (10) From this day forever, we shall have no power . . . to bring against you . . . suit or process." This division does not seem correct since, as far as I can tell, this clause does not introduce the main constitutive verbs and clauses but rather follows them: (10) . . . *zbn wyhbn* (11) *lk wrḥqn mnh mn ywm' znh wʿd ʿlmn* "We have sold and transferred (it) (11) to you and have removed ourselves from it (i.e., the house) from this day and forever." (*BP* 3; so Kraeling). Or, (8) . . . *brty šlyṭh bh mn ywm' znh «znh» ʿd ʿlm* (8) "My daughter owns it from this day forever" (*BP* 10). I therefore prefer to read in *AP* 20, "My heart is satisfied from this (this!) day forever; I Menaḥem and Ananiah—we renounce all claim (we are removed) from you (10) from this day forever. We will not be able, etc."

If this reading is correct, the terms *ṭyb lbby*, *rḥqt* and the transfer/investiture clause all employ the phrase "from this day forever" in exactly the same way; the three terms all describe legal states which begin "from this day" and continue "forever." E.g., "My heart is satisfied/I remove myself/You are (now) owner—from this day forever." Thus, the "satisfaction" of the seller's heart, like his relinquishment, is not a feeling of the moment but a state of mind which is to continue for all times; if the seller is not satisfied in the future, the transaction is not final. Cf. the discussion below.

The following should also be noted: the exact semantic parallel of the Aramaic clause has not yet been located. However, the two elements (a) "from this day" and (b) "forever" are found in the Ras Shamra Akkadian (a) *ištu ūmi annî* and (b)

'removed' [1]) from you (10-11) from this day forever. We are not able nor are our children . . . able to institute [2]) against you . . . formal process." [3])

---

ana dārīti (cf. *PRU* III, 16.353 and *passim*; see also Yaron's comments in "Aramaic Marriage Contracts from Elephantine," *JSS*, 3 (1958), p. 30). Even though the individual Akkadian and Aramaic terms are virtually identical, each tradition combines these elements into different syntactical structures: the Aramaic combines the two terms into one organic unit "from this day and forever" while the Akkadian does not. For a discussion of nonlegal Ugaritic and Biblical examples of the organic usage of "from this day and forever," cf. S. Loewenstamm, "Notes on the Alalakh Tablets," *IEJ*, 6 (1956), p. 222. To this list should be added *PRU* IV 17.353: 4 *ištu ūmi annî ina arki ūmi*. For the possible relationship between this clause and contemporary Egyptian deeds, cf. Alt, *Kleine Schriften*, III, pp. 155 ff. Finally, it should be noted that the sale of land *ana dārītim* "for all times" was quite common in Susa. Cf. *MDP* XXIV 349: 9; *ibid.* 351: 7 and *passim*.*

[1]) The meaning of the term *rḥqt* "I have removed myself" will be discussed below. In brief, the term expresses any relinquishment of rights by a former right-holder or any cessation of claims by a litigant.

[2]) The terms *grh* and *ršh* are virtual synonyms in the Aramaic documents. Furthermore, they are the cognates of the Akkadian *gerû* and *rašû* (cf. *AP*, p. xxix). Even though the roots *grh* and *ršh* may well belong to the indigenous lexical stock of Aramaic (so Kutscher, *New Aramaic Texts*, p. 238), nevertheless, their terminological use within stereotyped legal clauses is probably based on cuneiform models. Although the OB *rašû* is etymologically identical with the Aramaic *ršh*, the two terms differ in respect to their specific syntactical usage: the Aramaic *ršh* (and its synonym *grh*) both take a double object (*lʾ ʾgrnk/ʾršnk dyn wdbb* "I will not institute a formal suit against you"); the Akkadian term—at least in its OB usage—does not take an object (cf. *Schlussklauseln*, p. 44, n. 8). However, the Aramaic usage does have definite cuneiform prototypes: the OB deeds from Alalakh contain a clause which anticipates most of the lexical and syntactical features of the Aramaic. *AT** 11: 25 ff. reads: *ša ú-ra-am še-ra-a[m]* (26) *aš-[šum* *[al]*]*Na-aš-tar-bi* [*ki*] (27) *a-na Ya-ri-im-li-im di-nam i-gi-ir-ru-ú* "Whoever in the future (= Aramaic *mḥr ʾw ywm ʾḥrn* "tomorrow or some other day") shall sue Yarīm-Līm in a suit concerning the city of Naštarbi" Both the Aramaic *grh* and the Akkadian *gerû* take personal indirect objects (Aramaic: *lʾ ʾgrnk* "I will not sue you"; Akkadian: *ana Yarīm-līm . . . igerrû* "shall sue Yarīm-Līm") and impersonal direct objects (Aramaic: *lʾ ʾgrnk dyn wdbb* "I shall not institute against you a *formal process*"; Akkadian *dīnam igerrû* "[whoever] institute a *process*"). There is one other point of correspondence between the Aramaic and the Akkadian. Kutscher (*New Aramaic Texts*, p. 242) had noted the equivalence of Aramaic *bšm* with Akkadian *aššum*, both with the meaning "concerning." Kutscher's theoretical equation is now confirmed by a comparison of the Akkadian *aššum Naštarbi* "concerning Naštarbi" with *AP* 20: 12 *b[šm] nksn wksp* "(No one shall institute a formal process) concerning/in the matter of goods and money." Cf. also AP 8: 12; 13: 9; 14: 8.

In the Aramaic usage, the direct object is *dyn wdbb*, while the Akkadian usage only contains the first element—*dīnam*. However, this particular aspect of the Aramaic usage is already anticipated by the NA phrase: *ša elânni dēnu dabābu itti* PN *igarrûni iqabbûni kaspu lā gammur bītu kirû lā apil* "Whoever rises up (seeking) to institute a formal suit against PN saying: 'The money was not paid completely; the house and the garden were not paid for' " (*ARU* 163 and *passim*). The Aramaic *lʾ ʾgrnk dyn wdbb* thus equals NA *ša . . . dēnu dabābu itti* PN *igarrûni*. The only difference between the two clauses is that the Aramaic is subjectively formulated, while the Akkadian is objectively formulated.*

[3]) *dyn wdbb*: lit. "suit and process." The expression is a hendiadys and is therefore

2) *AP* 14 (441 B.C.)

Mibṭaḥiah was obligated by the court to clear herself by a purgatory oath concerning the goods she had held in common with her ex-husband, the Egyptian, Piʾ. Piʾ declared himself "satisfied" by the oath and thereupon relinquished all claims to the contested property.

(4) . . . *ʾdyn mwmʾh* (5) *mṭʾh ʿlyky wymʾty ly ʿlyhm bsty ʾlhth wṭyb lbby* (6) *bmwmʾh dkʾ zy ʿbdty ly ʿl nksyʾ ʾlky wrḥqt mnky mn* (7) *ywmʾ znh wʿd ʿlm lʾ ʾkhl ʾgrnky dyn wdbb*

"... Then an oath (5) was imposed [1]) upon you and you swore to me concerning them by Sati, the goddess, and my heart was satisfied (6) with that oath which you took for me concerning those goods of yours; and I hereby [2]) remove myself from you from (7) this day for ever. I will not be able to sue you in a formal process."

3) *AP* 6 (465 B.C.)

Dargaman raises a claim against Maḥseiah concerning a plot of land. The latter satisfied the heart of Dargaman with an oath of purgation.

(11) . . . *ymʾt ly byhw whwṭbt* (12) *lbby ʿl ʾrqʾ zk lʾ ʾkhl ʾgrnk dyn wdbb*

(11) ". . . You took an oath for me by *Yhw* and satisfied (12) my heart concerning this land; I will not be able to sue you in a formal process."

4) *AP* 67 (date not preserved)—fragment no. 5 preserves the following sequence:

---

translated as a "formal suit." For a study of hendiadys in Hebrew, cf. E. Z. Melamed, "Hendiadys in the Bible" *Tarbiẕ*, 16 (1945), pp. 173 ff. Cf. also by the same author, *Break-up of Stereotype Phrases*.

[1]) *mṭʾ*: lit. "to reach, to arrive." The concept "to impose (an oath) on someone/ to obligate (to take an oath) is also expressed in Elephantine Aramaic by the verb *ṭʿn*, lit. "to load." Cf. *AP* 6 : 6 *wṭʿnwk ly mwmʾh lmwmʾ* "And they (the judges) obligated you to take an oath on my behalf." This use of *ṭʿn* seems to be a loan-translation from the Akkadian *emēdu* "to load/ to force to take an oath." (Cf. *MDP* XXIII 393 : 13) The Elephantine term is probably the prototype of the Rabbinic *ṭāʿan* "to raise an objection" and *ṭāʿūn* "in need of" which are both based on the metaphor of lading: cf. the antonym of *ṭāʿan, pāraq* "to unload." Contrast Kutscher, *New Aramaic Texts*, p. 238 who derives the terms from the metaphor of piercing (cf. the Arabic *ṭaʿana*).

[2]) In Biblical Hebrew—and probably also in West Semitic in general—verbs in the first person perfect often have a present perfect aspect and should be translated: "I hereby . . ." Cf. the discussion of Driver, *Tenses*, pp. 15-17. This phenomenon was noted by several of the Jewish commentators of the Middle Ages; cf. the comments of Rashbam to Gen. 23:11 and those of Rashi to Gen. 14: 22.

*]w*ṭ*yb lbb[y*
*]r*ḥ*qt mnk mn* y[*wm*ʾ *znh*
*]*ʾ*yš ly* <*l*ʾ> *ygrnk d[yn*

"And [my] heart is satisfied . . . I hereby remove myself from you from [this d]ay [. . .] <no> one of mine will sue you in a pro[cess]."

5) *BP* 1 (451 B.C.)

Mika raised a claim against the *hyr/d* [1]) of Ananiah son of Azariah. The defendant paid a sum of money to the plaintiff, and thereupon the plaintiff declared that his heart had been satisfied and that he had no further claims. [2])

(3) . . . *yhbt ly ksp šqln* 5 *bdmy hyr/d*ʾ *zylk zy* (4) *qblt* ʿ*lyk*! *bgw* [*w*ṭ*y*]*b lbby bdmwh*[*y wl*ʾ] ʾ*khl* ʾ*grnk* (5) *dn wdbb*

(3) ". . . You have paid me 5 shekels of silver as the price of your *hyr/d* concerning which (4) I raised a complaint against you (!) and my heart is (now) [satisfied] with its pri[ce. I shall not] be able to sue you in (5) a formal process."

B. *The Term* ṭyb lbby *in Sale*

6) *BP* 3 (437 B.C.)

Bagazušt and his wife Ubil [3]) sell a house to Ananiah son of Azariah.

---

[1]) For the meaning of this difficult (foreign ?) term, cf. Kraeling's notes to *BP*, p. 135. Rosenthal (*apud BP*, p. 135) derives the word from the Syriac *hrr* "to litigate." This interpretation, however, was rejected by Kutscher (*New Aramaic Texts*, p. 234). Milik (*RB*, 61 [1954], p. 248) suggests several Egyptian terms for vessels or building objects.

[2]) The translation given above is based on the interpretations and emendations suggested by H. L. Ginsberg, "Brooklyn Museum Aramaic Papyri," *JAOS*, 74 (1954), p. 156.

[3]) Why was the wife included as a partner in the sale ? What is the legal significance of the wife participating in the alienation of the property ?

The participation of the wife in the sale transaction may be akin to the later Demotic adhesions—additions to the sale contract written by the wife, in which she waived her rights to the property being sold. Such waivers were necessary because the wife had a lien on her husband's property for the payment of her dowry in the case of divorce. Furthermore, in some cases, husbands and wives acquired property jointly (cf. *BP*: 2 (11) *Tmt hy šly*ṭ*h bkl nksn zy yhwwn byn* ʿ*nny wtmt* "*Tmt* is the owner of all goods which may be acquired in common by Anani and *Tmt*"). Cf. also the Ras Shamra Akkadian stipulation that she, upon the death of her husband is the sole owner of: (*RS* 8.145: 4) *mi-nu-um-me-e* (5) *ša i-ba-aš-ši a-na ya-ši* [Aramaic: *yhwwn byn*] (6) *ša ta-ar-te-ši* *fBi-da-wa* (7) *it-ti-ya* "of everything which shall accrue unto me, or/namely that which Bidawa shall acquire in common with

(3) . . . *zbn wyhbn* [1]) (4) *lk byth zy ʾpwly br msdy*

Condition of property [2])

(5) . . . *ʾnḥn zbnhy lk wyhbt* (6) *ln dmwhy . . . wṭyb lbbn* (7) *bdmyʾ zy yhbt ln*

Boundaries of property [3])

(10) . . . *ʾnḥn zbn wyhbn* (11) *lk wrḥqn mnh mn ywmʾ znh wʿd ʿlmn*

(3) . . . "We have sold and transferred (4) to you the house of *ʾpwly* son of *Msdy.*"

---

me" (Thureau-Dangin, "Trois contrats de Ras-Shamra," *Syria*, 18 (1937), p. 249). In such cases, obviously the wife's participation or at least passive consent was needed to insure the finality and the incontestability of the sale. The Aramaic documents themselves indicate that women could contest legal transactions as effectively as men. (Cf. the regular Aramaic clause of no-contest: *AP* 8: 10 —*lʾ ʾyty ly br wbrh ʾḥrnn ʾḥ wʾḥh wʾnth* (11) *wʾyš ʾḥrn šlyṭ bʾrqʾ zk lhn ʾnty* . . . "I have no other son(s) or daughter(s), brother sister or wife (11) or anybody else related to me who is owner of this land except you . . .")*

[1]) The Aramaic *zbn wyhb* lit., "he sold and transferred" is another example of the hendiadys construction. In all probability, the phrase is similar in function to the Middle Assyrian *iddinma — ušappi* (*iddin* = *zbn*; *ušappi* = *yhb*) "he effected a final sale." For a discussion of the terms, cf. Koschaker, *NKRA*, pp. 27-30.

[2]) The description of the condition of the property is one of the characteristics of the Aramaic (and the Demotic) deeds of sale. In *BP* 3, the description is the following: *ʾgrwh qymn wtrbṣh* (5) *ʾrʿ hy wlʾ bnyh wkwyn bh wgšrn lʾ ʾḥd* "Its walls are standing and its courtyard is unbuilt land; it has windows but is not fitted/supplied with beams." (Cf. the comments of Kutscher, *New Aramaic Texts*, p. 235 on the meaning of the terms *ʾrʿ* and *ʾḥd*; Kutscher also pointed out some significant late Demotic parallels to this clause. The same Demotic source is also quoted by Rabinowitz in his *Legal History*, p. 7. For similar description of the condition of the property, cf. *BP* 4: 8 *ʾḥd gšwrn wkwn* "fitted with beams and windows;" cf. *BP* 9: 13; *BP* 10: 2-3; *BP* 12: 13. If one can judge from the limited number of extant early Demotic conveyances (cf. for example, Malinine, *Choix de textes*), the practice of describing the condition of the land being sold, although known from a later period, was not employed during the early Demotic period (roughly contemporaneous with the Aramaic documents). Could it be that the later Demotic deeds were influenced by the early Aramaic practice? So Kutscher, *New Aramaic Texts*, p. 235.

Yaron, *LAP*, p. 119 has pointed out the cuneiform parallels from the NA and NB documents and from the OB lexical series *ḪAR.ra* = *ḫubullu* and *ana ittišu*. Although rare in OB documents of lower Mesopotamia, such a description is attested to in Meissner, *Beiträge*, No. 35: a house was sold (4) *qa-du-um i-ga-ra-ti-šu* (5) *ka-li-ši-na i-ga-ru-um* (6) *ša gu-šu-ru ku-nu* "Together with all its walls. The wall (6) which is fitted with a beam (Aramaic *gšwr ʾḥd*)." However, descriptions of the condition of the property are fairly common in the OB sale deeds from Susa. Cf. also *MDP* XXII 44-47.

[3]) In *BP* 3, the boundaries are described in the following manner: "Now these are the boundaries of the house which we are selling you: *lʿlyh lh* . . . (ll. 7-8) . . . *lthth lh* (l. 8) . . . *mwʿh šmš lh lmʿrb šmš lh* (l. 9). For the meaning of the terms "above" and "below," cf. the interpretation of H. L. Ginsberg, "The Brooklyn Museum Aramaic Papyri," p. 154. The designation of boundaries is also found in the Demotic deeds (cf. Malinine, *Choix de textes*, No. 9 and 11). The designation of boundaries is also common in NB and Arsacid texts. The practice is also known from OB times. Cf. Gautier, *Archives de Dilbat*, Nos 1, 3-5, and *passim*.

Condition of property

(5) . . . "We have sold it to you and you have payed (6) us its price . . . and our heart is (now) satisfied (7) with the price you have payed us."

Boundaries of property

(10) . . . "We have sold and transferred (11) (it) to you and we have removed ourselves from it from this day and forever."

7) *BP* 12 (401 B.C.)

Ananiah son of Azariah and his wife *Tpmt* sell the house they had bought from Bagazušt (cf. *BP* 3) to Anani son of Ḥaggai. The scribe evidently began to write the whole transaction and for some reason did not finish. He began the whole transaction all over again on the same sheet of papyrus. Thus, two versions of the transaction (A and B) are preserved on the same sheet: lines 1-9 (A) contain the operative section of the uncompleted deed; lines 10-35 (B) contain the complete version of the same transaction. Thus, *BP* 12 contains two versions of the same operative section. [1]) The second recension is quoted first because of its similarity with that of *BP* 3.

b)

(12) . . . *zbn wyhbn lk bytn* . . .

Condition of property

(13) . . . *wyhbt ln dmwhy* . . . (14) *wṭyb lbbn bdmy' zy* (15) *yhbt ln*

Description of property

a)

(3) . . . *zbn wyhbn lk bytn* . . .

Condition etc.

(5) . . . *wyhbt ln dmy bytn* . . . (6) . . . *wṭyb lbbn bgw zy l' 'št'r ln ʿlyk mn dmy'* . . .

b)

(12) . . . "We have sold and transferred you our house."

Condition etc.

(13) . . . "And you gave us its price (14) . . . and our heart is satisfied with the price which (15) you gave us."

Description etc.

a)

(5) . . . "And you gave us the price of our house . . . (6) . . . and our heart is satisfied in that none of the price is outstanding against you on our account." [2])

[1]) For this interpretation, cf. Ginsberg, *JAOS*, 74 (1954), p. 161.

[2]) This clause is taken from the law of obligations. Cf. *AP* 11: 9 *wmrbyth zy yšt'r*

C. *The Relationship Between* ṭyb lbby (*Sale*) *and* yhbt lk brḥmn *Gift*)

It was noted above (in the comments to the distribution chart, p. 25) that the expression *hwṭbt lbby/ṭyb lbby* is limited in usage to sale and *mrḥq*. It is conspicuously absent from deeds of gift. Furthermore, its slot is not left empty but is filled with a parallel set of contrasting terms: 1) *yhbt lk bḥyy wbmwty* "I (hereby) give to you in my lifetime and after my death"; 2) *yhbt lk brḥmn/t* "I (hereby) give to you in affection/as a gift"; 3) *ʿšt lk bḥyy(brḥmn)* . . . *wyhbt lk/šbqtky bmwty* "I (hereby) turn my thoughts to you during my life (in affection) . . . and assign to you/free you upon my death."*

1) *AP* 8 (460 B.C.)

Maḥseiah gives to his daughter Mibṭaḥiah a gift of a house on the occasion of her marriage to Yezaniah ben Uriah.

(3) . . . *ʾnh yhbt lky bḥyy wbmwty byt 1 ʾrq zyly*

(3) ". . . I (hereby give to you for my lifetime and after my death a house and land belonging to me."

BP 10 (402 B.C.)

Anani gives a gift of a house to his daughter.

(11) . . . *wʾnty ʾm šlyṭh bbytʾ znh* . . . *bḥyy wbmwty* [1]*ʾp* (12) *lʾ ykhl* [2])

ʿly "And the interest which is outstanding against me . . ." Cf. the Demotic, Hebrew, Arabic, and Akkadian examples cited by Kutscher, *New Aramaic Texts*, p. 242. Cf. also the use of the Aramaic word *ʿl* in the Aramaic dockets (*Delaporte, Épigraphes araméens*, p. 13). See also the Canaanite examples cited by Tur-Sinai, p. 34, and the Nabatean ones cited by Rabinowitz, *Jewish Law*, p. 104.

[1]) When the expression *bḥyy wbmwty* is used, it indicates that the gift is final from the moment of donation and is not affected by the death of the donor: the gift is for all time. (So *LAP*, p. 78.) The same expression is used later on in the fragments of documents preserved in the Talmud. The Talmudic discussion of the term (*TB*, *Bāḇā Baṯrā* 153a) is as follows: "There was a certain (deed of) gift, in which it was written *beḥayyīm uḇemāweṯ* 'in life and in death.' Rab said: 'This has the force of a *mattenāṯ šekiḇ meraʿ* (a gift made by a sick man that can be revoked if the man recovers).' And Samuel said: 'This has the force of a *mattenaṯ bārīʾ* (a gift made by a healthy man which is not revocable).' " Cf. the discussion of this and other related passages in Yaron's *Gifts*, pp. 120 ff.

Even though the opinion of Samuel was usually followed, in this case, the law was decided according to Rab's interpretation. However, to judge from the older Elephantine usage, Samuel's interpretation was the more historically correct: it is quite clear from the Aramaic usage that gifts made *bḥyy wbmwty* were final and irrevocable, i.e., they were *mattenaṯ bārīʾ*. This is not the only case in which the legal theory of the Rabbis conflicts with the ancient common-law practice reflected in the actual documents.

[2]) The Aramaic *lʾ ykhl* "he shall not be able" means in this context "he is not allowed." Kutscher has pointed out (*Words*, pp. 78 ff.) that Hebrew and Aramaic

br ly wbrh ly . . . zy yršnky dyn wdbb wyqbl ʿlyk (13) *wʿl bnyky lsgn wmrʾ* [1]) *lhʿdyh* [2]) *bytʾ znh mn qdmyky* [3]) *bḥyy wbmwty*

(11) . . . "And you, moreover, are the owner of this house . . . in my lifetime and after my death. Nor (12) shall son or daughter of mine . . . who institute against you a formal process or who lodge against you (13)

(and one may possibly add Akkadian as well) originally lacked a means of expressing the idea of "forbidden" and "allowed." The earlier layer of language expressed this concept by the negative jussive: "he shall not do it" (*ibid.*). It seems that Elephantine Aramaic reflects a stage later than the jussive but earlier than the use of *ʾasūr* "forbidden" and *muttār* "allowed": in these documents, the negative jussive is strengthened by the word *khl* "to be able." "He shall not be able" stands for "he is not allowed." Rabinowitz (*Jewish Law*, pp. 104 ff.) noted that the same usage is found several times in Deuteronomy—Deut 12: 17 *lōʾ tūḵal leʾeḵōl bišeʿārêḵā* "you may not partake (of the tithes) in your settlements"; Deut 21: 16 *lōʾ yūḵal lebakker ʾeṯ ben haʾăhūḇā* "he may not treat as first-born the son of the beloved (wife)." Rabinowitz (*ibid.*) notes that the Targum already understood these verses in the same way. My colleague Dr. David Weiss of the Jewish Theological Seminary notes that the interpretation of Onqelos is also reflected in Rabbinic tradition preserved in Hoffmann, *Midrasch Tannaïm*, pp. 51, 92, 129 and 155. Rabinowitz (*ibid.*) considers the Aramaic *lʾ ykhl* to be a Hebraism. (Cf. also Rabinowitz's discussion of Hebraisms in his article, *Jewish Elements*, p. 442, n. 24). More likely, it seems that the different branches of West Semitic solved the same problem in similar ways. [Cf. Addenda.]

1) Cf. *MDP* XXIV 330: 25-27 *aš-šum ap-lu-ti-šu* (26) *šarram ù da-a-na-am* (27) *ù-ul i-ma-ḫa-ar* "concerning his inheritance, he shall not approach a king or a judge (with a complaint)." See the comments of J. J. Rabinowitz, "The Susa Tablets, the Bible and the Aramaic Papyri," *VT*, 11 (1961), pp. 63-66.

2) *lhʿdyh*: from the Aramaic *ʿdw/y* "to pass away." Even though *lhʿdyh* is not found again in this sense in the Aramaic legal documents, the expression seems to be used here as a technical term with the meaning "expropriate." Rabinowitz has pointed out the presence of a *šṭr ʿdw* in a Nabatean legal deed ("A Clue to the Nabatean Contract from the Dead Sea Region," *BASOR*, 139 [1955], p. 12). He translates the words as "deed of seizure." If he is correct in his interpretation, the Aramaic and the later Nabatean usages are somehow related.

3) The term *qdm*, lit. "before, in the presence of" means in this context "from the possession of." The Aramaic *qdm* is similar in meaning to the NA *ana pāni*, lit. "in the presence of, before" which is used in NA deeds of loan in the sense of "at the disposal, in the possession of the creditor." (Cf. *NKRA*, p. 93, n. 6). Terms meaning "before, in the presence of" are frequently employed in a similar sense in the legal documents of Wadi Murabbaʿat. Thus, if the debtor does not repay the loan, all that he will acquire is *lqwblyk* "at your (the creditor's) disposal" (cf. *Les grottes de Murabbaʿat*, p. 101, 1. 8). In several of the deeds of sale from Wadi Murabbaʿat* edited by Milik ("Deux documents inédits du désert de Juda," *Biblica*, 38 (1957)), we find the statement that the seller is obligated *lmrqʾ wlqymʾ zbnh zk qdm[kn] wqdm yrtkn* "to clear this sale (of all claims) and to secure it in your possession and in the possession of your heirs"—lit. "to make it stand before you" (p. 259, l. 12'). Milik (*ibid.*, p. 263) points out the same use of *qdm* in the Talmudic clause *wʾwqym qdmk* "I will restore it to your possession/ I will establish your right to it" (*Bāḇā Meṣīʿā*, 15a). Finally, it may be noted that the term *qdm* is found in the Aramaic dockets to the NA legal documents with the meaning "at the disposal of/in the possession of" (cf. Delaporte, *Épigraphes araméens*, p. 81).

or against your children a complaint before prefect or lord be able to remove this house from your possession, whether it be in my lifetime or after my death."

2) *BP* 4 (434 B.C.)

Ananiah makes a gift of a house to his wife *Tmt*

(2) . . . *'nh yhbt* (3) *lky plg try rbt'* . . . (4) . . . *yhbth lky brḥmn zylky hw mn ywm' znh* (5) *'d 'lm* . . . (12) . . . *'nh 'nnyh yhbth lky brḥmn l' 'khl* (13) *'nh 'nnyh 'ršnky 'ldbrh dyn*

(2) ". . . I have given (3) you half [1]) of the greater *try* [2]) . . .(4) . . . I have given it to you in affection/as a gift; it is yours from this day (5) for ever . . . (12) . . . I, Ananiah, have given it to you in affection. I will not be able (13)—I, Ananiah—to institute a process against you concerning it."

BP 6 (440 B.C.)

Ananiah gives his daughter Yehoyishma a part of a house as a gift. (14) . . . *'nh 'nny yhbt lk bty' 'lh brḥmh l' 'khl* (15) *'nh 'nny 'hnṣl m[n]ky wl' 'khl 'mr npš* 'ḥryt *'hnṣl mnky* [3])

(14) ". . . I, Anani, have given you these houses in affection/as a gift. I will not be able, (15) I, Anani, to take (them) away from you, nor will I be able to command someone else to take them away from you."

3) *BP* 9 (404 B.C.)

Ananiah reconfirms the gift recorded in *BP* 6. [4])

---

[1]) The sale or donation of part of a house was quite common in antiquity; cf. the cuneiform, Greek and other examples cited by Cuq, *Études*, p. 185. Cf. also the Mishnah, *Bāḇā Baṯrā*, Chapter IV.

[2]) According to Kutscher, *New Aramaic Texts*, p. 235, the term is Egyptian and means "cell" or "side." See also the interpretation of B. Couroyer, *RB*, 61 (1954), p. 252 and his article "Termes égyptiens dans les papyri araméens du musée de Brooklyn," *ibid.*, p. 557.

[3]) This clause is reminiscent of the Babylonian *kudurru* monuments in which the donor of the property places under the ban not only those who personally raise claims against the gift but also those who instigate or hire others to do so. Cf. King, *BBSt*, No. 3, col. V: (32) *ša il-lam-ma* (33) *i-na mu-uḫ Bit-* [I]*Ta-kil-a-na-ili-šu* (34) *i-da-ab-bu-bu i-rag-gu-mu* (35) *ú-šar-ga-mu ú-ma-'-a-ru* (36) *ú-ša-aḫ-ḫa-zu ú-šad-ba-bu* (37) *ú-šat-ba-lu* . . . (32) "Whoever will rise up (33) and against Bīt Takil-ana-ilišu (34) will bring an action or make a claim (35) or cause a claim to be made, or will send (another) (36) and cause him to take, or lay claim to, or seize (it) . . ." Similar clauses are found in almost all the *kudurru* documents. For a comprehensive survey of this type of transaction, cf. Steinmetzer, *Grenzsteine.**

[4]) H. L. Ginsberg, *JAOS*, pp. 159 f.

(2) . . . *'nh 'štt*[1]) *lky bḥyy*[2]) *wyhbt* (3) *lky qṣt mn byty* . . . (5) . . . *brḥmn* . . . (11) . . . *'nty šlyṭh*[3]) *bh byt' znh* . . . (12) . . . *'nh 'nny br 'zryh yhbth lk brḥmn* . . . (16) . . . *'nh 'nny yhbth lyhwyšm'* (17) *brty bmwty brḥmn lqbl zy sbltny*[4]) *w'nh ymyn sb l' khl hwyt bydy wsbltny 'p 'nh* (18) *yhbt lh bmwty*

(2) ". . . I have turned my thoughts to you in my lifetime and I give (3) to you part of my house . . . (5) . . . in affection/as a gift . . . (11) . . . You are (now) in possession of this house . . . (12) . . . I, Ananiah bar Azariah (hereby) give it to you in affection/as a gift . . . (16) . . . I, Anani, have given it to Yehoyishma (17) my daughter at my death in affection/ as a gift because she has diligently taken care of me in my advanced years, when I could not take care of myself. I on my part, (hereby) assign (it) to her (as final property) after my death." [5])

BP 5 (427 B.C.)

Meshullam bar Zakkur liberates his slave-girl *Tpmt* and her daughter Yehoyishma. The terminology used in this deed of manumission is similar to that regularly used in deeds of gift. Evidently, manumission was considered as the "donation" of personal freedom. [6])

---

[1]) Cf. the Hebrew verb *hiṯ'aššeṯ* "to be mindful of" in Jonah 1: 6; the Akkadian equivalent is *ḫasāsu* "to think about" and *naplusu* "to look at, to consider." For the partial overlap between these two Akkadian verbs, cf. J. J. Stamm, *Die akkadische Namengebung* (Leipzig, 1939), p. 167, n. 4. Cf. below, p. 135.*

[2]) Note that *bḥyy* is not used here together with *bmwty* as it is in the examples cited above. Cf. *LAP*, p. 78 and Yaron, *Gifts*, pp. 120 ff.

[3]) The *šlyṭ* transfer clause is somewhat unusual in this deed: first of all, unlike most conveyances, it does not state that the gift is (a) "from this day forever"; (b) that it belongs to the donee and his children; (c) that it can be given as a gift or freely alienated—all indicators of an immediate and permanent transfer. Instead, the *šlyṭ* clause lists the various rights the donee has in the property: (a) certain building rights; (b) the rights to use the gate; (c) the rights to use the stairs (ll. 11-15). This may indicate that the transfer was not complete at the moment of donation. [Cf. Addenda.]

[4]) The Aramaic *sbl*, lit. "to bear/ to carry" is used here in the sense "to provide for/ to take care of. It is the interdialectal variant of the Akkadian *našû* "to bear/ to provide for." Cf. Schorr, *Urkunden*, No. 24: 6 and No. 25: 10. In Biblical Hebrew, *sābal* and *nāśā'* are used as synonyms (cf. Is 46: 3-4). However, as far as I can tell, the Biblical usage is limited to "carrying"; unlike the Akkadian and the Aramaic, it does not have the extended meaning of "providing."*

[5]) A full treatment of this particular expression must be reserved for a separate discussion.

[6]) The Old Babylonian formula: *ša ramāniša šī*: *mala libbiša maṣiat* "She belongs to herself: she is able/allowed to (do) her heart's desire" (cf., for example, Schorr, *Urkunden*, p. 54) is, in essence, a transfer/investiture clause similar to the Aramaic: *zylk hw 'nt šlyṭ l* . . . "It is yours; you are allowed to . . ." The only difference between the two clauses is that in the Aramaic clause the old right-holder invests the

(3) . . . *'nh ʿšt lky* (4) *bḥyy 'zt*[1]) *šbqtky*[2]) *bmwty*

(3) ". . . I turned my thoughts to you (4) during my lifetime that you be set free upon my death."[3])

2. The Interpretation of the Texts

A. *The Contrast of* ṭyb lbby *with* yhbt lk brḥmn

The terms *yhbt lk brḥmn* "I have given you in affection" and *ṭyb lbby bdmy'* "my heart is satisfied with the money" contrast with each other (cf. above, p. 36). Since this is so, the definition of *yhbt lk brḥmn*, although not our prime concern, will aid us, at least negatively, in defining *ṭyb lbby*: the meaning of the newly defined *yhbt lk brḥmn* can be eliminated as a possible parallel to the undefined *ṭyb lbby*. Any limitation in the range of possible meanings of an undefined term is, thus, in itself a partial definition.

Fortunately, the meaning of *yhbt lk brḥmn* is not as elusive as that of *ṭyb lbby*. The latter has never been adequately defined; on the other hand, the correct interpretation of the former term was suggested as early as 1906 by Sayce-Cowley but,[4]) unfortunately, their correct observations were not incorporated in Cowley's re-edition of the texts (1923) and, thus, escaped later scholarly notice. Sayce and Cowley compared the Aramaic expression *yhbt lk brḥmn* "I have given you in

---

new right-holder with property, while in the Akkadian clause, the old right-holder (the slave owner) invests the slave with the gift of his freedom.

[1]) Many authorities have independently interpreted the term *'zt* as the Persian *azāta* "free." Cf. J. de Menasce, "Mots d'emprunt et noms propres iraniens dans les nouveaux documents araméens," *BiOr*, 11 (1954), p. 161; I. Gerschevitch, *JRAS*, 1954, p. 126; É. Benveniste, *JA*, 242 (1954), p. 299; Rosenthal, *Concept of Freedom*, p. 13, n. 32a. See also *LAP*, p. 51, and pp. 155 and 170. As a rule, languages usually borrow terms which are lacking in the borrower. Did Aramaic lack a term "free"? In Biblical Hebrew, the complex "to set free" is expressed by the common *laḥofši yešalleḥennu*; cf. Ex 21 : 26. Interestingly enough, the Targum has to paraphrase this verse as *lebar ḥōrīn yifterinnē*. It seems quite possible that Aramaic could express the concept "a free person" (*bar ḥōrīn*) but lacked the adverbial complement (to set) "free." The same situation seems to exist in Akkadian. This may *possibly* account for the use of a Persian loan word in a situation where the resources of Semitic seem quite adequate.

[2]) The same root is found in the deed of divorce from Wadi Murabbaʿat; cf. *Les grottes de Murabbaʿât*, No. 19:21 (p. 105); significantly, divorce and manumission use the same term—*šbq*. The (partial) affinity between these two transactions was noticed by the Talmud (cf. *TB*, *Giṭṭin* 9a).

[3]) The Talmud was also acquainted with gift transactions in which ownership passed immediately to the donee but the usifruct was to be retained by the owner. The formula employed was *mehayyōm ule'aḥar mīṯā* "from today and after death." (Cf. *TB*, *Bāḇā Meṣīʿā* 19a = *Bāḇā Baṯrā* 135b. Cf. also the discussion of Yaron, *Gifts*, p. 114. Cf. also, *LAP*, p. 78.

[4]) *Aramaic Papyri Discovered at Assuan*, p. 47.

affection" with the common Neo-Babylonian legal expression *ina ḫūd libbišu iddin* "he gave in the joy (= volition) of his heart." Both the Aramaic *brḥmn* and the Akkadian *ina ḫūd libbišu* expressed the idea of willingness or uncoerced action. [1])

The volitional overtones of the expression *yhbt lk brḥmn* are supported by the clearly volitional function of the term *rḥm* "to wish, to like" in other Aramaic contexts. The term is found in the following contexts (besides the one already discussed above):

1) As a supplement to the transfer clause.

The transfer/investiture clause *zylk hw ʾnt šlyṭ bbytʾ* "it is yours; you are (now) owner of the house" is often supplemented by the phrase: "you may sell it for money or give it to whomever you wish." [2])

This supplement is found in two parallel formulations:

a) *lmn zy rḥmt/y tntnn* (*AP* 8:9-10; *AP* 13:8; *AP* 25:9; *BP* 9:21; *BP* 12:23)

b) *lmn zy ṣbyt/tṣbyn hbhy* (*AP* 13:16; *AP* 28:7; *BP* 3:12)

Ṣby is the Aramaic term of volition par excellence. In this context at least, *ṣby* and *rḥm* are synonymous variants: *rḥm* "to like/love" can only mean here "to wish/to will."

2) The term is also used as a supplement of the *Schlussklauseln*.

The usual formulation of the *Schlussklauseln* is the following:

[1]) Cf. San Nicolò, *Beiträge*, pp. 158 and 182. The Akkadian terms of volition will be discussed in greater detail in Chapter V, pp. 128 ff.

[2]) The function of the transfer/investiture clause is the publication of the transfer of ownership. The legal declaration (a) *zylk hw* "it is (now) yours"; (b) *ʾnt šlyṭ* "you are (now) the master" are general statements in need of greater specification. The need for specification was especially great since the concept of "ownership" was not clearly defined in cuneiform law (cf. Cardascia, *Propriété*, pp. 19 ff.), where it seems to have been understood as a type of control. Accordingly, the most efficient way of defining ownership was to spell out the various types of control the new right-holder was allowed to exercise over his property. Since no greater control over property exists than the voluntary relinquishment of control either by donation or sale, the general terms *zylk hw* and *ʾnt šlyṭ* were defined by the more specific clauses *wlmn rḥmt tntnnh ʾw tzbn bksp* "And you may give it to whomever you want or sell it for money." I have no doubt that the whole clause was based on older cuneiform elements which were reworked by the Aramaic scribes. Cf. clauses like *ana kaspi ul inamdin ana rēmūtu ul irêm* "He (the donor) shall not sell it for money or to give it as a gift (*NRVU* 12)" or the Arsacid transfer/investiture clause *ul išallaṭ-ma ana kaspi ana rēmūti* ... *ana mimma gabbi ana mamman šanamma gabbi elat* the buyer *ul iddin ul inamdin* "(The seller) is not allowed to give or have given (the property now being transferred) for money, to give or have given it as a gift ... or for any other purpose to any one other than the buyer." Cf. Krückmann, *BRVU*, pp. 48 ff. The Aramaic scribes converted these negative formulations into a positive statement of property rights, something which as far as I can tell, had not been done before in cuneiform legal documents. Cf. below, pp. 132 ff.

"We will not sue you or your children in a formal suit." However, this clause is often supplemented with any one of the three main elements of the operative section: *ṭyb lbby, rḥqt mnk,* or *zylk hw*: *lmn rḥmt/ṣbyt tntnnh.* Thus, we find the formulation:

"We will not be able to sue you—or anybody to whom you have sold the property or given it as a gift (*brḥmn/t*)."

This variant is found in two forms:

a) *'pl' nkhl nršh lbr wbrh lkm . . . 'w gbr zy tzbnwn lh . . . 'w zy brḥmn tntnw lh*

"And furthermore we shall not be able to institute (formal process) against any son or daughter of yours . . . or against any person to whom you may sell it . . . to whom you may give as a present." (*AP* 25: 10-11)

b) *l' nkhl nršh lbnyk wbntk wzy tntn lh bksp 'w rḥmt*

"We will not be able to institute (formal process against your sons and daughters or against anyone to whom you may sell it for money or give it as a gift." (*BP* 12: 26)

3) The *Schlussklauseln* of gift transactions employ the term *rḥm* in yet another way: the donor obligates himself not to contest the gift in the future by saying, "I gave you the gift in affection and now I want to take it back" (*AP* 18:2-3; *BP* 7:41-42; *BP* 10:9-10). [1]) The formulation in *AP* 18—slightly more explicated than the others—reads as follows:

[1]) The legal function of the clause is not clear. Why should the statement: "Since I have given this gift in affection" motivate the litigation: "Now I want to take it back"? The key to this difficult clause is provided by Ehrlich, *Randglossen* I, p. 102, in his interpretation of the legal background behind the sale of the Cave of Machpela. Why did Abram insist on paying the full price of the field instead of receiving it as a gift from Ephron? Ehrlich suggests the following reason: "Jemand macht uns ein Geschenk, weil er ein gute Meinung von uns hat und uns dadurch seine Achtung bezeigen will. Möglich jedoch, dass er sich in uns täuscht und wir seine gute Meinung nicht verdienen. In solchem Falle verdienen wir auch sein Geschenk nicht, und dieses wird daher auch nicht unser ehrliches und wahres Eigentum." Since Abram did not want to bury his wife in land which might have been contested by Ephron at some future time, Abram insisted on paying the full price to insure the finality and incontestability of the transaction.

On the basis of Ehrlich's insight, the Aramaic clause under discussion must be understood eliptically: "Since I gave you this gift in affection—and your ownership of the gift depends on my constant feeling of affection toward you—I now want to take it back—because I no longer feel the same affection for you." In order to prevent such contingencies and to insure the finality of the gift, the donor specifically states: "I will not be able to say, 'Since I have given the gift in affection I now want it back.'"

wl' t[kh]l yhwḥn . . . [t'mr lh] (2) *wlslw' brth kzy nksy'* [']*lh wksp' zy ktybn bspr' znh brḥmn yhbt lkm k'n ṣbyt* (3) *'hnṣl hm hn t'mr kyt*! *ḥybh hy l' yštm' lh*

(1) ". . . And Yehoḥan will not be ab[le/allowe]d . . . [to say to him] (2) and to Sallua' her daughter, 'Since I gave these goods and the money set forth in this deed to you as a free gift, now I desire (3) to take them back.' If she says so(!), [1]) she is liable (to pay a fine); she shall not be listened to." [2])

To sum up: the term *rḥmt/rḥmh* is the equivalent of the Akkadian *rēmūtu* "a free-will gift." [3]) A *rḥmh/rēmūtu* is a gift given *brḥmn/ina nar'amāti* i.e., in affection, willingly. To give a gift *brḥmn/ina nar'amāti* is to give it *lmn zy rḥmt/ana ša irammu* "to whomever you/he want/s." The volitional meaning of *rḥm/rêmu(râmu)* in these particular contexts is thus clearly established. [4])

The positive definition of the term *yhbt lk brḥmn/t* has negative implications for the meaning of the contrasting term *ṭyb lbby*: if *yhb brḥmn* is the Aramaic expression of volition, *ṭyb lbby* probably expresses some other legal idea which remains to be identified. Thus, there is already an *a priori* argument against the volitional interpretation of Seidl.

B. *The Definition of the Term* ṭyb lbby *in Sale and* mrḥq

The underlying principles of sale and *mrḥq* contrast sharply with

[1]) *AP* reads *kzt* "like this" with a question mark over the second letter. To judge from the parallels in *BP* 7: 33 and 39 the word should be read *kwt* "thus, so" (Kutscher, orally).

[2]) The Aramaic expression seems to be derived from the common NA *dayānu dēnšu lā išammû* "the judge shall not listen to his case i.e., he shall not accept his argument as valid" (*ARU* 167, 195-200 and *passim*). A similar clause is also found in the contemporary Hieratic conveyances: "quant à celui qui ferait une contestation à leur sujet, sa déposition ne sera entendue dans aucune des Archives" *DJE* 2, p. 14. Whether or not the Hieratic clause was derived from Near Eastern antecedents—possibly through an Aramaic medium—cannot be determined at this stage of the investigation. However, in the light of the close relationship between the Aramaic with the cuneiform tradition on the one hand, and the relationship of the Aramaic with the Demotic and abnormal Hieratic on the other, the possibility of such a transmission seems quite plausible. Nevertheless, the possibility of independent development, although less probable, still must be allowed for.

[3]) Cf. Ungnad, *Aramäische Papyrus*, p. 52, n. 3.

[4]) Concerning the use of the Akkadian *rêmu* in gift contexts, see for the time being, Steinmetzer, *Schenkungsurkunde*, pp. 15 ff. The Aramaic usage suggests that a *rēmūtu* "gift" is that which is given *ina nar'amāti* "in affection" *ana ša irammu* "to whomever one wants" (cf. S. E. Loewenstamm, "The Foundation of the Alalakh Dynasty," *BIES*, 20 [1950], p. 15 for a similar line of thought). For semantic difficulties of this equation, cf. below, p. 132.

those of gift. In gift transactions, it is the spontaneous state of mind that precedes the transaction—the willingness and volition of the donor expressed by the term *rḥmh*—that motivates the transfer of goods and constitutes its legal basis.

In sale and *mrḥq* transactions, however, it is the payment of an *Entgelt* (compensation, consideration), the tendering of some necessary performance (usually on oath of purgation) and the resultant satisfaction of the former right-holder's mind that are the constitutive elements in the transaction. The compensation/consideration or oath of purgation induce the right-holder, whether seller or claimant, to relinquish his property and the rights thereto:

"You have given us the price of our field and our heart is satisfied" (*BP* 3 and 12).

"You have tendered us an oath and our heart is satisfied therewith" (*AP* 6 and 14).

If, however, the payment of the consideration were the only necessary element in the transfer, the scribes would not have added the expression *ṭyb lbby bdmy'* in between the record of payment and the record of relinquishment. The deeds do not read: *yhbt ln dmwhy wrḥqn mnk* "you have given us its price and we have removed ourselves from you"—but *yhbt ln dmwhy wṭyb lbbn bgw . . . rḥqn mnk/h* "you have given us its price and our heart is satisfied therewith . . . we have removed ourselves from you/it (the property)." Therefore, it is logical to assume that the reaction of the right-holder to the receipt of the compensation must have some constitutive significance within the structure of the conveyance transaction. The answer may be along the following lines:

Sales are only considered final and incontestable by the courts if the consideration is paid in full or the necessary performance is completed. If they are not, the right-holder can always raise a claim. However, the mere objective notation that the full price was paid may still not insure the transaction against future claims by the seller or the litigant: he may claim that he was not actually "satisfied" with the amount received, and still demand more payment. In order to prevent that eventuality, the scribes also recorded the personal acknowledgement by the former right-holder that he had received the payment in full and that he is satisfied therewith. "Satisfaction" indicates the cessation of desire: nothing more is wanted and nothing more can be demanded in the future. In this context, therefore, "my heart is satisfied with the money you have given me" means: "I am quitted after the receipt of full payment or performance." The personal acknowledgement of the former right-holder that he had received the compensation and was quitted therewith heightens the obligatory power of the following oath of no-contest. [1])

Thus analyzed, *ṭyb lbby* proves to be a many-faceted term of considerable subtlety. It implies the presence of a necessary performance (payment or a purgatory oath); it records the receipt of final payment; it expresses the concommitant idea of quittance; it also anticipates the final relinquishment of rights expressed in the *Schlussklauseln*. From a temporal point of view, the reaction of the former right-holder expressed by the term *ṭyb lbby* is the bridge between the performance recorded in the operative section and the obligatory effects of the final clauses.

In the following paragraphs, an attempts will be made to explicate the various nuances inherent in the term such as a) the relationship between *ṭyb lbby* and performance/consideration; b) the relationship between *ṭyb lbby* and the completeness of payment; c) the relationship between *ṭyb lbby* and the idea of quittance expressed in the term *rḥqt*

---

[1]) According to San Nicolò (*Schlussklauseln*, pp. 76 ff.), the cuneiform conveyance was not an obligatory instrument, i.e., it did not in itself obligate the two parties to complete the promised performances. Therefore, in order to insure a perfect performance, extra obligatory instruments had to be added to the body of the transaction. The classical OB obligatory instrument was the oath, either by the god or the king or by both. In the provincial areas of Susa, Nuzi, Kültepe, Assyria, and the Diyala region, the obligatory function of the oath was usually filled by fines (especially in Nuzi), the death penalty (in Kültepe), and all sorts of physical punishments such as the removal of the tongue (Susa, Diyala) and right hand (Susa, Alalakh) or death by hot pitch (Ḫana). For a study of the subject, cf. Oppenheim, *Studien*, pp. 153 ff. The legal praxis of the more recently discovered cities of Mari and Alalakh also fits into this provincial pattern. Cf. the use of hot lead as a punishment in the Alalakh documents: **AT* 8 : 32 and **AT* 28 : 25-6 or the threat of taboo violation—*asak šarrim īkul* "he (the contract breaker) has eaten the taboo of the king": Boyer, *ARM* VIII, pp. 165 ff. Of all the areas of cuneiform law, the obligatory instruments of Nuzi and especially of Ras Shamra are the mildest: in the Ras Shamra legal documents, fines and other punishments, although known, are not common; their place is taken by the warning—*urram šēram mannumma lā ilaqqīšu ištu qāt A* "In the future, no one shall take it (the property) from the possession of A (the new owner)." Similar abstract warnings are often found in the deeds of Nuzi: *ištu ūmi annî A aššum kirî ina arki B lā išassi* "from this day, A shall not raise claims against B," Speiser-Pfeiffer, No. 15: 16-19 and *passim*. However, the more usual Nuzi pattern is a combination of warning, fine, and obligation to clear the property of all claims (cf. *ibid.*, No. 19). This is exactly the pattern reflected in the Aramaic conveyance *BP* 3 (the possibility of some historical relationship between the two patterns seems quite plausible and is worth further investigation). Since the Aramaic and the Nuzi documents rely neither on the oath of the gods nor on the threat of physical punishment, their obligatory instruments, viewed from a comparative point of view, are relatively weak. Therefore, the declaration of the seller that his heart was satisfied with the price and that he demands no more payment is not at all superfluous: it is probably a means of heightening the rather weak obligatory powers of the Aramaic conveyance.*

"I have removed myself" which often follows *ṭyb lbby* and forms with it a type of cluster.

The First Phase: ṭyb lbby *and Performance.* The phrase *ṭyb lbby* is closely related to performance or payment of a consideration. In fact, whenever the expression is found in the Aramaic documents, it is always preceded by the description of some constitutive action. For example: "you have given me the price of my house and my heart is satisfied" (*BP* 3 and *BP* 12). Or, "you have taken an oath in my behalf and my heart is satisfied" (*BP* 6 and *BP* 14). Thus, if *ṭyb lbby* does not actually describe the action, it is always preceded by a description of such an action.

The relationship between the idea of satisfaction and that of performance is seen most clearly in the active form of the expression—*hwṭbt lbby b* "you have satisfied my heart with" which is often used instead of the passive *ṭyb lbby* in the litigation-*mrḥq* (*AP* 6 and *AP* 20). In this active formulation, the two ideas of satisfaction and performance—usually expressed by two sets of terms: a) *yhbt ly dmwhy/ym't ly* "you have given me its price/you have taken an oath in my behalf" and b) *wṭyb lbby bgw* "and my heart is satisfied therewith" are fused into one term of satisfactory performance: *hwṭbt lbby b* "you have satisfied my heart with (the payment or the performance)."

Compare—

"You have satisfied our heart with these goods" (*AP* 20) with—

"You have given us the price of our house and our heart is satisfied" (*BP* 3).

And—

"You have satisfied my heart with the oath" (*AP* 6) with—

"You have taken an oath in my behalf and my heart is satisfied" (*AP* 14).

Thus, if the necessary performance is only echoed in the passive *ṭyb lbby* ,it is clearly stated in the active *hwṭbt lbby*, which is not merely a term of receipt and quittance but also a term of performance. This active form can be translated:

> "By tendering me necessary performance or full payment, you have induced me to quit my property and all claims thereto."

The most archaic use of the terms is preserved in *AP* 20:8 *hwṭbtm lbbn b'lk nksy' wṭyb lbbn bgw* "You have satisfied our heart in regard to these goods and our heart is satisfied therewith." The active/passive cluster formed here is virtually identical with similar constructions well known from Ugaritic and Biblical poetry. Cf. for example, *r^e^fā'ēnī YHWH w^e'ērāfē' hōšī'ēnī w^e'iwwāšē'a* "Heal me, O Lord, and I shall be healed; save me and I shall be saved" (Jer 17:14).[1] In all such constructions, the second element is always the passive form used as an emphatic complement. This passive verb reflects a situation which is the outcome of the action described by the preceding active verb. Thus, the relationship between the two terms is always causal: *ṭyb lbby* is clearly not an independent state of mind but the result of the preceding performance expressed by the verb *hwṭbt*—"my mind is (now) satisfied because you have (just) satisfied it."

This archaic usage is preserved in only one text (*AP* 20). All other texts employ either the active *hwṭbt/m* or the stative *ṭyb*. The breaking up of the cluster, however, does not seem to affect the legal force of the expression. When used together in a cluster, *hwṭbt/m* expresses the idea of complete performance and *ṭyb* the resultant state of mind. When used separately, however, each term conveys its own special emphasis, yet echoes the overtones of the other: thus, *hwṭbt/m*, when used alone, stresses performance but anticipates receipt-quittance, while *ṭyb lbby*, when used alone, stresses receipt-quittance but echoes the previous performance.

The Second Phase: Completeness of Payment. In deeds of sale, the satisfaction clause usually reads: *wṭyb lbby bdmy' zy yhbt ly* "And my heart is satisfied with the money you have given me." It was suggested above that "satisfaction" indicates full payment. This particular nuance of the term is seen most clearly in the operative section of *BP* 12 (ll. 6-7 version 1): *wṭyb lbbn bgw zy l' 'št'r ln ʿlyk mn dmy'* "our heart is satisfied in that none of the price is outstanding against you in our account" (= "we are quitted since you do not owe us any more money"). There can be no room here for misunderstanding; the reason for the satisfaction is clearly spelled out: satisfaction is the immediate result of full payment. Full payment, and nothing short of full payment, satisfies the heart. Since Aramaic sale, like Old Babylonian sale, was probably *Barkauf* (sale for cash),[2] only the sale which has been paid for in full is considered final and incontestable. Thus, *ṭyb lbby* reflects an organic complex of ideas: the receipt of the full price which announces the finality and incontestability of the transaction.

The Third Phase: ṭyb lbby *and the Quittance Term* rḥq. It was pointed out in the preceding section that *ṭyb lbby* contrasts with *rḥm* and is therefore not a term of volition. Furthermore, inductive investigation

[1]) Cf. U. Cassuto, "Biblical and Canaanite Literature," *Tarbiz*, 14 (1942), p. 10. Cf. M. Held, "The Action-Result (Factitive-Passive) Sequence of Identical Verbs in Biblical Hebrew and Ugaritic," *JBL*, 84 (1965), pp. 272-82. For more examples of this phenomenon cf. below, p. 71 and p. 122.

[2]) Cf. San Nicolò, *Schlussklauseln*, p. 7. For a contrasting conception of the nature of cuneiform sale, cf. Boyer, *Formation de vente*, pp. 55-85.

has shown it to be a term which records quittance after the receipt of a necessary consideration. The quittance overtones of *ṭyb lbby* are confirmed by its close association with the abstract quittance term *rḥqt mnh/k.*

Ṭyb lbby and *rḥqt mnh* often appear together as a cluster:

AP 14 (5) . . . *wṭyb lbby* (6) *bmwm'h* . . . *wrḥqt mnky*
(5) . . . "And my heart is satisfied (6) with the oath . . . and I hereby remove myself from you."

AP 20 (8) . . . *hwṭbtm lbbn b'lk nksy'* (9) *wṭyb lbbn bgw* . . . *rḥyqn 'nḥnh mnk*
(8) . . . "You have satisfied our heart with these goods (9) and our heart is satisfied therewith . . . we are removed from you."

AP 67 (5) *wṭyb lbb*[*y* . . .]*rḥqt mnk*
(5) "And my heart is satisfied [. . .] I hereby remove myself from you."

In these examples, the two terms are used in a contiguous cluster; there is, however, one case in which they are used together in a broken cluster:

BP 3 (3) . . . *zbn wyhbn lk* . . . condition of property . . . (6) *yhbt ln dmwhy* sum enumerated *wṭyb lbbn* . . . description of boundaries . . . (10) *zbn wyhbn lk* (11) *wrḥqn mnh*
(3) . . . "We have sold and transferred to you . . . condition of property . . . (6) you have given us its price (sum enumerated) and our heart is satisfied . . . boundaries . . . (10) . . . We have sold and transferred it to you (11) and have removed ourselves from it."

Rḥq is the Aramaic quittance term par excellence; it expresses the relinquishment of rights and claims and nothing else; it is abstract and unmotivated and does not convey overtones of performance. Its basic meaning is reflected most clearly in the transfer-*mrḥq* deeds (*AP* 13 and *AP* 25). These deeds record the peaceful transfer and relinquishment of property: no motivation is given; no mention is made of volition, consideration, litigation or oath of purgation; *ṭyb lbby* is not used. The main clauses are: a) *rḥqt mnk* "I hereby remove myself from you;" b) *zylk hw* "It (the property) is yours."

If *ṭyb lbby* already conveys the idea of quittance, why was the extra quittance term *rḥq* added? The answer must be sought along the following lines: scribes often added extra terminology to strengthen the obligatory powers of a deed. This is especially true when a term would otherwise be ambiguous. Since *ṭyb lbby* has overtones of completeness, performance and receipt—as well as of quittance—, the scribes may have added *rḥqt mnk* "I hereby remove myself from you"—the unambiguous relinquishment/quittance term—to explicate the quittance meaning latent in the many-faceted *ṭyb lbby*. However, *ṭyb lbby* when used alone can, if necessary, express the full range of meaning, including that of quittance, without the use of extra explicatives. Thus, if we are correct in our interpretation of the two terms, the use of *rḥqt* with *ṭyb lbby* is complementary rather than necessary or constitutive.

The close relationship between *ṭyb lbby* and *rḥqt*, and the complementary role of *rḥqt* in the cluster, are seen clearly from a juxtaposition of the two extant sale transactions, *BP* 3 and *BP* 12.

BP 3	*BP* 12
Operative	Operative
'nḥn zbn wyhbn lk byth . . . (3-4)	*zbn wyhbn lk bytn* . . . (12)
condition of the house	condition
'nḥn zbnhy lk wyhbt ln dmwhy . . . *wṭyb lbbn bdmy'* . . . (5-7)	*wyhbt ln dmwhy* . . . *wṭyb lbbn bdmy'* . . . (13-14)
boundaries	boundaries
zbn wyhbn lk wrḥqn mnh . . . (10-11)	*zbn wyhbn lk* . . . (17)
Final Clauses	Final Clauses
l' nkl ngrnk dyn . . . *bšm byt' znh zy 'nḥn zbn wyhbn lk wrḥqn mnh* (12-13) [1]	*l' nkhl nršnk dyn* . . . *bšm byt' znh zy zbn wyhbn lk wyhbt ln dmwhy* . . . *wṭyb lbbn bgw* (25-26) [2]

1) Whereas *BP* 3 employs the sequence *ṭyb lbby-rḥqt*, *BP* 12 simply uses *ṭyb lbby* without any explicatives; the force of the two documents, is nevertheless, exactly the same: *rḥqt* can therefore be omitted without weakening the structure of the transaction.

---

[1]) "We have sold and transferred to you the house of . . . condition of the house. . . We have sold it to you and you have given us its price (. . .) and our heart is satisfied with the price (5-7) . . . boundaries . . . We have sold and transferred (it) to you and have removed ourselves from it . . . (10-11). Final Clauses. We will not be able to sue you in a suit . . . concerning this house which we have sold and transferred to you and removed ourselves therefrom (12-13)."

[2]) "We have sold and transferred to you our house . . . condition . . . You have given us its price . . . and our heart is satisfied with the price (14-15) . . . boundaries . . . We have sold and transferred it to you . . . (17). Final Clauses. We will not be able to institute against you a (formal) suit concerning this house which we have sold and transferred to you and you gave us its price and our heart is satisfied therewith (25-26)."

Paraphrased into Akkadian syntax, the final clause of *BP* 3 should read: "we will not be able to contest the sold, transferred, and ceded house." Similarly, the final clause of *BP* 12 should read: "we will not be able to contest the sale of the house which was transferred after the payment of satisfactory payment."

2) In the final clauses, *wrḥqn mnh* of *BP* 3 is functionally identical with *wyhbt ln dmwhy ... wṭyb lbbn bgw* of *BP* 12.

More light is shed on the relationship of *ṭyb lbby* to *rḥqt* from the litigation-*mrḥq, AP* 6. Dargaman lodged a complaint against his neighbor Maḥseiah concerning a plot of land. Maḥseiah thereupon "satisfied Dargaman's heart" with a purgatory oath. The usual formula in this type of deed is: *hwṭbt lbby bmwm'h wrḥqt mnk* "you have satisfied my heart with the oath and I have removed myself from you." Since the deed is specifically called a *spr mrḥq* in the docket (l. 22), we would naturally expect the term *rḥqt* to be used in the main part of the deed. Instead, we find simply: (11) ... *ym't ly byhw whwṭbt* (12) *lbby ʿl 'rq' zk* "... You took an oath on my behalf by YHW and satisfied (12) my heart concerning this land." The explanation of this rather strange phenomenon is the following: since *ṭyb lbby* is both a term of receipt/ payment and quittance—and in its latter phase is a virtual synonym of *rḥqt* (at least in *entgeltliche* transactions)—it can often fill the slot demanded by *rḥqt* according to the structural logic of the deed.

CHAPTER THREE

Ṭyb Lbby IN CONTEXTS OTHER THAN CONVEYANCE

1. The Texts

The term *ṭyb lbby* is found in three other contexts:

A. The term records the reaction of the father of the bride to the receipt of the *mohar* from the groom.

1) *AP* 15 (about 441 B.C.)

Asḥor marries Mibṭaḥiah; he pays the *mohar* to her father, Maḥseiah and declares:

(4) ... *yhbt lk mhr* (5) *brtk mpṭḥyh* ... *ʿl ʿlyk wṭb lbbk* (6) *bgw*

(4) "... I have given you the *mohar* (5) of your daughter, Mipṭaḥiah ... You have received it and your heart is satisfied (6) therewith."

2) *BP* 7 (420 B.C.)

Ananiah bar Ḥaggai marries Yehoyishma; he pays the *mohar* to her brother, Zakkur bar Meshullam and says:

(4) *wyhbt lk mhr ʾḥtk yhyšmʿ* (5) *ksp* ... *ʿl ʿlyk* [*wṭyb lbbk bg*]*w*

(4) "... And I have given you the *mohar* of your sister Yehoyishma (5) (so much) silver ... You have received it [and your heart is satisfied there]with."

B. The term also records the reaction of the groom to the receipt of the evaluated dowry (*tkwnh*) [1]) of the bride.

1) *AP* 15 (about 441 B.C.)

Asḥor receives the *tkwnh* of Mibṭaḥiah, evaluates each item and after the grand total, declares:

(14) *wdmy nksyʾ* ... (15) ... *ʿl ʿly* [*wṭ*]*yb lbby bgw*

(14) "And the (total) value of the goods ... (15) ... I have received (them) and my heart is [satisfi]ed therewith." [2])

---

1) Cf. the word *tkwnh* "wealth" in Nahum 2: 10. Dr. Moshe Greenberg (orally) has suggested the semantic parallel between *tkwnh*—from *kwn* "to be ready, available,"—and the Rabbinic *mezummānīm* "ready-cash."

2) In some of the marriage settlements (*BP* 7: 20-21; *AP* 15: 15, 16), after the grand total and the husband's declaration of receipt, various other items the wife brings into her husband's house—mostly oil and small amounts of cosmetics—are also listed; their value, however, is not given. It would seem that because of their

C. The term also records the acknowledgment of the consignees of goods-to-be-delivered that they had received the goods and that the goods actually received tallied exactly with the amount recorded in the bill of lading.

AP 2 (484 B.C.)

Hoshea and Aḥiab received from Espemeṭ a consignment of barley and lentils which they undertake to deliver to the government officials in Syene.

(3) ... *yhbt ʿl ydn śʿ[rn ...]* (detailed amount of goods) ... (9) *wṭyb lbbn bgw ʾnḥnh nbl ʿbwrʾ [znh ...]* (11) ... *ʾnḥnh nntn dy[n qdm rb mʾtʾ wrbny]* (12) *byt mlkʾ wqdm spry ʾwṣrʾ* ... (13) ... *[whn lʾ nntn kl ʿbwrʾ zy]* (14) *lk bmnyn* ... (15) *ʾnḥnh nḥwb*

(3) "... You have consigned to us ba[rley ...] (detailed amount) ... (9) and our heart is satisfied therewith. We will deliver [this] grain [. . .] (11) ... We will render an acco[unt before the company commander and the authorities of the] Government House and the clerks of the treasury ... (13) ... [If we do not deliver all of the grain that is] (14) yours in full, ... (15) we shall be liable (to you for the some of etc.)"

2. The Explanation of the Texts

In all of the three contexts just cited, *ṭyb lbby* records a reaction to receipt. The objects received differ: *mohar*, dowry, goods-to-be-delivered. The legal implications of these various types of receipt differ from one another. Furthermore, not all of these implications are identical with those found in the conveyances (sale and *mrḥq*). Thus, the underlying meaning of the term is elusive, to say the least. One thing, however, is certain: all known contexts that employ the term are intimately related to receipt. Furthermore, the reaction to the receipt expressed by the term *ṭyb lbby* must have had some constitutive function; otherwise it would not have been so carefully recorded.

The close relationship between *ṭyb lbby* and the idea of receipt is most clearly seen in the *mohar* receipt clause. Here, *ṭyb lbbk* is preceded by the unambiguous receipt teım *ʿl ʿlyk* "You have received it (the *mohar*) and your heart is satisfied therewith." [1])

perishable nature and small value, they were not included in the list of valuables the husband obligated himself to return. Cf. the discussion of Ginsberg, "The Brooklyn Museum Aramaic Papyri," *JAOS*, 74, (1954) p. 156, n. 4. The Aramaic practice seems to have been based on a Neo-Assyrian model: cf. B. Parker, "The Nimrud Tablets, 1952—Business Documents," *Iraq*, 16 (1954), pp. 37 ff. (The deed is *ND* 2307). Contrast Epstein, *JJLG*, 6 (1908/09), p. 366, n. 5.

[1]) This is not the first time that *ṭyb lbby* has been associated with other complementary terms and phrases. Each of these complements explicates some specific

A. *The Implications of the Use of* ṭyb lbby *in the* mohar *Clause*

In sale and *mrḥq*-litigation, the term *ṭyb lbby* always indicates the receipt of an *Entgelt* or the acknowledgement that some performance was tendered. This limited definition of the term certainly fits the use of *ṭyb lbbk* in the *mohar* contexts cited below: the father of the bride receives the *mohar* from his son-in-law and declares that he is "satisfied" therewith. So far *mohar* receipt agrees with conveyance receipt.

It was noted above that in conveyance contexts *hwṭbt lbby/ṭyb lbby* is more than a neutral term of receipt: it is also, and essentially, a term which describes the tendering of some necessary consideration and/or the receipt thereof. Furthermore, the party who declares himself quitted ("satisfied") is always a former right-holder (either seller or plaintiff) who has been induced to part with his property or rights after having been "satisfied" by some performance. Thus defined, *ṭyb lbby* is intimately related to the transfer of rights and property. In a sense, it is the conveyance term par excellence.

How does the conveyance meaning of *ṭyb lbby* relate to the *mohar*

---

aspect of this rather complex term. When the active form *hwṭbt lbby* precedes the stative *ṭyb*, the idea that *ṭyb* is the result of some specific performance is stressed. The clause *bgw zy lʾ ʾštʾr ln ʿlyk mn dmyʾ* "in that none of the price is outstanding against you on our account" stresses the completeness of the payment. When *rḥqt* follows *ṭyb lbby*, the relationship between "satisfaction" and quittance is more clearly explicated. In the case under discussion, the clause *ʿl ʿlyk/ ʿly* "it has been received by you/me" explicates the relationship between *ṭyb lbby* and receipt. Thus, if the term were to be defined on the basis of its explicatives it would mean: "quit after the receipt of final consideration." However, these explicatives express only part of *ṭyb lbby*'s rather complex meaning. Since the whole is greater than any of its parts, neither *rḥq* nor *ʿl ʿly* is a real synonym of *ṭyb lbby*; at the most, each overlaps one sector of the term's broad semantic range.

Logically, however, a cluster of *ʿl ʿly wrḥqt mnk* would more or less cover the legal functions of *ṭyb lbby*. Such a cluster is never actually employed. Furthermore, the Aramaic scribes never explicated more than one of the term's meanings by the use of explicatives at any one time. Thus, we find *ʿl ʿly wṭyb lbby bgw* or *ṭyb lbby wrḥqt* or *ṭyb lbby bgw zy lʾ ʾštʾr* but never *ʿl ʿly wṭyb lbby bgw zy lʾ ʾštʾr wrḥqt mnk*. Such over-explication would have rendered *ṭyb lbby* otiose and all but superfluous.

Furthermore, the Aramaic formulation, by explicating only one nuance at a time, allowed *ṭyb lbby* to express the other aspects of the term. Thus, when *ṭyb lbby* precedes *rḥqt*, it stresses the idea of consideration received; however, when *ṭyb lbby* follows *ʿl ʿly*, it expresses the idea of quittance which follows receipt. To some degree, therefore, the meaning of the term is dependent on its contextual relationship with its various complements.

In the preceding analysis, I have attempted to demonstrate the wide semantic range of the term and its subtle contextual variations. However, there is a possibility that by the fifth century, the term had become stereotypic and non-evocative and that the scribes, even if they employed the term in ways which may seem subtle to us, were merely following time-honored usage whose original significance was not always clear to them.

receipt meaning of the same term? Is *ṭyb lbbk,* like its conveyance alloform *ṭyb lbby,* not merely a term of receipt but also one which reflects the relinquishment of property rights upon the receipt of a necessary consideration? In other words, does the use of the same term in marriage and conveyance signify some affinity between the underlying legal principles of the two transactions? The following analogy between the two transactions is certainly worthy of consideration:

1) The father's heart is satisfied with the *mohar* as the seller's heart is satisfied with the sale price.
2) The seller relinquishes title to his property after having been satisfied; likewise, the father of the bride relinquishes "title/ownership/control" over his daughter after having declared himself satisfied.
3) Only after the declaration of satisfaction does the transferred property actually become the property of the buyer: only then can the declaration of "investiture"—"It is yours from this day forever"—be made. Likewise, only after the father's declaration of satisfaction is the bride really the groom's; only then can the groom declare: "I am her husband and she is my wife from this day forever."
4) The *mohar* is to marriage what sale price is to sale: both are the necessary considerations that establish the legal ground for the transfer of control/ownership, whether of land or wife.

It is, therefore, inherently possible that the use of *ṭyb lbby* in marriage as well as conveyance reflects the underlying structural affinity between the two types of transaction. Identical conclusions based on entirely different material were reached by Koschaker. [1]) However, this does

---

[1]) Concerning the structural affinity between sale and marriage, cf. Koschaker, *Eheschliessung*, especially his concluding remarks: "Der Rechtshistoriker ist Jurist, seine Aufgabe ist es, die Rechtsbegriffe und die juristische Struktur von Geschäften, Rechtsakten der Vergangenheit zu erforschen, wie sie *objektiv* [emphasis Koschaker's] bestanden. Was sich die Beteiligten in concreto dabei dachten, kann ihm gleichgültig sein. Wenn er, wie ich gezeigt zu haben glaube, herbei zum Ergebnis kommt, dass die juristische Struktur der Eheschliessung dieselbe ist wie diejenige des Kaufs, so ist er berechtigt, von Kaufehe zu sprechen (p. 234)."

Koschaker's arguments were based on OB marriage practice and, to some degree, on the actual documents themselves. Babylonian deeds are formulated from the point of view of the new right-holder who takes possession of the goods. Koschaker noted that the husband *īḫuz* "took" his wife from the father exactly as the buyer *ilqi* "received" the land from the seller. In neither case is the reaction of the former rightholder recorded.

The Aramaic deeds on the other hand, stress the inter-action between the two parties, whether the seller and buyer or husband or father-in-law. The reactions of the old right-holder are carefully recorded since they are of constitutive value. My arguments are based on the affinity between the reactions of the seller to the

not mean to imply—nor did so Koschaker [1])—that because of certain objective-structural affinities between conveyance and marriage, the wife was considered an object of barter: nothing could be further from the social realities of both Mesopotamia and the Elephantine community. The deeds themselves bear witness to the independent position of women in the Jewish colony: they could run their own business, [2]) testify in court, [3]) and even institute divorce proceedings against their husbands [4]) —hardly reflections of a chattel-like status. Nevertheless, the economic independence of the woman and its obvious sociological implications should not blind us to the legal and philological realities of the deed itself: the presence of conveyance terms like *ṭyb lbby* in the marriage contract and the declaration of the father that he is quitted of the *mohar* after the manner of the seller who is quitted of the sale-price—these are not meaningless phenomena. *Ṭyb lbby,* even in this context, seems to indicate some relinquishment of "ownership" in return for a consideration. If the father did not actually "own" his daughter, he certainly exercized a degree of "control" over her in virtue of *patria potestas.* [5])* It is well known that ancient Near Eastern society had not clearly defined the concept of ownership, [6]) anymore than the mediaeval

---

receipt of the sale price and the reactions of the father upon the receipt of the *mohar/terḫatu.*

[1]) Koschaker, *ibid.*, p. 235: "Denn eines ist ausser Zweifel: niemals und nirgends wurde die Ehefrau als eine Ware gekauft."

[2]) All of the Aramaic legal documents belong either to the family archive of Mibṭaḥiah or to that of Ananiah bar Azariah (cf. *LAP,* p. 14). The fact that one of the two extant archives belonged to a woman is but one of the many indicators of the independent status of women at Elephantine.

[3]) Cf. *AP* 14.

[4]) Cf. *AP* 15 and *BP* 7.

[5]) The whole topic deserves an independent investigation. For the time being, of the discussion of Seidl, *ÄRg,* pp. 48 ff.; for the Bible, see Nu 30: 4 ff. and especially the expression *bᵉḇēṯ ʾaḇīhā bineʿūrēhā* "before attaining her majority, while still in her father's house." Cf. also de Vaux, *Ancient Israel,* p. 20. For remnants of *patria potestas* in the Aramaic documents, cf. *BP* 7: 28 where it is stipulated that if Yehoyishma should repudiate her husband *thk lbyt ʾbwh* "she goes (back) to the house of her father." (Cf. the cuneiform analogue in CH 142: *ana bīt abīša ittallak* "she shall go back to her father's house.") That the divorced wife was not always required to return to her father's house is reflected in the parallel clause *AP* 15: 25 *wthk [l]hʾn zy ṣbyt* "and let her go [wher]ever she wants."

[6]) Cf. the discussion on the nature of "ownership" in cuneiform law by Cardascia, *Propriété,* pp. 19 ff. Cf. for example, his statement "c'est de l'absence de termes appropriés que nous avons inféré l'absence d'une catégorie précise de la propriété (p. 26)." Or: "En d'autres termes, *bêlu* sert à exprimer non la puissance absolue, mais la relation à la fois la plus générale et la plus directe entre un sujet et un objet (p. 23)." This statement may be accepted with the reservation that not every concept operative in a given civilization has its exact terminological reflex.

Germans or Anglo-Saxons:[1]) the concepts of ownership and control were virtually interchangeable.

Furthermore, even if this structural affinity between sale and marriage is admitted—with the reservation that the father merely "controlled" but did not "own" his daughter—it may be argued that such affinity was simply an echo of archaic legal norms long forgotten. This, however, is for the sociologist to determine. The philologian can only point out the objective legal and linguistic parallels.

B. *A Possible Atypical Use of* ṭyb lbby *in Deeds of Delivery*

In all of the texts examined so far, the declaration *ṭyb lbby* "my heart is satisfied" has been made by a former right-holder who was induced to give up some right in return for a payment of a specific performance. In sale transactions, the seller declares that he is quitted with the *Entgelt* and thereupon relinquishes his property. In litigation transactions, the plaintiff declares himself satisfied with the oath or payment of the defendant and thereupon desists from all further suit and litigation. It has been pointed out above that the very use of *ṭyb lbby* in the *mohar* clause reflects the same structural pattern: the father's heart is satisfied with the *mohar* as the seller's heart is satisfied with the sale price; both are right-holders who relinquish claims in return for consideration.

There are only two further uses of *ṭyb lbby* that have not as yet been considered: *ṭyb lbby* in the deed of delivery *AP* 2, and *ṭyb lbby* in the dowry-*tkwnh* receipt clause of *AP* 15. The usage of the term in these contexts seems to be at variance with the conveyance-*mohar* meaning of the term: in these two contexts (*AP* 2 and 15), the term does not express the relinquishment of rights but the creation and acceptance of new responsibilities and obligations. Let us first consider *AP* 2.

In this deed, two colonists, Aḥiab and Hoshea, are hired by Espemeṭ to deliver grain to the garrison at Syene. The deed is written from the point of view of the agents who obligate themselves to deliver the grain. They declare:

(3) . . . *yhbt ʿl ydn śʿ[rn* . . .] (exact amount) . . . (9) *wṭyb lbbn bgw ʾnḥnh nbl ʿbwrʾ* . . . (13) . . . [*whn lʾ nntn kl ʿbwrʾ zy*] (14) *lk bmnyn* . . . (15) *ʾnḥnh nḥwb lk ksp* . . . (16) . . . *wʾnt šlṭ bprsn zy byt mlkʾ* . . . (17) . . . *ʾnt šlṭ lmʾḥd ʿd ttmlʾ bʿbwrʾ* . . .

(3) ". . . You have consigned to us barley . . . (exact amount) . . . (9) and our heart is satisfied therewith. We shall deliver the grain . . . (13) . . .

---

[1]) The same situation obtains in German law. Cf. Heubner, *Germanic Private Law*, p. 227. Cf. also Petschow, *Pfandrecht*, p. 135, n. 406.

[And if we do not deliver all the grain that is] yours in full, (15) we shall be liable (to you) silver . . . (16) . . . and you have a right to our wages from the Government House . . . (17) . . . you have the right to seize our wages until you are indemnified in full for the grain."

In this deed, the parties who declare that their hearts are satisfied are not former right-holders who are relinquishing some right or claim in return for an *Entgelt* or necessary performance; they are not sellers who are relinquishing land in return for a sale price; nor are they like the father who cedes control over his daughter in return for the *mohar*/bride-price. Instead, Aḥiab and Hoshea are servants/agents hired by a master; they themselves are not property-owners or right-holders and, therefore, have no property, rights, or claims to give up. Their declaration of satisfaction does not record the receipt of a necessary payment and the concommitant quittance: it simply records the fact that they have received the goods their master consigned to them. On the surface, it is only this one idea—that of receipt—which the two polar uses of *ṭyb lbby* seem to have in common.

Does the term, in this rare context, merely record the receipt of the consigned goods by the agents? Since this idea is already expressed by the opening clause, *yhbt ʿl ydn śʿrn* "you consigned to us barley," it would seem reasonable to assume that *ṭyb lbby* filled some more specific constitutive function other than that of simple receipt. If the term did not convey some other specific idea, it would not have been used by the scribes.

The expression *ṭyb lbby* in *AP* 2 is the nexus between two aspects of the transaction: the delivery of the goods to the agents by the owner; and the obligation of the agents to perform as hired. The term *ṭyb lbby* is at once the constitutive reaction of the agents to the performance of the owners, and the reason for their obligating themselves to deliver the goods in the future:

"You have given us; our heart is satisfied; we shall deliver."

Conversely, if their hearts had not been satisfied with the goods actually received, they would not have obligated themselves to deliver the goods *bmnyn* "in full measure." In this context, *ṭyb lbby* is somehow related to the idea of obligation to perform rather than with quittance; the absence of this term therefore would weaken the obligatory power of the deed.

At first glance, there can be no possible relationship between the two polar meanings of the term. How can the same term express the relinquishment of rights after the receipt of an *Entgelt* and the creation of an obligation to perform? Further investigation, however, may uncover the underlying meaning common to both uses of the term.

Until now, I have stressed the close relationship between the term *ṭyb lbby* and the payment of an *Entgelt* which induces an owner to part with his property. Since these aspects are totally absent from *ṭyb lbby* as used in the delivery document, let us, for the moment, focus our attention on other significant aspects of the term: the ideas of completeness and incontestability. These ideas may shed some light on the problem of the underlying elements which unite the polar aspects of the term.

Conveyances are incontestable only if the full price has been paid. Analogously, deeds of delivery are incontestable only if the full amount of goods was delivered: a) by the owner to the agents at the inception of the transaction b) or by the agents to the owner at the culmination of the transaction. If the agents delivered less than was specified in the deed, the owner will seize the property (in this case, their wages) in satisfaction. The agents will counter-attack by instituting a suit against the owner, claiming that they delivered as much as they received and that the owner shortchanged them by delivering less than the amount he obligated them to deliver in the deed.

Thus, the promises of the agents to perform lack sufficient obligatory basis as long as some possibility of litigation remains. The potential claims of the agents can be obviated in only one way: by a declaration of receipt and quittance. The agents are, therefore, obligated upon receipt of the consignment from the owner to check the goods received in order to determine whether the goods actually received tally with the goods they were hired to deliver. If the two amounts tally with each other, the agents declare that their heart was satisfied with the goods received; they do not want or demand any more from the owner. If they now deliver less than the amount stipulated, they hereby admit that it is not the owner's fault: they have no claims against him; the responsibility to deliver the goods in full, therefore, is all theirs. Thus, in this context at least, the relinquishment of all future claims and litigations against the owner is by implication equivalent to the acceptance of an obligation to be performed.

C. ṭyb lbby *in the Dowry-Acceptance Clause*

The same affinity between receipt and acceptance of an obligation is reflected in the use of *ṭyb lbby* in the dowry-receipt clause *AP* 15:15. The marriage document lists each item the bride brought into (Aramaic *hnʿlt*; Akkadian *ušērib*) her husband's house, together with its exact value. The dowry list concludes with the grand total of valuables and the husband's reaction to the receipt of the goods: *ʿl ʿly wṭyb lbby bgw* "It (the goods) has been received by me and my heart is satisfied therewith." What is the meaning of the term in this context? It certainly does not express quittance of rights after the receipt of an *Entgelt.* It is quite possible that *ṭyb lbby* is used here exactly as it was in *AP* 2: as a term that records the acceptance of an obligation to deliver or return goods with which one has been entrusted. We know from the deed itself that the husband was obligated to return the wife's dowry in case of divorce:

(26) . . . *mḥr ʾw ywm ʾḥrn yqwm ʾsḥwr bʿdh* (27) *wyʾmr śnʾt* [*lʾn*]*tty mpṭḥyh mhrh* [*y*]*ʾbd wkl zy hnʿlt* (28) *bydh thnpq mn ḥm ʿd ḥwṭ*

(26) ". . . If tomorrow or another day, Asḥor should stand up in the congregation and say: (27) 'I hereby repudiate my [wi]fe Mipṭaḥiah,' his dowry shall be forfeited and everything she had brought (28) in with her, she shall take away, be it straw or string." [1])

---

[1]) According to its syntactical structure—*mn . . . ʿd*—, the expression is a *merismus*; cf. A. M. Honeyman, "*Merismus* in Biblical Hebrew," *JBL*, 71 (1952), pp. 11 ff. The term has both Biblical and cuneiform analogues. Functionally, the expression is identical with the OB inheritance-division clause *zīzū gamrū ištu pê adi ḫurāṣim aḫum ana aḫim ul iraggam* "they have divided completely; from straw to gold, one shall not raise a claim against the other" (Schorr, *Urkunden*, No. 186: 16-19 and *passim*). A similar clause is used in the liquidation of *tappûtu*-partnerships (Schorr, *Urkunden*, No. 169 and *passim*). From a structural point of view, the liquidation of common property by a husband and wife in case of divorce is virtually identical with the liquidation of *tappûtu*-property; however, instead of taking everything that belongs to her "from straw to gold," the wife takes everything of hers "be it straw or string (*mḥm wʿd ḥwṭ*)." (The functional equivalence of the Akkadian and Aramaic terms was noticed already by H. Pick in the *OLZ*, 11 [1908], p. 317.)

Etymologically, the Aramaic *mḥm wʿd ḥwṭ* is virtually identical with the Biblical expression *mḥwṭ wʿd śrwk nʿl* "be it string or sandal-lace" Gen 14: 23 on the one hand, and with the Akkadian *ḫāmu u ḫuṣābu* (Speiser, *JAOS*, 54 [1934], pp. 100-03; for the meaning of the Akkadian term, see *CAD*, VI, "*ḫāmu*" (p. 73a) and "*huṣābu*" (p. 259a)). Unfortunately, until recently, the Akkadian expression was known only from literary texts; it was not known in deeds of division. On the other hand, *ištu pê adi ḫurāṣim*, although functionally identical with the Aramaic expression, is etymologically dissimilar. Inner-Aramaic investigation, therefore, raised the interesting Assyriological question: did the Aramaic scribes have before them cuneiform texts in which the expression *ḫāmu u ḫuṣābu* was used in exactly the same contextual matrix as the Old Babylonian *ištu pê adi ḫurāṣim*, or, did the scribes borrow an old Akkadian term and apply it to a new context? On the basis of newly published Neo-Assyrian documents, the cuneiform origins of the Aramaic expression can be established without much doubt. Cf. Deller, *Terminologie*, p. 34 who cites *ADD* 1252 = *AJSL*, 42, p. 267, r. 1-5: (ḪA.LA É.AD . . .) PN_1 (2) *a-na* PN_2 (3) *ib-ta-*<*at*>*-qa it-ti-din* (4) *lu-u ḫa-a-mu*! *lu-u ḫu-ṣa*!*-bu* (5) *ib-ta-taq* „dass Erbe des Vaterhauses hat PN_1 dem PN_2 geteilt (und) gegeben; (bis zum letzten) Strohhalm und Holzsplitter hat er (es) geteilt." Cf. below, p. 182.

Thus, the husband is actually the guardian of the wife's property. [1]) His position is much like that of the agent who obligates himself to guard and deliver the goods that have been entrusted into his care. The agent promises to deliver the goods "in full" (*bmnyn*). The husband, for his part, obligates himself to return the wife's dowry in full. In the marriage document, the abstract *bmnwn* "in full,"/"according to (exact) count" is replaced by the more concrete *merismus* "from straw to string" i.e., everything, no matter how insignificant. Contextually, *ṭyb lbby* here means: "I have received the dowry from you in full and hereby obligate myself to return it to you in full, be it straw or string, in case of divorce."

The explanation of this atypical use of the term follows the line of reasoning employed in the delivery clause, *AP* 2, below. In all probability, the husband had the right to use the dowry for his own purposes. The obligation to return the property—or its equivalent—must have been a great economic hardship for the husband: the money may have already been invested in his business. [2]) We know from the Ras Shamra [3]) legal

[1]) So E. J. Bickerman, "Two Legal Interpretations of the Septuagint, "*RIDA*, 3e série, 3 (1956), p. 85.

[2]) According to Talmudic law (*TB*, *Ketubboth* 82b; *TP*, 23b-c; *Tosefta*, *Ketubboth* 12, 1), the bride price was given originally to the father-in-law; then the father-in-law gave the bride-price back to the husband and made him the trustee of the wife; at a later stage, the husband could use this sum for his own purposes and all his property was placed as security for the payment of the sum in case of divorce. According to Ginsberg ("The Brooklyn Museum Aramaic Papyri," *JAOS*, 74, pp. 156 f.), a similar practice is reflected in the Elephantine deeds: the *mohar* was returned as part of the *tkwnh*. The problem is whether the husband was simply the trustee of the goods—which remained the wife's property and could not be touched by the husband (Bickerman, *op. cit.*, p. 88)—or whether he could also use the goods for his own purposes with the condition that he return them (or their value) in case of divorce. Some light may be shed on this question from older Ras Shamra sources; In *RS* 17.159 (= *PRU* IV, p. 126), the daughter of Bentišina, the king of Amurru, is divorced by Ammistamru king of Ugarit, her husband. She is allowed to take everything she had brought into the house of Ammistamru (as her dowry) and depart: (14) *ša ina bīti Ammistamri* (15) *ultēribu* (16) *lilqīma ištu* (17) [*bī*]*ti Ammistamri littalak* = Aramaic *kl zy hnʿlt bydh thnpq mn ḥm wʿd ḥwṭ wthk lh'n zy ṣbyt*. However, if Ammistamru sold (?) any of her property, let the sons of Ammuru take an oath, and Ammistamru will reimburse them: *mīnummē* (19) *ša Ammistamri i-na-ki-ru* (20) *mārū Amurri litmūma* (21) *Ammistamri lišallimšunūti*. If *i-na-ki-ru* means *aliéné* as Nougayrol interprets it (tacitly reading the form as *unakkiru*?), then it seems that the husband, either according to right or custom, had some use of his wife's property. Possibly it is unsound to infer anything from a royal marriage. However, whether the husband had actual use of his wife's *tkwnh* or was merely its trustee, the return of the money in case of divorce, was often the source of court action. See the discussion below.*

[3]) The relevance of the Ugaritic passage cited in note 2 for the interpretation of the Elephantine documents was also noted by Yaron, "A Royal Divorce at Ugarit," *Or*, 32 (1963), pp. 27 f. According to his interpretation, some list enumerating the

documents and from the Elephantine deeds [1]) themselves that the divorce settlement was often the cause of litigation between husband and wife; in such a contingency, the only way the wife could establish her claim to her property was by an oath—to judge from the Akkadian sources, a legal instrument that was not looked on favorably by either party.

Just such a litigation seems to be reflected in *AP* 14. Here, Mibtaḥiah takes an oath of purgation for Pi', her ex-husband. The object of the litigation was:

(3) . . . *ksp* (4) *w'bwr wlbwš wnḥš wprzl kl nksn wqnyn wspr 'ntw 'dyn mwm'h mṭ'h* (5) *'lyky wym'ty ly 'lyhm bsty 'lhth wṭyb lbby* (6) *bmwm'h*

(3) "... concerning money (4) corn, garments, copper, and iron, all goods and acquisitions, and the marriage document. Then an oath was imposed (5) on you and you swore on my behalf concerning them by the goddess Sati and my heart was satisfied (6) with the oath." [2])

In order to forestall such litigations, the Elephantine marriage contracts recorded the exact value of each item and added to this list the acknowledgment by the husband that he had actually received the goods recorded in the deed. He cannot, therefore, claim, on a later occasion, that he did not receive such goods. By declaring, "My heart is satisfied

---

dowry of the daughter of Bentišina must have existed. Yaron explains the clause *mīnummē ša i-na-ki-ru* not as "that which he (the king) had sold" but "that which he denied." Thus, the king denied that he had received the full amount of the dowry; this forced the sons of Bentišina to defend the rights of the divorced queen with an oath (*mārū ša Bentišina litmūma*).

Nougayrol's interpretation is difficult grammatically: *nakāru* can only be used as a term of alienation in the *D* form. Therefore, Yaron's suggestion should be seriously considered.* However, whatever the case may be, litigations connected with return of dowry were usually settled by an oath, whether at Ras Shamra or Elephantine. Furthermore, while dowry-lists and obligation-creating terms like *ṭyb lbby* were added to the marriage document in order to preclude possible litigation, it is clear that such legal instruments did not always succeed in their purpose.

[1]) Yaron, *ibid.*, p. 27.

[2]) Several parallels from Demotic and Talmudic sources should be mentioned in this context. In slightly later Demotic marriage contracts, the husband promises his wife that "I cannot impose and oath on you about your *nkt.wns.hm.t* (the paralel of the Aramic *tkwnh*) above (mentioned), saying: 'You have not (really) brought them with you to my house'." Cf. *Pestman*, p. 96 and especially Pestman's interpretation of the meaning of the clause: "The husband might refuse to part with the goods [even if the amount of goods is listed in the deed], drive matters to legal proceedings and put her on oath before the court of justice in which she would have to swear that she indeed brought the disputed goods along with her into her conjugal domicile and thus now has the right of claiming them." (p. 96) Virtually the same stipulation not to force the wife to defend her rights by an oath is also found in Rabbinic sources. Cf. *TB*, *Ketubboth* 86b; *Tosefta*, *Ketubboth*, 9, 3; for a discussion of these rabbinic sources, cf. Epstein, *Jewish Marriage Contract*, p. 257.

with the amount received," he relinquishes any claim, suit, or litigation he might raise against his wife in the future; thus, by relinquishing any claim he might have against his wife, he acknowledges the claim of his wife against him: the obligation to return the dowry in full.

This interpretation is fully confirmed by contemporary Demotic marriage documents. In Papyrus Berlin 3109 (225 B.C.) we read:

"Das Verzeichnis deiner Frauensachen (= Aramaic *tkwnh*), die du gebrachst hast in mein Haus mit dir" . . . detailed list . . . grand total . . . "um voll zu machen" . . . total . . .: "Wert deiner Frauensachen, die du gebrachst hast in mein Haus mit dir. Empfangen habe ich sie aus deiner Hand, indem sie vollständig sind ohne Rest (= Aramaic: *ʿl ʿly wṭyb lbby bgw zy lʾ ʾštʾr mn nksyʾ*). Mein Herz ist zufrieden mit ihnen. Bist du drinnen, so bist du drinnen mit ihnen. Bist du drausen, so bist du draussen mit ihnen. Dein ist ihre Bestimmung, mein ist ihre Verwahrung.

Entlasse ich dich (als) Ehefrau, oder beliebst du zu gehen, (so werde) ich geben dir deine Frauensachen welche (oben) geschrieben sind, oder das Silber gemass dem, was oben geschrieben ist.

Nicht soll ich können (geben) einen Eid hinter dich wegen deiner Frauensachen . . . sagend: Nicht hast du sie gebracht in mein Haus mit dir." [1])

---

[1]) Cf. Lüddeckens, p. 43. These Demotic and Talmudic parallels were independently seen by Yaron in his article, "A Royal Divorce at Ugarit," Or, 32 (1963), pp. 27 ff.

CHAPTER FOUR

LIBBAŠU ṬĀB

1. *Libbašu ṭāb* IN DEEDS OF SALE: A PRELIMINARY INVESTIGATION

In spite of the widespread use of *libbašu ṭāb* in various types of Old Babylonian legal transactions, no systematic study has been devoted to the definition of its legal function(s), the charting of its somewhat unusual distribution patterns, and the establishment of typological and historical *Sitz im Leben*. Thus, the Aramaic or Demotic legal historian interested in the cuneiform background of the Aramaic *ṭyb lbby* or the Demotic *m-ʾib-hr* will find no *Vorstudien* but merely sporadic comments on *libbašu ṭāb* in the Assyriological literature.

Paradoxically, it is the study of the Elephantine legal terminology that calls for a re-evaluation of the juridical significance of the Akkadian cognate *libbašu ṭāb* and for its redefinition on the basis of all the available material: the full range of contexts—both typological and geographical —in which it is used; and on the basis of all its semantic equivalents, complements, and contrasts. Only after the legal function of *libbašu ṭāb* has been established philologically can the historical problems of dependence be approached with some degree of control.

A. *Previous Studies of* libbašu ṭāb *in Sale and Division*

Even though *libbašu ṭāb* is used quite frequently in OB conveyances, there is little or no discussion of the term in San Nicolò's classic study of Old Babylonian sale law. In one note, San Nicolò states that *libbašu ṭāb* is found only in Sippar conveyances and that its origins are uncertain since it is not found in pre-OB documents. [1]) He makes no attempt to determine its meaning or juridical function. Could it be that San Nicolò, like Yaron, overlooked the specific juridical function of *libbašu ṭāb* because of its "narrative" and unterminological character? [2]) Or is it that *libbašu ṭāb*, in reflecting the reactions of the seller to the sale transaction, did not fit into a discussion of OB conveyances, regularly formulated from the point of view of the buyer? [3]) Whatever the case may

---

[1]) San Nicolò, *Schlussklauseln*, p. 25, n. 45.

[2]) Cf. Yaron, *LAP* [Hebrew], p. 107.

[3]) Concerning formulations *ex latere emptoris* and those *ex latere venditoris*, cf. *Schlussklauseln*, pp. 27 ff.

be, San Nicolò's study, although vital to the understanding of many phases of NE law, contributes little to the definition of the term under discussion.

Another scholar to comment on the term was J. Klíma. In his study of OB inheritance law, [1] Klíma noted the presence of the clause *zīzū gamrū libbašunu ṭāb* "they have divided; they are finished; their hearts are satisfied" in several OB division documents, mainly from Sippar. [2] Since the clause is used rather infrequently—its more common variant being: *ištu pê adi ḫurāṣim zīzū gamrū* "they have completely divided, from straw to gold"—Klíma has little to say about its specific juridical function. However, he does make the following comment: "Diese Wendung *libbašu* bzw. *libba-šunu ṭāb* stellt eine Willenserklärung der Verfügungen dar. Die Parteien wollen damit besagen, dass sie mit der durchgeführten Teilung in jeder Weise einverstanden sind und sie mit nicht anfechten werden." [3]

The volitional-consensual interpretation suggested by Klíma for the division clause *zīzū gamrū libbašunu ṭāb* can be applied with some cogency to the sale usage of *libbašu ṭāb*. The following cluster of three clauses is quite common in Sippar conveyances: (a) *bukannu šūtuq* "the *bukannu* was passed"; (b) *awassu gamrat* "its transaction (i.e., that of the property) is completed";* (c) *libbašu ṭāb* "his heart (i.e., the seller's) is/was satisfied." Thus, the direct antecedent of *libbašu ṭāb* would seem to be the completed transaction (= *awassu gamrat*; cf. the division formula *zīzū gamrū libbašunu ṭāb*). The clause would then mean: "He (the seller) agreed to the completed transaction."

The volitional interpretation of the term is supported not only by the order of the clauses but also by certain etymological considerations. In commenting on the meaning of certain Mari legal expressions based on the stem *ṭābu*, G. Boyer had the following to say: "Les . . . mots *annûm ṭûbu* peuvent s'expliquer comme exprimant le plein approbation des parties à l'opération. Elle équivaudrait ainsi à la mention *ina ṭûb libbim* des N°s 13 et 15, ou *libbašu ṭâb* = 'son coeur est satisfait'. . . ." [4] Many other such terms of volition based on the stem *ṭābu* could be adduced in favor of this consensual-volitional interpretation, the most notable being the OB Susa clause *ina ṭūbātišu ina nar'amātišu* "of his own free

---

[1]) Klíma, *Untersuchungen*, p. 35.

[2]) Klíma quotes W 78, whose origin is not known. The term is also found sporadically in deeds of division from Kiš and Larsa. For these texts, cf. the end of this chapter.

[3]) Klíma, *Untersuchungen*, p. 35.

[4]) Boyer, *ARM* VIII, p. 189.

will and voluntarily." [1] Thus, both the order of the clauses and considerations of etymology seem to support the volitional interpretation of the term.

According to the interpretations of San Nicolò, Klíma, and Boyer, the subject of *libbašu ṭāb* is the seller who has agreed to the completed sale transaction. By the term "transaction" they mean the payment of the price and the agreement to complete the performance; the actual transfer of the goods by the seller and the *ḥazaqah* [2] of the buyer are not included in the term "transaction" or in the verb *išām* "he bought." Szlechter, in a recent study of OB deeds from the Diyala region, has offered a new interpretation of the terms *išām* and *libbašu ṭāb.* [3] According to Szlechter, the term "transaction" includes the transfer of goods and the concomitant *ḥazaqah* of the buyer. Accordingly, *išâm* does not mean "he bought" but "he took into possession." Thus, the clauses *bukannu šūtuq, awassu gamrat,* and *libbašu ṭāb* all reflect situations which take place after the owner has taken possession of his goods. According to Szlechter's interpretation, *libbašu ṭāb* reflects the final stage in the process of *ḥazaqah*: it does not refer to the seller who has agreed to the finished transaction but rather to the buyer whose heart is satisfied after having completely taken possession of his new property. [4]

B. *A New Interpretation*: libbašu ṭāb—*A Term of Receipt and Quittance*

Both the volitional and *ḥazaqah* interpretations of *libbašu ṭāb* have been rejected by Simmons in his study of early OB sale documents from the Diyala region, especially from Ḥarmal. [5] In the Ḥarmal conveyances, the active form of the term *libbam uṭīb* [6] "he satisfied the heart" regularly alternates with the more common passive *libbum ṭūb* "the heart is satisfied." [7] The same alternation is also found in the contemporary OB conveyances from the neighboring Khafajah: *libbum/libbašu ṭūb* [8] // *libbam/libbašu uṭīb* "the/his heart was satisfied//he satisfied the/his heart." Clearly, argues Simmons, the active form can only mean "the buyer

[1] Cf. *CAD, I/J*, p. 12, for this translation.
[2] Cf. above, p. 24, n. 2 and p. 26.
[3] Szlechter, *Tablettes juridiques*, pp. 44, 48-49.
[4] *Ibid.*, pp. 48-49.
[5] S. D. Simmons, "Early Old Babylonian Tablets from Ḥarmal and Elsewhere," *JCS*, 13 (1959), pp. 71 ff.; 105 ff.; *ibid.*, 14 (1960), pp. 23 ff., 75 ff., 117 ff.; *ibid.*, 15 (1961), pp. 49 ff. and 81 ff. Simmons' comments on the distribution and meaning of *libbašu ṭāb* are found in the first part of his study, *JCS*, 13 (1959), p. 90.
[6] *Simmons, Ḥarmal*, Nos. 46 : 14; 47 : 9; 48 : 11; 49 : 12.
[7] Simmons, *Ḥarmal*, No. 70 : 11.
[8] Harris, *Khafajah*, pp. 31 ff. For the active form, cf. Nos. 61, 72 and 74; for the passive form, cf. Nos. 56, 60, 75, 81.

satisfied the heart of the seller." Accordingly, the passive can only mean "the heart of the seller is/was satisfied." Such a reading obviously removes the basis of Szlechter's interpretation. [1]

The order of the clauses in the oldest conveyances from the Diyala region is used by Simmons to refute the volitional-consensual interpretation of *libbašu ṭāb*. In the Sippar deeds of sale, the order of the clauses is: (a) *bukannu šūtuq* (b) *awassu gamrat* (c) *libbašu ṭāb*. Thus, the direct antecedent of *libbašu ṭāb* is the completed transaction. Simmons was the first to point out the incongruity of the term in this final position. After the payment of the full price, the passing of the *bukannu*, and the declaration that the transaction was terminated, the statement that the heart of the seller is satisfied is anticlimactic, to say the least. [2] Agreement should precede rather than follow the passing of the *bukannu* and the perfection of the transaction. Simmons notes that this more logical order—and probably the original one—is exactly the order most common in the Diyala conveyances; this order is found in all of the Ishchali [3] deeds of sale (where the term of satisfaction appears immediately after the payment of the price, and before the passing of the *bukannu* and the perfection of the transaction), in all of the Ḥarmal deeds and in most of the deeds of Khafajah. A typical example of this variant order is Ḥarmal 46: (12) šám.til.la.ni.šè (13) kù.bi in.na.lal.e (14) *li-ba-am ú-ṭì-ib* (15) giš.gan íb.ta.bal (16) *a-wa-sú ga-am-ra-at.**

Simmons infers from the order of the clauses that "coming directly after the statement that the buyer has paid the price it, stresses the fact that it was the seller who accepted the money and is satisfied with the amount received." [4]

Clearly, the term records the following: (a) that the complete sale price had been tendered by the buyer—the subject of the expression *libbašu uṭīb*; (b) that the full price had been received by the seller—the subject of the expression *libbašu ṭūb*; (c) that the price received was to his satisfaction; [5] that he had enough and wanted no more; (d) that, in short, he was quitted and would not contest the transaction in the future. [6]

---

[1]) Simmons, *JCS*, 13 (1959), p. 90.

[2]) *Ibid.*

[3]) *Ibid.*

[4]) *Ibid.*

[5]) Cf. Gordon, *Smith College Tablets*, pp. 32-34. Gordon translates the OB clause *leqû libbašu ṭāb* as "they (the containers of grain) have been received; his heart is gratified." In his paraphrase, Gordon renders the idiom as „reimbursed to full satisfaction." Although Gordon does not explicate this translation, it is clear that he did not take the term in a volitional sense.

[6]) Ferris Stephens, "Notes on Some Economic Texts of the Time of Urukagina,"

The term *libbašu ṭāb* records the constitutive reaction of the seller to the essential aspect of the transaction—the payment of the full price. This reaction is the psychological motivation of the clauses of perfection which follow: (a) *awassu gamrat* (inim.bi al.til) "its transaction is completed"; and (b) *bukannu šūtuq* (giš.gan íb.ta.bal) "the *bukannu* was passed." It should be noted, in passing, that if the interpretation just suggested is correct, the legal functions of the Aramaic and Akkadian terms of satisfaction are virtually identical.

Simmon's interpretation of *libbašu ṭāb* was based on the order of clauses in the Ḫarmal conveyances. However, even Simmons assumes that this order is limited to the deeds of the Diyala region and that *libbašu ṭāb* is always found in last place in the Sippar conveyances. [1] Clearly, a reinvestigation of the Sippar order of clauses is now in order.

The Order of Clauses in Sippar Conveyances. The distribution patterns of the Sippar conveyances are virtually identical with those reflected in the early OB conveyances of Khafajah where *libbašu ṭāb* appears either (a) immediately after the record of payment, [2] or (b) following the perfection of the sale by the passing of the *bukannu* or the declaration *awassu gamrat* (Sum. inim.bi al.til) "its transaction is completed." [3]

	Payment—*libbašu ṭāb* [4]	Perfection—*libbašu ṭāb* [5]
Sumulael		*HG* 247=*R* 8 383=*CT* IV 48b
Immerum	*HG* 376=*CT* VIII 47b 379=*R* 5	*HG* 242=*M* 35

RA, 49 (1955), p. 132, n. 4, compares the Sumerian expression used in the Reform Text of Urukagina with the common OB expression *libbašu ṭāb*. Concerning the latter terms, Stevens notes: "The latter is used to indicate that an account is settled." This is certainly one of the nuances inherent in the term.

[1] Simmons, *JCS*, 13 (1959), p. 90.

[2] Harris, *Khafajah*, Nos. 47: 7, 63: 8, and *passim*.

[3] *Ibid.*, No. 58: 9 and *passim*.

[4] I have not cited every published Sippar conveyance. My selection is based on the material contained in San Nicolò's *Schlussklauseln* and in the volumes of *HG*. As far as I can tell, most OB documents edited since the time of the *Schlussklauseln* and *HG* (1922 and 1923) are from central and southern Mesopotamia; therefore a selection based on older publications still insures an adequate control. However, it should still be understood that this distribution chart is illustrative rather than exhaustive. To achieve exhaustive citation would have expanded this work considerably. Cf. below, p. 97, n. 5.

[5] Two different orders of clauses have been included under this heading: (a) giš. gan íb.ta.bal, inim.bi al.til, šà.ga.ni al. dùg; (b) inim.bi al.til, giš. gan íb.ta.bal, šà.ga.ni al.dùg. Included under the heading "payment—*libbašu ṭāb*" are all cases where šà.ga.ni al.dùg is found after the payment of the price, whether or not the term of satisfaction is followed by a perfection clause. The many conveyances in which šà.ga.ni al.dùg was not used were not listed.

	Payment—*libbašu ṭāb*	Perfection—*libbašu ṭāb*
Ilumaila	*HG* 370=*CT* VIII 26b 371=*CT* VIII 38b 373=*R* 2	
Ṣabium		*HG* 251=*R* 13 = Schorr, *Urkunden* 86 384=*CT* II 3 386=*CT* II 37 = Schorr, *Urkunden* 95
Apil-Sîn	*HG* 396=*CT* VIII 31a 1597=*W* 45	*HG* 393=*CT* IV 16a 1598=*W* 55
Sîn-muballiṭ	*HG* 933=*VS* VIII 49.78	*HG* 262=*M* 32 264=*CT* II 37 265=*CT* IV 44b 266=*CT* IV 45b 268=*CT* VIII 4b 269=*CT* VIII 20b 957=Como 4
Ḫammurabi	*HG* 287=*R* 22 288=*CT* VI 45 293=*CT* VIII 13a 403=*CT* II 42 425=*CT* VIII 43c 427=*CT* VIII 35b 943=*VS* IX 165	*HG* 286=*CT* VIII 18b 295=*CT* VIII 13b 296=*CT* IV 40a 423=*CT* II 25 424=*CT* VIII 22b 440=*R* 37 939=*VS* IX 10.11 961=*VS* VIII 121.122 1623=*VS* XIII 25 1637=*CT* XXXIII 38
Samsuiluna	*HG* 338=*R* 57 341=*CT* VIII 24a 356=*CT* VI 49c 360=*S* 87 361=*CT* II 28 362=*R* 63 364=*CT* IV 18a 407=*R* 61 409=*CT* VI 20a 1577=*CT* XXXIII 35	*HG* 316=*M* 33 325=*CT* IV 11b 331=*CT* IV 46a 339=*CT* IV 17c 357=*CT* IV 17b 363=*CT* VIII 9b 406=*CT* VIII 15b 410=*CT* IV 19b

	1638=*W* 63 1641=*W* 46	
Abi-ešuḫ		*HG* 366=*R* 76 437=*M* 2
Ammiditana	*HG* 367=*R* 88	
Ammiṣaduqa		*HG* 368=*R* 105
Undated	*HG* 1631=*W* 43	

Statistically, *libbašu ṭāb* in last place is slightly more common than *libbašu ṭāb* in first place after the record of payment; this may account for the impression that *libbašu ṭāb* was always found in last place in the Sippar documents. However, as is evident from the distribution chart, this is not so. In some periods (Sîn-muballiṭ and Ḫammurabi) the two orders are about evenly divided; the same holds true for the early Old Babylonian period.

2. The Explication of the various Aspects of the Term on the Basis of its Grammatical Alloforms and Complements

Like the Aramaic *ṭyb lbby*, the Akkadian *libbašu ṭāb* is a many-faceted term: it records the payment of a consideration by the buyer, the receipt of the consideration by the seller, the acknowledgment of the seller that the payment is complete and that the transaction is therefore final, the quittance of the seller with the sale-price, and his relinquishment of all claims against the seller. This interpretation of the meaning and legal function of the term is confirmed not only by the order of the clauses in the Sippar-Diyala conveyances but also—and especially—by the grammatical structure of the term in the older documents and by the complementary terms used with *libbašu ṭāb* to explicate more clearly its various legal aspects.

A. *The Grammatical Structure of the Term*

As a general rule, the oldest forms of a term or an institution reflect more clearly the underlying structure of the term or institution being investigated. The latest—and "normative"—form of the Akkadian term of satisfaction is the G stative—*libbašu ṭāb* "his heart is satisfied." Logically speaking, *libbašu ṭāb* is a static state of mind, existing independently of any previous action either of the buyer or the seller. The "satisfaction" of the seller's heart is a spontaneous state of mind uninduced by any performance. Clearly, the volitional interpretation applied to the term by earlier scholars was in harmony with the stative structure of the term: "volition" cannot be induced; it either comes about spontaneously or not at all.

However, an entirely different picture emerges from a study of the more archaic Akkadian formulation of the term, used in most of the early OB conveyances from Sippar. In many of these conveyances, the expression is not *libbašu ṭāb* "his heart is satisfied" but *libbašu ṭūb* "his heart has been satisfied." [1]) In this older formulation, the term of satisfaction is not a G but a D stative: in other words, "satisfaction of the heart" is not a static condition, independent of or uninduced by any previous action or performance; rather, the D stative clearly echoes the preceding performance—*libbašu uṭīb* "he (the buyer) satisfied his (the seller's) heart"—of which *libbašu ṭūb* "his heart (the seller's) has been satisfied" is the direct result. Exactly such an active form—*libbašu uṭīb* —seems to be found in *HG* 383=*CT* IV 48b (time of Sumulael). Unfortunately, the text is slightly damaged, but the last two signs are clearly *ṭi-bu*. On the basis of a reconstructed [*u*]*ṭību*, demanded by the context, *HG* translates: "Betreffs des Geldes, des Preises ihres Gartens, hat Ilabrat-û-Sin ihr [the seller's] Herz befriedigt."

The Evidence of Ḥarmal-Khafajah. Fortunately, there is no need to rely on a reconstructed reading to confirm the fact that in its more archaic usage, the term of satisfaction consisted of an active expression of performance—*libbašu uṭīb* "he (the buyer) satisfied his (the seller's) heart"—and a factitive stative *libbašu ṭūb* "his (the seller's) heart has been satisfied" that recorded the result of the preceding performance: the receipt of the payment, the acknowledgment of its perfection, and the quittance therewith. The deeds of Ḥarmal and Khafajah, most of them from the early OB period [2]) and therefore parallel to the oldest conveyances from Sippar, clearly and unmistakably confirm this suggestion. Usages which are rare and archaic in Sippar are common and contemporary in the Diyala region.

The form *libbašu ṭāb* is never found in the Ḥarmal conveyances. The

---

[1]) *HG* contains eleven Sippar conveyances from the time of Sumulael to Ṣabium. One of them (*CT* IV 48b; Sumulael) is formulated in the active voice; two of them are formulated in Sumerian (*CT* VIII 47b; Immerum and *CT* II 3; Ṣabium); one deed (*CT* VIII 26b; Ilumaila) uses the form *ṭāb*; the rest of the deeds use the D stative *ṭūb* (*R* 8 [Sumulael], *R* 5, *M* 35 [Immerum], *R* 2, CT VIII 38b [Ilumaila], Schorr, *Urkunden* 86 and 95—the latter from the time of Ṣabium).

[2]) For the date of the Ḥarmal conveyances, cf. Simmons, *JCS*, 13 (1959), pp. 74-82. According to Harris, *Khafajah*, p. 49, the Khafajah documents were written slightly after the beginning of the First Dynasty of Babylon.

regular form is either the active *libbam uṭīb* "he (the buyer) satisfied the heart (of the seller)" or *libbum ṭūb* "the heart (of the seller) has been satisfied" (used only once). [1] A similar situation is reflected in the conveyance of Khafajah: *libbam uṭīb/libbašu uṭīb* "he satisfied the/his heart" alternates with *libbum/libbašu ṭūb* "the/his heart has been satisfied." [2] It should be noted that once again the overlap between the Akkadian and Aramaic terms of satisfaction is nearly complete: the Aramaic *hwṭbtm lbbn/ṭyb lbbn* [3]: the Akkadian *libbam uṭīb/libbum ṭūb.* In both cases, the stative form is the direct result of a preceding (implied) performance.

The Active-Stative Cluster. The Aramaic usage differs from the Akkadian in only one respect: the active and stative forms combine to form a cluster *hwṭbtm lbbn . . . wṭyb lbbn bgw* "you have satisfied our heart . . . and our heart is satisfied therewith" (*AP* 20:8-9). In Akkadian texts, on the other hand, although both active and stative forms are known and may alternate with each other in the same collection of deeds, the cluster *libbašu uṭīb-libbašu ṭūb,* to the best of my knowledge, is not found in any of the documents published so far.

Although this syntactical construction is common in West Semitic, it is also known from Akkadian documents. Such a cluster is found in the Old Assyrian legal documents of Kültepe: *kaspam* (6) *u ṣipassu Ušḫuba* (7) *u Asīd Aššur-nā'da* (8) *ušabbīšunu kasapšunu šabû* "Aššur-nā'dā (the debtor) satisfied Ušḫuba and Asīd (the creditors) with the money and its interest; they are satisfied with their money" (*EL* 194).

The construction is also found in the Akkadian legal documents of Ras Shamra; cf. *PRU* III, p. 32 (*RS* 16.129): (1) *iš-tu ūmi^{mi} an-ni-i-im* PN . . . (3) *ú-za-ki* PN_2 *mār-šu* (4) *iš-tu bīti^{ti}-šu iš-tu eqlāti^{pl}-šu* . . . (6) *za-ka₄* PN_2 "(1) From this day, PN . . . made his son PN_2 (3) quit; (4) from his estate, from his fields . . . (6) PN_2 is quit (= disinherited)." A similar complementary use of the active-stative forms is found in the Neo-Assyrian sale formula: Sold property the buyer *iṣṣirip issiqi*; sold property *ṣarip laqi* = "The buyer bought the property completely; the property is (now) completely acquired (*ARU* 38 and *passim*)." According to Koschaker [4]) and Meissner, [5]) an active-stative cluster is also used in the MA sale formulary; (a) *eqla* the seller *ana šīm gamir ana* X *šikil kaspam* the buyer *iddin-ma ušappi* "the seller sold and transferred the

---

1) Cf. *Ḫarmal,* No. 70: 11.
2) Cf. above, p. 65, n. 8.
3) *AP* 20: 8-9.
4) Koschaker, *NKRA,* p. 29. Landsberger (*apud* Koschaker) doubts whether *ušappi* and *uppû* are derived from the same stem.
5) Meissner agrees with Koschaker against Landsberger, *MAOG,* 7 (1933), p. 58.

field to the buyer for the full price—so many shekels of silver—; (b) *eqlu uppû laqi* "the field is now transferred and sold."

The forms *ušabbīšu-šabû, uzakki-zakû, ušappi-uppû* clearly indicate the possibility of active-stative constructions in Akkadian. Was a similar cluster **libbam uṭīb-libbum ṭūb* once used in the Diyala formulary? Although it is quite possible that the Aramaic scribes created the cluster "you have satisfied my heart; it is (now) satisfied" on the basis of West Semitic linguistic patterns, it is equally possible that the late Aramaic usage simply echoes older cuneiform traditions. Only future publications of early OB conveyances will tell.

B. *The Relationship Between Payment and Satisfaction*

The close relationship between the payment of the price and the satisfaction of the heart is clearly reflected in the active form *libbam uṭīb*. This relationship is also inferred from the position of *libbašu ṭāb* immediately after the payment of the price in the Diyala conveyances and in many of the Sippar ones. However, even those Sippar formulations which place *libbašu ṭāb* immediately after the clauses (a) ki seller . . . Buyer in.ši.in.šám "from the seller . . . the buyer bought"; (b) šám. til.la.bi.šè kù.babbar ì.na.an.lal "as its full price he measured out the silver" are ambiguous or at least unclear: the immediate cause of the satisfaction is not clear from the wording of the clause itself and has to be inferred from the order of clauses which is not very consistent in the Sippar tradition. Without the more explicit Ḥarmal-Khafajah evidence to rely on, it is no wonder that the term was never accurately defined. And yet, as in the case of the grammatical structure of the term, the older Sippar conveyances often contain archaic usages which clearly reflect the true meaning and original juridical functions of the term.

The Early OB Complement: kaspam šīm bītišu gamram. In the oldest Sippar conveyances, the term of satisfaction is usually formulated in Akkadian. These archaic Akkadian formulations are frequently accompanied by a complement which clearly explicates the immediate reason for the satisfaction of the heart.

HG 242=*M* 35 (Immerum)

a-na ga-me-ir-tim (10) *i-šam a-na ši-mi-šu* (11) *ga-am-ri-im kaspam iš-qú-ul* . . . (14) *kaspam ši-im bīti*[ti]*-šu* (15) *ga-am-ra-am* (16) *li-ba-*<*šu*> *ṭú-ub*

"(The seller) bought (the property) completely. (10-11) He weighed out the money as its full price . . . (14-16) [His heart] has been satisfied with the complete money, the price of his house."

HG 370=*CT* VIII 26b (Ilumaila)

(11) *ši-im eqli-šu kaspam* (12) *li-ba-šu ṭà-ab*

(12) "His heart is satisfied (12) with the money, the price of his field."

HG 371=*CT* VIII 38b (Ilumaila)

(8) *kaspam li-ba-šu ṭú-ub*

(11) "His heart has been satisfied with the money."

HG 373=*R* 2 (Ilumaila)

(2) *kaspam li-ba-šu ṭú-ub*

HG 247=*R* 8 (Sumulael)

(28) *kaspam ga-am-ra-am ši-im bītit*[i]*-šu-nu* (30) *li-ba-šu-nu ṭú-ub*

(30) "Their heart has been satisfied (28) with the complete money, the price of their house."

HG 379=*R* 5 (Immerum)

(13) *ši-im eqli-šu-[nu]* (14) *kaspam ga-am-ra-[am]* (15) *li-ba-šu-nu ṭú-ub*

(15) "Their heart is satisfied (14) with the complete money, (13) the price of their field."

HG 376=*CT* VIII 47b is not altogether clear. The deed is formulated in Sumerian: kù.babbar šà.ga.ni . . . The following signs are not clear; they seem to be ì.dùg or something like them. However, the beginning of the line already indicates the relationship between the heart and the money.

It should be noted at this point that the early OB usage is virtually identical with the later Aramaic: the Akkadian explicates the term "his heart is satisfied" with the complement "with the full sum of money —the sale price of his house"; the Aramaic explicates the term "my heart is satisfied" with the complement "with the money you have given me" or with the clause "in that nothing is outstanding against you on our account."

The Transition from the Akkadian to the Sumerian. In all of the oldest Akkadian conveyances from Sippar, whether the term of satisfaction is found after the payment of the price or after the perfection of the sale, there is never any doubt as to the cause of the satisfaction: it is the immediate reaction of the seller to the receipt of the *kaspam šīm bītišu gamram* "the complete (sum of) money—the price of his house." After the time of Apil-Sin,[1]) however, the clearly explicated Akkadian gives way to the abridged Sumerian formulation šà.ga.ni al.dùg, in which the relationship between the payment and the satisfaction is left out.[2]) Thus, after the abridged Sumerian formulation was placed after the perfection clauses inim.bi al.til or giš.gan.na íb.ta.bal, one could quite naturally interpret the term to mean: "the seller agrees to the completed sale," or following Szlechter, as the acknowledgment of the buyer that he had taken full possession of the newly acquired property.

There is one document from the time of Ṣabium which seems to reflect some of the confusion which resulted from the ambiguity of the un-explicated Sumerian formulation.

R 13=Schorr, *Urkunden* 86

(18) šám.til.la.bi.[šè] (19) kù.babbar in.nan.[lá] (20) giš.gan.na íb.ta.[bal] (21) inim.bi al.[til] (22) šà.ga.ni ì.dùg (23) *kaspam ši-im bīti-šu-nu* (24) *li-ib-ba-šu-nu ṭú-ub*

(18) [In Sumerian] "As its full price (19) he weighed out the money. (20) The *bukannu* was passed; (21) the transaction is completed; (22) his heart is satisfied. (23) [In Akkadian] With the money, the price of their house, (24) their heart has been satisfied."

Why was the clause of satisfaction included twice in this deed, once in Sumerian (l. 22) and once in Akkadian (ll. 23-24)? Could it be that the newer Sumerian formulation was ambiguous and was therefore explicated by the archaic Akkadian codicil? Could it be that the Akkadian term *libbašu ṭāb*, in a more Sumerian milieu, lost some of the constitutive powers it had exercised in early Diyala and Sippar conveyances? Translated into Sumerian, stripped of its explicatives, and relegated to the end of a series of archaic, Sumerian perfection clauses—inim.bi al.til etc.— it was conservatively preserved as a fossilized stereotype, its legal function attenuated—and who knows—even forgotten.[3]) This possibility will be discussed in greater detail in a later section.

[1]) CT VIII 47b from the time of Immerum is formulated in Sumerian. Like the early Akkadian versions of the clause, it is clearly explicated: "his heart is satisfied in respect to the money."

[2]) As far as I can tell, the Akkadian formulation *libbašu ṭāb* does not appear in the documents of the later OB period. According to San Nicolò, the term is used for the last time in BE VI[1] 105: 26 (Schorr, *Urkunden* 92) from the time of Ammiṣaduqa (cf. *Schlussklauseln*, p. 25, n. 45). The situation does not differ radically in the OB texts now being edited by J. J. Finkelstein (oral communication).

[3]) The implication being that the term is of Akkadian origin. (Cf. the last section of this chapter for more detailed argumentation.) Even if the term were considered as Sumerian in origin, the late Sippar usage would still have to be considered

In passing, the following should be noted: the fifth century term *ṭyb lbby* still preserves the clear relationship between payment and satisfaction which was lost in the documents of the OB period. [1]) Fifth century *ṭyb lbby* is closer in function to early OB deeds than to later ones.

The OB Alalakh Complement Apil. The term *libbašu ṭāb* is also found in the conveyances from Alalakh (cf. *AT* * 52:16-17; *AT* *53 rev. 1-2; *AT* *58:10; *AT* *61:12). The regular formula is: *ana šīm gamir išām; apil libbašu ṭāb* "He bought (the property) at full price; he (the seller) is paid off; his heart is satisfied." This formulation is much more explicit than those from Sippar or even from the Diyala region. In the Alalakh conveyances, the legal function of *libbašu ṭāb* is not obscured by an ambiguous association with the perfection clauses *bukannu šūtuq* and *awassu gamrat* as it is in the Sippar deeds (the clauses of perfection are not found in the Alalakh conveyances). Instead, the clear relationship between the payment of the money (*ana šīm gamir išām*) and the resultant satisfaction of the seller's heart (*libbašu ṭāb*) is explicated by the receipt-payment term *apil* "he has received payment; he is paid off." In this context, *libbašu ṭāb* is more than a simple term of receipt (the idea of receipt being expressed by *apil*); it reflects the state of mind which results from receipt, namely, quittance. Even though the clause *apil libbašu ṭāb* is not found in Sippar sale or division documents, similar clauses—*leqi/maḫir/apil libbašu ṭāb* "he has received/accepted (the money)/he is paid off; his heart is satisfied" are regularly found in almost all Sippar deeds of quittance. I therefore tentatively suggest that the original *Sitz im Leben* of *libbašu ṭāb* was the quitclaim and that the term was later incorporated into those sale transaction where the receipt of the price and the quittance therewith played some constitutive role.

Once again, the Akkadian and the Aramaic usages are virtually identical: the Akkadian *apil libbašu ṭāb* "he has received the money and his heart is satisfied" is identical with the Aramaic *ʿl ʿly/k wṭyb lbby/k bgw* "I/you have received the money and my/your heart is satisfied therewith." The overlap of *ṭyb lbby* with *libbašu ṭāb* may be the product of parallel development; however, the concatenated overlap of two terms and their explicatives hardly seems the result of such a coincidence.

---

residual. This judgment is similar to that of Kraus concerning the OB use of the perfection clauses inim.bi al.til and giš.gan.na íb.ta.bal (cf. Kraus, *Nippur und Isin*, p. 106.)

[1]) The relationship between payment and satisfaction is clearly explicated in the Aramaic: "my heart is satisfied with the money you have paid me in that none of the money is outstanding against you on our account." The fact that the use of *ṭyb lbby* is more alive and functional than that of šà.ga.ni al.dùg is merely another reflection of the uneven tempo of cultural development in the Near East.

C. libbašu ṭāb *and the Completeness of Payment*

In the preceding section, the relationship between the notion of satisfaction and the payment of the price has been discussed in some detail. The immediate reason for the satisfaction of the seller's heart is not the tendering of part of the price or a down-payment but the payment of the full price. The early OB conveyances express the idea of completeness by the clauses *kaspam šīm bītišu gamram libbašu ṭūb* "his heart has been satisfied with the complete money—lit. silver—the price of his house" (M 35). Even more explicit is the clause *kaspam gamram šīm bītišunu libbašunu ṭūb* (*R* 8) or *šīm eqlišunu kaspam gamram libbašu ṭūb* (*R* 5).

The Aramaic expresses the idea of complete payment quite clearly: *ṭyb lbbn bgw zy lʾ ʾštʾr ln ʿlyk mn dmyʾ* "our heart is satisfied (with the money you have given us) in that none of the price is outstanding against you on our account" (*BP* 12:6). Although the early OB clauses quoted above are functionally identical with the Aramaic clause, their etymological dissimilarity precludes the possibility of their having served as the models of the Aramaic clause. On the other hand, the Aramaic clause seems to have served as the model for a much later Gaonic clause. The following clause is found in a deed recording the sale of a house, in the Formulary of Hai Gaon: *wʾp lʾ ʾštyyr mn dmy! zbyny! ʾylyn ʿl plny šwm mydʿm bʿlmʾ mšwy prwṭh wlʿylʾ* "and moreover none of this price* at all —from a penny's-worth and up—is outstanding against PN on my account." [1])

The cuneiform background of the Aramaic clause and the Gaonic one derived from it can now be determined on the basis of the rare NA terms recently published by Deller. Deller notes that the term *riāḫu* "to remain" has not appeared in any hitherto published NA legal texts. "Um zu betonen, dass eine Schuld vollständig bezahlt (und nicht nur eine Abschlagungszahlung geleistet) ist, wird häufig die Formel „1 Sekel, 1/2 Sekel ist nicht übrig" gebraucht, z.B. 1 1/2 *GÍN lā* (11) *re-e-ḫe* VAT 16512, 10-11; 1 1/2 *GÍN lā re-ḫe* VAT 8737,7 . . . Dass der Ausdruck 1 (*GÍN*) 1/2 *GÍN* Formel, unserem „Heller und Pfennig" entsprechend, ist, geht u.a. auch daraus hervor, dass er gelegentlich durch *memeni* ersetzt wird: *me-me-ni la re-ḫe* VAT 14451,11 „nichts is übrig." Beide Gebrauchweisen können noch durch Beifügung adverbiell zu zu verstehenden *ina muḫḫi* "darüber hinaus" erweitert werden." [2])

[1]) Asaf, *Formulary*, p. 26, l. 12.

[2]) Deller, *Terminologie*, pp. 41 f. It should be noted that in spite of its brevity, Deller's article has been of the greatest use to me in determining the proximate antecedents of the Aramaic formulary. During the course of this study, I attempted

The equivalence of the Elephantine-Gaonic clause with the NA is almost mathematical: *l' 'št'r/ l' 'štyyr* = *lā rēḫe* "nothing remains"; the Gaonic *myd'm* = NA *memēne*; the Gaonic *šwy prwṭh* "nicht ein Pfennig" = 1 (*GÍN*) 1/2 *GÍN*; *ina muḫḫi* = *l'yl'* "and above it." There can be no doubt that both the Elephantine and the Gaonic clauses were based on proximate NA Assyrian models which in their way attempted to express the same legal concept as the early OB conveyances did by the use of the clause *kaspam gamram šīm bītišu libbašu ṭūb*.

3. The Quittance Use of *libbašu ṭāb* Outside of Conveyance

All earlier investigators of *libbašu ṭāb* have tacitly assumed that the *Sitz im Leben* of the term was the conveyance and the closely related deed of division. Few if any have attempted to define the term on the basis of its wide contextual range, which includes quitclaims, marriage settlements, the *ṭuppi lā ragāmim*,[1]) and deeds of loan. Furthermore, it is quite possible that the original context of the term was not the many-staged sale transaction, where the role of *libbašu ṭāb* is so ambiguous that it was not clearly appreciated, but rather the quitclaim whose sole function was to record the receipt of goods by a right-holder and his quittance therewith. In this context, *libbašu ṭāb* plays the central and constitutive role.

A. libbašu ṭāb in the Quitclaim

The whole deed usually consists of one or two clauses:

aššum kaspi ša A eli B iršû leqi/maḫir/apil; libbašu ṭāb

"Concerning the money which is owed to A by B, A has received (it); his heart is satisfied." The idea of receipt is expressed by the first term—*leqi/maḫir/apil*—and the idea of the concomitant quittance by the second term—*libbašu ṭāb*.

Various kinds of right-holders draw up quitclaims:

1) A depositor on the return of his deposit

---

to convert many of the Aramaic terms and clauses back into the "original" cuneiform state. Many of these "conversions" were verified only by the new material published by Deller. I am therefore convinced that the next stage in Aramaic legal research depends on further publications of the Neo-Assyrian material. Furthermore, the fact that the Aramaic formulary is so dependent on the Neo-Assyrian legal tradition should cast new light on the historical significance of the latter tradition. Cf. below, pp. 180 ff.

[1]) Lit. "deed-of-no-contest." For a discussion of this type of document, cf. Lautner, *Streitbeendigung*, pp. 1 ff. The Aramaic *spr mrḥq* filled the same juridic function as the *ṭuppi lā ragāmim* (cf. Lautner, *Streitbeendigung*, p. 2, n. 5; p. 37, n. 116 and p. 41, n. 3).

M 28 = Schorr, *Urkunden* 235. (Warka; Ḫammurabi)

(1) *aš-šum kaspim* (2) *ša Zi-ik-rum* (3) *ù Ṣa-bi-tum* (4) *a-na Ṣi-lí-Ištar* (5) *a-na ma-uṣ!-ṣa-ar-tim* (6) *id-di-i-nu* (7) *li-e-qú-ú* (8) *li-ib-ba-šu-nu ṭa-a-ab*

"Concerning the money which Zikrum and Ṣabitum intrusted with Ṣilli-Ištar; (7) they have received (it); (8-9) their heart is satisfied."

2) An owner of a garden upon the receipt of his rent:

M 29

(1) 15 *šiqil kaspam* (2) *ša er-bu kirî* . . . (5) *li-e-qú* (6) *li-ib-ba-šu* (7) *ṭa-ab*

(1) "15 shekels of silver (2) of the rent of a garden . . . (5) he has received; (6) his heart (7) is satisfied."

3) A nursemaid upon the receipt of her wages:

CT IV 13b = Schorr, *Urkunden* 242 (Sippar; undated)

(5) . . . *epram* (6) *piššatam lubuštam ma-aḫ-ra-at li-ib-ba-ša ṭāb[ab]*

(5) ". . . Rations (6), oil (and) clothes she has received; her heart is satisfied."

Cf. also *VS* VII 37 = Schorr, *Urkunden* 241; *TD* 197:8-9 = Schorr, *Urkunden* 243

4) The most common quitclaim is that written up by an heir upon the receipt of his inheritance share:

M 27 = Schorr, *Urkunden* 245 (Sippar; Ḫammurabi)

(1) 10 *šiqil kaspam* (2) *ša i-na ku-nu-uk* (3) *zi-i-it-ti-šu* (4) *a-na Ṣi-lí-[d]Šamaš* (5) *ša-ak-nu* (6) *itti Ṣi-lí-Ištar* (7) *ù A-wi-il-ì-lí aḫīšu* (8) *[I]Ṣi-lí-[d]Šamaš* (9) *il-te-qí* (10) *li-ib-ba-šu* (11) *ṭa-a-ab* (12) *ú-ul i-ta-a-ar* (13) *ú-ul i-gi-ir-ri*

(1) "Ten shekels of silver (2-5) which were set aside/allotted for Ṣilli-Šamaš in his division tablet, (6-8) Ṣilli-Šamaš (now) received from Ṣilli-Ištar and Awēl-ili, his brother. (10) His heart (11) is satisfied. (12) He will not return; (13) He will not contest."

Cf. also *KU* IV 1045 = Schorr, *Urkunden* 230 (Sippar); cf. also Harris, *Khafajah*, No. 25 (a quitclaim).

B. *The Incorporation of the Quitclaim into Other* Entgeltliche *Transactions*

The relinquishment of rights over persons or property in return for a satisfactory consideration is an essential element in many different types of transactions: (a) the seller relinquishes his rights to the property in return for the sale price; (b) the *aḫḫē lā zīzūte*—brothers who hold ancestral property in common—relinquish their rights to a percent of all the undivided property in return for a concrete share; [1]) (c) the claimant in a litigation will often settle out of court and desist from his suit in return for some consideration tendered by the defendant; (d) the father of the bride relinquishes his *patria potestas* over his daughter in return for the *mohar/terḫatu*. [2])

In each of these cases, the idea of quittance upon the receipt of a consideration would naturally be expressed by the term *libbašu ṭāb*—at least during the OB period. "His heart is satisfied" can apply with the same legal cogency to the father of the bride, the brother who has received his share, the litigant who has settled out of court as it can to the seller who is quitted of the sale price. In each case, the declaration of satisfaction reflects a relinquishment of claims.

A separate quitclaim may have originally been drawn up to supplement each of these *entgeltliche* transactions. However, even if such independent quitclaims did actually exist, scribes began to incorporate them or their central term—*libbaṣu ṭāb*—into the very body of the deed. Thus, sale, marriage, division, and litigation documents became composite instruments; each one records some specific legal situation plus the receipt of a consideration. This thesis is supported by Kraus' study of the Old Babylonian conveyances from Isin and Larsa. According to Kraus, the Ur III sale transaction consisted of two separate phases, each with its own legal instrument: (a) a deed of sale: the agreement to sell and the stipulation of the price; (b) the quitclaim: the payment of the price; the quittance of the seller; the perfection of the transaction by the clauses inim.bi al.til "its transaction is completed"; the passing of the *bukannu*. When, at a later period, both phases of the transaction took place at the same time, quitclaim elements were incorporated directly into the deed of sale: (a) the record of payment was placed between the amount of the price and the verb in.ši.šám "he bought from him"; the quittance elements inim.bi al.til and the passing of the *bukannu* were placed at the end of the transaction, before the *Schlussklauseln*. [3])

The thesis that *libbašu ṭāb* originated in an independent quitclaim which was later incorporated into the structure of the conveyance—and other *entgeltliche* instruments as well—parallels Kraus' theory concerning the quitclaim origins of the Sippar clauses of perfection. It is no coincidence, therefore, that the three quittance clauses—inim.bi al.til, giš.gan.na íb.ta.bal, and *libbašu ṭāb*—terms which may have

[1]) Cf. Koschaker, *NKRA*, pp. 40 ff.
[2]) Cf. the discussion above, Chapter III, pp. 53 ff.
[3]) Cf. Kraus, *Nippur und Isin*, pp. 104 ff.

been derived from different legal traditions, [1]) were listed together at the end of the Sippar conveyance.

Furthermore, the original juridical functions of these three terms seem to have been attenuated by the (end of) the OB period; the terms are preserved as stereotypic fossils of legal processes which, at some earlier date, must have played constitutive roles within the structure of the archaic conveyance. This does not mean to say that the process of attenuation was universal [2]) or that it took place at the same rate in all areas and in all transactions. [3]) *Libbašu ṭāb* still preserves its juridical significance in deeds where it is the only or the central term.

1) *Conveyance.* The most cogent proof that the conveyance use of *libbašu ṭāb* is related to—and probably derived from—the independent quitclaim can be adduced from the OB Alalakh use of the term. The Alalakh conveyance formula is: the property A *ana* x *šiqil kaspam ana šīm gamir išām* "A bought the property at full price at x shekels of silver"; *apil libbašu ṭāb* "he (the seller) is paid; his heart is satisfied." In this context, there can be no doubt as to the receipt-quittance function of the term: (a) since the Sumerian perfection clauses in inim.bi al.til and giš.gan.na íb.ta.bal are not used in the Alalakh conveyance, the role of *libbašu ṭāb* is not obscured by its association with clauses whose juridical functions had already been lost; (b) placed after the complement *apil* "paid," *libbašu ṭāb* plays a clearly defined role in the transaction as a term of receipt and quittance.

Significantly, the original juridical function of the term is more vividly reflected in this provincial context—and for that matter in the widely separated [4]) but equally provincial contexts of the Diyala deeds—than in the deeds of central Mesopotamia (Sippar). Moreover, the virtual identity of the Alalakh conveyance formula *apil libbašu ṭāb* with the Sippar quitclaim clause *apil/leqi/maḫir* + *libbašu ṭāb* seems to confirm the suggestion that *libbašu ṭāb* originated in the legal *Sitz im Leben* of the quitclaim.*

2) *Division.* The regular clause in Sippar division documents is *zīzū*

[1]) The two perfection clauses inim.bi al.til and giš.gan íb.ta.bal are of Sumerian origin (*ibid.*, p. 106). The clause of satisfaction *may* be of Akkadian origin.

[2]) The original meaning of the term is still preserved in the OB Alalakh clause *apil libbašu ṭāb* "he is paid; his heart is satisfied" and in the Diyala *libbam uṭīb* "he satisfied the heart."

[3]) Although šà.ga.ni al.dùg may be stereotypic and non-evocative in Sippar conveyances and deeds of division, it is still quite alive and functional in Sippar quitclaims, marriage documents, and in the *ṭuppi lā ragāmim*.

[4]) The preservation of archaic forms in widely separated areas is a well-known linguistic phenomenon. Cf. Bloomfield, *Language*, Chapter XIX: "Dialect Geography."

gamrū libbašunu ṭāb "they have divided, they are finished, their hearts are satisfied." According to Klíma, *libbašunu ṭāb* indicates the consent and agreement of the heirs to the completed division. However, in the light of the preceding discussion, it is clear that in this context, as in conveyance, *libbašu ṭāb* is not a term of volition but a term of receipt-quittance. *Libbašu ṭāb* does not mean "he (the heir) agrees to the completed transaction" but "he is satisfied with the individual share he has received; he is satisfied with that which he has received and, in the future, will not raise claims against his brothers for added property; he is quit." Unfortunately, the immediate antecedent of *libbašu ṭāb* is as ambiguous in the division documents as it is in most Sippar conveyances. In the clause *zīzū gamrū libbašunu ṭāb,* the finished transaction (cf. conveyance *awassu gamrat libbašu ṭāb*) seems to be the direct antecedent. Fortunately, this ambiguous clause is explicated by a more archaic OB text (*M* 101):

(8) *zi-zu ga-mi-ir* (9) *zi-ta-šu ga-mi-ir* (10) «*li-ba*» *li-ib-ba-šu ṭa-ab* (8) "He has divided; he is finished; (9) with his complete share (10) his heart is satisfied."

In this context, the immediate reason for the satisfaction is spelled out: the receipt of a full inheritance share. Because it is full, the heart of the heirs is satisfied and, therefore, he will never raise claims against the other heirs for the completion of the division. The complement *zittašu gamir* (*libbašu ṭāb*) in this archaic division deed parallels the complement *ana kaspam gamram šīm bītišu* (*libbašu ṭūb*) found in the archaic Sippar conveyances.

3) *The* ṭuppi lā ragāmim. In Mesopotamia, litigations were brought to an end either by a court case or, more frequently, by settlements out of court. [1]) In either case, the plaintiff's relinquishment of all claims against the defendant was formalized by the drawing up of a *ṭuppi lā ragāmim* "a deed of no contest." If the immediate motivation for the plaintiff's relinquishment was a settlement tendered by the defendant, the receipt of this settlement and the plaintiff's quittance therewith was usually recorded in the body of the *ṭuppi lā ragāmim*; the term of receipt-quittance was *libbašu ṭāb*/*libbašu uṭīb.**

VS VII 16 = Schorr, *Urkunden* 279 (Dilbat; Samsuiluna)

[1]) Such settlements were preferred both in cuneiform and Talmudic law; cf. Walther, *Gerichtswesen*, pp. 231 ff. For the Talmudic law, cf. *TB*, *Sanhedrin* 6b and *Tosephta San.* 1.3. Settlements out of court were probably preferred because they avoided the necessity of taking the oath.

A parcel of land was contested. After remeasuring, the land was found to be larger than stipulated in the conveyance. The case was settled by the payment of a sum of money for the extra land.

(31) *ša wa-tar-ti bīti-šu a-pí-il libbašu ṭābab*

(31) "Concerning the excess (land) of his plot, he is paid off. His heart is satisfied."

VS III 101 = Schorr, *Urkunden* 306 (Sippar; Ḫammurabi)

(1) *IMa-ta-ni* (2) *a-na Ib-ni-dŠamaš* (3) *ir-gu-um!-ma i-di-nu-šu-nu-ti-ma* (4) *ru-gu-ma-ni-ša ma-aḫ-ra-at*

(1) "Mattani raised claims against Ibni-Šamaš. (3-4) After (the judges) judged them; she received her claims; her heart is satisfied."

AO 1765 = Schorr, *Urkunden* 308 (Sippar; Samsuiluna)

This deed concerns a litigation over unpaid rent. The parties come to an agreement and part of the rent is paid.

(19) *ma-ḫi-ir li-ib-ba-šu ṭābab* "He has received the rent (and) his heart is satisfied."

Cf. also *CT* VIII 9a = Schorr, *Urkunden* 295.

Once again the uses of the Akkadian *libbašu ṭāb* and the Aramaic *ṭyb lbby* overlap: both are key terms in deed of no-contest (Akkadian *ṭuppi lā ragāmim* = Aramaic *spr mrḥq*); in both cases, the terms of satisfaction record the plaintiff's receipt from the seller of some performance-payment which induces him to desist from his suit. The prevalence of the active form *hwṭbt lbby b* "you have satisfied my heart with" in the Aramaic deed of no-contest was noted above. A similar situation obtains in the Akkadian material: even though the active *libbašu uṭīb* is almost never found in Sippar conveyances, there are several cases of its use in Sippar deeds of no-contest.

CT VI 33b = Schorr, *Urkunden* 304 (Sippar; Apil-Sin)

[Two brothers raise claims against Šāt-Aya concerning the price of a house they had sold to her which was still outstanding. The judges obligated her to clear herself by an oath of purgation. At the last moment, however, the parties come to an amicable solution of their differences (*imtagrū* "they came to an agreement [out of court]," 1. 13) and:]

(14) *ù libbi(?) dMarduk-mu-ba-li-iṭ* (15) *ù dSin-i-din-nam aḫīšu* (16) *Ša-at-dAya* (15) *ú-ṭì-i-ib*

(14) "And Šāt-Aya satisfied the heart of Marduk-muballiṭ and Sin-iddinam his brother."

Unfortunately, the method of satisfaction was not specified. The usual method in the Aramaic *spr mrḥq* was an oath: *hwṭbt lbby bmwm'h zy 'bdt ly* "you have satisfied my heart with the oath you have taken on my account" (*AP* 6:11; *AP* 14:5) or by a monetary settlement: *hwṭbtm lbbn b'lk nksy' wṭyb lbbn bgw* "you have satisfied our heart with these goods and our heart is satisfied therewith (*AP* 20:8)."

Since this deed was drawn up as a result of a settlement out of court, it stands to reason that the method of satisfaction was the payment of a consideration: parties usually settled out of court (*imtagrū* "they came to an agreement") precisely in order to avoid the need to take the oath. This assumption seems to be confirmed by another litigation—*CT* VIII 17a = Schorr, *Urkunden* 303—concerning an outstanding sale price. Here too the defendant satisfies the plaintiff's heart; here, however, the mode of satisfaction is clearly stated: (7) *kaspam*^{am} *li-ba-šu uṭ-ṭe-*[*ib*] "he (the defendant) satisfied the heart (of the plaintiff) with money."

The active form: *libbi* Plaintiff Defendant *uṭīb*—is also found in a Susa litigation concerning inheritance property—*MDP* XXIII 330. The plaintiff, Ibbi-Ninšubur, raises a claim against the children of Tan-Uli (the father of Puzur-maṣat and the ancestor of Ibbi-Ninšubur ?). The litigation is brought to an end after: (15) *ap-lu-ú ša Puzur-ma-ṣa-at* (16) *li-ba-šu ú-ṭe*$_4$*-bu* "The heirs of Puzur-maṣat satisfied his heart (i.e., of the plaintiffs)." The method of satisfaction is not specified. Conceivably, however, it was a money settlement. As far as I can tell, the satisfaction which motivated the plaintiff in an OB litigation to relinquish his claims was always some concrete monetary settlement; in this respect the Akkadian usage differs from the Aramaic where the plaintiff relinquished claims after having been satisfied by the oath of purgation declared by the defendant at the order of the court. However, even though the Egyptian and Aramaic modes of satisfaction may sometimes differ, the legal function of the active Akkadian form *libbašu uṭīb*, like its Aramaic analogue *hwṭbt lbby*, is the same; both terms mean: to induce the litigant to relinquish his claims by tendering him some satisfactory consideration or performance; to pay him off; to make him quit his claim by payment.

4) *Loan*. The active form of the expression is also found in a deed of loan (*Riftin* 6:5-7—Larsa, Rim-Sîn): *waraḫ simānim* (6) *kaspam li-ib-ba-šu* (7) *ú-ṭa-ab-bu* "in the month of Simanu, (7) they (the debtors) shall satisfy (6) his (the creditor's)heart (6) with the money (owed)." In this context, *libbašu uṭīb* means: "he (the debtor) satisfied his heart (i.e., the creditor's) with the full amount of money owed; he made the creditor quit by tendering him full payment." In a later section, the equivalence of the OB *libbašu uṭīb* with the MB *rašâ uzakki* "he satisfied/

paid off the creditor" will be discussed in greater detail. (For more examples of this usage, see *HG* 873 = *P* 65; *HG* 895 = *P* 16; *HG* 908 = *P* 25; *HG* 909 = *P* 27; *HG* 917 = *P* 20. All these documents stem from Nippur and were written either during the reign of Ḫammurabi or Samsuiluna).

5) *A Common Wall.* [1]) The same expression is also used in deeds that record the building of a common dividing well between two neighbors, in which one neighbor builds the wall and lays out the original expenses. It seems that under certain circumstances, in order for the second neighbor to use the newly erected wall, he had to pay some consideration to the first neighbor who has built the wall and laid out its expenses.

TD 185 = Schorr, *Urkunden* 201 (Sippar; undated)

(4) *i-ga-ar bi-ri-tim* (5) *Warad-ᵈŠamaš i-pu-uš-ma* (6) *ma-na-ḫa-at i-ga-ri-im* (7) *Be-li-sú-nu li-ib-ba-šu* (8) *uṭ-ṭi!-ib*

(4) "After Warad-Šamaš had built a common wall, (6-8) Bēlissunu satisfied his heart (Warad-Šamaš's) with the expenses of the wall."

The same expression is found in a Sumerian formulation in a deed from Nippur, *HG* 805 = Schorr, *Urkunden* 199 (Ḫammurabi)

6) *Marriage.* In several OB marriage contracts, the parents or the relatives of the bride receive the bride-price from the groom in a manner which is similar to the receipt of the sale price by the seller and his quittance therewith.

a) *CT* VIII 7b = Schorr, *Urkunden* 3 (Sippar; Ammiṣaduqa)

(9) 4 *šiqil kaspam tir-ḫa-at* (10) *ᶠEl-me-šum mārat Am-mi-ya* (11) *Šu-mu-um-li-ib-ši mār Am-mi-ya* (12) *ú Ki-ṣi-ir-tum aḫassu ma-aḫ-ru*

(11-12) "Šumum-libši, the son of Ammiya, and Kiṣirtum his sister, received (9) 4 shekels of silver as the bride-price (10) of Elmēšum, the daughter of Ammiya."

b) Chiera, *UM* VIII², p. 127: (*CBS* 1404; Ammiṣaduqa)

(14) 5 *šeqel kasap te-ir-ḫa-as-sà* (15) *i-na qa-ti Zi-me-ir- ᵈŠamaš* (16) *ᴵA-ta-na-aḫ-ì-lí a-bu-šá ma-ḫi-ir* (17) *li-ib-ba-šú ṭa-ab*

---

[1]) The legal structure of this type of transaction is discussed in some detail by Lautner, *Rechtsverhältnisse*, pp. 76-95. In passing, it should be noted that, in all probability, *AP* 5 is an Aramaic adaptation of this common Near Eastern legal tradition. The relationship between the two types of deeds deserves a more extensive discussion. Cf. above, p. 26, end of note 1.

(16) "Ātanaḫ-ili, her father (i.e., the father of the bride) received (14) 5 shekels of silver as her bride-price (15) from the hand of Zimir-Šamaš (the groom); (17) his heart is satisfied."

One of the distinctive features of the Aramaic marriage contracts is that these deeds contain two receipt-lists: (a) the receipt of the bride-price by the father of the bride; (b) the receipt of the wife's dowry by the husband. The key term in both receipts is *ṭyb lbby/k* "my/your heart is satisfied." In the few marriage documents published, receipt clauses of either kind are quite rare: in the OB marriage deeds cited on p. 84 of the present study, a few bride-price receipt clauses with the term *libbašu ṭāb* have been cited: a Neo-Assyrian marriage document (*ND* 2307 = Parker, "The Nimrud Tablets, 1952—Business Documents," *Iraq*, 16 (1954), p. 37) contains a list of the wife's dowry but no record of the bride-price. However, the only document I know of that records both the receipt of the bride-price and that of the dowry, and uses *libbašu ṭāb* at least in the first case, is *CBS* 1404 = Chiera, *UM* VIII². The parallel between the OB and Aramaic usages is unmistakable and is certainly more than a historical coincidence.

c) *M* 90 = Schorr, *Urkunden* 2 (Sippar; Samsuiluna)

(7) [*x*] *šeqel kaspam kasap* (8) [*te*]-*ir-ḫa-sà* (9) *u-la-nu-ma ma-aḫ-ra-at* (10) [*libb*]*aša ṭāb*

(9) "She has already(?) received (7) [x] shekels of silver, the money of (8) her (daughter's) bride-price. (10) Her heart is satisfied."

d) *W* 72 = *HG* 1418 (Samsuiluna)

(7) 6 *šiqil kasap te-ir-ḫa-sà* (8) *Ša-mu-uḫ-tum mārat Ḫa-ya-am-di-du-um* (9) [*m*]*a-aḫ-ra-a*[*t*] (10) *li-qí-a-at li!-ib!-ba-ša* (11) *ṭa-ab.*

(8) "Šamuḫtum daughter of Ḫayamdidum (9) has received and taken (7) 6 shekels of silver as her (daughter's) bride-price; (10) her heart (i.e., the guardian's) is (11) satisfied."

The formal equivalence between the receipt of the bride-price in these marriage contracts and the receipt of the sale price in conveyances is unmistakable: [1]) in both transactions, the receipt of some constitutive payment, whether it be sale price or bride-price, is expressed by the term *libbašu ṭāb*. It was pointed out before that the same structural parallelism between the receipt clauses of sale and marriage is also reflected in the Aramaic documents: *ṭyb lbby/k* records the acceptance

[1]) The structural similarity between sale and marriage was pointed out by Koschaker, *Eheschliessung*, pp. 210 ff.

of the *mohar* as well as the sale price. In all probability, the father relinquished his *patria potestas* over his daughter upon the receipt of a satisfactory consideration as the seller relinquished his ownership over his property in return for a satisfactory consideration. [1] However, the structural parallelism between the two transactions does not necessarily indicate that a daughter was sold like a piece of property; [2] as Cuq [3] and other scholars have pointed out, marriages could take place without the payment of a *terḫatu*; even when a *terḫatu* was paid, its value was too little to be considered the actual "price" of the bride.

4. *libbašu ṭāb* in Borrowed Legal Forms

In all of the texts examined so far, *libbašu ṭāb* records the reaction of a former right-holder—seller, claimant, father of the bride, heir—who has relinquished some right in return for a payment of a necessary performance. This is also the regular use of *ṭyb lbby*, a term which was used in almost all the same contexts as its Akkadian analogue. However, it was noted above that the Aramaic *ṭyb lbby* has a second legal function reflected in the deed of consignment (*AP* 2) and in the dowry-receipt clause (*AP* 15). In these two contexts, *ṭyb lbby* still records a reaction to the receipt of goods. However, the receivers are not right-holders and, therefore, they do not relinquish any right upon the receipt of the goods since they have no rights to relinquish. Their declaration of satisfaction does not express the relinquishment of rights upon the receipt of an *Entgelt* but rather an acknowledgment that they are thereby obligated to perform a given service. [4]

The same meaning of the term *ṭyb lbby* is reflected in *AP* 15. The husband declares that he has received his wife's dowry and that his heart is satisfied therewith. In this case, the husband does not relinquish any rights upon declaring that his heart is satisfied with the goods: on the contrary, in case of divorce, he is obligated to return all of his wife's dowry "be it straw or string." He is therefore considered as the guardian of his wife's property and is responsible for its complete return. His declaration of satisfaction does not record the relinquishment of a right but the creation of an obligation.

---

1) Cf. the fuller discussion above, Chapter III, p. 54.

2) So also Koschaker, *Eheschliessung*, p. 235; also above, p. 55

3) Cf. Cuq, *Études*, pp. 30 ff.; also Van Praag, *Droit matrimonial*, Chapter VI: "Les dons nuptiaux," pp. 128 ff. Concerning the independent social status of women in some areas of cuneiform culture, cf. L. Matouš, "Quelques remarques sur les récentes publications de textes cunéiformes économiques et juridiques," *ArOr*, 27 (1959), p. 441.

4) Cf. below, pp. 56 ff.; also pp. 163 ff.

In the light of the close functional and linguistic correspondence between the regular meanings of the Akkadian and the Aramaic terms, it is not altogether unlikely that the atypical obligatory meaning of the Aramaic term may have its Akkadian analogue. Is this inference made from the study of the Aramaic deeds confirmed by actual cuneiform usage; does the Akkadian *libbašu ṭāb* ever express the creation of an obligation rather than the relinquishment of a right? A usage, similar but not identical with the Aramaic is reflected in *CH* 264:

šum-ma [siba] *ša* áb.gud.[ḫ̮á] *ù lu* ganám.[udu.ḫ̮á] *a-na ri-*[*im*] *in-na-*[*ad*]*-nu-šum* id—*šu ga-am-ra-tim ma-ḫ̮i-ir li-ib-ba-šu ṭa-ab* áb. gud.ḫ̮á *uṣ-ṣa-aḫ̮-ḫ̮i-ir* ganám.udu.ḫ̮á *uṣ-ṣa-aḫ̮-ḫ̮i-ir ta-li-it-tam um-ta-ṭi a-na* ka *ri-ik-sa-ti-šu ta-li-it-tam ù bi-il-tam i-na-ad-di-in*

"If a herdsman to whom cattle or sheep have been given to tend, having received his full wages and his heart having been satisfied, reduces the cattle (or) reduces the sheep (or) diminishes the offspring, he shall give offspring and products (to their owner) according to the terms of his contract."

The legislator clearly stresses that the wage of the shepherd had been paid in full and that his heart was satisfied therewith. If this clause had not fulfilled some constitutive function within the structure of the transaction, it would not have been added to the paragraph. The implication of the law is that if the wage had not been paid in full and the heart of the shepherd had not been satisfied, the shepherd would not have been liable for negligence and damages—or at least not for their full amount. As long as the master had not fulfilled his part of the bargain with the shepherd, the shepherd was not fully obligated to complete his part. Only when the shepherd has received full payment does the owner have a claim to the services of the shepherd. Until then, the shepherd has a claim to the payment of the owner. This implication was also seen by Driver-Miles:

"The meaning may be that he has been paid in full before the claim against him has been made; but, however this may be, the requirement of full payment of the wages must indicate some matter of importance. It may then be surmised that its object is to protect the shepherd, a poor man, against extortion by a rich owner of cattle. The Laws therefore provide that the shepherd must have been paid his full wage before default on his part be made by his employer." (Driver-Miles, *The Babylonian Laws*, I: *Legal Commentary*, p. 456.)

The Derivation of Obligation from Quittance. The relationship between these two, almost antithetical, uses of the term *libbašu ṭāb* seems somewhat puzzling. However, the relationship between these two functions will be more understandable if it is recalled that *libbašu ṭāb* records not only the relinquishment of property rights in return for a consideration—by a seller or an heir—but also the desisting from a litigation in return for a consideration tendered by a defendant. It is this second nuance of the term which probably engendered the atypical obligatory meaning. The transition from relinquishment of a claim to the creation of an obligation can be conceived in the following manner:

Superficially, the hire transaction seems to create but one claim—that of the hirer on his shepherd's service—and one obligation—that of the shepherd to perform the services due his mater. However, in reality, the transaction creates two sets of interrelated claims and obligations:

a) the obligation of the owner to pay the wages;
b) the obligation of the shepherd to perform the services.

Furthermore, these obligations are not simultaneous: the claim of the owner for the services of the shepherd does not go into effect until the claim of the shepherd for the payment of his wages is cancelled. The term *libbašu ṭāb* by recording the cancellation of the shepherd's claim—for wages, immediately activates the claim of the owner for the complete performance of the shepherd.

In this context, *libbašu ṭāb* still retains its original meaning: it still records the receipt of an *Entgelt* by a right-holder and the concomitant relinquishment of rights and claims. However, since this declaration of quittance triggers an interrelated obligatory transaction, *libbašu ṭāb* also assumes this second function. One could almost say that *libbašu ṭāb* in *CH* 264 carries an obligatory meaning by contextual association rather than in essence.

The Contrast Between the Aramaic and the Akkadian. If the obligatory meaning of the Akkadian *libbašu ṭāb* still clearly preserves its connection with the regular quittance-receipt meaning of the term, this connection, if it ever existed, has been almost completely obliterated in the Aramaic usage. In order to understand the difference between the Aramaic and the Akkadian obligational nuances of the respective terms of satisfaction, *AP* 2 will be reconstructed according to the pattern of *CH* 264:

A hired B to deliver grain.

Two sets of obligations are created:

1) the obligation of the owner to pay the wages in full;

2) the obligation of the agents to deliver the grain in full.

The second obligation only goes into effect after the first obligation has been cancelled. Thus, when the agents declare that their heart had been satisfied with their wages, the claim of the owner for the full performance of his agents is activated.

If this were the situation reflected in the Aramaic deed, the Aramaic and the Akkadian obligational uses would overlap completely. However, this is not quite the situation reflected in *AP* 2. Instead, the following legal transaction takes place:

A hires B to deliver goods.
Two sets of obligations are created:

1) the obligation of the owner not to cheat the agents: he must consign to them exactly the amount they are obligated to deliver according to the stipulations of the bill of lading;

2) the obligation of the agents to deliver the goods exactly as specified in the deed.

The obligation of the agents to deliver the goods in full is activated only after the obligation of the owner to deposit the full amount of goods into the custody of the agents is cancelled. Or, formulated conversely: the owner has a claim against the agents for full delivery only if the agents have no claim that the full amount of goods was never intrusted to them. When they declare that they are satisfied with the amount of grain actually received, they trigger the claim of the owner for full performance. Thus, the term of receipt is in effect a term of obligation. It should be noted that *ṭyb lbby* is no longer a term which records the receipt of an *Entgelt* by a former right-holder and his subsequent relinquishment of rights. In this, the Aramaic openly contrasts with the Akkadian.

The formal parallelism between the use of *libbašu ṭāb* in *CH* 264 and *ṭyb lbby* in *AP* 2 is unmistakable in spite of the substantial differences between them. Furthermore, it is fully justified to consider the Aramaic usage as the natural development of the Akkadian. In certain types of many-staged transactions, the receipt of an *Entgelt* by a former right-holder (usually a hired hand) triggered the claim of the new right-holder (the hirer). The term, however, still preserved its original connections with *Entgeltlichkeit*. Once the term developed this added obligational nuance, it was extended to contexts where the receivers were not right-holders and the sum received was not an *Entgelt*. Such cases of borrowed legal forms are well known from ancient Near Eastern legal history. (Cf. Boyer, *Emplois de fiction*, pp. 73 ff.)

5. The Origins of the Term *libbašu ṭāb*

In the preceding section, an attempt was made to define the term *libbašu ṭāb* on the basis of the various contexts in which the term was employed, and to determine, as far as possible, which of these—sale, division, litigation, receipt, etc.—was its original contextual *Sitz im Leben*. In the present section, the geographic and linguistic distribution of *libbašu ṭāb* will be charted in an attempt to identify the particular legal tradition from which the term was derived and, by doing so, to illuminate further its underlying meaning and legal function.

In many respects, this section is the most theoretical of the whole study. More questions are raised than can be answered, and most of the answers should simply be considered as suggestions of various degrees of probability. To quote Gunkel in his introduction to Genesis: "Schliesslich bitte ich den Leser, die vielen „Vielleicht", „Wohl", „Kann", „Mag" u.s.w. nicht zu übersehen. Ich habe mich bemüht, die verschiedenen Grade der Wahrscheinlichkeit, Möglichkeit, Gewissheit der einzelnen Aufstellungen wohl zu unterscheiden." [1]

A. *Traditions of Cuneiform Law: A Problem of Method*

In spite of its great continuity [2] and inner stability, [3] cuneiform law was not monolithic. Several well-defined subtraditions can be isolated. From which of these traditions was *libbašu ṭāb* derived? Before this question can be answered, however, something must be said about the traditions themselves and about the problems connected with their historical interpretation.

The marked contrast between the Assyrian and the Babylonian legal traditions was pointed out by San Nicolò. [4] Then Oppenheim [5] called attention to an even more significant series of contrasts: between the language, formulary, and legal practice of central and southern Mesopotamian deeds and that of the deeds written in the fringe areas of Susa, Nuzi, and Kültepe. [6] The deeds of the South were written pre-

---

[1] H. Gunkel, *Genesis* (Göttingen, 1901), Vorwort.

[2] San Nicolò, *Beiträge*, p. 253. Cf. above, p. 13, n. 3.

[3] *Ibid.*, p. 256.

[4] *Ibid.*, p. 1.

[5] In a series of studies: *Der Eid*; *Studien*; "Ein Beitrag zum Kassiten-problem," *Analecta Orientalia*, 12 (1935), pp. 266 ff.

[6] Cf. especially *Der Eid*.

dominantly in Sumerian; the deeds of the provinces were written mainly in Akkadian. The deeds of the South were formulated objectively; the deeds of the provinces were often formulated subjectively. [1]) In the South, the incontestability of transactions was insured by the oath; in the provinces, it was insured by fines, physical punishment, or a combination of both. [2])

Oppenheim further noted that this contrast was vertical as well as horizontal: the MB, NB, and NA deeds all have marked affinities with the provincial tradition. [3]) This is even more true of the later Arsacid formulary [4]) and of the Aramaic formulary used at Elephantine.

The historical evaluation of these various traditions is somewhat more complicated than their description. According to Oppenheim, the provincial tradition is a reflection of the indigenous law of the local population that inhabited the highlands that surrounded the Tigris-Euphrates basin. [5]) This interpretation, however, is to be rejected in favor of the theory of Koschaker [6]) and Speiser [7]) that the legal documents of the fringe area preserve archaic legal norms introduced into these areas in the wake of the Sargonic conquests, that were later lost in the South, the land of their birth, due to its progressive Sumerianization. [8])

On the other hand, the formulary and the legal norms of the OB deeds are derived in the main from the Sumerian praxis of the preceding Ur III

---

[1]) Cf. *Der Eid*, pp. 254 ff.

[2]) Cf. *Studien*, pp. 161 ff. Cf. above p. 45, n. 1.

[3]) Cf. *Der Eid*, pp. 261 ff. Cf. above, p. 15, n. 5.

[4]) Cf. Krückmann, *BRVU*, p. 38.

[5]) Cf. *Der Eid*, pp. 242 ff.

[6]) Cf. *Randnotizen*, p. 224 and *Keilschriftrecht*, p. 13 ff.

[7]) Orally. Jacobsen is of the opinion that the provincial formulary preserves archaic norms lost in the core-land. He is not as definite as to their "Akkadian" or "Sumerian" origins.

[8]) This would account for the predominantly Akkadian formulation and the sparse use of Sumerian logograms in the provincial formularies (cf. Koschaker, *Randnotizen*, p. 224). For the primitive character of the few logograms used in these formularies, cf. Koschaker, *NKRA*, p. 16, n. 1.

After Gelb's publications of Old Akkadian conveyances, Koschaker's thesis concerning the Akkadian origins of the provincial documents can be substantiated by actual documentary evidence. First of all, the first person, subjective formulations common in the provincial formularies (cf. Oppenheim, *Der Eid*, pp. 255 ff.) are already found in the Old Akkadian documents (cf. Gelb, *Akkadian Inscriptions*, Nos. 8, 10 and 21). Secondly, seller-oriented conveyances known from Middle Assyrian times are clearly rooted in the Old Akkadian praxis (cf. Gelb, *ibid.*, Nos. 3 and 4). Furthermore, the presale-measuring and publication of property known from MA and Nuzi documents also have clear Old Akkadian antecedents (cf. Gelb, *ibid.*, p. 189, where the legal background of the terms *išdud/imdud* "he measured" is discussed). Attention should be called to Koschaker's discussion in *NKRA*, pp. 27-36 and 67-81.

period. [1]) Thus, the contrast between "core" (or "Old Babylonian") and "provincial" seems to be the natural continuation of an even older contrast between "Akkadian" and "Sumerian" law.

The terms Old Babylonian and provincial are fairly clear: they describe nothing more than the geographical provenience of the formularies or the period in which they were used. On the other hand, the terms Akkadian and Sumerian, whether applied to the general cultural milieu of the ancient Near East, [2]) or more specifically to legal matters, are somewhat ambiguous. Are the distinctions merely formal, i.e., do the terms Sumerian and Akkadian simply describe the language in which the deeds were written, or the given period—Old Akkadian or Ur III—when the deeds were written? Or do the terms describe contrasting ethnic traditions, legal as well as religious?

Recently, the whole problem has been the subject of a symposium [3]) on the part of Edzard, [4]) Falkenstein, [5]) Kraus, [6]) Gelb, [7]) and Kramer. [8]) Since an attempt will be made in the following pages to derive *libbašu ṭāb* from one of these two traditions, the further clarification of the terms "Akkadian" and "Sumerian" is most germane in this context.

The ethnic position was first formulated by Koschaker in his *Rechtsvergleichende Studien*. [9]) He suggested that the Code of Ḫammurabi was, in part, a harmonization of two ethnic-legal traditions, the Sumerian and the Akkadian. Recently, Korošec has studied the specific norms of

---

[1]) Cf., for example, Kraus, *Nippur und Isin*, pp. 98 ff., where the relationship between the Isin-Larsa formulary and the Ur III deeds is traced in great detail, especially the relationship between the various conveyance formularies. It should be remarked in this context that the real understanding of the development of cuneiform law will only be possible after the archaic deeds of the third millennium have been thoroughly studied. Then Old Babylonian law, which seems like the *fons et origo* of all later formularies, will appear in its true light: as the end product of many previous developments and traditions.

[2]) Cf. especially Jacobsen's study on the problem of Sumerian-Akkadian relations, "The Assumed Conflict Between Sumerians and Semites in Early Mesopotamian History," *JAOS*, 59 (1939), pp. 485-495.

[3]) Printed under the general title, "Aspects du contact suméro-akkadien," *Genava*, 8 (1960), pp. 241 ff.

[4]) D. Edzard, "Sumerer und Semiten in der frühen Geschichte Mesopotamiens," *Genava*, 8 (1960), pp. 241-258.

[5]) A. Falkenstein, "Kontakte zwischen Sumerern und Akkadern auf sprachlichem Gebiet," *Genava*, 8 (1960), pp. 301-314.

[6]) F. R. Kraus, "Ein zentrales Problem des altmesopotamischen Rechtes: Was ist der Codex Hammu-rabi," *Genava*, 8 (1960), pp. 283-296.

[7]) I. J. Gelb, "Sumerians and Akkadians in their Ethno-Linguistic Relationship," *Genava*, 8 (1960), pp. 258-271.

[8]) S. N. Kramer, "Sumero-Akkadian Interconnections: Religious Ideas," *Genava*, 8 (1960), pp. 272-283.

[9]) Pp. 1 and *passim*.

CH in the light of Koschaker's thesis, using the newly discovered pre-Ḫammurabi "codes" as his control, in an attempt to define more clearly its various ethnic-legal components. [1])

Furthermore, both Falkenstein and Edzard assume a clear contrast between the legal practice of Akkadians and Sumerians during the third millenium B.C. The contrasts noted by these scholars are in the realm of sale and marriage law. (A) In Sumerian society, land was owned either by the temple-city or by the city-state and could not be alienated by private citizens; in Akkadian society, however, land was owned privately and could be alienated, [2]) even though its sale was often subject to certain restrictions, remnants of an earlier tradition of collective ownership. (B) Akkadian marriage law was based on the payment of the bride-price (*terḫatu*); Sumerian marriage, on the other hand, was based on the delivery of gifts by the groom to the bride (the later Akkadian *nudunnû*). [3])

Some of the arguments adduced in favor of ethnic contrasts in the realm of legal practice are not substantiated by a re-examination of the evidence. Thus, the recent investigations of Matouš, [4]) Gelb, [5]) and Djakonoff [6]) clearly demonstrate that in early Sumerian society, land was often privately owned and freely alienated. The rejection, however, of one example does not necessarily invalidate the whole approach.

Recently, the whole approach has been subjected to a methodological criticism by F. R. Kraus. [7]) According to him, the Akkadians and Sumerians had so completely intermingled—at least by the Ur III period—that it was no longer possible to speak of separate Akkadian and Sumerian legal traditions. Thus, what is commonly called "Sumerian" law, is either the law practiced in the Sumerian city-state, or law written in the Sumerian language. The same holds true for the term "Akkadian" law. [8])

Kraus' analysis certainly applies to much of the cuneiform legal

---

[1]) V. Korošec, "Le Code de Ḫammurabi et les droits antérieurs," *RIDA*, 8 (1961), pp. 11-27.

[2]) A. Falkenstein, "La cité-temple sumérienne," *Cahiers d'Histoire Mondiale*, 1 (1953), pp. 802 f.; Edzard, *ZZB*, pp. 4 f., especially nn. 20, 21 and 39.

[3]) Cf. Edzard, *ibid.*, p. 6. Cf. also Korošec, *RIDA*, 8 (1961), pp. 15-17.

[4]) Matouš, *Ausdrücken*.

[5]) I. J. Gelb, "Social Stratification in the Old Akkadian Period," *Proceedings of the International Congress of Orientalists* (Moscow), 1962, pp. 225 ff.

[6]) "Sale of Land in the Most Ancient Sumer and the Problem of the Sumerian Rural Community [in Russian]," *Vestnik Drevney Istorii*, 1951/2-1954/6, pp. 10-40; reviewed in *RA*, 52 (1958), p. 243.

[7]) *Genava*, 8 (1960), pp. 295 f.

[8]) *Ibid.*, p. 296.

material; much that is called Akkadian or Sumerian is simply common-Mesopotamian. In certain cases, however, the Koschaker-Falkenstein approach may interpret the data more correctly. Originally, the Sumerians and the Akkadians must have had their own unique traditions in law as they did in religion. In the course of their mutual assimilation, these contrasts were often lost. However, there is always the possibility that even as late as the Ur III period, some of these ethnic-legal contrasts were still in force. Thus, although the suggested contrast between Sumerian and Akkadian conveyance law cannot be accepted, the suggested contrast between Sumerian and Akkadian marriage law may yet prove to be correct.

A third possibility should also be considered. It is quite conceivable that the Akkadian and Sumerian legal traditions, which originated with two distinct *ethne*, became dislodged from their original ethnic matrix and were preserved simply as contrasting linguistic conventions, used by all, regardless of ethnic affiliation. Thus, when Sumerians wrote in Akkadian (let us say, during the OA period), they followed Akkadian legal procedure. Conversely, when Akkadians wrote in Sumerian (during the Ur III period), they followed Sumerian legal procedure.

This third possibility was suggested to me by Jacobsen's discussion of the royal inscriptions found at Ešnunna. [1]) He notes that two inscriptions, one in Akkadian and the other in Sumerian, although both describing the same objective set of facts, seem to follow different literary patterns. These patterns probably originated in two different ethnic-cultural milieus, one Akkadian, the other Sumerian. However, by the time of the Ešnunna inscriptions, although the ethnic contrast was no longer in force—kings, whatever their ethnic affiliation, had inscriptions written in both languages—a contrast still existed in the form of two literary or linguistic conventions. An inscription written in the Akkadian language, followed the "Akkadian" pattern, while an inscription written in Sumerian followed the "Sumerian" pattern.

To sum up the discussion concerning the various traditions of cuneiform law: (a) in the first and second millennia, two main traditions of cuneiform law can be identified: 1) the OB "core" tradition and 2) the "provincial" tradition; (b) the proximate source of the first is the praxis of the Ur III period; the linguistic vehicle of these traditions was Sumerian; (c) the proximate source of the provincial tradition was the praxis of the Old Akkadian documents; the linguistic medium of these traditions was the Akkadian language; (d) in the following discussion, when the terms

---

[1]) Jacobsen, *Notes on Eshnunna*, p. 25.

"Akkadian" or "Sumerian" are used, I mean the law of the Old Akkadian period, or that originally written in Akkadian, and the law written in the Ur III or Early Dynastic periods, or that written in Sumerian, respectively; (e) the ultimate origins of these two traditions are complex: they may be 1) common Mesopotamian (*pace* Kraus); 2) contrasting ethnic traditions (*pace* Koschaker-Falkenstein); 3) traditions which originally contrasted ethnically, but which at a later date simply contrast as linguistic conventions used by all.

In the first of the following two sections, an attempt will be made to place *libbašu ṭāb* within one of the two traditions, "core" or "provincial.' In the second section, the older, third millennium roots of the term will be further investigated.

B. *The Geographic and Linguistic Distribution of* libbašu ṭāb

The Geographic Distribution in Sale. Except for two examples from Larsa, [1] I have not been able to find the term *libbašu ṭāb* in the conveyances of central and southern Mesopotamia. On the other hand, it is a regular element in the early OB conveyances of Ḫarmal and Khafajah, and in the slightly later deeds of Ishchali. Outside of the Diyala region, the term is a regular element in the oldest conveyances of the nearby city of Sippar and is still used, although less frequently, in the deeds of the Ḫammurabi and Ammiṣaduqa periods. [2]

The distribution pattern in the provinces is somewhat uneven. Even though *libbašu ṭāb* is found in the OB deeds of Susa, it is never used in conveyances. Nor is it used in the conveyances of Mari. However, it is a regular component of the Alalakh conveyance formulary. In fact, the receipt quittance function of the term is more clearly reflected in these provincial documents than in the deeds of Sippar or the Diyala region. [3] Significantly, the closest parallel to *libbašu ṭāb*—the Old Assyrian term *šabû* "satisfied"—comes from the northern and non-Sumerian area of Kültepe in Asia Minor. [4]

Superficially, at least, the concentration of *libbašu ṭāb* in the conveyances of the North and its almost total absence from the conveyances of the South suggests a northern and Akkadian origin. Of course, there is always the possibility that the usage was of a Sumerian origin, conserv-

---

[1] Cf. Leemans, *SLB* I/2, No. 4 (*LB* 1034), l. 14. This deed records the exchange of a house during the time of Warad-Sîn. Cf. also No. 7 (LB 1037), line 6. This deed records the exchange of a house during the time of Rîm-Sin.

[2] The relevant texts from these sites are quoted above in Chapter IV, b.

[3] Above, p. 80.

[4] Cf. the discussion in the following chapter, pp. 120 ff.

atively preserved in the North with other archaic terms and practices, while it was lost in the South. [1]) However, the presence of its isogloss at non-Sumerian Kültepe does not support the Sumerian derivation. Furthermore, as far as I can tell, the term is not found in the Sumerian deeds of the Ur III or early dynastic periods. [2])

---

[1]) The *bukannu* and inim.bi al.til clauses so common in the OB conveyances of northern Babylonia are remnants of Ur III quitclaims which were no longer used in the South; cf. Kraus, *Nippur und Isin*, p. 106. Cf. also the preservation of the law of the primogeniture—long considered a Sumerian praxis (cf. Klíma, *Untersuchungen*, p. 33, with some reservations)—in the deeds of Mari (cf. Kraus, *Genava*, 8 (1960), p. 296, for texts and discussion).

[2]) Dr. Jacobsen calls my attention to the Reform Text of Urukagina, §§ 13 and 14. For the text and translation of these sections, cf. Deimel, *Grammatik*, pp. 72-73: "Wenn einem šub.lugal (niedrige Soldatenklasse) ein guter Esel geboren wurde, (und) wenn sein Vorsteher ihm sagt: 'ich will (ihn) kaufen'; wenn er ihn kaufen will, soll er (der šub.lugal) ihm sagen: 'mit Geld, welches (mir) im Herzen gut (scheint) [kug $šag_4.ga_2.a$ $šag_5.ga$], zahle mir.' Wenn er ihn nicht verkaufen will (er ihm nicht feil ist), soll der Vorsteher ihm den Zorn licht fühlen lassen."

The same expression—kug $šag_4.ga_2.a$ $šag_5.ga$—is also used in § 14: "Wenn das Haus eines Grossen (Reichen, mächtigen Mannes, lu_2.gu.la) an das Haus eines sub.lugal grenzt und wenn dieser Grosse sagt: 'Ich will (es) kaufen'; wenn er es verkaufen will (es ihm feil ist), soll (der šub.lugal) ihm sagen: 'mit der Gelde, welches mir im Herzen gut (scheint) [kug $šag_4.ga_2.a$ $šag_5.ga$], zahle mir."

According to this interpretation, the term kug $šag_4.ga_2.a$ $šag_5.ga$ is neither one of performance or of quittance-receipt. Therefore, it is not the prototype of the later *libbašu ṭāb/utib*. Deimel's interpretation is followed by most modern interpreters (cf. S. N. Kramer, "Sumerian Historiography," *IEJ*, 3 [1953], p. 231, where the expression is rendered, "pay me as much as I think fair"). Cf. also M. Lambert, "Les 'réformes' d'Urukagina," *RA*, 50 (1956), p. 181, where the term is translated: "Pèse-moi un argent qui fasse réjouir mon coeur"; cf. also Sollberger, *Le système verbal*, p. 169: "En argent agréable à mon coeur, paye-moi!" The only interpretation I am aware of that differs from this reading is that of Ferris J. Stephens ("Notes on Some Economic Texts of the Time of Urukagina," *RA* 49 [1955], p. 132). According to him, the overseer rather than the šub.lugal is the subject of the sentence: "pay . . . me." Furthermore, the overseer is conceived as a type of profiteer who buys up the debts of the poor—among them those of the šub.lugal—from the government and then seizes the choice property of his debtors as "satisfaction" for the money owed. The overseer says to the šub.lugal: "Pay me the silver to settle my account [kug $šag_4.ga_2.a$ $šag_5.ga$] (so Stephens)." Stephens then compares the Sumerian expression with the OB *libbašu ṭāb*. The later expression is correctly interpreted as one which indicates that an account has been settled.

If Stephens is correct in his interpretation, the OB *libbašu ṭāb* has a good Sumerian prototype. However, his interpretation of the syntax of the sentence and its legal Sitz im Leben seems a bit forced. The natural interpretation seems to be that of Deimel, Kramer, and M. Lambert: the šub.lugal is the subject of the sentence "pay me . . ." and the term "money that makes my heart glad" means something like a "just price." Thus, the Sumerian term expresses volition and consent rather than receipt-quittance. It is thus related to the OB *ša elišu ṭāb* "which seems good to him" rather than to *libbašu ṭāb*. Cf. Chapter IV, 5 for a discussion of this contrast of homogeneous terms.

Distribution in Other Contexts. It is only in the deeds of Sippar that the rich contextual range of *libbašu ṭāb*—sale, division, quitclaim, litigation, and marriage—is fully represented. The deeds of the Diyala region, which otherwise preserve so many original features of the term, reflect only the conveyance use of *libbašu ṭāb*. Since only a limited number of legal genres are represented in the Sin Archive of Khafajah and in the Ḫarmal deeds published by Simmons, the lacuna in the use of *libbašu ṭāb* may be due simply to the accidents of excavation.

The term is found sporadically in the Old Babylonian deeds of Susa:* once in marriage, [1]) once in receipt, [2]) and once in litigation. [3]) *Libbašu ṭāb* is also found in one Mari deed of division. [4]) Except for the Alalakh conveyances uses, these are the only examples of *libbašu ṭāb* known to me from the deeds of the provinces.

Among the thousands of Old Babylonian deeds of central and southern Mesopotamia, I have only been able to locate a handful of texts in which *libbašu ṭāb* was used. Even though some examples have no doubt

---

[1]) *MDP* 24 383: 8. The meaning of the term *libbašu ṭāb* in this context is not clear because of the poor condition of the tablet. The deed is cited by the editor as follows: (1) [Id]*Šušinak-mu*[!]*-ba-li-iṭ* (2) *ù I-lí-ša-ḫi-in-ga-al* (3) *i-na ti-iḫ zu-uk-ki-e ša Ta-ta* (4) *ù Te-im-ti-a-gu-un in-na-aḫ-zu* (5) *ù ma* (?) [. . .] *a-na* [d]*Šušinak-mu*!*-ba-li-iṭ* (6) . . . [I]*I-lí-ša-ḫi-in-ga-al* (7) *aš-ša-as-sù iš-ku-nu-šu* (8) [. . .] *li-ib-ba-šu ṭà-ab.* Scheil offers the following translation: "Šušinak mubaliṭ et Iliša ḫingal, auprès de la chapelle de Tata et Temti-agun, se sont épousés, (5) et . . . à Šušinak mubaliṭ (les magistrats) ont constitué Iliša ḫingal pour femme . . ., son coeur est satisfait." The text does not seem to mention any *terḫatu* (cf. Van Praag, *Droit matrimonial*, pp. 85 and 140) whose receipt would be recorded by *libbašu ṭāb* as in the OB marriage contracts from Sippar. If the subject of *libbašu ṭāb* in this text is the husband, this would be the only case known to me where *libbašu ṭāb* does not record the receipt of an *Entgelt* by a former right-holder. Scheil's interpretation would seem to support the volitional interpretation of the term. However, it is also possible to interpret this deed in the light of the established Sippar usage. In the Sippar documents, *libbašu ṭāb* records the receipt of the *terḫatu* by the father of the bride. If the subject of the verb *iškunūšu* "they made her (his wife)" is taken to be the parents of the bride (following Van Praag, *ibid.*, p. 85), it is quite possible that the subject of *libbašu ṭāb* is the father of the bride who has just received the *terḫatu*.

This interpretation, however, is open to certain objections. First of all, the space in line eight is not large enough for the suggested reconstruction. Furthermore, if the parents of the bride were the subject of the verb *iškunūšu*, the plural *libbašunu ṭāb* instead of the singular *libbašu ṭāb* would be expected. Finally, the text should be interpreted, as far as possible, from its own structural logic and not forced into patterns which were typical of Sippar but which may have been foreign to Susa. Unfortunately, because of the lacunae in the text, the exact function of *libbašu ṭāb* in this context cannot be adequately defined.

[2]) *MDP* XXIII 241 : 8'. The word *ṭāb* is reconstructed; *libbašu*, however, is spelled out.

[3]) *MDP* XXIV 330 : 16.

[4]) Boyer, *ARM* VIII, No. 84 : 10.

escaped me, [1]) the general distribution pattern is clear: *libbašu ṭāb* is used so rarely that it cannot be considered as a term of constitutive significance; at best, it is a fossilized remnant of an older usage, Akkadian or Sumerian. Yet it is significant to note—if one can judge from less than twenty examples—that when the term does appear in the deeds of the South, it is usually in nonconveyance contexts. In these contexts—payment of a debt, quitclaim, and litigation—the payment-receipt functions of the term (often formulated in the active voice) are still alive and clearly felt. The distribution pattern of the term *libbašu ṭāb* in the deeds of central and southern Mesopotamia is as follows:

Kiš once in the receipt of inheritance property (Akkadian). [2])

Nippur several times in deeds of loan (A); [3]) once in a deed concerning a dividing-wall (Sumerian). [4])

Larsa twice in sale (A and S); [5]) sporadically in division (S); [6]) several

---

[1]) I have not gone over every Old Babylonian deed published; to do so would delay the completion of this work unnecessarily. I think I have checked a sufficient number of texts to establish a general pattern. There can be no doubt as to the distribution pattern of the term *libbašu ṭāb* in the deeds published before 1922/23, the years in which the last volume of *HG* and San Nicolò's *Schlussklauseln* were published. Recent publications of deeds from Ur, Nippur, and Larsa, such as Figulla-Martin, *UET* 5; Alexander, *BIN* 7; *ARN*; Faust, *YBT* 8; the *SLB* publications of Leemans—all seem to confirm the distribution patterns established on the basis of the early publications. The Figulla-Martin Ur texts have been carefully studied by Kraus in his article, "Neue Rechtsurkunden der altbabylonischen Zeit," *WO*, 2 (1955), pp. 120-136. The same scholar has also subjected the Nippur texts to a thorough examination, with special emphasis on the various schemata and formulae used, in his book, *Nippur und Isin*. Fortunately, the Larsa material edited by Leemans was not merely presented in the cuneiform originals, but was translated and carefully annotated. Citations of parallel passages are usually complete. Furthermore, the Larsa material has also been studied by Matouš in a series of important articles: L. Matouš, "Some Remarks to the Economical Sources from Larsa (In Margine of Two Publications by W. F. Leemans)," *ArOr*, 23 (1955), pp. 465 ff.; "Zur Chronologie der Geschichte von Larsa bis zum Einfall der Elamiter," *ibid.*, 20 (1952), pp. 288 ff.; Matouš, *Partage*. Thus, even though I have not personally gone over each of the newly published texts, the formulary of these deeds has been studied either by Kraus, Matouš, or Leemans, who have carefully noted the peculiarities of the local formularies. Therefore, the possibility that a significant number of examples of *libbašu ṭāb* has escaped identification does not seem very great.

[2]) *HG* 1434=*PSBA* 33 Pl. 28 (Edin. 09-405-28; Ṣabium).

[3]) *HG* 873=P 65; Nippur, Samsuiluna. *HG* 895=*P* 16; Ḫammurabi. *HG* 908=*P* 25; Samsuiluna. *HG* 909=*P* 27; Samsuiluna. *HG* 917=*P* 20; Samsuiluna.

[4]) Cf. Schorr, *Urkunden* 199=P 14; Ḫammurabi, year 38. Is it possible that the use of this term in the deeds of Nippur reflects a northern influence? All of the Nippur examples of the term date from a time somewhere after Ḫammurabi's conquest of Mesopotamia.

[5]) Both examples have been cited above p. 95, n. 1.

[6]) Cf. the examples cited by Matouš, *Partage*, p. 155.

times in receipts (A); [1]) several times in the payment of loans (A); [2]) once in a votive tablet (S). [3])

Ur once in a litigation (A). [4])

The Linguistic Distribution. Both the Sumerian šà.ga.ni al.dùg and the Akkadian *libbašu ṭāb* are used. Was the term originally Sumerian and later translated into Akkadian, or was it originally Akkadian, later translated into Sumerian? Or was the term of general Mesopotamian origin? The linguistic distribution of the term, although not decisive in itself, is certainly worthy of investigation.

If the term was originally Sumerian, one would expect that the South Mesopotamian formulations of the term would be entirely Sumerian. However, this is not the case: Akkadian formulations are found in the deeds of Kiš, Nippur, Larsa, and Ur. The Akkadian formulation (and the active voice) of the Ur tablet is noteworthy: in the heartland of the Sumerian South, one should have expected a Sumerian formulation. The presence of Akkadian formulations in the South, although not decisive in itself, does suggest that the term was originally Akkadian.

The fact that the term appears in an Akkadian formulation in the provincial deeds is to be expected. In general, the language of the provincial formularies was Akkadian, with only a minimal use of the most rudimentary Sumerian logograms. According to Koschaker, the absence of Sumerian—or at least its relative rarity—in the provincial formularies

---

1) Two such unpublished documents have been called to my attention by the Rev. George Dole of Cambridge, Mass. These deeds record the receipt of rent and use *libbašu ṭāb* as the main quittance clause. The deeds are *HSM* 7532, probably from the time of Rim-Sîn the second; the second text is *HSM* 7602; the date is not clear. The first text is in Akkadian, the second in Sumerian.

2) Cf., for example, Riftin 6. The term is certainly found in Faust, *YBT* VIII, No. 111: 11-12 and probably in 100: 14-15. The active form may be found in No. 52: 5. Nos. 100 and 111 are listed by Faust as "List of taxes" and "Receipt of royal taxes" which would agree quite well with the basic meaning of the term.

3) V. Scheil, "La promesse dans la prière babylonienne," *RA*, 12 (1915), p. 69. This genre of document is extremely rare in cuneiform literature. In it, a devotee of a god makes an oath that if the god listens to the prayers of his servant, he will then be obligated to pay a sum of money to the god. This conditional promise is solemnized by a legal document which, for all intents and purposes, is a deed of obligation in which the god is the creditor, the devotee, the (conditional) debtor. The debt exists only if the god shows his kindness. The liquidation of the obligation is expressed by the clause: kù.babbar šà Šamaš lugal.ani al.dùg "with the silver, the heart of Šamaš his lord will be satisfied" (or: "he will satisfy the heart of Šamaš, his lord, with the silver").*

4) Cf. Kraus, *WO*, 2 (1955), p. 131. The term *libbaka nuṭâb* is found in Figulla-Martin, *UET* V, No. 268 (Samsuiluna). The clause is translated: "für Schaf[e], Gerste und ‚Silber' für die Lohnarbeiter ..... kommen wir dir auf."

is an indication of their derivation from the Old Akkadian legal tradition.[1]) Thus, the presence of the Akkadian *libbašu ṭāb* in the provincial deeds strongly suggests that it is somehow related to archaic Akkadian legal praxis. The presence of its Akkadian isogloss in the Kültepe documents only supports this suggestion.

However important the evidence gleaned from the few provincial and South Mesopotamian documents, it is to the deeds of the Diyala region and especially to the deeds of the neighboring Sippar that one must turn to properly investigate the term and its linguistic distribution. It is in the deeds of this area that the oldest, widest, and most fully explicated usages of the term are preserved. Even more significantly, it is here that the number of documents that employ the term is large enough, and sufficiently stratified historically, to insure the success of a statistical analysis.

Almost all the early OB deeds from Ḫarmal are formulated in Akkadian. [2]) On the other hand, the slightly younger deeds from Ishchali are formulated in Sumerian. [3]) An intermediate position is taken by the Khafajah praxis: the conveyances employ both Akkadian and Sumerian formulations. [4]) Thus, the evidence of the Diyala documents regarding the original linguistic formulation of the term seems inconclusive, to say the least.

However, further examination of the Khafajah documents sheds some

---

[1]) Cf. Koschaker, *Randnotizen*, p. 222.

[2]) Cf. Simmons, *Ḫarmal*, Nos. 46-49 and 70. No. 50 uses the Sumerian formulation. Cf. Simmons' discussion, *JCS*, 13 (1959), p. 90.

[3]) Cf. Lutz, *Ashjali*, Nos. 5, 8, 12, 13. Cf. Simmons, *JCS*, 13 (1959), p. 90.

[4]) Cf. Harris, *Khafajah*, Nos. 55, 56, 60, 61, 72, 74, 75, 81, 87, 89 (Akkadian); Nos. 57, 58, 63, 67, 68, 70, 80, 82, 84, 91, 93 (Sumerian); all the rest of the conveyances do not have terms of satisfaction. Many of the documents do not seem to fall into clearly definable patterns. One document (No. 59) follows a more or less normal schema (kù.babbar *a-na šīmišu gamrim* ì.la.e giš.ga.an *šūtuq*) but ends with the symbolic-magical gestus: (10) *ša-am-na qá-qá-sú-≪nu≫ pa-ši-iš* "their heads were annointed with oil."* There are no *Schlussklauseln*. No. 81 follows the abnormal pattern—*išām šīmam gamram libbašu ṭūb* and ends with the symbolic gestus: (7) *ki-ša-du-ma* (8) *a-na li-ti a-ba-aḫ*! "I passed from neck to cheek." There are several document which contain archaic features that are found only in Old Akkadian or Old Babylonian deeds from Susa; cf., for example, the expression *ana šīm gamir* šu.ba.an.ti in No. 56 (cf. Harris' discussion *ad loc.*) or the expression *ana šīmim iddin* in No. 88 (cf. Harris *ad loc.*). I have little doubt that these documents are the transitional stage from the Old Akkadian tradition preserved in the Susa documents to the Old Babylonian formulary reflected in the Sippar deeds. The close association of *libbašu ṭāb* with these archaic features (symbolic gestus, lack of *Schlussklauseln*, etc.) only confirms the conclusion arrived at on the basis of other evidence that the term has archaic origins. The fact that the most archaic usage of the term is found in the Akkadian documents supports the conjecture that *libbašu ṭāb* is of Akkadian rather than Sumerian provenience.

suggestive light on the problem of origins. First of all, it should be noted that the Akkadian-formulated conveyances often follow a schema which differs significantly from that employed in the Sumerian conveyances. The Akkadian conveyances seem to follow an independent tradition which, as far as I can tell, is not attested in other collections of OB documents. First, the term is frequently used in the active voice. [2]) Secondly, the term is often not *libbašu ṭāb* but *libbum ṭūb* or *libbam uṭīb*; the pronominal element is often missing. More significantly, the Akkadian conveyances often do not contain the regular *Schlussklauseln*. [1]) These deeds often simply end with the term *libbum ṭūb*, some archaic symbolic action, or a combination of both. [3])

---

[1]) Cf. Simmons, *Ḥarmal*, Nos. 46-49; Harris, *Khafajah*, Nos. 61, 72, and 74.

[2]) Deeds are classified as Akkadian if their main sale clauses are written in Akkadian; Sumerian, if their main sale clauses are written in Sumerian; some deeds are difficult to classify. Generally, but not always, it is the Akkadian deeds that lack *Schlussklauseln* and contain other archaic features; the Sumerian deeds follow the well-known patterns of North Mesopotamia: šám.til.la.ni.šè kù. babbar in.na.lá giš.gan.na íb.ta.bal inim.bi al.til, etc. The normal Sumerian deeds are the following: Nos. 57, 58, 62, 63, 65-68, 70, 75-77, 80, 82-84, 90-93, 95. There are, however, several Sumerian deeds that do not follow this pattern. For example, No. 69 has the following schema: x gán a.šà ki seller, the buyer in.ši.šám giš.gan.na íb.ta.bal, witnesses. The rest of the normal clauses, especially the *Schlussklauseln*, are missing. The formulary of No. 85 is somewhat fuller (šám.til.la.ni.šè ì.na.lá); the deed lacks *Schlussklauseln* and ends simply with the *bukannu* clause. No. 86 also lacks *Schlussklauseln*.

The only normal Akkadian document in the collection is No. 75, which has the regular clause *ana šīmim gamrim* kug.babbar *išqul* and ends with the *Schluss-klauseln*. All the rest of the Akkadian conveyances have abnormal or archaic features. These Akkadian deeds can be divided into the following classes: (a) those which have the schema: *A x ikû išām* (nos. 71, 78) and (b) those whose schema is *šīmam gamram išām*+ *libbum ṭūb/libbam uṭīb* (Nos. 60, 61, 72, 81, 87) or *ši-ma-a-a i-ša-am ši-ma-am ga-am-ra-am* "the property (which) he bought was acquired completely, lit., a complete buying" (No. 96). First of all, the use of the active *libbam uṭīb* is probably an archaic feature. Furthermore, the clause *šīmam gamram išām* is clearly archaic in origin. It should be distinguished from the common sale clause: *ana šīmim gamrim kaspam išqul* "he paid out the money as the full price" (No. 75). The early Khafajah *šīmam gamram išām/ šīmā išām šīmam gamram* is paralleled by the early Old Babylonian deeds from Ḥarmal where the clause appears as *šīmātim ša išāmu* . . . *ana gamertim išām* "the saleable property which he bought . . . he bought completely" (Ḥarmal, No. 51). Cf. also *ana gamertim išām* "he bought completely" in Ḥarmal, No. 79. One cannot argue that *šīmam gamram išām* and *ana šīm gamir kaspam išqul* are synonymous, since the two clauses are found together in the same early Old Babylonian deed from Sippar; their legal functions are clearly differentiated: (1) *a-na ga-me-ir-tim* (10) *i-ša-am a-na ši-mi-šu* (11) *ga-am-ri-im kaspam iš-qú-ul* . . . (15) *kaspam ši-im bīti-šu* (15) *ga-am-ra-am* (16) *li-ba-*<*šu*> *ṭú-ub* (*M* 35) "(The property which the buyer bought), he bought completely. As its full price he weighed out the money . . . With the money, the full price of his house, his heart has been satisfied." Furthermore, it should be noted that in both the Diyala and the early Sippar deed just quoted the clause *šīmam gamram/ana gamertim išām* is found together with another archaic feature—the D stative *ṭūb*.

[3]) Cf. the texts cited at the end of the preceding note.

The presence of symbolic actions in the Khafajah documents is a clear indication of their archaic provenience. Recent studies by Cassin, [1] Boyer, [2] Koschaker, [3] and Matouš [4] on the nature and structure of the oldest Mesopotamian sale transactions have demonstrated that all kinds of symbolic actions—the dressing of the buyer in the seller's coat, [5] throwing a clod of earth into a nearby canal, [6] raising the seller's foot from the sold property and placing the buyer's foot in its place [7]—were employed to magically sever the almost physical tie which bound the owner to his land. Once the magical action had been performed, the tie was severed forever: the old owner had ceded his rights and could no longer raise claims against the new owner.

According to Boyer [8] and Matouš, [9] these symbolic actions filled the same juridical functions as the later Ur III and OB *Schlussklauseln*. In fact, historically, the *Schlussklauseln* are the natural terminological transformation of the older symbolic actions. In the light of this analysis, there can be no doubt that the Akkadian-formulated Khafajah conveyances are a reflex of a very archaic tradition.

Furthermore, it should be noted that in these deeds the place of the *Schlussklauseln* is filled by two different elements: (a) by the symbolic actions; (b) by the term *libbum ṭūb*. The fact that the symbolic actions stand in the place of the *Schlussklauseln* clearly confirms the theory of Boyer and Matouš concerning the evolution of the instruments employed to insure transactions against litigations. Of immediate significance to this study, however, is the presence of *libbašu ṭāb* in such an archaic *Sitz im Leben*.

First of all, it can be safely assumed that its presence in deeds which lack *Schlussklauseln*—an instrument already present, and probably developed in, the Ur III period—is definite proof of its archaic background. Significantly, none of the Old Akkadian conveyances—whether they be deeds which record the measuring (*išdud/imdud*) and transfer

[1] Cassin, *Symboles de cession*, pp. 107-162.
[2] Boyer, *Formation de vente*, pp. 49-55.
[3] Koschaker, *Begriff des Kaufs*, pp. 118 ff.
[4] Matouš, *Vente*, pp. 11-67; Matouš, *Ausdrücken*, pp. 434 ff. Cf. also, Klíma, *Reglung des Kaufs*, pp. 11-67 and Koschaker, *Eheschliessung*, pp. 210-296.
[5] Koschaker, *Eheschliessung*, pp. 253 ff.
[6] Cf. Cassin, *Symboles de cession*, pp. 108-120.
[7] *Ibid.*, pp. 120-129.
[8] Boyer, *Formation de vente*, pp. 54 f.
[9] Matouš, *Ausdrücken*, p. 442: "In dieser präventiven Einrichtung [the extra payments] kann mann erste Spuren der sog. Nichtanfechtungsklausel sehen, deren ursprünglicher Sinn war, das Grundstück, das aus dem gemeinsamen in das Private Eigentum überging, vor den Ausprüchen anderer Mitglieder dieser Gemeinschaft, die eigentlich auch Miteigentumer des verkauften Grundstuckes waren, zu schützen."

of the fields or those which record the receipt of the price (*imḫur*)—contain *Schlussklauseln*. Thus, the assumption that *libbašu ṭāb* is somehow associated with the Old Akkadian legal tradition gains added confirmation.

Secondly, the fact that *libbum ṭūb* fills the same contextual slot as the early symbolic actions and of the later Sumerian *Schlussklauseln* suggests that the term filled the same juridical function as these above-mentioned instruments. Thus, when *libbum ṭūb* stands at the end of a deed, it probably insured the transaction against future litigation as effectively as did the early symbolic actions and the later *Schlussklauseln*.

The linguistic distribution pattern of the Sippar documents was analyzed in a previous section; however, the basic outlines of this pattern should be recalled in this context: (a) most of the early OB examples of the term are in Akkadian; the later examples are all in Sumerian; (b) the function of the early Akkadian examples is clear and unambiguous, since the clause of satisfaction is placed immediately after the record of payment and is fully explicated by the phrase *šīm bītišu gamrim* "(his heart has been satisfied) with the full price of his house." On the other hand, the function of the later Sumerian formulations is ambiguous, since the explicatives have been eliminated and the position of the clause has been changed.

Thus, to judge merely on the basis of the Sippar evidence—the most representative both in terms of numbers of examples as well as the range of contexts employed—the Akkadian formulation clearly takes precedence over the Sumerian in reflecting the original—or at least the most operative—juridical function of the term. (A similar phenomenon is known from the deeds of Alalakh where Akkadian formulae tend to dominate in level VII while Sumerian ones are the most prevalent in level IV; oral communication, E. A. Speiser.)*

An Argument from Syntax. There is yet another consideration, syntactical rather than juridical, which seems to tip the scales in favor of an Akkadian origin. It was pointed out above that in the oldest Sippar conveyances the form employed was not *libbašu ṭāb* but the D stative, *libbašu ṭūb*, to be translated "his heart has been satisfied" rather than "his heart is satisfied." Thus, the satisfaction of the heart is not an independent state of mind but a condition induced by some preceding activity or, more specifically, by some preceding performance.

The stative form *libbašu ṭūb* implies the existence of the active—and primary—form **libbašu uṭīb* "he (the buyer) satisfied his (the seller's) heart." Thus conceived, the stative term of receipt is a derivative of an original (active) term of performance. On the basis of the early Sippar form *libbašu ṭūb*, I posited the existence of the active *libbašu uṭīb*. This inference was confirmed by the older Khafajah usage: some of these conveyances use the active *libbum uṭīb*, while others use the stative form *libbum ṭūb*.

This active-passive aspectuality has some bearing on the linguistic background of *libbašu ṭāb*. Is this aspectuality a sign of its Akkadian origin, or can it be interpreted as an indication of its ultimate Sumerian provenience? Logically, both interpretations are possible.

In defense of its Sumerian origin, it could be argued that this aspectuality is a secondary (Akkadian) development. The problem of the active-passive aspectuality of the Sumerian verb has not as yet been satisfactorily solved. However, it seems clear that potentially any Sumerian verbal root is either active/transitive or passive/intransitive. [1]) Because of this ambiguity, Akkadian scribes could—and did on occasion—render the same Sumerian verbal form either as an active or as a passive. Thus, for example, the Sumerian an.da.gál "he has" was rendered either as the active *naši* "he carries", or as the stative, *elišu baši* "there is to/on him". [2]) It could be argued that the Akkadian aspectuality *libbašu uṭīb*/*libbašu ṭūb* is simply the result of two different attempts to render the aspectually ambiguous šà.ga.ni al.dùg into Akkadian.

However, attractive as this argument may seem at first glance, there are many serious considerations which militate against its acceptance. First of all, exactly the same active-stative aspectuality is reflected in the slightly older Kültepe isogloss *šabû* "he (the seller) is satisfied." The active form *ušabbīšu* "he satisfied him"—parallel to the OB *libbam uṭīb*—is also attested to. [3]) Furthermore, the Kültepe terms form an active-stative cluster *ušabbīšu-šabû* "he (the buyer) satisfied him (the seller) and he (the seller) is satisfied (with the price)." [4]) Such clusters are well known from Biblical and Ugaritic poetry, and have recently been found in the Aramaic deeds of Elephantine, in Ras Shamra Akkadian, and possibly in Middle Assyrian legal documents. [5]) If, following Jacobsen, one does not distinguish too dogmatically between West Semites and Akkadians, [6]) it stands to reason that this active-

---

[1]) Sollberger, *Le système verbal*, p. 36; Falkenstein, *Grammatik* I 48 and *OLZ*, 1931, pp. 791-794. See also Jestin, *Verbe*, p. 87; Poebel, *Grammatik* § 447-485, and *AJSL*, 50 (1933/34), pp. 143-170. Cf. also Jacobsen, "Introduction to Chicago Grammatical Texts," *MSL* IV, pp. 49* ff.

[2]) *MSL* IV 70, line 61 and *Izi* A III 13.

[3]) Cf. the evidence collected in the following chapter, pp. 120 ff.

[4]) Cf. the following chapter, p. 122.

[5]) Cf. below, p. 47

[6]) Orally.

passive aspectuality, and, more specifically, the active-passive clusters arising from it, would not be altogether foreign to Akkadian.

Furthermore, if one is guided by the rule that the more original the formulation of a term, the more clearly reflected is its equal underlying juridical function, why is it that the later Sumerian formulations used in the Sippar conveyances are totally obscure and give the impression of being legal fossils, while the early Akkadian formulations reflect legal and linguistic usages which are still alive, functional, and unambiguous? If the Sumerian formulation were the original, it, instead of the Akkadian, should reflect the clearest and most functional use of the term. Evidently, then, the Akkadian formulation, at least to judge from the Sippar evidence, is the older form of the term.

There is another argument against the Sumerian thesis. It should be noted that the legal functions and contextual uses of the active *libbašu uṭīb* do not overlap those of the passive *libbašu ṭāb*. In fact, the active form is employed in contexts where the passive form is out of place. For example, in the context: "In the month of Simānum, they (the debtors) will satisfy his heart (the creditor's) with silver," [1]) it is impossible to assume that this clearly differentiated functional distinction between the active and passive forms of the terms is the result of two different and halting renderings of an aspectually ambiguous Sumerian model. Clearly, the aspectuality of the Akkadian is primary. It is a characteristic of the term which would never have found adequate linguistic formulation if it were known only from its Sumerian usage.

C. *Unique Characteristic of* libbašu ṭāb *and Archaic Sale Law*

Although *libbašu ṭāb* is not found in deeds earlier than the OB period, its use in the archaic Khafajah documents, its predominantly Akkadian formulation, its presence in the deeds of Sippar, all suggest that the term was derived from an older and probably Akkadian tradition. This suggestion is confirmed by the presence of the isogloss *šabû*, "he is satisfied," in the older non-Sumerian deeds of Kültepe, deeds which have well-known associations with Old Akkadian legal praxis.

The actual term is not found in the Sumerian deeds of the Ur III period nor in the Old Akkadian documents. As far as I can tell, it is not attested in the deeds of the Early Dynastic or Proto-Literate periods. Although the term itself is limited to the OB period, and its root metaphor of satisfaction is no older than the Old Assyrian period, nevertheless the legal background out of which the term developed is the archaic sale

[1]) Cf. Riftin 6 and P 14: 9 (above, p. 83).

law of the third millennium B.C. It is in this archaic sale tradition that the answers to several unanswered questions concerning the nature and function of *libbašu ṭāb* are to be found.

Libbašu ṭāb *and the Role of the Seller.* All OB conveyances, except those which use *libbašu ṭāb*, are formulated from the point of view of the buyer and completely ignore the person of the seller. The reactions of the seller to the transactions seem to be devoid of any legal significance and are not recorded.

Libbašu ṭāb, in recording the receipt of the price by the seller and his satisfaction therewith, breaks with this consistent OB schema.

The Sumerian deeds of sale from the Ur III period are, like their later OB reflex, formulated from the point of view of the buyer. However, on the basis of the evidence examined in the preceding section, it is not in the Ur III deeds that one would logically expect to find the origins of *libbašu ṭāb* but rather in the more archaic deeds of the Old Akkadian period. Significantly, all of the OA conveyances I have studied, whether they record the measuring [1]) and transfer of the property, [2]) or the receipt of the price and the *iškinū*, [3]) are all formulated from the seller's point of view.

This type of formulation seems to have been typically Akkadian since the older Lagaš conveyances, like the later Ur III and OB deeds of sale, are formulated from the point of view of the buyer. [4]) Significantly, the Sargonic practice of formulating the deeds from the seller's point of view is rooted in even older Akkadian praxis. [5])*

Libbašu ṭāb *and the Receipt Clause.* More specifically, *libbašu ṭāb* describes the seller not so much as the transferer of goods as the receiver of the price. Once again, *libbašu ṭāb* reflects an older Mesopotamian practice, this time Sumerian as well as Akkadian, of recording the

---

1) Cf. Gelb, *Akkadian Inscriptions*, Nos. 1: 12′ (*išduda*), 2: 4 (*išdud*), 9: 21′ (*imdud*).

2) For example, *ibid.*, Nos. 3: 10 and 4: 5.

3) Cf. Gelb, *MAD* I, Nos. 51, 58, and *passim*.

4) Cf. M. Lambert, "Textes commerciaux de Lagaš (III)," *ArOr*, 23 (1955), pp. 558 ff.; the regular formula is e.ne.šè.šám.

5) In *MAD* II, pp. 3-5, Gelb lists a series of pre-Sargonic stone inscriptions dealing with the transfer of property. In one of these documents (Allote de la Füye, *DP* I 2, from Lagaš ?), the main verb of the transaction is *iš-du-du* "they measured," which is exactly the term used later on in the conveyances of the Old Akkadian period (cf. above, n. 1). However, one cannot draw any definite conclusions from this text concerning the Akkadian provenience of the practice since according to Koschaker, *Begriff des Kaufs*, pp. 118 ff., the oldest (unpublished) Sumerian sale transactions stressed the measuring, publication, and transfer of the property as well as the payment of the price. Thus, it is quite possible that the pre-Sargonic *išdud* and the Sargonic *išdud* are reflexes of an older Sumerian or common-Mesopotamian praxis.

receipt of the price within the deed of sale or within an independent quitclaim.

The receipt of the price by the seller is recorded in the deeds of the Ur III period; the term used there is šu ba.ti "he received." [1] The Akkadian version of this term is reflected in the older, Sargonic *imḫur* "he received." [2] Both go back to the even older, Lagaš formula šu ba.ti. [3]

The Contextual Matrix of the Term. One would have expected that since *libbašu ṭāb* stresses the role of the seller as receiver of the price, deeds of sale using *libbašu ṭāb* would also stress the role of the seller as the transferer of the property. Thus, a schema like *iddin libbašu ṭāb* "he sold; his heart is satisfied" would have been expected. [4] This, however, is not the case. The Sippar schema is: (a) *išām* "he bought"; (b) *libbašu ṭāb* "his heart is satisfied." Nor can one argue—as I formerly did—that the schema of the Sippar conveyance resulted from the incorporation of an Akkadian, seller-oriented clause (*libbašu ṭāb*) into a Sumerian, buyer-oriented structure, since exactly the same schema—"the buyer bought; the seller is satisfied"—is found in the Old Assyrian deeds of Kültepe which seem to reflect little or no trace of Sumerian influence. [5]

Is the schema Old Akkadian as one would expect from all that is known about the historical affinities of the Kültepe-Sippar deeds? Two kinds of OA conveyances are known: (a) one which records the receipt of the price and the *iškinū* by the seller; [6] (b) one which records the measuring (and the transfer) of the property by the seller. [7] Thus, even

---

[1]) Cf. the examples cited by Kraus, *Nippur und Isin*, pp. 99-102. For other Sumerian examples of various periods, cf. Hackman *BIN* VIII, Nos. 38, 80, 170-172, 174.

[2]) All of the examples are collected by Gelb in *MAD* III under "*MḪR maḫārum*," pp. 171-172.

[3]) Cf. M. Lambert, "Textes commerciaux de Lagaš (III)," *ArOr*, 23 (1955), p. 558 and *passim*.

[4]) Such a combination of "the seller sold" and the "seller received the price," although not found in regular Old Akkadian deeds, where each of these elements is recorded in a different type of deed (contrast the deeds in Gelb's *Akkadian Inscriptions* with those published in *MAD*, I), nevertheless is found in an Old Akkadian deed from Susa, *MDP* XXIV 361 (1) *zi-ti Ga-[at-n]e-im* (2) *a-na Puzur-ma-ṣa-at i-ti-in* (3) kug.bi *x šiqil kaspam* (4) *a-na šīmim* (5) *ga-am-ri-im* (6) šu.ti.a. This schema looks like an amalgamation of the two regular OA schemata: (a) *ana šīmim nadānum* (b) *ana šīmim maḫārum.**

[5]) Cf., for example, *EL* 107.

[6]) Cf. the conveyances in Gelb, *MAD* I.

[7]) Cf. the conveyances in Gelb, *Akkadian Inscriptions*; cf. Leeman's review in *BiOr*, 12 (1955), p. 75.

if the two deeds were combined into one, the Kültepe-Sippar schema would not emerge.

It seems that even though the actual terms *libbašu ṭāb* and *šabû* are Akkadian in origin, the over-all schema—"the buyer bought; the seller received"—reflects an archaic Sumerian, or common Mesopotamian, legal tradition. Even though private Ur III deeds are extremely rare, [1]) and most of the known conveyances of this period do not agree with the Sippar-Kültepe schema, at least one deed, recently published, does. [2]) Furthermore, this schema, which is rare in Ur III deeds, is common in the conveyances from Early Dynastic Lagaš where the regular schema is: e.ne.šè.šám "he bought"; níg.šám.bi níg.ba.bi šu ba.ti "he (the seller) received its sale price (and) its ni.g.ba." [3])

The Metaphor of Satisfaction. In the preceding paragraph, the distribution of third millennium conveyance receipt clauses was traced. The Old Akkadian *imḫur* "he received" and the Ur III šu ba.ti "he received" are both reflexes of the older, Lagaš šu ba.ti. The Old Babylonian formulary, in both its Akkadian and Sumerian versions, breaks with this century-old tradition: the southern deeds eliminate the receipt clause altogether, while the Akkadian deeds, instead of using the Old Akkadian term *imḫur*, replace it with the new term *libbašu ṭāb*.

However, *libbasu ṭāb* is not a simple isogloss of *imḫur*. The former term contrasts with *imḫur* and šu ba.ti in several respects. First of all, while the older terms have but one function—that of receipt—and are essentially passive or intransitive, [4]) the Old Babylonian term of satis-

[1]) Cf. M. Çiğ; H. Kizilyay; A. Falkenstein, "Neue Rechts- und Gerichtsurkunden der Ur III-Zeit aus Lagaš aus den Sammlungen der Istanbuler Archäologischen Museen," *ZA* 19 (1959), p. 51.

[2]) *Ibid.*, No. 19. The beginning of the deed is broken; however, the following lines are clear: [in].ši.lá(4′) Ur.[d]Satarana (5′) dumu.ša$_x$.dub.ba (6′) šu ba.ti(7′) inim.bi ì.[til]. Thus, the deeds record the payment by the buyer (in.ši.lá) and the receipt by the seller (šu ba.ti). Cf. the same schema in the OA deed from Susa cited above, p. 107, n. 4.

[3]) Cf. the texts edited by Lambert, "Textes commerciaux de Lagaš (III)," *ArOr*, 23 (1955), pp. 557 ff. The schema cited above in the text is found in ENAN II (= *DP* 31), p. 562, of Lambert's study. In most of the other Lagaš texts, šu ba.ti records the receipt of the níg.ba alone. Cf. the conveyances in *MAD* I, where *imḫur*—the OA equivalent of šu ba.ti—records both the receipt of the sale price and of the *iškinū*—the Akkadian equivalent of the níg.ba.

[4]) From a formal grammatical point of view, *maḫārum* may be considered an active-transitive verb, since the money received constitutes the direct object of the action reflected in the verb. However, from a psychological point of view, the role of the receiver is essentially passive; he certainly does not do anything to the money. The passivity of the receiver is more clearly expressed in the OB and MB formula *apil maḫir* "he is paid off; he has received." For a discussion of the various uses of *maḫāru* and for a different interpretation, cf. Rowton, *Permansive* pp. 239 and 243 f.

faction has two clearly distinguished but organically related functions: (a) as the stative *libbašu ṭāb* it is a term of receipt; (b) as the active *libbašu uṭīb* it is a term of performance, more specifically, a term of payment. Thus, the terms šu ba.ti and *imḫur* only overlap with the passive *libbašu ṭāb* [1] but not with the active *libbašu uṭīb*. The earlier conveyances express the idea of payment by other terms. [2]

Secondly, šu ba.ti and *imḫur* are objective terms; *libbašu uṭīb/ṭāb*, on the other hand, are subjective terms. By this I mean the following: the first set of terms places the emphasis on the objective receipt of the sale price; the terms of satisfaction, on the other hand, place the emphasis on the subjective reactions of the seller to the receipt of the price. Contrast the two syntactical structures: (a) "he paid the price to the seller" (Sumerian) with (b) "he satisfied the heart of the seller with the price" (Akkadian). In the first case, the objective price is the direct object; the seller, the indirect object. In the second case, the person of the seller is the direct object; the price, on the other hand, is conceived as the indirect object. In all probability, these contrasting syntactical orders reflect underlying contrasts in the structure of the sale transaction: Sumerian sale reflected in the term šu ba.ti stressed the role of the price, while Akkadian sale, reflected in *libbašu uṭīb*, stressed the reactions of the seller.

Thirdly, while *imḫur* and šu ba.ti are abstract terms, *libbašu ṭāb* is certainly not. In fact, probably the most distinguishing characteristic of the term is its metaphorical, poetical, and almost non-terminological nature. It was this "narrative" quality of the term that has led some scholars into actually denying its specific terminological function. [3]

Each of these three qualities that distinguish *libbašu ṭāb* from šu ba.ti-*imḫur*, namely, (a) its two functional aspects as a term of payment as well as receipt; (b) its subjectivity, i.e., its stress on the reaction of the seller rather than on the objective price; (c) its concrete and poetic quality—are all probably rooted in an older legal milieu. The roots of the last characteristic—the poetic, non-terminological quality of the expression—will be examined first.

1) As a general rule, the more poetic and metaphoric a term, the closer

---

[1] And then, only partially. The terms *imḫur* and šu ba.ti convey only the idea of receipt; *libbašu ṭāb* conveys the idea of quittance as well. In order to convey the idea of quittance upon the receipt of full price, the Sumerian deeds often add inim.bi al.til "its matter is settled" after šu ba.ti. Cf. Çiğ-Kizilyay-Falkenstein, *ZA*, 19 (1959), No. 19, cited above, p. 108, n. 2, and Hackman, *BIN* VIII, No. 172. (Even though for our immediate purpose šu ba.ti and *imḫur* seem functionally identical, it is quite possible that further investigation will point out significant contrasts between these two archaic terms of receipt.)

[2] Cf. the verb sum "give" (Hackman, *BIN* VIII, No. 174).

[3] *LAP* [Hebrew], p. 107.

it is to its preliterate and primitive origins. Many metaphorical terms seem to be terminological metamorphoses of early symbolic-magical actions. For example, the term *irtēq* "he removed himself"—the antonym of the common MA (*ul*) *iqerrib* "he shall (not) come close," i.e., "he has (no) claim,"—is probably the terminological reflection of an older gestus whereby the seller physically left the property as a concrete symbol of his relinquishment. [1]) Similarly, the expressions *ullil, ubbib, uzakki* "he purified," "he cleansed," "he made clean," when used in the abstract terminological sense "he liberated, freed from obligation," seem to be reflections of an earlier practice whereby the manumitted slave was ceremonially purified [2]) or anointed with oil. [3]) (For anointing in sale, cf. below, p. 137, n. 2.)

Therefore, the metaphorical nature of *libbašu ṭāb* suggests that the term is the terminological translation of some older prelegal gestus or mentality. What, then, is the psychological *Sitz im Leben* of a term of "satisfaction"? On the most primitive level, one is satisfied after having eaten a good meal. After having eaten one's full and having been satisfied, one leaves the table; nothing more is demanded. Is it possible that at some early stage of legal development the price was conceived as food, fed to the seller by the buyer? This would certainly explain why the term "his heart is satisfied with the price" is a term of quittance: having "eaten" as much of the price as he wants and having been "satisfied" therewith, the seller-eater demands no more; he makes no further claims.

Such a derivation would explain why the declaration of satisfaction is the concrete expression of cession, quittance, and relinquishment. It would also explain why the term can fill the functional slot of the early symbolic actions or of the later *Schlussklauseln* in the archaic conveyances of the Khafajah.

In this case, the logical construction suggested above can be confirmed —at least to some degree—by the actual documents. There is ample evidence that at the beginning of Mesopotamian civilization, the price consisted of grain and other foods, and that the seller who

---

[1]) Cf. above, p. 21, n. 4.

[2]) In the OB manumission formula *pussu ullil* "he (the owner) purified his (the slave's) forehead," the purification is still taken quite literally: in some cases, the purification is actually accompanied by the symbolic gestus *ana ṣīt šamši pānīšu iškun* "he (the master) placed his face (the slave's) toward the rising sun" (Schorr, *Urkunden*, No. 27 = *CT* VIII 48a). In later times, *uzakki* was probably used as an abstract term equal without necessarily mirroring any symbolic gestus.

[3]) For the anointing of a manumitted slave, cf. *PRU* III, RS 8. 208 (p. 110); cf. also the discussion of Harris, *Khafajah*, p. 92.

received the price was called "the eater of the grain" (lú šám.kú). [1])

To properly evaluate this evidence, let us record once more the distribution of the receipt terminology used in the oldest conveyances.

	Akkadian	Sumerian
OB	*libbašu uṭīb-libbašu ṭāb*	
OAs	*ušabbīšu šabû*	
Ur III		šu ba.ti
OAkk.	*imḫur*	
Lagaš		šu ba.ti
Kiš	šám . . . kú (= *šīmam īkul* ?) [2])	
Šuruppak	lú šám.kú	

All of the receipt terms used in the early conveyances are ultimately derived from the Šurrupak designation for the seller: "the man who eats the price/grain." The original nominal expression used in the Šuruppak conveyances was later explicated in two different ways:
(a) in an abstract manner, which was typical of the Sumerian documents;
(b) in a concrete manner, which was typical of some of the Akkadian deeds.

In a pre-Sargonic conveyance from Kiš, [3]) the older nominal form lú šám.kú "the man who eats the price" is reflected in the verbal form šám . . . kú (to be read *šīmam īkul* ?) "he ate the price." The concreteness of the original expression is still preserved. The Early Dynastic Lagaš praxis, on the other hand, although it preserved the ancient níg.ba, has already modernized the ancient tradition by converting the prelegal "eating of the price" into the abstract and terminological "receiving of the price." In this respect, the Old Akkadian *imḫur* "he received" is simply a reflection, and probably a translation, of the abstract Sumerian šu ba.ti; in both terms, all traces of the prelegal situation have been eliminated. Only the presence of the níg.ba or the *iškinū* indicates the antiquity of the legal *Sitz im Leben*.

Nevertheless, some of the Akkadian deeds from the North did preserve later reflexes of the older tradition. Thus, for example, in the Stele of Maništusu (Old Akkadian), the seller is called the *ākil kaspim* "the eater of the price." [4]) As noted above, the Ur III šu ba.ti and the Old Akka-

[1]) Cf. Cassin, *Symboles de cession*, pp. 140 ff.; also Boyer, *Formation de vente*, pp. 49-52 and Deimel, *Fara*, pp. 11 * f.

[2]) Cf. James B. Nies, "A Pre-Sargonic Inscription on Limestone from Warka," *JAOS*, 38 (1918), pp. 188 ff.

[3]) *Ibid.*, p. 189; the document has been given a Sumerian transliteration for convenience. Nies strongly suggested that the deed was written in Semitic and that it came from Kiš. Cf. now Gelb, *MAD* II, p. 3.

[4]) The passages are cited by Cassin, *Symboles de cession*, p. 157, n. 1.

dian *imḫur* are the reflexes of the more modern terminological trend. For reasons that will be discussed later, the Sumerian deeds of the Old Babylonian period break with time-honored tradition and eliminate the receipt clause from the conveyance. On the other hand, the OAs, Sippar, and Diyala conveyances from the Akkadian North still continue the practice—now archaic—of recording the receipt of the sale price. However, instead of recording the receipt of the price by the abstract Old Akkadian *imḫur* "he received," the Old Babylonian scribes—and the Old Assyrian ones before them, employ the concrete and metaphorical terms "he (the buyer) satisfied him" and "he satisfied his heart" with the full price.

To me, the expressions *ušabbīšu* and *libbašu uṭīb* seem like the terminological reflexes of the Old Akkadian *ākil kaspim* and the even older, common-Mesopotamian lú šám.kú "the eater of the price." Furthermore, lú šám.kú and *libbašu ṭāb* are mutually illuminating. The existence of the first term, which conceives the receipt of the price as the eating of grain, lends documentary support to the suggestion offered below that the term "his heart was satisfied with the price" was derived from the metaphor of eating. On the other hand, the term *libbašu ṭāb* seems to explicate the underlying legal function of lú šám.kú. The expression "he ate the grain" would mean something like: "he received the price and is satisfied therewith; he is full and demands no more; he is quit and will raise no more claims in the future." Such an interpretation underlies Nies' translation of šám kú as "with the price (of the field) he is satisfied." [1])

What is merely implied in the objective act of eating the grain is spelled out in its (possible) terminological reflex—*libbašu ṭāb*. Šám kú describes the outer action; *libbašu ṭāb* describes the psychological reaction—an inner state of mind. Thus, the new formulation of the archaic gestus achieves greater clarity without losing the overtones of the original prelegal *Sitz im Leben*.

2) If *libbašu ṭāb* is in reality a late terminological reflex of lú šám.kú and šám . . . kú, an explication of the underlying principles behind these early terms may throw more light on some of the problems raised by *libbašu ṭāb* and *šabû*, namely, the emphasis these terms place on the reactions of the seller rather than on the objective payment of the price and the fact that the same term, in its different aspects, is both a term of payment and of receipt-quittance.

The following reconstruction of archaic sale is based on the research

---

[1]) *JAOS*, 38 (1918), p. 192.

of Koschaker, [1]) Boyer, [2]) Matouš, [3]) and Cassin [4]) in this area. The most extensive treatment of the subject is that of Cassin. According to her, the sale of land was not effected merely by the payment of an objective sum of money. Owners—even those who expressed willingness to part with their property—did not part with their property so easily. One could say that they were bound to their land by emotional ties that bordered on the physical. [5]) The land was part of their patrimony; it was a link with preceding generations; it was to be kept in the family and to be handed down as an inheritance to later generations. One can compare the attitude of the ancient landowner to his property to that of Naboth, who, when offered a price for his land by Ahab, replied: "The Lord, forbid, that I should sell to you the inheritance of my fathers." [6])

Furthermore, there is good reason to believe that, at least in very early times, the land was held collectively* by the family or clan. [7]) Each member of the family had a partial claim on all of the property. Even when private individuals obtained the right of alienation, the members of the family still had residual rights to the land; they still could object to its being sold outside of the family group. Thus, even as late as the Code of Ešnunna, a reflex of the ancient mentality can be seen in the stipulation that if a man wants to offer his land for sale, he has to offer it first to a member of his family, and at a reduced price. [8]) A similar attempt to preserve the family property is reflected in the Biblical story of the daughters of Zelophehad (Nu 36:1 ff.). Since Zelophehad had no sons, his daughters inherited his property. However, in order to keep the property within the clan, the daughters were forbidden to marry outside of the tribe.

Now both the personal attachment of the individual to his land and the residual claims of the relatives and neighbors of the owner constituted

---

[1]) Koschaker, *Begriff des Kaufs*, pp. 118 ff.

[2]) Boyer, *Formation de vente*, pp. 49-55.

[3]) Matouš, *Ausdrücken*, pp. 434 ff.

[4]) *Symboles de cession*, n. 149.

[5]) This is the basic assumption of Cassin's essay.

[6]) I Kings 21: 3.

[7]) This point is stressed by Matouš (*Ausdrücken*, p. 140 f.), where extensive Russian literature on this subject is cited. For the remnants of collective-tribal ownership in later times, cf. Cuq, *Études*, pp. 89, 99 ff. For remnants of rabbinic inhibitions against the sale of ancestral property, cf. the discussion in Gulak, *The History of Jewish Law during the Talmudic Period: the Law of Immobila* (Jerusalem, 1929), pp. 41 ff. [in Hebrew]. When a man would sell a piece of ancestral property, his neighbors would gather together near his house and say: "PN is cut off from his estate." The custom was known as *qᵉṣāṣā* or "severance."

[8]) *LE*, No. 38. Cf. Klíma, *Reglung des Kaufs*, pp. 95 ff. and Cassin, *Symboles de cession*, p. 152, n. 1.

formidable obstacles against its free alienation. These obstacles were overcome by tendering all kinds of considerations to the owner. Some of these considerations were roughly identical with what is now called the sale price. However, besides the price—which was originally in the form of grain—gifts of food, money, clothes, and metal utensils—whose value sometimes exceeded that of the formal sale price—were often tendered. [1]) The function of these gifts was to induce the seller to cede his land. He had to be bribed and cajoled by these considerations. A similar mentality is not unknown in some of the more backward areas of the modern world. [2])

Furthermore, it may be assumed that the price itself was less an objective sum whose payment insured the immediate and automatic transfer of ownership than another type of gift or inducement. If this construction is correct, the formal payment of the price did not necessarily transfer the title to the buyer. As Cassin suggests, it may have conferred as much "ownership" as a creditor had over a pledge. [3])

The constitutive activity of the seller was not the tendering of the objective price to the seller; rather it was the winning of the seller's heart by the different forms of gifts. It is the seller's mind, not the objective price, which is the focal point of the transaction. The activity of the seller in presenting the gifts aims at, and hopefully anticipates, his favorable reaction.

The final stage in the sale transaction was the formal acknowledgment of the seller that all his past ties with his land were now severed for all time. This severance of ties was effectuated by different kinds of symbolic-magical actions, some of which were described above. [4])

If *libbašu ṭāb-libbašu uṭīb* were really the terminological reflex of the older šám . . . kú, many of the characteristics of the Old Babylonian terms of satisfaction which seem unusual against the background of *imḫur* and šu ba.ti find their natural explanation in the context of the

[1]) These various performances were called níg.ba, níg.diri, and níg.gar in Sumerian. The Akkadian equivalent of the níg.diri is the *watru*, and the equivalent of the níg.gar is the OA-OB *iškinū*. Cf. Matouš, *Ausdrücken*, and Cassin, *Symboles de cession*, pp. 140 ff. For later reflexes of these performances, cf. San Nicolò, "Zum *atru* und anderen Nebenleistungen des Käufers beim neubabylonischen Immobilarkauf," *Or*, 16 (1947), pp. 273 ff.

[2]) In his book *Bitter Lemons* (New York, 1957), the writer Lawrence Durrell describes his stay in Cyprus before the Enosis war of independence. Among other things, Durrell describes the acquisition of a house according to the archaic customs still followed on the island. This sale procedure ("How to Buy a House," pp. 47 ff.) is remarkably like that of ancient Mesopotamia, according to the reconstructions of Cassin and others.

[3]) Cassin, *Symboles de cession*, p. 150.

[4]) *Ibid.*, pp. 108-139.

more archaic receipt terms. Thus, one could easily paraphrase the archaic sale transaction by using the OB terms of satisfaction: the buyer did not merely pay an objective sum of money to the seller to acquire title to the land. The attachment of the seller to his property was so strong that the seller had to be induced, cajoled—"satisfied"—by the gifts and money tendered by the buyer into relinquishing his claim to the land. The whole performance of the buyer was concentrated on one end: to dislodge the owner from his attachment by satisfying his heart. Only when the seller had finally received enough payment, when "his heart was satisfied," did he really relinquish his claim; this relinquishment was not merely formal and external; it was essentially an inner state of mind—he no longer had any formal claims or inner mental reservations against the sale: he was quit, now and for all time.

Thus, the terms *libbašu uṭīb* and *ušabbīšu* both express legal principles latent in the older actions. By coining these terms, the OB and OAs scribes brought the archaic mentality reflected in lú šám.kú to a higher degree of consciousness and rational expression.

CHAPTER FIVE

SEMANTIC EQUIVALENTS AND CONTRASTS

In the previous section, *libbašu ṭāb* has been defined inductively [1]) on the basis of its various contextual usages, its complements and explicatives, and its grammatical-syntactical structure. The conclusions reached in the preceding section can be independently confirmed by a study of its semantic equivalents and contrasts.

1. The Isoglosses of *libbašu ṭāb*

There are various types of functional equivalents: (a) synonyms (= free variants within the same dialect); (b) isoglosses (= functionally identical but mutually exclusive terms belonging to different branches of the same language); (c) interdialectal variants [2]) (= functionally identical terms belonging to different languages of the same family. These terms are often unrelated etymologically). [3]) Synonyms can best be isolated by a study of glosses, by the examination of parallel recensions of the same narrative, [4]) and especially by a study of the *parallelismus membrorum* of poetic texts. Unfortunately, none of these methods is applicable to *libbašu ṭāb*. On the other hand, *libbašu ṭāb* has a series of important isoglosses. All of these terms fill the same role within the

---

[1]) Concerning the difference between etymological and inductive-contextual definition, cf. M. Held, "*mḫṣ/*mḫš* in Ugaritic and Other Semitic Languages," *JAOS*, 79 (1959), pp. 169 ff.

[2]) This is the term employed by Held following Landsberger (*ibid.*, p. 169). In the course of this study, the less formal term "semantic equivalent" is often used interchangeably.*

[3]) For example, interdialectal variants of the Hebrew *ʿāmad* "to stand" are the Akkadian *uzzuzu*, the Aramaic *qām*, and the Arabic *waqafa*. Even though the Hebrew *ʿāmad* and the Akkadian *emēdu* are based on the same radicals (i.e., they are cognates), their semantic ranges have almost nothing in common. Unfortunately, except for the article of Held and sporadic comments of Landsberger, *Gesetz und Recht*, p. 223, n. 20, where Hebrew *ḥoq* is equated with Akkadian *parṣu* "norm" and of Speiser (who has in his classes equated the Hebrew *ʾalōṯ habbᵉrīṯ* "a covenant sealed by oaths containing imprecations" with the Akkadian *adê māmīt ilāni*),* most Semitic lexica still reflect the older method of stressing etymological equivalence and ignoring functional identity. The present study is in a limited sense an exercise in comparative legal lexicography based on the principles of interdialectal distribution. The nature of the legal material, especially the parallelism inherent in the various dialectal formulations of the same type of legal genre, makes the legal material the ideal genre for such comparative lexicographical studies.

[4]) Cf. Talmon, *Synonymous Readings*, pp. 335 ff.

documents of their particular period or dialect as *libbašu ṭāb* fills within the OB documents of the Sippar-Diyala region.

A. *Sippar* libbašu ṭāb = *Susa* duppur

In the previous section, it was noted that the clause *zīzū gamrū libbašunu ṭāb* is found sporadically in the division deeds of Sippar and in the division deeds of Larsa and Kiš. The clause means: "they have divided; they have finished; their hearts are satisfied (with the portions received)." *Libbašu ṭāb* records the receipt of the individual portions by the heirs, their satisfaction therewith, and the relinquishment of all rights and claims to the property received by the other heirs.

A clause which is functionally identical with the Sippar *zīzū gamrū libbašunu ṭāb* is a regular element in almost all of the Susa deeds of division. The clause reads: *zīzū mesû duppurū.* [1]) Syntactically, the Sippar and Susa clauses are identical: both are stative clusters consisting of three terms, the first of which is the division term *zīzū* "they have divided." It stands to reason that *mesû* is the equivalent of *gamrū* and that *duppurū* is the synonym of *libbašunu ṭāb*. In all probability, *mesû*, in this context, has nothing to do with the regular Akkadian *mesû* "to wash." It is simply a rare or archaic legal term with the same range as the regular *gamāru* "to finish." The term *duppur* is equivalent to *libbašu ṭāb,* at least functionally. According to most authorities, it is a term of receipt and quittance. [2]) The whole clause would then read: "they have divided; they are finished; they are quit." The translation "quit" renders the sense rather than the etymology. According to *CAD* [3]), against Koschaker, Matouš, and Von Soden, the term is related to the rare poetic expression *dapāru* "to slake the thirst, to be satisfied" used of Enkidu in the Gilgamesh Epic.

According to this interpretation, *duppur* "satisfied" is not only the functional equivalent of *libbašu ṭāb* but is also based on the same root metaphor of satisfaction. However, there are several objections to this interpretation: (a) *dapāru* in Gilgamesh is rare and poetic; *duppur* in Susa is common and legal; (b) the Gilgamesh usage is in the G, while

---

[1]) For a study of these deeds, cf. Klíma, *Elamischen Erbrecht*. For the use of the clause *zīzū mesû duppurū*—and the alternate order, *zīzū duppurū mesû*—cf. *ibid.*, p. 9, n. 27. Cf. Matouš, *ArOr*, 32 (1964), p. 132.

[2]) So Klíma and Koschaker, *Göttliches Recht*, p. 56.

[3]) *CAD* contains two entries for the root *dpr*: (a) *dapāru* "to be sated" applied to Enkidu in the expression *itti būlim mašqâ idappir* "he sates himself with the animals at the drinking place" (Gilg. I ii 40). The expression *zīzū duppurū mesû* is listed under this entry and is translated: "they have divided (the property), they are satisfied, they have cleared up the matter" (*CAD, D*, p. 104); (b) *duppur*, which means either "go away" or "drive away" (*CAD, D*, pp. 186 ff.).*

the Susa usage is in the D form. [1]) Since the closely related D form *udappar* "he goes away, runs away" is used regularly in OB legal documents to describe the illegal departure of slaves or other servile persons from their masters' services, [2]) it seems methodologically sounder to interpret the Susa clause *zīzū mesû* duppurū* as "they have finished dividing; they have removed themselves," i.e., they are quitted. This is also the interpretation of Koschaker and Von Soden. [3]) It is also confirmed by several other considerations. The lexical tablets equate *duppur* with *rêqu* (the Aramaic *rḥq*). [4]) If the interpretation just suggested is correct, *duppur* has two aspects: a) that of a right-holder who removes himself from his property; b) that of a servile person who removes himself (illegally) from his master's service. The same aspectuality is reflected in the isogloss *rêqu*: an owner of property *irêq* "removes himself from his property" [5]); an indentured hand *irêq* "removes himself" from his owner's service. [6]) Furthermore, to support the argument with comparative evidence, the use of the metaphor "to remove oneself" as a term of quittance and cession is clearly reflected in the Aramaic *rḥq*. [7]) There is one final argument against deriving *duppur* from the metaphor of satisfaction. *Duppur* is also used several times in Susa deeds of litigation. [8]) The party that loses his rights and claims is *duppur nasiḫ*. [9])

[1]) The problem of intransitive verbs in the D stem is discussed by Von Soden in his discussion of *duppur* (*Or*, 18 [1949], p. 395). Intransitive Piel forms are also known from Biblical Hebrew; cf. Is 60: 11 *ūfittᵉḥū šᵉʿārāyiḵ tāmīḏ* "And your gates shall be open continually."

[2]) Cf. the texts cited in *CAD, D*, p. 187.

[3]) Cf. Koschaker, *Göttliches Recht*, p. 56: "sie halten sich (nach der Teilung) fern." Also Von Soden, *Or*, 18 (1949), p. 395.

[4]) Cf. *CAD, D*, p. 186, where *duppur* is also equated with *nesû* "to go far away/to be far away" in various lexical series.

[5]) Cf. *JEN* 221 : 18.

[6]) Cf. *HSS* V 105 : 18. The term *ruʾāqum* is used quite frequently in Old Assyrian legal documents as a synonym of *ḫalāqum* and *abātum* "to run away." The two latter terms are applied regularly to slaves who run away from their masters. The three terms—*ruʾāqum, ḫalāqum,* and *abātum*—are also applied to capital investments which "run away" from their masters, i.e., which are lost to their owners because of nonpayment of debts (cf. J. Lewy, "Grammatical and Lexicographical Studies," *Or*, 29 (1960), pp. 25 ff.; cf. especially p. 25, n. 5, where the identity of the OAs *ruʾāqum* with the *OB rêqum* is established.)

[7]) Cf. the end of Chapter II of this study.

[8]) *MDP* XXI 379: 18; 375: 2′ and 4′.

[9]) *MDP* XXIV 379: Gimil-Adad bequeathes all his property to his wife, Bēltani. Any child of Gimil-Adad who contests the donation "shall not enter her house and eat her (!) bread (lines 13-14)." The next few lines are broken. Line 17 reads: *ú-ul i-qa-ab-bi* "he shall not say" followed by *na-sí-iḫ du-up-pu-ur*. In this context, these terms can only mean: "(whoever says thus) is disinherited and removed." The preceding is contrasted to the following stipulations (lines 19 ff.): "The child who serves her (faithfully) (*ša palāḫša īpušu*) shall enjoy her favor (*maḫriša uššab*)."

The second term *nasiḫ* is well known from OB texts: it means "uprooted/removed/deprived of rights/forfeited." [1]) Clearly, in this context *duppur* cannot be translated "satisfied." Only one translation is possible, "far removed." [2]) The Aramaic *rḥq* also has the same semantic range: *rḥyq* "removed" is often applied to a litigant who has no more claims and rights. [3])

To sum up: *duppur* is essentially a term of quittance; it is also an exact semantic parallel of the Akkadian *rêqu*. It expresses one basic idea—the severance of an owner relationship—from two points of view: (a) that of the owner or claimant who—voluntarily or involuntarily—relinquishes/forfeits his rights/claims; (b) that of the servile (*gewalt-unterworfene*) person who legally or illegally severs the servile relationship. In its first aspect, *duppur* is often used in the Susa documents as a term of quittance after the receipt of an inheritance share.

Since *libbašu ṭāb-libbašu uṭīb* when used in the passive voice and in certain specific contexts, along with the nuances of completed payment and receipt, also expresses the idea of quittance, its semantic range sometimes overlaps that of *duppur*. Thus, in the correspondence between Sippar *zīzū gamrū libbašunu ṭāb* "they have finished the division; their

[1]) The semantic range of this root and its interdialectal distribution deserve an independent study. For the time being, the following observations may be made: Even though the root is usually translated "to uproot", more often than not, it conveys the idea of "removal" and "transfer" (cf. *ARM*, IV, 4: 11'). Similarly, *nasāḫu* is the regular Akkadian term for deportation; in this sense, it probably refers as much to the removal of populations from their place of dwelling and their transplantation to another as it does to the idea of uprooting them (cf. the West Semitic variant *hwrd* "to deport," lit. "to bring down" used in Karatepe I: 20 and Isaiah 10: 13 (according to the interpretation of H. L. Ginsberg).

Furthermore, as well as the transitive meaning "to remove," "to take away," the term also has a less well-known intransitive meaning: "to go away," "to pass." Cf. the common expression b a . z a l=*issuḫ* "(time) passed." See also the expression found in a deed of hire: *i-na-pu-uš i-na-sa-aḫ i-na-ad-di it-ta-al-la-ak i-na idi-šu i-te-el-li* "If he (the hired hand) runs away, departs, is lax, goes away, he shall forfeit his wages" (*UM* VIII_2 196). (Cf. the same transitive-intransitive aspectuality reflected in *duppur*.)

In legal texts, *nasāḫu* means "to remove, to cancel (a claim)." More specifically, it is applied to judges who reject the claims of a litigant (*rugummê nasāḫu*, lit. "to remove claims": Schorr, *Urkunden*, No. 257: 9=*CT* VIII 28a; No. 274: 15=*CT* VI 42a); to parents who disinherit their children (*ina aplūtim nasāḫum*, lit. "to remove from the status of heir"; Schorr, *Urkunden*, No. 258: 14=*CT* II 31; No. 215: 34=*CT* VIII 20a; cf. also *CH* 158 and, in a slightly different context, *LE* 59 and the discussion of Koschaker, "Zur Interpretation des Art. 59 des Codex Bilalama," *JCS*, 5 (1951), p. 110, n. 20 where extensive literature is cited).

[2]) Cf., however, the contrasting interpretation of Klíma, *Donationes*, p. 139 where *nasiḫ duppur* is translated: "(das Geschäft) ist klargebracht, erledig." *

[3]) Cf. *AP* 20: 15 *hw ʾpm rḥyq mn ʾlh nksyʾ* 'he (the contestant), moreover, is removed (= *nasiḫ*, *duppur*) from these goods."

hearts are satisfied, i.e., they are quit" and the Susa *zīzū mesû duppurū* "they have finished dividing; they have removed themselves (from each other), i.e., they are quit," *libbašunu ṭāb* and *duppurū* have more in common with each other than the passive *libbašu ṭāb* has with the active *libbašu uṭīb* or than *duppur*[a] (the right-holder's relinquishment) has with *duppur*[b] (the departure of the servile person from a master's ownership). [1])

The equivalence of *duppur* both with *rḥq* and with *libbašu ṭāb* is paralleled by the partial overlap of the Aramaic *ṭyb lbby* "my heart is satisfied" with the closely related term *rḥqt mnk.* [2]) It was noted above that *rḥqt mnk,* the Aramaic quittance term par excellence, is often used as a complement to *ṭyb lbby* to explicate the quittance nuance inherent in the many-faceted performance-receipt-quittance term, *ṭyb lbby.* On occasion, *ṭyb lbby* is used where *rḥqt mnk* is demanded by the structural logic of the deed. The fact that the partial overlap of *ṭyb lbby* with *rḥqt* parallels a similar overlap between *duppur/rêqu* and *libbašu ṭāb* hardly seems to be produced by coincidence; the partial overlap of the Aramaic/Akkadian terms of "removal" and the Aramaic and: Akkadian terms of "satisfaction" seems to me to be one more indicator of the historical relationship between the two traditions.

B. *The Sippar* libbašu ṭāb = *Kültepe* šabû*

The Susa *duppur* is only a partial isogloss of *libbašu ṭāb,* since it only takes the place of *libbašu ṭāb* in Susa division contracts; however, it does not take the place of *libbašu ṭāb* in the Susa deeds that record receipt of wages, in Susa litigation, or in marriage. Furthermore, besides the quittance function which both terms hold in common, each has a broad semantic range not shared by the other: *libbašu uṭīb* expresses the completion of a payment, while *udappar* describes the severance of a servile relationship. Nor do the terms share a common root metaphor: *duppur(ū)* is based on the metaphor of "removal-departure"; *libbašu ṭāb* on the metaphor of "satisfaction."

The closest semantic equivalent of *libbašu ṭāb* is the slightly older Old Assyrian term *ušabbīšu-šabû* used quite frequently in the deeds of Kültepe. [3]) The two terms overlap in almost all respects: syntax and grammar, complements, semantic-contextual range, and root metaphor.

---

[1]) Expressed schematically as follows:

Payment	*Quittance*	*Liberation* (a gewaltunterworfene person "departs")
libbašu uṭīb	*libbašu ṭāb*	
	duppur[a]	*duppur*[b] (= *udappar*)

[2]) Cf. above, the end of Chapter II.

[3]) For the date of the Kültepe documents, cf. Goetze, *Kleinasien,* pp. 64 ff., and P. Garelli, *Les Assyriens en Cappadoce,* pp. 31-79.

Šabû *in Sale.* The term is used frequently in deeds of sale.

EL 107 (= *KTS* 46)

(1) *bītam*$^{bi_4\text{-}tám}$ *ša iš-ti I-ku-nim* (2) *mēr Sà!-ma-a* «TA» *Pè-ru-a* (3) *mēr Wa-lá-aḫ-ší-na* (4) *a-na* 1/2 *manêm* 4 *lá* 1/4 *šiqlī* (5) *iš-ú-mu iš-tí* (6) *Pè-ru-a a-na* 1/2 *manêm* 4 *lá* 1/4 *šiqlī* (7) *Um-mì-na-ra* (8) *ta-áš-a-am-šu kaspam* (9) *ša-bu.* Witnesses.
(1) "The house which from Ikūnum (2) son of Samāa, Peru'a (3) son of Walaḫšina (4) for 1/2 mina, four-minus 1/4 shekels (5) bought. From (6) Peru'a for 1/2 mina, four-minus 1/4 shekels (7) Umminara (8) bought it. With the money (9) he is satisfied.

Šabû *in Litigation. Šabû,* like its isogloss *libbašu ṭāb,* is also used in litigation settlements.

EL 11 (= *TC* 79)

The following situation is recorded in this deed: Ikuppia owed money to Pūšu-kēn. Pūšu-kēn died; his son, Aššur-mutabbil and a certain *rābiṣu* claimed the money. They received it according to the decree of the court. In this deed, the sons and daughters of Pūšu-kēn promise not to raise claims in the future. The following clause of quittance is found at the end of the deed:

(24) *ma-lá dí-in a-lim*^{ki} *kaspam* (25) *me-er-ú Pu-šu-ki-in* (26) *ù mērat Pu-šu-ki-in ša-bu-ú*

(24) "In accordance with the decree of the 'city' (25-26), the sons and daughters of Pūšu-kēn are satisfied with the money (i.e., they are quitted and will raise no future claims)."

The deed does not state specifically that the debtor actually "satisfied" the creditors with the money owed. However, if this was not the case, why was *šabû* "they are satisfied" used? Or can *šabû* express abstract quittance without the receipt of some satisfactory consideration? The former assumption seems more plausible.

Quitclaims. It was suggested above that the quitclaim was the original Sitz im Leben of the term *libbašu ṭāb.* The frequent use of the isogloss *šabû* in such documents is amply attested:

EL 191

(1) 16 1/2 *šiqlī kaspam* (2) *ša Pì-lá-aḫ-A-šur* (3) *i-ṣé-er Šu-A-nim* (4) *i-šu-ú kaspam* (5) *Pí-lá-aḫ-A-šur* (6) *ša-bu-ú* (7) *Pí-lá-aḫ-A-šur w[a-ar]-ki-šu* (8) *a-na Šu-A-nim* (9) *ú-lá i-tù-wa-ar*

(1) "(Concerning the) 16 1/2 shekels of silver (2) which to Pilaḫ-Aššur is (3) owed by Šū-Anum; (5) Pilaḫ-Aššur is satisfied with the money. (7) Pilaḫ-Aššur (9) will not contest (7) with (8) Šū-Anum."

The term *šabû* is also found in many other quitclaims. Significantly, in all of these deeds, the reason for the "satisfaction" is clearly stated: the creditor is "satisfied with the money" (*EL* 197, 202, 210, and 212), "with his money" (*EL* 206), or with "the price of his slave girl" (*EL* 213). In this practice of specifying the immediate reason for the satisfaction, the Old Assyrian deeds are identical with the earliest conveyances from Sippar where the clause *libbašu ṭūb* "his heart has been satisfied" was usually supplemented by *kaspam šīm bītišu gamram* "with the complete money, the price of his house." [1])

Active-Passive Cluster. The Akkadian and Aramaic terms of satisfaction emply both the active (*libbašu uṭīb/hwṭbt lbby*) and the passive (*libbašu ṭāb/ṭyb lbby*) voices. In all of the Kültepe texts quoted so far, only the passive *šabû* "satisfied" has been used. However, there is at least one text which employs the active form *ušabbīšu* "he (the new right-holder) satisfied him (the old right-holder)."

EL 194

This deed records the repayment of a loan. The term *šubbû* "to satisfy" is used here exactly as *libbašu uṭīb* was used in Sippar deeds recording the repayment of debts.

(1) 1/3 *manêm kaspam* (2) *ša A-šùr-na-da a-na* (3) *Uš-ḫu-ba mēr Ḫa-al-gi₅-a-šu* (4) *ù A-ší-i-id mēr Lu-ùḫ-ra-aḫ-šu* (5) *i-ḫi-ib-lu-ni kaspam* (6) *ù ṣí-pá-sú Uš-ḫu-ba* (7) *ù A-ší-i-id A-šùr-na-da* (8) *ú-ša-bi-šu-nu kasapáp-šu-nu* (9) *ša-bu-ú.*

(1) "(Concerning) the 1/3 mina of silver (2) which Aššur-nā'dā from (3) Ušḫuba son of Ḫalgiašu (4) and Ašīd son of Luḫraḫšu (5) borrowed.* With the money (6) and its interest (7) Aššur-nā'dā (8) satisfied (6-7) Ušḫuba and Ašīd. (8) With their money (9) they are satisfied."

In this deed, the active *ušabbīšu* "he satisfied him" is used together with the stative *šabû* to form an active-passive cluster, a syntactical structure common in the Bible and Ugaritic poetry, and used sporadically in Akkadian documents as well. The cluster *ušabbīšu-šabû* is a perfect

[1]) The expression *nisḫāssu watrā šaduāssu šabû* is quite common in certain types of business transactions. The expression is translated by Goetze as "die Steuer dafür ist beigefügt, mit den Gebühren dafür sind sie gestättigt." The subject of this clause must be the palace officials. For examples, discussion, and literature, cf. Goetze, *ibid.*, p. 76, n. 6.*

semantic and syntactical parallel of the Elephantine *hwṭbtm lbbn wṭyb lbbn* (*AP* 20) "you have satisfied our heart-our heart is satisfied." The presence of *ušabbīšu-šabû* in the Old Assyrian documents and its echo in the Aramaic *hwṭbtm-ṭyb* seems to add support to the conjecture that the Aramaic was derived from an original cluster *libbašu uṭīb-libbašu ṭūb*.

Historical Implications. The fact that the isoglosses of *libbašu ṭāb* are found in the Old Assyrian deeds of Kültepe and in Old Babylonian Susa—both areas whose legal traditions are mainly derived from the archaic Sargonic praxis [1])—lends further support to the thesis that *libbašu ṭāb* is more a reflection of the archaic Akkadian legal tradition than of the Sumerian.

C. *OB* libbašu ṭāb = *MB* zakû

Just as the Old Assyrian *ušabbīšu-šabû* gave way to the OB *libbašu uṭīb-libbašu ṭūb*, so the latter gave way to the MB, MA term *uzakkīšu-zakû* "he made him quit-he is quitted." Although *zakû* is based on the metaphor of "purity" instead of "satisfaction," it is functionally identical —in certain specific contexts—with *libbašu ṭāb*.*

The Alalakh Evidence. The semantic equivalence of *zakû* with *libbašu ṭāb* is definitively established by a comparison of the OB conveyances from the city of Alalakh with the MB conveyances of the same city.

Old Babylonian

**AT* 52

(14) *a-na ši-im ga-me-ir*	(14) "at full price,
(15) *i-ša-am* (16′) *ap-lu li-ib-ba-šu-nu*	(15) he bought; (16′) They (the
(17′) *ṭa-a-ab*	sellers) are paid off; their heart 17′ is satisfied."

(Cf. also **AT* 58:9-10; **AT* 61:12-13, and **AT* 53: 1′-2′.)

Middle Babylonian

AT 66

(4) *ᴵIlim-ilim-ma* (5) 50 *kaspu*^{pu} (6) *il-qí-šu* (7) *ù ši-im-šu* (8) *a-pil za-ku* (4) "Ilim-ilimma (5) (for) 50 shekels of silver (6) bought him (i.e., the slave). (7-8) With his price, he (the buyer) is paid (and) quit."

Significantly, the structure of the clause remains constant: *aplū* plus a term of quittance; only the term of quittance which fills the last position changes from period to period. The dialectal change which replaced

[1]) The relationship between the Kültepe deeds, other provincial traditions —especially the Susan—and the Old Akkadian documents is worthy of an independent discussion. For the time being, cf. p. 45, note 1.

Alalakh level seven (OB) conveyance *libbašu ṭāb* with level four (MB) conveyance *zakû* took place all over the Near East: Cf. Middle Babylonian —*maḫir apil zakû* "received he (the price); he (seller) is paid, quit" (Peiser, *Urkunden*, 139 : 11)—and Middle Assyrian—*šīm eqlišu maḫir apil zakû* "the price of his field, he (the seller) has received; he is paid, quit" (KAJ, 27 : 20). Thus, *zakû* becomes the classic term of quittance during this period and well into the Neo-Babylonian era. Unfortunately, its wide diffusion and distribution from MB-MA times on tended to obscure the quittance functions of the older isoglosses, *libbašu ṭāb* and *šabû*.

However, it should not be assumed that the "sudden" disappearance of *libbašu ṭāb* and its replacement by *zakû* reflects the supposed breakdown of societal norms during the "second dark ages." [1]) Significantly, the over-all structure of the Alalakh conveyance does not change that radically from level seven to level four: both conveyances contain a clause of receipt and quittance. Furthermore, even though *zakû* does take the place of the older *libbašu ṭāb*, it should not be assumed that the term itself is a Middle Babylonian innovation; on the contrary: the expression *kirâm . . . izūzū za-ku-ú* "they divided (the property) and are quit" is already found in an Old Babylonian document. [2])

The equivalence of OB *uzakkû/ubbibū*, lit. "they purified," contextually, "they made (a right-holder) quit" seems to be reflected in a series of OB deeds recording the liquidation of a *tappûtu*-partnership. [3]) The partners usually divided the common property into individual shares in the temple. In *R* 15 (Schorr, *Urkunden* 170; Sippar, Ṣabium), the division transaction takes place in the *ašar tēbibtim* (line 16), lit. "the place of purification." The division clause itself reads: (3) *ma-ḫa-ar* *^{d}Šamaš* *a-ḫu-[um libb a-ḫi-im]* (4) *ú-ṭí-[ib]* "In the presence of Šamaš, each satisfied [each other's] heart." The expressions means: "by giving a share of the whole property to partner B, partner A induced B to relinquish any residual claim he may still have against the share that A received." "To satisfy the heart" means to make someone quit. Significantly, the procedure takes place in the place of *tēbibtum* "purification"; in this context "purification" seems to mean "liquidation, quittance." In another text—*M* 79 (= Schorr, *Urkunden* 169; Sippar, Ṣabium)—the clause is *iš!-tu pi-e* (16) *a-na ḫurāṣim ú-za-ku* "they made each other quit

---

1) Cf. Speiser, "The Alalakh Tablets," *JAOS*, 74 (1954), pp. 18 ff.

2) *TLC* XI 141 : 14; cf. *CAD*, *Z*, p. 27.

3) Cf. Eilers, *Gesellschaftsformen*, pp. 27 ff., especially p. 28, n. 2 for a discussion of the *tappûtu* relationship in general and, more specifically, for a discussion of the term *tazkītum*.

(16) from straw to gold." The equivalence of *uṭībū* with *uzakkû* seems fairly certain. A third text—*M* 78 (= Schorr, *Urkunden* 171; Warka, Ḫammurabi)—the clause reads: (4) *a-na ta-az-ki-tim* (5) *da-ya-ni ik-šu-du-ú-ma* . . . (15) *zi-i-zu-ú* (16) *i-na bīt* ^{d}*Šamaš ù* ^{d}*Sîn* (17) *iz-ku-ru a-ḫu-um a-na a-ḫi-im* (18) *ú-ub-bi-bu-ú* (4) "They went before the judges for a settlement . . . (15) they divided; (16) in the temple of Šamaš and Sîn (17) they pronounced (an oath); (18) they declared each other *eb* "pure/quit."

Thus, the equation *aḫum ana aḫim ubbibū/uzakkû/uṭībū* seems to emerge. All these expressions mean essentially the same thing: to make a right-holder quit by tendering a satisfactory consideration. Furthermore, since the parties to the transaction recorded in *M* 78 *ubbibū* "clear each other" in the *tazkītum* ("purification/quittance") ceremony, *ubbubu* would seem to be the synonym of *zukkû*. On the other hand, in *R* 15, the parties to the transaction "satisfy each other's hearts" in the *ašar tēbibtim* "in the place of purification/quittance." This would seem to confirm the equation *libbi* PN *uṭīb* = *ubbubu/zukkû*. [1])

One more observation concerning the contextual range of MB *zakû*. In a deed of loan from Larsa quoted above, [2]) the following stipulation is found: In the x day of y month, the debtor *libbi* creditor *uṭâb*. Once again, the term means "to make a right-holder quit by paying an *Entgelt* or money owed." A similar type of transaction is found in later Babylonian deeds: *ša il-lam-ma i-qab-bu-ú um-ma-a kaspu ul nadin ù ra-ša-a ul ú-zak-ki* "whoever shall rise up saying: 'the silver was not paid; he has not satisfied the creditor'" (King, *BBSt* 9 IV A: 27). The translation of *uzakki* by "satisfy" (cf. King and *CAD*) [3]) is independent confirmation of the equivalence of *libbašu uṭīb* and *zukkû*.

D. *OB* libbašu ṭāb = *MB* zakû = *Late NB* eṭir

Sometime during the late Neo-Babylonian period, the regular receipt-quittance formula *maḫir/nadin zakû* undergoes a significant change: the quittance term *zakû* is replaced by a new term *eṭir*. [4]) The dictionaries

---

[1]) *CAD, E*, p. 6, interpret the Mari use of *tēbibtum* in the light of the OB evidence. However, a different societal pattern may be reflected in the Mari usage (cf. E. A. Speiser, "Census and Ritual Expiation in Mari and Israel," *BASOR*, 149 (1958), pp. 117-125).

[2]) Cf. Chapter IV, p. 83. The text is *Riftin* 6: 5-7.

[3]) *CAD, Z*, p. 30, col. ii.

[4]) Cf. the frequent occurrence of the term in the quitclaims (*giṭṭānu*) in G. Cardascia, *Les archives des Murašû*, pp. 108 ff. Cf. BE, IX, 84: 9 *maḫ-ru-ʾ e-ṭir-uʾ*; BE, X 6: 11 *ma-ḫir e-ṭir*; BE, X, 115: 14-15 *ma-ḫir e-ṭir* and *passim*. Cf. also the texts cited by *CAD, E*, pp. 404 ff. The term is also used in the quittance clause of NB conveyances (cf. Petschow, *Kaufformulare*, p. 16, n. 27: "Neben *maḫir* finden

are at a loss to explain the relationship between the regular *eṭēru* "to remove" and the late NB term *eṭēru* "to pay off" and the stative *eṭir* "to be paid off; to be quitted." [1]) However, the semantic development of a term of "removal" into a term of "quittance" is not without precedent: in several OB deeds from Susa the buyer *utīr qāssu* "removes his hand (the seller)" from the sold property by tendering the seller the full price: in another deed, the seller's hand has been removed (*qāssu turrat*) upon receipt of the full price. *Qāssu turrat* contextually means: he is quitted. [2]) A similar semantic development is reflected in the Gaonic Hebrew *sillēq* the creditor *min* "he (the debtor) removed the creditor (by payment)." [3]) *Eṭir* simply means "removed" therefore quitted. One could hardly ask for a closer semantic parallel to the Aramaic *rḥyq* "removed/quit" or to the Susa *duppur* "removed/quit."

E. *Degrees of Overlap among* šabû, libbašu ṭāb, *and* zakû

To what degree do the semantic ranges of these various isoglosses really overlap? At the outset, a clear contrast emerges between *šabû* and *libbašu ṭāb* on the one hand, and *zakû* on the other. The terms *šabû* and *libbašu ṭāb* seem to overlap in all significant respects. However, they convey nuances not expressed by *zakû*, while *zakû*, although partially overlapping with *šabû-libbašu ṭāb*, has a whole range of meaning not found in the first two terms. The three terms overlap in one fixed context alone: the receipt-quittance clause.

1) *šabû* and *libbašu ṭāb*

---

sich: gelegentlich *eṭir* (Pohl 2; 3; 8; NRV I 40; 51), regelmässig *apil* und in der Texten der assyrischen und frühen chaldäischen Zeit *zaki* (später selten, z.B. in Cyr 3)."

[1]) *CAD* lists the two aspects of the same root under different entries and comments (*E*, p. 404): "The two spheres of meaning of *eṭēru* ,"to take away," and "to save," can be connected if we interpret "to save" as "to take way from disaster, death, etc."; that a semantic connection exists is shown by the logograms KAR and SUR, which are common to both spheres. The NB verb *eṭēru* "to pay," although it, too, has the same logograms, has been treated separately as *eṭēru* B." Von Soden in his *AHw* also treats the concepts of "removal" and "payment" as two separate lexical entities.

[2]) For the expressions *qāssu utīr* "(the buyer) removed his (i.e., the seller's) hand" and *qāssu turrat* "his (i.e., the seller's) hand has been removed," cf. *MDP* II, "Kudurru de Nazimaruttaš," p. 87, line 17 and *MDP* IV, No. 14, p. 190, line 16 (for the later Hebrew analogue *sillēq* the creditor *mn* "to remove the creditor from"/ "to pay him off," cf. *Ben Yehudah*, p. 4084-5). For a later Aramaic reflex of the NA *uṭṭur* "to be removed/to relinquish claims" (cf. *ADD* 155: 6; *ND* 2337: 7; *VAS* I 97: 8), cf. the Talmudic deed of slave sale called *ʿyṭrʾ* or "deed of removal" cited in *TB*, *Bāḇā Baṯrā* 29b and *Bāḇā Meṣīʿā* 39b. The relationship between these terms deserves an extensive discussion.*

[3]) Cf. the preceding note.

These terms have the following common characteristics:

The subject of these terms can only be a former right-holder (a seller or a claimant); a slave cannot be *šabû* of his master.

The active forms *ušabbīšu* and *libbašu uṭīb* record the rendering of a satisfactory consideration.

The passive forms clearly echo the preceding performance: *šabû* and *libbašu ṭāb* mean: quit after having been tendered full performance. Thus, *libbašu ṭāb* is at once a term of receipt and quittance with clear overtones of performance. These various nuances are inherent in the metaphor of "satisfaction" and are not the result of contextual association.

2) *zakû*

This term, like its equivalents *el* and *eb* "to be free, quit" based on the metaphor of purity, is a term which usually described the freedom of property, either animate or inanimate, from its owner, or from the burden of taxes or feudal obligations. [1]) Correspondingly, the active form *uzakki* meant "to liberate from ownership and/or obligations." [2]) On rare occasions, *zakû* could be applied to a right-holder who surrendered his rights. [3])

During the MB period, several important developments took place: First of all, *zakû/uzakki* replaced the older *el/ullil, eb/ubbib*. [4]) Secondly, the receipt-quittance terms *šabû** and *libbašu ṭāb* disappeared. [5]) Thirdly, the semantic range of *zakû* is extended to include that of *libbašu ṭāb*. Now *zakû* commonly expresses the quittance of a right-holder as well as the freedom of a *gewaltunterworfene* person. [6]) The extension of the range of *zakû* was based on rare OB models. In this extended usage, *uzakki* comes to mean "to satisfy by tendering payment/to make a rightholder *zakû* quit." [7])*

Libbašu ṭāb is essentially a term of performance and receipt; its quittance function is a result of the performance-receipt functions. On the other hand, *zakû* is essentially a pure quittance term like the Aramaic

[1]) For extensive citation, cf. *CAD, Z*, pp. 25-31.
[2]) *Ibid.*, especially pp. 28 ff.
[3]) Cf. *TCL* XI 141: 14: *kirâm . . . izūzū zakû* "they divided the garden and are free (from mutual claims)."
[4]) I do not know of any legal use of these terms after the OB period. Cf. *CAD, E*, pp. 6 ff. and pp. 81 ff.
[5]) I have not found the term in documents of a later period.
[6]) As in the receipt-quittance clause *apil maḫir zakû*.
[7]) As in the expression *rāšâ ul uzakki* "he has not satisfied the creditor."

rḥq and the Akkadian *rêqu* and *duppur*. Its receipt nuance is a result of its contextual associations rather than its essential nature.

2. Contrasting Terms and Clauses

In the Aramaic section of this study, the following contrast between the structure of sale and that of gift was established: the constitutive element in the gift transaction is the spontaneous volition which motivates the donor to part with his property without the receipt of some counter-donation; this volition is expressed by the clauses *yhbt lk brḥmn* "I hereby give you in affection" and *ʿšt lk bḥyy yhbt lk bmwty* "I have turned my thoughts to you during my lifetime and have given you (the property) after my death." On the other hand, the constitutive elements in the sale transaction are the payment of the full price by the buyer, the receipt of the price by the seller, and his satisfaction-quittance therewith. Performance, receipt, and quittance are all expressed by the clause *ṭyb lbbn bdmyʾ zy yhbt ln* "our heart is satisfied with the money you have given us." [1] Do similar contrasts between terms of volition in *unentgeltliche* transactions and terms of performance, receipt, and quittance in *entgeltliche* transactions exist in related Akkadian legal documents? Or, to formulate the question from the Assyriological point of view: if *libbašu ṭāb* really expresses quittance upon receipt of consideration, how is volition expressed in cuneiform legal literature? Do these Akkadian terms of volition contrast with *libbašu ṭāb*?

A. *The Verb* ḫadû *"to rejoice" as a Term of Volition*

The most common term of volition in cuneiform legal documents is the Neo-Babylonian expression *ina ḫūd libbišu iddin* "he (the right-holder) gave in the joy of his heart." In this context, "joy" is used as the legal metaphor for spontaneous volition, willingness to part with the property." [2] The volitional function of the term is confirmed by its synonym *ina migir libbišu* "with the agreement of his heart." [3] In Neo-Babylonian documents, the clause is found at the beginning of deeds recording the sale of mobilia [4] and in most dialogue documents. [5] In the later Arsacid documents, the use of the clause is extended to almost all transactions, including the sale of land. [6] In none of these deeds are terms of volition limited to *unentgeltliche* transactions.

---

1) Above, Chapter II.
2) Cf. San Nicolò, *Beiträge*, pp. 158 and 182.
3) *Ibid.*, p. 181.
4) Cf. Petschow, *Kaufformulare*, pp. 45 ff.
5) Cf. San Nicolò, *Beiträge*, pp. 181 ff.
6) Cf. Krückmann, *BRVU*, pp. 28 ff.

San Nicolò considered the use of terms of volition to be the innovation of the Neo-Babylonian period. [1]) He seriously doubted the presence of real terms of volition in deeds earlier than the NB period. [2]) However, his negative verdict does not seem to be confirmed by a reexamination of the earlier sources. Even though terms of volition may not have been used as widely as they were in the NB period, they are attested in MB/MA and OB periods. [3]) In fact, most of the earliest terms of volition were either based on the root *ḫadû* "to rejoice" or on one of its synonyms *ṭābu* "to be happy" or *râmu* "to like."

OB Use of ḫadû. The volitional use of *ḫadû* in the OB period is reflected in the following source:

CT VIII 49a (= Schorr, *Urkunden* 14; Sippar, Apil-Sîn)

Šī-lamassi adopts Ḫunābatiya and bequeathes to her adopted daughter all of her property. At the same time, the father of the girl presents gifts to his daughter and her new mother.

(25) *i-nu-ma Ši-la-ma-sí* (26) *a-na ma-ar-ti-ša iš-ṭu-ru*! (27) *ᵈEnlil-ma-lik iḫ-du-ma* (28) *ištēn ˢᵃᵍwardam* . . . (35) *a-na Ši-la-ma-sí-i* (36) *ù Ḫu-na-ba-ti-ia* (37) *ᵈEnlil-ma-lik i-di-in*

(25) "When Šī-lamassi (26) recorded (Ḫ.) as her daughter, (27) Enlil-mālik rejoiced; (28) one slave . . . (35-7) to Š. and Ḫ. he gave."

CAD correctly renders the terms *iḫdūma . . . iddin* as a hendiadys: "he gave voluntarily." Significantly, the transaction is *unentgeltlich.*

Ras Shamra Use of ḫadû. The oldest known use of the noun form *ina ḫūd libbi* is found in the Ras Shamra Akkadian document *PRU* III = *RS* 16. 129:3 ff.

PN *ardu ša* PN_2 . . . *iddû u ana muḫḫi* gud.áb.meš *uza[kk]ūšu* PN_2 *ina ḫūd libbišu ana [ri]ʾītu ša* gud.áb.meš *ana* PN_3 *ittadin**

"PN_2 (who is selling his prebend to PN_3) of his own free will gave his slave, PN, whom he had marked (with the spade and the stylus on his hand) and

[1]) San Nicolò, *Beiträge*, p. 181: "Erst im neubabylonischen Recht lassen sich die ersten Anzeichen einer bewussten Hervorhebung des Willenselementes, also einer Willenstheorie . . . beim Geschäftsabschluss wahrnemen. Das Erfordernis des freien . . . Willens bricht sich in der Klausel *ina ḫūd* (*migir*) *libbišu* . . . Bahn".

[2]) *Ibid.*, p. 181. Cf. also the negative verdict of Koschaker (*Rechtsvergleichende Studien*, p. 16, n. 20) and of Walther (*Gerichtswesen*, p. 21, n. 1). Koschaker (*OLZ*, 1932, p. 320) also doubted the volitional function of the NB *ina ḫūd libbi* and the MA *ina migir ramnišu.*

[3]) The presence of volitional terms in OB legal documents was maintained by Cuq, "Les actes juridiques Susiens," *RA*, 28 (1931), p. 61.

whom he had released (on the condition that he) serve (with) the cattle (belonging to the prebend), PN_3, for the tending of the cattle" (so *CAD, Z*, p. 29b).

MA, Nuzi, and Kudurru Uses. The volitional character of *ḫadû* is clearly reflected in the regular Nuzi expression *ašar ḫadê illak-inaddin* "he may go/give wherever/to whomever he wants" [1]) (the Nuzi isogloss or the OB *ašar ṭābušim inaddin* "he may give whomever he wants") and in the Middle Assyrian expression *ḫadi . . . ḫadi* "if he wants . . . if he wants." [2])

One of the least noticed uses of *ḫadû* as a term of volition is found in a ninth century Babylonian *kudurru*. [3]) The most common function of this type of document was the publication of property rights and the insurance of these newly created rights by the magical imprecations written on the boundary-stone. Such *kudurrus* were literally stones erected on the boundary between the property of two neighbors. However, the *kudurru* form was later employed simply as a charter which conveyed rights or bestowed exemptions from feudal service. *Kudurru* documents were sometimes written in the name of a god who bestowed upon his elected king the rights of his office, or in the name of a king who invested his high priest with his revenues. [4]) In one of these investiture-*kudurrus*, [5]) Nabû-apla-iddina, the king of Babylon, bestows priestly revenues upon Nabû-nādin-šum, the priest of Sippar. The actual donation of rights is preceded by the following, rather florid, introduction describing the king's state of mind as he made the donation:

(36) *ša* *^{d}Nabû-apla-iddina^{na}* (37) *š[ar] Bābili* (38) *lib-ba-šu iḫ-du-ma* (39) *im-me-ru zi-mu-šu* (40) *eli* *^{Id}Nabû-nādin-šum* (41) *šangû Sippar^{ki}* *^{lú}bārû* (42) *it-ru-ṣa bu-ni-šu* (43) *ina bu-ni-šu nam-ru-ti* (44) *zi-me-šu ru-uš-šu-ti* (45) *damqāti^{meš} īnā^{II}-šu ḫa-diš* (46) *ip-pa-lis-su-ma* . . . Col. V (13) *arad-su i-rim*

"The heart of Nabû-apla-iddina the king of Babylon rejoiced. His countenance became bright. He turned his attention on Nabû-nādin-šum, the priest of Sippar. With his bright gaze,* shining countenance (and)

---

[1]) Cf., for example, *JEN* 465: 10-12.

[2]) Cf. The Assyrian Laws, § 55. Cf. *CAD, Ḫ*, p. 27a.

[3]) Concerning the functions of the *kudurru*, cf. Steinmetzer, *Grenzsteine* and Hinke, *Boundary Stone*; cf. also the discussion of Thureau-Dangin, "Une acte de donation de Marduk-zâkir-šumi," *RA*, 16 (1919), pp. 117 ff.

[4]) Cf. the documents published by Thureau-Dangin in the preceding note. Of especial interest is the second deed published in the study (pp. 141 ff.) in which the goddess Nanâ bestows the temple income on her high priest. Note also the same expression of joy—*ina būnīšunu namrūti . . . ḫadīš ippalsūma*—as was used in the *kudurru* under discussion.

[5]) King, *BBSt.*, No. 36, Cols. IV-V (nineth century).

sparkling eyes, he joyfully looked upon him . . . and granted his servant (these revenues)" (King, *BBSt.* No. 36, Cols. IV and V).*

The grant of priestly rights is not a matter of poetry, poetic language notwithstanding. The granting of priestly revenues is as much a formal legal conveyance as the sale of land. However, many of the grants recorded in the *kudurrus* were *unentgeltliche.* The legal instability of such donations is well known. In some cases, some fictive counter-performance was tendered by the donee in order to assimilate the transaction to *Entgeltlichkeit* and thereby insure its validity and incontestability. [1]) In other cases—the deed under discussion being one of them —the validity of the conveyance is secured by the donor's energetic declaration of his total willingness and volition to part with his property for all time. After such a declaration, the donor could not later invalidate the transaction by claiming that the grant was made with mental reservations.

It was pointed out above that *iḫdû* "he rejoiced" is a common way of expressing volition in cuneiform legal documents. Quite clearly, the expression *ša šar Babili libbašu iḫdû . . . arassu irīm* "the heart of the king of Babylon rejoiced . . . he bestowed on his servant" is virtually identical both in function and formulation to the OB *iḫdû . . . iddin* "he rejoiced . . . and gave" and to the NB *ina ḫūd libbišu iddin* "he gave in the joy of his heart." Thus, the rather poetic introduction is, in reality, a legal formula which expresses the eternal and uncoerced will of the donor. This introduction, therefore, is really the legal basis of the whole transaction.

However, considering the seriousness of the situation and the majesty of the donor, a simple statement that the "heart of the king of Babylon was glad" did not suffice. The joy reflecting the willingness of the king had to be orchestrated with a commensurate solemnity. The joy of the king is so great that it is reflected in his whole countenance: his face lights up and his eyes sparkle. [2]) Unfortunately, the beauty of the description has long obscured the legal nature of the situation.

Furthermore, the joy/volition of the king is not a diffused mood; it has been stimulated by and is focused on a particular person: the donee, the priest of Sippar. The narrative expressions "the king turned his gaze" (*itruṣa būnīšu*) and "he looked at him" (*ippalissu*) are not so much

[1]) Cf. the use of counter-donations in the Nuzi praxis (Koschaker, *Randnotizen,* p. 209. Cf. also Krückmann, *BRVU,* p. 38.

[2]) For the outer manifestations of inner joy—bright eyes and a shining countenance—cf., Dhorme, "L'emploi métaphorique des noms de parties du corps en hébrew et en akkadien," *RB,* 30 (1921), pp. 383 ff.

actions of the eyes as of the mind: "looking at someone" in idiomatic Akkadian often means "to think about, to consider." [1]) Taken together, the expressions convey the idea that the king intended (*ippalis*) with full volition (*ḫadīš*) to bestow (*irīm*) a gift on his servant.

The last term *rêmu* [2]) "to bestow a gift" is of great significance for

[1]) *Ibid.*, p. 384; cf. also L. Oppenheim, "Idiomatic Akkadian," *JAOS*, 61 (1941), p. 256: the expression *pānam šakānu* when used of divinity means "to look favorably at somebody." More specifically, *naplusu* means "to look at somebody with the intent of showing mercy or bestowing a favor." Cf. Böllenrücher, *Gebete*, p. 14, ll. 15 ff.:

áš-sum gam-ma-la-ta be-li as-sa-ḫar ilu-ut-ka
áš-sum ta-a-a-ra-ta eš-te-ʾ-ú-ka
áš-sum mu-up-pal-sa-ta a-ta-mar pa-ni-ka
áš-sum ri-mi-ni-ta at-ta-ziz maḫ[ar-ka]
ki-niš naplis-an-ni-ma ši-me [qa-ba-a-a]
"Weil du gütig bist, O Herr, wende ich mich an deine Gottheit;
weil du voll Erbarmen bist, suche ich dich auf.
Weil du gnädig blickst, schaue ich auf dein Angesicht;
weil du voll Vergeben bist, stehe ich v[or dir].
Treulich sieh mich an, erhöre [mein Rufen]."

Just as *muppalsāta*=*rēmēnēta* in this poetic context, so *ippalissu* "he looked upon him" is closely related to *irēnšu* "he bestowed upon him" in the legal context of the *kudurru*. For another example of *ippalis* / / *irīm* in *kudurru* texts, cf. Belser, *Kudurru-Inschriften*, p. 116. Furthermore, just as the donor of the gift looks favorably at the donee (*ḫadīš ippalis*) when the gift is given, so he calls on the gods to look with punitive anger (*ilāni rabūti ezziš likkelmūma*; *ibid.*, p. 126) upon the person who attempts to contest the donation.*

[2]) The etymology of the terms *rêmu* "to give a gift" and *rēmūtu* "a gift" is somewhat complicated. Since the Aramaic terms *yhb brḥmn* "to give a in affection," *rḥmt*/*rḥmh* "a gift," and the clause *lmn rḥmt tntnnh* "give it to whomever you wish" are organically related (one gives a gift in affection to whomever one wishes), it seems logical that a similar relation exists between *ina narʾamātišu iddin* "he gave in affection/willingly" (=*yhb brḥmn*), *rēmūtu*/*rêmu* "a gift/to give a gift" (=*rḥmh*/*rḥmt*) and the clause *ana ša irammu inaddin* "he may give it to whomever he wants" (=*lmn rḥmt tntnnh*). There is no doubt that functionally the Aramaic and Akkadian terms are identical. However, although the Aramaic evidence suggests that all of these Akkadian terms are derived from the same root, this inference is misleading.

In Aramaic, the root *rḥm* means both "to love" and "to be merciful, to show kindness." However, this is not the case in Akkadian: the two concepts are expressed by contrasting stems; *rêmu*—whose present and preterite forms are in the present study, contrasted artificially as *irêm* and *irīm* "to have mercy, to show kindness" and is derived from an original *rḥm*; *râmu-raʾāmu*—whose present form is *irâm* (sometimes *iraʾ ʾamu*)—means "to love" and is derived from an original *r-ʾ-m* (Arabic رأم). This contrast was established by J. Barth, *ZA*, 22 (1909), pp. 1-5, and is an accepted fact of modern Assyriology. (Cf. Jacobsen, *JNES*, 5 (1946), p. 132.)

There is good reason to believe that the term "to bestow a gift" is derived from *rêmu* "to be kind to" rather than from *râmu* "to love." (Cf. especially Von Soden, *GaG*, § 98k: *rêmum* "sich erbarmen; schenken.") This is established by the contrast between *irâm* "he loves" and *irêm* "he bestows a gift" in MB texts (cf. Aro, *Glossar*, p. 87); *irêm* "he bestows a gift" is identical in form with *irêm* "he is kind to."

comparative purposes: there can be no doubt that the common Aramaic expression *ntn/yhb brḥmn/* [1]) *brḥmh/* [2]) *brḥmt/* [3]) *rḥmt* [4]) "to give (something) in affection/as a gift" [5]) is clearly related with the Akkadian term.

Thus, the bestowing of a gift was conceived as an extension of the concept "to show kindness to someone, to be beneficent"; a gift was simply conceived as a "kindness." In a Neo-Babylonian document from the time of Nabû-na'id, the "showing of mercy" is expressed in the same contextual matrix as the "bestowing of a gift." Cf. H. Lewy, "The Babylonian Background of the Kay Kâûs Legend," *ArOr*, 17[2] (1949), p. 52: (19) *pa-ni-šu tu-saḫ-ḫi-ram-ma* (20) *ina bu-ni-šú nam-ru-ti* (21) *ki-niš tap-pal-sa-an-ni-ma* (22) *túš-ri-im-mi ra-am-ma* "And she (the goddess Gula) turned her countenance toward me (Nabû-na'id); with her shining face she faithfully looked at me and actually caused (him, i.e., Marduk) to show mercy." Furthermore, the Susa isogloss of *irīm* is *īnun* (cf. *MDP* XXIII 282 : 5)—from *enēnu* "to be kind to" [Heb. *ḥānan*]. Thus, *irīm* is to *rēmūtu* as *īnun* is to *ennu* "grace/mercy," *ennanātu* "favor" and possibly to *taḫanatu* "benefaction."

In the light of this discussion, the volitional terms *ina nar'amātišu* "in his affection, willingly" and *ana ša irammu* "to whomever he wishes" (for the volitional character of this clause, cf. Koschaker, *JCS*, 5 [1951], p. 108) contrast etymologically with *rêmu* "to bestow a gift" and *rēmūtu* "a gift." However, since Aramaic makes no distinction between the concepts "to love" and "to be kind to"—expressing them both by the stem *rḥm*—the etymological contrast between *ina nar'amātišu* "willingly" and *ana ša irammu* "to whomever he wants" on the one hand, and the term *rēmūtu* "a gift" on the other, disappears as soon as the Akkadian terms are translated into Aramaic: a *rḥmt* (= *rēmūtu*) is given *brḥmn* (= *ina nar'amāti* to *mn zy rḥmt* (= *ana ša irammu*": a gift is given in affection to whomever you want. (The problem of the relationships between the Akkadian *râmu* and *rêmu*, the Arabic *rḥm*, *rḫm*, and *r'm*, and the Hebrew and Aramaic *rḥm* is most complicated and deserves an independent discussion.)

[1]) Cf. *AP* 18: 2; 25: 11, 14; *BP* 4: 4, 12; 7: 41; 9: 5, 12, 17.

[2]) *BP* 6: 14.

[3]) *AP* 43: 3.

[4]) *AP* 9: 7; *BP* 12: 26, 31.

[5]) The expression *brḥmn* "in affection" is clear and unambiguous. This is not true of the other expressions. Is the final *t* in the expression *lmntn rḥmt* to be taken as an adverbial element like the Syriac—*āiṯ* or —*aṯ* (cf. the adverbial interpretation of the clause *'mrn lh mṣryt* "they call it in Egyptian" *BP* 6: 5 suggested by Ginsberg, *JAOS*, 74 [1954], p. 161)? The expression seems to have been taken adverbially by Nöldeke, *ZA*, 20 (1907), p. 142. However, the presence of the variant forms *brḥmt* and *brḥmh* would seem to invalidate this interpretation: the latter two forms are clearly nouns. The form *b^{e}raḥmā* (*brḥmh*) is not problematic: it is a noun in the absolute state. However, what is the construction reflected in the form *brḥmt*? Is it the construct state of *brḥmh*? This cannot be since it is not followed by a genitive. Is it then an abstract noun *b^{e}raḥ^{a}mūṯ*? Both interpretations are considered as possibilities by Leander, *Laut- und Formenlehre*, p. 119. In the light of the functional correspondence between the Akkadian *ana rēmūti ul irêm* and the Aramaic *l' šlyṭ 'nt . . . lmntn rḥmt l'ḥrnn* "you are not allowed to give it as a gift to anyone else" (*AP* 9: 6-7), the nominal interpretation seems the more likely. Even though *-ūt* is usually written *wt* (cf. Leander, p. 112), nevertheless there is at least one example—*šrt* "meal-time" (cf. *AP* 72: 2, 3, 10)—where *-ūt* is written simply as *t*. However, if the form *rḥmt* (=*raḥmūt*) is a noun in the absolute case, one would expect the form *raḥmū* (cf. *'ntw* "marriage"; cf. Leander, p. 112). However, if the term *rḥmt* is a loan-word or loan translation from the Akkadian *rēmūtu*, this departure from Aramaic linguistic patterns would find its natural explanation.*

Furthermore, the gap between the Aramaic and the MB sources can be eliminated since *rêmu* with this particular meaning is found in both NA and NB texts. The NA usage is almost identical with the MB: *eqlāte bītāte u nišē šunātunu ša* PN [RN] *šar Aššur uzakkīma irīmu* "these fields, houses and personnel of PN, which RN, king of Assyria, granted him with freedom from taxation." [1]) The NB and Arsacid uses of *rêmu* are different from the MB and closer to the Aramaic: *ana kaspi ul inamdin ana rēmūti ul irêm maškānu ul išakkan* [2]) "he shall not sell it for money, he shall not give it as a gift, he shall not give it as a pledge." This clause is virtually identical with the Aramaic: *lʾ šlyṭ ʾnt lzbnh wlmntn rḥmt lʾḥrnn* "You are not allowed to sell it nor to give it to anyone as a gift" (*AP* 9:6-7).[3]) The relationship, however, between the Aramaic deeds of gift and Babylonian *kudurru* is not limited to the term *rêmu/rḥm*. In the Aramaic deeds of gift, the expression *ʿšt lk* "I have turned my thoughts to you" often appears together with *yhbt lk brḥmt* "I have given it to you willingly/as a free-will donation." Functionally, the Akkadian *ḫadīš ippalissu arassu irīm* "he thought about him joyfully (= willingly) and bestowed upon his servant" is identical with the Aramaic *ʿšt lk brḥmt wyhbt lk* "I have thought about you affectionately and have given you." The Akkadian *naplusu* "to consider/think about" and the Aramaic *ʿšt* "to think about" both focus the volition of the donor (*ḫadīš/rḥmt*) on the recipient of the gift.

It may be objected that *naplusu* only means "to think about" by extension. The equation, therefore, can be confirmed only if the more literal equivalent of the Aramaic *ʿšt*—the Akkadian *ḫasāsu* "to think about" can be found in a context identical with the earlier *kudurru*, filling the slot of *naplusu*. Such an inner-cuneiform variant is found in a *kudurru*-type charter of one of the Neo-Assyrian kings.

(8) [*I*]*ᵈNabû-šarru-uṣṣur ˡᵘ́ràb rēši* (9) [*š*]*á ᴵᵈAššurˢᵘʳ-bān-apli šàr ᵏᵘʳÁš-šurᵏⁱ* (10) [*bēl ṭ*]*a-ab-ti bēl di-iq-ti* . . . (14) *ina maḫ-ri-y*[*a i-na ki-na-a-ti i-zi-z*]*u-ma* (15) *it-tal-l*[*a-ku šal-me-iš*] (16) *qi*[*-rib ekalli-ya* . .] (18) [*i-na bi-*]*bíl libbi-ya mi-li*[*k ra-ma-ni-ya i-n*]*a at-ta-šu aḫ-su-us-ma ú-*[*kin* . . .]*-šu* (20) *eqlētiᵐᵉš kirâtiᵐᵉš* [. . .] (21) *šá i-na ṣilli-ya* [*iq-nu*]*-ú* (22) *e-pu-šú bīt* [*ra-me*]*-ni-šu* (23) *ú-zak-ki-ma aš-ṭur*

---

[1]) *ADD* 661: 24—cited by *CAD, Z*, p. 31.

[2]) *NRVU*,; No. 12 = *VS* V 21, Nabû-naʾid.

[3]) Cf. the Arsacid sale formula: *ul išallaṭ-ma*: *ana kaspi ana rēmūti ana mammam šanamma gabbi elat* the buyer *ul iddin ul inamdin* "he (the seller) is not empowered to have sold or to sell (this property) or to have given or give it as a gift to anyone else except the buyer" (cf. Krückmann, *BRVU*, p. 48). Compare this with the positively formulated Aramaic transfer clause: *ʾnt šlyṭ bh . . . wlmn zy rḥmt tntn ʾw zy tzbn lh bksp* (*BP* 12 : 23-24). Cf. below, p. 41, n. 2 for discussion.*

(8) "Nabû-šar-uṣṣur, the general (9) of Aššurbanipal the king of Assyria (10), a friend and companion, . . . (14) who served me faithfully (15) and who loyally performed (16) his duties in my palace* . . . (18) By my own resolve and the decision of my heart (19), I lifted my eyes and considered (him) and confirmed [. . .] of his: (20) the fields and gardens which, under my aegis, he had acquired and incorporated into his private estate—(all of these) I acknowledged in a written document as free from taxation (*ARU*, No. 16; 655 B.C.).

Clearly, the phrase *ina bibil libbiya milik ramniya* "by my own resolve and the decision of my heart" explicates the more poetic *kudurru* clause *ina būnīšu namrūti damqāti īnāšu ḫadīš ippalissu arassu irīm* "he joyfully regarded his servant with his shining countenance and sparkling eyes and bestowed upon (him)." *Ḫadīš* "joyfully/willingly" = *ina bibil libbiya milik ramniya*. Furthermore, there can be no doubt as to the correspondence between the *kudurru ina īnāšu . . . ippalissu* "he looked at him with his eyes" and the NA *īnā attaši aḫsusma* "I lifted my eyes and thought about/considered." Clearly, the *kudurru naplusu* "to look at" means the same thing as Assyrian *aḫsus* "I thought about." Furthermore, the latter term is the proximate model of the Aramaic term *ʿšt lk brḥmn* "I have turned my thoughts to you in affection."

Finally, the Assyrian charter gives some indication why the thoughts of the donor were of such constitutive significance in these transactions. All of the charters and contracts studied so far record the *unentgeltliche* transfer of goods. Even though a formal consideration was not tendered in these transactions with the consideration of inducing a right-holder to part with his goods, nevertheless all of the recipients of grants recorded in the deeds studied did serve their lords faithfully.

In a sense, the gifts were bestowed as a reward for long years of service. Although not formally an *Entgelt*, this service is certainly a "consideration." The king's regard for this consideration prompts him to bestow the gift on the servant.

A similar situation is reflected in *BP* 9. Ananiah bar Azariah says to his daughter Yehoyishma: (2) *ʾnh ʿšt lky bḥyy wyhbt* (3) *lky qṣt mn byty* . . . (16) *ʾnh ʿnny yhbth lyhwyšmʿ* (17) *brty bmwty brḥmn lqbl zy sbltny wʾnh ymyn sb lʾ khl hwyt bydy wsbltny* (2) "I have turned my thoughts to you during my lifetime and have given (3) you part of my house . . . (16) I, Anani have given it to Yehoyishma, (17) my daughter, in affection upon my death since she took care of me when I was old in years and unable to take care of myself; she took care of me."

B. Ṭābu *"to be happy" as a Term of Volition*

One of the most common synonyms of the Akkadian *ḫadû* "to rejoice" is the verb *ṭābu* "to be sweet/to be happy." [1] The equivalence of the two terms is clearly reflected in the common phrase: *ina ḫūd libbi ṭūb šēri* "in happiness of mind and joy of body." [2] Like its synonym *ḫadû, ṭābu* is often used as a term of volition in legal texts, especially OB ones: (a) *ašar ṭābušim inaddin* = *ašar ḫadê inaddin* "he may give to whomever he wants"; (b) *ina ṭūb libbi* = *ina ḫūd libbi* "in the joy of his heart, i.e., willingly."

(1) *ašar ṭābušim inaddin*

CT VI 47a (= Schorr, *Urkunden* 289; Sippar, Ṣabium)

A husband gives a gift to his wife and stipulates that she may give it to whomever she wishes.

(15) *a-ša-ar tābu*[bu]*-ši-im* (16) *ap-lu-sà i-na-di-in*

(15) "To whomever she wants, (16) she may give her inheritance."

CT IV 7a (= Schorr, *Urkunden* 310; Sippar, Apil-Sîn)

This *lišānsu*-type deed records the sale of a house. The seller received a sum of money and a house in return for his house. He may dispose of the house according to his own discretion.

(30) *a-šar e-li-ya ṭābu*[bu] (31) *a-na-ad-di-in*

(30) "To whomever I please, (31) I may give it."

The synonym of *ašar ṭābu inaddin* is *ša irammu inaddin*
CT II 41 (= Schorr, *Urkunden* 19; Sippar, Ḫammurabi)

---

[1]) I doubt whether *ṭābu* is ever used in Akkadian to express moral goodness. Most frequently, *ṭābu* simply means "sweet" as in the expression *šēr nišī ṭubbum* "to make sweet/happy the flesh of men" (*CH, i*: 47-48) or in the expressions *karānu ṭābu* "sweetened wine" and *karānu lā ṭābu* "unsweetened wine." A similar, if not identical situation exists in West Semitic. In *PRU* II, No. 84=16.127: 1-3 a distinction is made between three kinds of wine: *yn.ṭb, d.l.ṭb,* and *yn.ḥlq*. Since the last kind of wine is "spoiled" (=Akk. *ḫalqu*), the first kind must be "sweetened" and the second "unsweetened" (Moshe Held, oral communication). Similarly, *qānē haṭṭōḇ* in Jer 6: 20 means "the fragrant sugar cane." (Cf. the Arabic *ṭīb* "fragrant smell"; *ṭayyib* "sweet, perfumed.")

Ṭōḇ in Hebrew often means "happy." For example: *wᵉlēḇ Nāḇāl ṭōḇ ʿālaw* "And Nabal's spirits were very high" I Sam 25: 36; cf. also Koheleth 2: 1 *ureʾe bᵉṭōḇ* "and be sated with joy" (cf. H. L. Ginsberg, *Koheleth*, p. 66 and *passim*). For a discussion of this use of *ṭōḇ* in rabbinic literature, cf. E. Z. Melamed, "Comments on the Language of *ʾĀḇōth* [Hebrew], *Lᵉšōnēnu*, 20, p. 232. In passing it may be noted that the rabbinic expression *bᵉṭōḇāṯō šᵉlō bᵉṭōḇāṯō* "willingly or unwillingly" is based on the nuance joy and gladness implicit in the root (literally: "gladly or not gladly") and is exactly like the Akkadian *ina ṭūbātišu* "in his joy/willingly."*

[2]) Cf. Dhorme, *RB*, 30 (1921), pp. 379 ff.

(30) *i-na aḫ-ḫi-ša ša ana ta-ra-mu-ú* (31) *ap-lu-sà i-na-di-in*

(30) "to whichever brother she wants (31) she may give her inheritance."

The semantic equivalence of *râmu* with *ṭābu* is confirmed by Waterman 22 (= *HG* 1749). The inner text reads: *a-ša-ar e-ra-mu*; the outer envelope reads: *a-ša-ar ta-bu-ši-im*. All of these expressions are the OB equivalents of the Nuzi/MA clause *ašar ṭābu(šim)*.

(2) *ina ṭūb libbi/ṭūbāti iddin*

ARM VIII, 13

5 sar é.dù.a (2) *ᴵÌ-lí-pa-ḫa-lum* (3) *ᴵIa-ri-im-ᵈAddu* (4) *in-ḫi-il* (5) *i-na ṭú-bi li-bi-im* (6) 11 5/6 SU kù.babbar (7) *ᴵYa-ri-im-ᵈAddu* (8) *ᴵÌ-lí-pa-[ḫa-lum]* (9) *in-ḫi-[i]l* . . . witnesses (11′) *ka-ra-am i-ku-lu* (12′) *ka-sa-am iš-tu-ú* (13′) *ù ša-am-na-am* (14′) *ip-ta-šu*

(2) 5 *sar* of built land (2) Ili-paḫalum (3) to Yarīm-Addu (4) gave as an ancestral portion. (5) In the joy of his heart (= willingly) (6) 11 5/6 shekels of silver (7) Yarīm-Addu gave to Ili-paḫalum as his (9) ancestral portion ... witnesses (11′) They ate bread(?); (12′) they drank the cup; (13′) and with oil (14) they anointed themselves."

Petschow was the first to recognize that *ina ṭūb libbim* is a term of volition and the early isogloss of the NB *ina ḫūd libbi*.[1]) The use of a term of volition in this conveyance may be connected with the unusual type of transaction recorded in this deed: the use of inheritance terminology (*naḫālu*), symbolic actions (*kāsam ištû, šamnam iptaššū*), and an expression of volition seem to have been employed to disguise the sale of land by converting it into a (fictive) division of inheritance property. [2]) However, whatever the case may be, there can be no doubt as to the volitional functions of *ina ṭūb libbi*.

The same expression is also found in *ARM* VIII 15 : 9-10 *i-na ṭù-ub li-bi-im i-za-iq!-da* "they divided/exchanged (?) in the joy of heart." The meaning of the verb *zaqādu** and the nature of the transaction are not clear. Some sort of unrequitable transaction is recorded whose nature

---

[1]) San Nicolò-Petschow, p. 27, n. 2.

[2]) Cf. Boyer, *ARM* VIII, p. 195. Anointing of oil in the sale transaction is also mentioned in the Khafajah conveyances (cf. Harris, *JCS*, 9 (1955), p. 92, n. 59) as well as symbolic actions. Thus, a clear relationship is established between the Diyala formulary and that used in Mari. On the other hand, the use of *naḫālu* "to bequeath an inheritance" is reflected in the rare Biblical usage of *nāḥal* (Qal) with the meaning of the Hiphil: "to bequeath" (cf. Nu 34 : 17 and Jos 14 : 1).

can only be surmised. [1]) A related expression is found in the regular requitable conveyance *ARM* VIII 8 : 5 *an-nu-ú-um ṭú-bu ú-ul nu!-la-nu* "this (sale) (took place) willingly, without deceit." [2]) The clause is thus a direct antecedent of the Neo-Babylonian *ina ḫūd libbi iddin* "he gave in the joy of his heart" and more specifically of the Gaonic and Arabic clauses of volition which specify not only the willingness of the donor but also the fact that the transaction took place without mental reservation, deceit, or coercion. [3])

The same expression is found in *M* 107 (Schorr, *Urkunden* 195; Sippar, Ammiṣaduqa). A brother divides ancestral property with another brother *ina ṭūbātišu* (line 14). The term should not be translated "aus Gutwilligkeit" (Schorr) but rather "freely and voluntarily." A similar expression is found in MAH 15916 (= Szlechter, "Les tablettes ... d'Abî-Ešuḫ ... de Genève," *JCS*, 7 (1953), p. 92. Ubarrum, a *qaqqad redūtim*, and Ili-iqīšam, his *taḫḫu*, settled their common property after some disagreement. After the division was over, Ili-iqīšam *i-na ṭú-ba-ti-šu* (17) *2 ka-lu-ma-tim a-na U-ba(r)-rum (18) id-di-in* "gave two lambs to Ubarrum *ina ṭūbātišu*." This last term was correctly rendered by Szlechter as "de sa propre volonté." There is also an unrecognized

[1]) Boyer, *ARM* VIII, p. 197.

[2]) Cf. Von Soden, *Or*, 28 (1959), p. 316. He corrects Boyer's reading *be-la-nu* and compares *LE* No. 6. The term is rendered "widerrechtliche Handlung" and is contrasted with *ṭūbu* "freiwillige Handlung."

[3]) Most early Near Eastern clauses of volition are formulated positively: thus, Susa *ina nar'amātišu ina ṭūbātišu iddin*, and so all Neo-Babylonian and Arsacid volition clauses. The same holds true for the Elephantine volition clauses *ʿšt lk* and *yhbt lk brḥmn* and for the volition clauses used in the deeds of Wadi Murabbaʿat (cf. *Les grottes de Murabbaʿât*, No. 19 or No. 24—*mn rʿty/mrṣwny* "of my own free will"). However, in the Gaonic amplification and reworking of older Aramaic and cuneiform prototypes, the older positive clause is now explicated by an antithetical, negative complement: *bṣbw npšy kdl' b'ns wl' bmrʿ wl' bšgw wl' bšlw 'l' blb' šlym' wbdʿt šlmt'* "(I declare) by my own volition, uncoerced and not under the influence of sickness, without confusion or mistake but with full control of my heart and mind . . ." (cf. Asaf, *Formulary*, p. 20). The same negative explication is also found in medieval Arabic documents. In these deeds, the clause reads: *fī ṣiḥḥah min ʿaqlihi wa-badanihi . . . ghayr mukrah wa-lā-mug̮bar* "(PN entered into the transaction) being sound of mind and body, not forced and not coerced." Cf. A. Grohmann, *Arabic Papyri in the Egyptian Library*, Vol. I. (Cairo, 1934), No. 59 : 10-11 and *passim*.*

To me there seems little doubt that the later Gaonic and Arabic—and probably similar volition clauses in contemporary Coptic and Byzantine deeds—are derived from older Aramaic reworkings of ancient cuneiform legal traditions. However, the exact relationship between these later traditions is a most complicated problem and deserves an independent investigation. Furthermore, the possibility that the Aramaic-Gaonic tradition was also influenced by the Arabic or Greek praxis must also be considered. For the time being, cf. Rabinowitz, *Jewish Law*, p. 167 and the literature cited there.

example of this usage in the legal documents of Ras Shamra. *RS* III 16.143 records a gift made by the king of Ugarit to one Abdu. Upon receipt of this gift from the king, Abdu cedes part of this gift to his son Kalbu. At the end of the deed, Abdu declares: (28) *ù a-na-ku i-na ṭābi-ma* (or should this be read *ina ṭūbāti-ma*) (29) *bīta*^{ḫa} *eql[a*^{ḫa} *a]t-ta-ad-na-šu*. The clause should not be rendered "pour moi, de bonne façon, maison et terre je lui ai donné" (so Nougayrol) [1]) but "I, on my part, have given him house and land willingly."

(3) *ina ṭūbātišu ina nar'amātišu* in the deeds of Susa

The examples of *ina ṭūbi/ṭūbātišu* cited so far have been sporadic and often unrecognized. However, the clause *ina ṭūbātišu ina nar'āmātišu* "of his own free will and voluntarily" [2]) is a regular element in many of the Old Babylonian documents from Susa and Mâlamir. The clause is used in adoption, [3]) division [4]) (where it is almost never missing); it is most common in deeds of gift [5]) and is found occasionally in deeds of rent. [6]) It is not common in the deeds of sale from Susa [7]) but is found regularly in the Mâlamir conveyances. [8])*

Finally, a comment about the use of *nar'amātišu*. The relationship between *ṭābu* and *râmu* is analogous to its relationship to *hadû*: *ašar ḫadê inaddin*: *ina ḫūd libbišu iddin* = *ašar ṭābu inaddin*: *ina ṭūbātišu iddin* = *ša irammu inaddin*: *ina nar'amātišu iddin*.

Summary

In the preceding chapter, some of the contextual reasons why the quittance-receipt meaning of *libbašu ṭāb* was not isolated were pointed out: *libbašu ṭāb* was studied on the basis of its late OB use in conveyances

---

[1]) *PRU* III, p. 83.

[2]) So rendered by *CAD*, *I/J*, p. 12. For the grammatical structure of the term *ina nar'amātišu* as well as its meaning, cf. Koschaker, *OLZ*, 35 (1932), p. 321.

[3]) Cf. *MDP* XXII 1 : 2-3; 3 : 2; and *passim*.*

[4]) Cf. *MDP* XXII 6 : 3-4; 7 : 4; 9 : 6-7; 10 : 2-3. For a study of the Susa division documents, cf. Klíma, *Elamischen Erbrecht*, p. 39 where the use of the clause *ina ṭūbātišu ina nar'amātišu* is discussed. Cf. also Klíma, *Donationes*, pp. 229 ff.

[5]) Cf. *MDP* XXII 135 : 2-3; 136 : 2; 137 : 1-2 and *passim*.

[6]) *MDP* XXIII 246 : 2. Cf. also the deed of lease, *MDP* XXII 84 : 1.

[7]) Cf. *MDP* XXIII 206 : 4; 234 : 3. In both these texts it is stated quite clearly that the property sold was ancestral property (*isqātu*). Since people did not easily part with property they had inherited from their fathers, and any such sale might seem as the result of the coercion of the buyer. To dispel such suspicions, it may have been necessary to add the declaration of volition which was not usually employed in conveyances not specified as "ancestral land." This interpretation is but a suggestion which needs further investigation.

[8]) Cf. *MDP* XXII 53 : 3-4; 71 : 5-6; 72 : 7-8 and *passim*, for the contrast between the use of the clause in the Mâlamir conveyances and its absence in the Susa deeds of sale, cf. Koschaker, *OLZ* 35 (1932), p. 320.

where its original position after the payment of the price was replaced by a less meaningful order, where its original active-passive modality was lost and its explicatives shorn away; a study based on the more archaic Diyala and Alalakh conveyances where the older order, modality, and explicatives are still preserved clearly establishes the original receipt-quittance function of the term.

A study of the various isoglosses of *libbašu ṭāb*—especially the Kültepe *šabû* and the *MA zakû*—helped to conform the results of the contextual study. Furthermore, this study of isoglosses, by pointing out that the root metaphor of *libbašu ṭāb* is that of "satisfaction" rather than "joy" provides yet another reason why the function of *libbašu ṭāb* has escaped adequate definition for such a long time: it was simply confused with the more common volitional terms *ina ṭūbi/ṭūbāti* based on the same root. Two contrasting concepts are homonymously expressed by the root *ṭābu*: (a) the idea of "joy" (*ina ḫūd libbi ṭūb šēri*), which in legal contexts is used metaphorically as an expression of "volition" (*ina ḫūd/ṭūb libbišu iddin*); (b) the idea of "satisfaction," which is used in legal contexts as an expression of quittance upon the receipt of a satisfactory consideration (cf. the Kültepe *šabû*). [1])

It was noted above that the Aramaic volitional expression *yhbt lk brḥmn* "I have given you in affection, willingly" used in unrequitable conveyances contrasts with *ṭyb lbby bdmy'* "my heart is satisfied with the money" used in requitable conveyances. Similar, but not identical, patterns and contrasts are reflected in the Akkadian material. The Akkadian *ina ṭūbātišu ina nar'amātišu iddin* "he gave of his own free will and voluntarily" contrasts with *ana šīm bītišu gamrim libbašu ṭūb* "his heart has been satisfied with the full price of his house." Furthermore, outside of Susa most of the terms of volition are found either in unrequitable conveyances (gifts) or in conveyances whose real requitable character is disguised by assimilating them to gifts or the division of

[1]) The following should be noted in passing: Yaron, *LAP* [Hebrew], p. 153, notes the gap between the Akkadian *libbašu ṭāb* and the Aramaic and Demotic terms of satisfaction. He finds one link between the two traditions: the expression *wayyīṭāḇ lēḇ hakkōhēn* Jud 18: 20. However, from the context this expression can only mean, "The priest was glad (=he agreed) to go." Here *ṭōḇ* as an expression of joy is, by extension, also a term of volition. It is thus related to *ina ṭūb libbi* (=*ina ḫūd libbi*) and therefore has nothing whatsoever to do either with *libbašu ṭāb* or *ṭyb lbby*. Etymological similarity is not necessarily the best indicator of functional identity.

(Lambert, *Wisdom*, p. 326, notes that the Babylonian *libbašu ṭāb* expresses satisfaction while the parallel Biblical expression indicates mirth. However, he misses the true juridical meaning of *libbašu ṭāb*: like Klíma and others before him he understands it as a term of agreement to the terms of the contract rather than as a term of quittance upon the receipt of the sale price.)

inheritance property (Mari). In the Susa deeds, the most common usage of the volition clause is in the deeds of division which are not strictly requitable, in gift and in adoption which are clearly unrequitable. The clause is almost never found in regular Susa sale. This distribution pattern would seem then to conform to the principle established above on the basis of the Aramaic material that terms of volition are limited to—or are most common in—unrequitable transactions. However, it should be noted that the expression *ina ṭūbātišu ina nar'amātišu* is used regularly in Mâlamir conveyances and in Susa deeds of hire. Furthermore, even if the contrast *Entgeltlichkeit*-satisfaction/*Unentgeltlichkeit*-volition is reflected—with some exceptions— in the MB and OB material, it virtually disappears in the NB material where clauses of volition originally used in *unentgeltlich* transactions—and related transaction such as the transfer of mobilia—are applied to almost all types of transactions in which a consideration is paid.

Excursus

There are several non-legal uses of the term *muṭīb libbi** in the Prologue to *CH* that deserve some comment. In the Prologue ii 7-9, Hammurabi is called *mu-ṭi-ib li-ib-bi Marduk be-lí-šu* "he who makes glad the heart of Marduk his Lord." In another passage (Prologue iii:3-4), he is called *mu-ḫa-ad-di li-ib-bi Ištar* "he who makes the heart of Istar rejoice." At first glance, these expressions seem similar to epithets applied to certain minor divinities who soothe the angry hearts of their divine overlords (cf. Tallqvist, *Akkadische Götterepitheta* [Helsinki, 1938] under *ḥdh* and *ṭyb*). Ḫammurabi, as the city-god of his people, would then have a similar function, i.e., to make his divine overlords happy when they are sad and calm when they are angry. However, since Ḫammurabi is never deified, and the contexts in *CH* are not sufficiently explicit, the expressions *muṭīb libbi Marduk* and *muḫaddi Ištar* are probably to be interpreted along the following lines: by furthering the public welfare, Ḫammurabi carries out the mandate of the gods to their satisfaction; the publication of the *dīnat mēšarim* demonstrate that the king is truely a *pāliḫ ilim*. It is this act which makes glad the heart of Marduk and makes the heart of Istar rejoice.

CHAPTER SIX

THE EGYPTIAN ANALOGUES OF Ṭyb Lbby

The overlap between the semantic range, the syntactical usage, complements, etc. of the Akkadian *libbašu ṭāb* and the Aramaic *ṭyb lbby* is so great that, in spite of the gap of over a thousand years that separates the two usages, some sort of historical relationship must have existed between them. From an Assyriological point of view, the cuneiform credentials of *ṭyb lbby* are beyond reproach.

Yet, the nature of the material is such that an equally convincing set of Demotic analogues can be adduced. In fact, as close as the Aramaic *hwṭbt lbby* "you have satisfied my heart" seems to be to the Akkadian *libbašu uṭīb* "he satisfied his heart" in some respects, in other respects the Aramaic term is virtually identical with the Demotic *dj.k-mtj ḥ3tj(.i)* "you have caused my heart to be satisfied." Thus, if the Assyriologist can claim the Aramaic legal papyri as an organic offshoot of cuneiform culture, the Demoticist can claim with equal cogency that the Aramaic papyri are a natural reflex of Demotic law. Significantly, the areas of overlap between the three traditions are not identical: thus, the Aramaic agrees with the Akkadian in some things, while it agrees with the Demotic against the Akkadian in others. Some may argue that the Aramaic was derived from the cuneiform and then took on certain Demotic characteristics; others, among them Kutscher, would argue that the Aramaic is a creative adaptation from the cuneiform which served as the model of the later Demotic formulary. However, whatever the case may be, all historical speculation is premature until the actual Egyptian terms are re-examined in the light of the Akkadian and the Aramaic.

1. Pre-Saitic Analogues to *ṭyb lbby*

Even though no direct historical relationship has been established between ancient Egyptian law (i.e., the law of the pre-Saitic periods) and the Mesopotamian legal tradition, [1]) there are some unnoticed

---

[1]) Cf. Seidl, *Einführung*, p. 18. However, the relationship between Egyptian and cuneiform law is somewhat more complicated than is commonly assumed. According to Alt, (*Kleine Schriften*, III, pp. 155 ff.), Egyptian law may have had some influence on the cuneiform formulary used at Ras Shamra. However, since most of the terms adduced by Alt also have good cuneiform antecedents, it seems likely that it was cuneiform law which influenced the Egyptian practice, rather than vice versa. The whole problem, of course, is in need of further investigation.*

analogues worthy of consideration. However, in this context, a few words concerning the marked contrast between the paucity of Egyptian legal documents and the ubiquity of this genre in the cuneiform legal tradition are in order.

While tens of thousands of legal documents are known from Mesopotamia, [1]) little over a hundred legal documents are known from the beginnings of Egyptian civilization until the eighth century B.C. [2])* Since the dry sands of Egypt have preserved every other type of writing, it stands to reason that this remarkable lacuna cannot be attributed entirely to the hazards of excavation: [3]) somehow, it must reflect an attitude towards the law which contrasts with that reflected in cuneiform culture. Several scholars have suggested that the autocratic atmosphere of Egypt where the king was a god and his word, the law, was not the ideal setting for the development of a legal praxis based on the objective deed. [4])* In Mesopotamia, on the other hand, where even the gods are subject to the cosmic norms, and kings are simply their human vicars, objective law, embodied in the legal document, is the very seal of the civilization. [5])

Nevertheless, the few ancient Egyptian legal documents which have come down to us do contain some significant parallels to the Akkadian terms of satisfaction and are therefore worthy of consideration. Furthermore, a discussion of these ancient terms will provide a needed control for the historical evaluation of the later abnormal Hieratic and Demotic terms.

a) The deed of sale of *Ṯntj* (IV-V dynasty; 2600-2350 B.C.) The house is transferred to the buyer; the seller obligates himself to "satisfy" the buyer, i.e., to insure the house against any faults or imperfections. [6])

"Sowahr der König lebt, ich veranlasse, dass es in Ordnung ist, woüber du zufrieden sein wirst (*ḥtp*), was die Existenz des gesamten Inventars

---

[1]) According to Oppenheim, (*Economic History*, p. 27): "The number of clay tablets dealing with these matters [i.e., legal transactions] increases by the thousands every year, and the number of published and unpublished documents approaches the hundred thousand mark with no end in sight."

[2]) The 1957 edition of Seidl's *Einführung* lists 109 entries and the number of deeds has not increased substantially since then.

[3]) Cf. especially, Griffith, *Catalogue of Demotic Papyri*, pp. 22 ff; Cf. also Malinine, *Choix de textes*, p. v.; for a contrasting view, see Seidl, *Einführung*, p. 21.

[4]) Cf. de Vaux, *Ancient Israel*, pp. 144 ff. Cf. also Speiser "Cuneiform Law and the History of Civilization," *Proc. Am. Phil. Soc.*, 107 (1963), p. 540.

[5]) Cf. Speiser, *ibid.*, p. 538.

[6]) For the Egyptian text, a detailed commentary, and a bibliography of previous studies, cf. *DJE* 1, pp. 3 ff.

dieses Hauses betrifft. Du hast umgekehrt diese Bezahlung voll entrichtet." [1])

Superficially, the term of satisfaction is reminiscent of the Akkadian *libbašu uṭīb* "he (the buyer) satisfied his (the seller's)heart." However, the marked differences between the Akkadian and the Egyptian terms are clear: (a) in the Akkadian usage, the buyer satisfies the seller; in the Egyptian, the seller satisfies the buyer. (b) In the Akkadian usage, the buyer has satisfied the seller with the payment of the full price; in the Egyptian usage, because the buyer has tendered the price in full, the seller obligates himself to satisfy the buyer, i.e., to insure the sale against all faults and imperfections.

b) Papyrus Kahun II, 1 (Middle Kingdom; XII dynasty, 2000-1788 B.C.). [2]) The deed records a litigation between two parties. Party A claims that his father, a priest, now deceased, had sold his prebend to party B but that B had never actually paid the price. Therefore, A now claims the prebend as his own. The deed of litigation describes the original sale transaction between the deceased priest (the seller) and party B (the buyer). After the completion of the sale, the officials of the court ask the priest the following question:

"'Bist du befriedigt damit (*hr.tj*), dass dir dieses Kapital, von dem gesprochen wurde, zusammen mit Aufhebung aller Bindungen, die dir zur Last gerechnet werden, gegeben wird als Gegenleistung für dein (Amt eines) Priesters bei der Phyle?' Darauf sagte mein Vater: 'Ich bin befriedigt' (*hr.kwj*) [3]) Thereupon, the parties take an oath: Nous sommes satisfaits (*hr. wjn*)." [4])

In this context, the expression of satisfaction is somewhat closer in function to the Akkadian *šabû* and *libbašu ṭāb*. When the priest answers the question of the court officials by the declaration: "I am satisfied," the term seems to be one of quittance after the receipt of the full price, and thus seems to be of the same order as *libbašu ṭāb*. However, we know from the deed of litigation that the price was not actually paid. [5]) Does the term of satisfaction, therefore, indicate agreement to the whole

[1]) Translation by Seidl in *Einführung*, p. 49.

[2]) For text, commentary, and bibliography, *DJE* 1, pp. 11 ff.

[3]) Seidl, *Einführung*.

[4]) *DJE* 1, p. 13.

[5]) According to Cuq, there seem to be cases in which the full price was not actually paid even though the term *libbašu ṭāb* was employed. Cf. "Commentaire juridique d'un jugement sous Ammi-ditana," *RA*, 7 (1908/10), pp. 136 f.

transaction rather than quittance with the price? If the term of satisfaction is also used by the buyer in the final oath, the term cannot be one of quittance; in that context "we are satisfied" can only mean "we have agreed to the stipulations of the contract."

c) Papyrus Berlin 9784 (Amenophis IV, XVIII dynasty).
A rents a slave to B, receives the price in advance and is quit. The renter further obligates himself to make up the work-time of the slave interrupted by the heat. [1])

„Da sagte er: ‚Ich bin gefüllt, befriedigt (*mḥ.kwj grḥ.kwj*) mit dem Preis meiner Sklavin. Bei Amûn, bei dem Herscher! Wenn die zwei Tage heiss sind, welche ich dir gegeben habe von der Sklavin *Ḥnw.t*, so soll Ring um Ring geleistet werden'." [2])

In this context, the Egyptian term of satisfaction (*mḥ.kwj grḥ.kwj*) fully corresponds with the Akkadian *šabû* and *libbašu ṭāb*. "I am satisfied" is clearly a term of quittance upon the receipt of the full price. Furthermore, the explicative "Ich bin gefüllt" indicates that the satisfaction is not a static state of mind but one that has been induced by some preceding performance. Thus, the clause "I have been filled; I am satisfied" describes the same process reflected in the cluster *ušabbīšu-šabû* "he satisfied him-he is satisfied" or in the D stative used in early Sippar and Diyala texts, *libbum ṭūb* "the heart has been satisfied."

Furthermore, the correspondence between the Akkadian and the Egyptian terms of satisfaction is greater than appears at first glance. The Akkadian term is usually applied to a right-holder (a seller or claimant) that relinquishes property or claims in return for full payment. However, in *CH* 264 the term is also applied to a shepherd who assumed complete responsibility for the welfare of the sheep entrusted to him only upon his receipt of his full wages and his quittance therewith. Exactly the same usage is reflected in the Egyptian text quoted above: in both cases, the declaration "I am satisfied" functions both as a term of quittance and as a term of obligation. Significantly, Seidl notes in his commentary that: "Eine künftig zu erfüllende Verpflichtung scheint nur dann gültig sein, wenn sie entweder mit einem Eide bekräftigt ist, oder wenn die Gegenleistung dafür bereits geleistet ist." [3]) Terms of satisfaction, in Akkadian, Aramaic, and Egyptian, by recording the receipt

[1]) *DJE* 1, pp. 25 ff.
[2]) Seidl, *Einführung*, p. 50. The basic meaning of *grḥ* is not 'satisfy' but 'finish, complete.' (Oral communication of Dr. Parker.)
[3]) Seidl, *ibid.*, p. 49.

of the *Gegenleistung* and the quittance therewith, serve by extension as terms of obligation.

d) The Stele of Euerot (950-730 B.C.—the period immediately preceding the emergence of the abnormal Hieratic and the Demotic formularies). [1]) The deed records the transfer of property. The pertinent clause reads:

"... ces 556 aroures de champ d'homme libre de diverses espèces, auxquels se rattachent leurs puits, leurs arbres, leur petit et grand bétail, qu'il a achetés en échange d'argent des hommes libres du pays, de plein gré (*n-ỉb-hr*) et sans injustice (*mn sp n ḥr gs*)." [2])

The term *n-ỉb-hr* "with a satisfied heart" clearly expresses the idea of willingness and volition. On the one hand, it is virtually identical with the older Egyptian expression *hr.wjn* "I am satisfied" which was discussed above. On the other hand, the Egyptian term and its negative complement "without injustice" is the functional equivalent of the Mari clause *ṭūbu ul nullānu* [3]) "willingly, without deceit/pressure," and other cuneiform and Near Eastern clauses of volition. [4]) Furthermore, it is the obvious prototype of the abnormal Hieratic expression *m-ỉb-hr* "with a satisfied heart, willingly."

None of these earlier Egyptian terms of satisfaction can be considered as the model of the Aramaic *ṭyb lbby*. It is to the deeds of the Saitic and Ptolemaic periods that one must turn for historically related analogues. In fact, some of the later Egyptian terms of satisfaction are so close to the Aramaic both in terms of specific semantic range and in general contextual usage that they must either be considered as models of the Aramaic or reactions to it.

In this context, a few words concerning the nature and origin of the later Egyptian legal documents are in order. Towards the end of the eighth century B.C., legal documents begin to appear in ever-growing numbers: twice as many deeds are known from the Saitic and Ptolemaic periods than from all other periods of Egyptian history combined. [5])

---

[1]) *DJE* 1, pp. 63 ff.

[2]) *Ibid.*, p. 44.

[3]) Boyer, *ARM* VIII, 8 : 5 (p. 18), with the emendation of Von Soden, *Or*, 28 (1959), p. 316; cf. *LE* 6 (A : 27).

[4]) Quoted above Chapter V, pp. 128 ff.

[5]) All the Egyptian material from the Saitic and Persian periods is listed at the end of Seidl's *ÄRg*: over 150 entries are recorded. Since the publication of Seidl's study (1956) a number of other early Demotic or abnormal Hieratic documents have been published by Malinine. Most of these more recent publications are listed above in Chapter I, p. 8, n. 1. For the Demotic deeds of later periods, Seidl, *PRg*, pp. 191-95.

These deeds are written in two distinct formularies: (a) abnormal Hieratic; (b) early Demotic. Even though the first formulary is somehow related to the older Egyptian tradition, the second seems to be without known antecedents. [1])

The sudden popularity of the legal document as an instrument of commerce and the emergence of the two new formularies have not been adequately explained. Some have suggested that these changes in Egyptian scribal praxis were the results of an inner Egyptian development. Others have stressed the possibility of Near Eastern influences. Trade with Asia Minior and the influx of foreign settlers acquainted with cuneiform legal traditions may have stimulated the Egyptians to develop their own formularies. [2]) Quite conceivably, cuneiform elements, in Aramaic or Phoenician garb, may have served as the proximate models of some of the newly coined Egyptian terms or clauses.

Significantly, the Demotic term of satisfaction is considered by some to be Near Eastern, i.e., cuneiform origin. [3]) It seems to me quite likely that the Aramaic term *ṭyb lbby* with its clear cuneiform background and its obvious Demotic affinities may have served as the bridge between the cuneiform tradition and the emergent Demotic scribal praxis. [4]) What has been suggested is simply a working hypothesis. Only the further study

---

[1]) For a discussion of these two formularies, their geographical distribution and their possible origins, cf. the introduction to Malinine, *Choix de textes*, especially pp. i-xxi.

[2]) All of these possibilities have been considered by Malinine, *ibid.*, pp. v-vi. He also notes that the problem of origins is most complicated and that "une analyse serrée du formulaire juridique attesté dans ces documents amènera les historiens du droit oriental ancien à une solution définitive de la question de son origine." Cf. also the statement of Griffith (*Catalogue of Demotic Papyri*, p. 10): "Probably several causes contributed to make legal documents suddenly more abundant in the Twenty-fifth Dynasty. The growth of trade by sea and land in the first millennium B.C. must have originated a new wealthy merchant class, causing property of all kinds to change hands rapidly, while contact with the crafty and business-like Phoenicians and other Semites opened the eyes of the Egyptians to the necessity of precision in their dealings. These influences would be felt most powerfully in Lower Egypt, Upper Egypt receiving them only at second hand."

[3]) Cf. for example, Seidl, *ÄRg*, pp. 41 and 71; Leibovitch, "Quelques égyptianismes contenus, dans les textes araméens d'Égypte," *BIE*, 18 (1936), p. 25.

[4]) Contrast Seidl's statement (*ÄRg*, p. 73): "Zusammenfassend wollen wir sagen: es könnte sein, das in einer vorhergehenden Zeit von der aramäischen Urkunde einiges aus der ägyptischen übernommen wurde. Davon abgesehen aber haben die Aramäer auch nach Elephantine ihr heimisches Recht mitgebracht, es aber dort Schritt für Schritt dem sie umgebenden frühdemotischen angeglichen. Dass aber durch die aramäischen Elephantine-Papyri vorderasiatisches Recht nach Ägypten vermittelt worden wäre, kommt überhaupt nicht in Frage." The rather dogmatic rejection of this last possibility cannot be accepted. Cf. the comments of J. Modrzejewski in his review of Seidl in *BiOr*, 14 (1957), p. 221.

of the late Egyptian material and its comparison with the well-defined Aramaic and Akkadian terms of satisfaction can establish its validity.

2. An abnormal Hieratic Analogue

The term *m-ỉb-hr* "with a satisfied heart" is found in the conveyances written in abnormal Hieratic. Even though it is based on the same root metaphor as the Aramaic *ṭyb lbby*, there is some question as to whether it fills the same juridical function. The term is used in the following deeds:

a) Papyrus Turin 247 (619 B.C.)

The deed records the sale of land.

"(9) . . . (je te les ai) vendues, de mon plein gré [*m-ỉb-hr*(.*ỉ*)] aujourd'hui. J'ai reçu de toi 5 deben d'argent . . . (10) comme argent (équivalant à) leur (prix);" [1])

There can be little doubt that in this context, the expression *m-ỉb-hr* "with a satisfied heart" is clearly an expression of volition. Furthermore, the abnormal Hieratic expression is directly related to the slightly earlier expression *n-ỉb-hr* used with the same volitional function in the Stele of Euerot quoted above. [2]) Significantly, this is not the only example of the relationship between the abnormal Hieratic formulary and older Egyptian legal traditions. [3])

Thus, the term *m-ỉb-hr*, although based on the root metaphor of satisfaction seems to be the semantic equivalent of *ina ḫūd libbišu* "willingly" rather than of *libbašu ṭāb* or *ṭyb lbby*. As far as I know, all interpreters have translated the term as one of volition.

However, there are several contexts where this reading seems open to question:

b) Papyrus Turin 246 (634 B.C.)

The deed records the sale or property

"(12) Nous te les avons vendus aujourd'hui de notre plein gré. Nous avons reçu de toi (13) 3 kite d'argent . . . comme argent (équivalent à) leur (prix),—de notre plein gré;" [4])

In this text, the expression *m-ỉb-hr* is used in two different contexts: (a) "I have sold to you *m-ỉb-hr*, willingly;" (b) "I have received from

---

1) Malinine, *Choix de textes*, p. 73-75.
2) P. 146.
3) Cf. Malinine, *Choix de textes*, p. x.
4) *Ibid.*, p. 59.

you *m-ib-hr*, willingly." The first use makes good legal sense and is confirmed by the older volitional use of the same expression in the Stele of Euerot and by cuneiform parallels. What, however, is the legal meaning of the expression "I have received from you, willingly." Can one accept the sale-price and yet be unwilling? Something like "I have received the price and am satisfied therewith" is expected. However, this interpretation is not supported by any Demotic authority. It should be noted that in Papyrus Louvre E 3228 e (707 B.C.)—a deed which records the sale of a slave—the expression *m-ib-hr* is used only with "I have received." [1]) The explanation of the second usage may be along the following lines: Talmudic literature gives ample evidence of sale transactions which were completed even though the seller was unwilling. Most land owners were so attached to their property that they sold only under economic duress. [2]) All that the Talmud required from a seller is that he passively acquiesce to the transaction by receiving the price; it did not demand from him a greater degree of volition. In a sense, his receipt of the price was done unwillingly. [3]) Furthermore, all kinds of mental pressure could be used against the seller to force him into receiving the sale-price; according to many authorities, even though the seller was under pressure from the buyer, once the money was received, the sale was considered valid. [4]) A similar legal background may be reflected in the abnormal Hieratic clause: "I have accepted the money willingly." The declaration of willingness was meant to cancel any suspicion that the receipt of the price—a seemingly free and spontaneous act—was the result of any sort of duress. It is also possible, however, that once the term *m-ib-hr* was used in the clause "I have given you the land willingly" it was applied in a stereotypic and non-evocative manner to the following clause: "I have received."

Whatever the case may be, the term is closer in function to the Akkadian *ina ḫūd libbišu* "in the joy of his heart, willingly" than to the Akkadian *libbašu ṭāb* or the Aramaic *ṭyb lbby*.

---

[1]) *Ibid.*, p. 37.

[2]) Cf. the statement in *TB*, *Bᵉrāḵōṯ* 5a that in most ordinary transfers of property, the buyer is happy while the seller is sad, i.e., he sells under economic duress and is therefore somewhat unwilling to part with his property.

[3]) Cf. the discussion of Gulak, *Jewish Law*, Vol. I, pp. 55 ff. According to Gulak, knowledge rather than volition, was the necessary prerequisite of Talmudic sale law: since few alienations were carried out willingly, all that could be demanded was the knowledge of the seller, and his acquiescence to the transaction.

[4]) According to *TB*, *Bāḇā Baṯrā* 47b, even if the seller was coerced into selling his property by physical violence, if he actually accepted the sale-price from the buyer, the sale was considered valid.

3. The Demotic Analogues of *ṭyb lbby*

It is in the Demotic deeds that the exact functional equivalent of the Aramaic and Akkadian terms of satisfaction is to be found. As far as I can tell, Pritsch was the first scholar who recognized the functional identity of the Demotic *dj.k-mtj ḥ3tj(.i)* "you have satisfied my heart (with the price)" with the Aramaic *hwṭbt lbby* "you have satisfied my heart" and the Akkadian *libbašu ṭāb* "his heart is satisfied." [1]) The terms seem so close both in their use of the common metaphor of satisfaction and in their semantic ranges that many scholars have posited the existence of some historical relationship between the terms. Seidl [2]) and Leibovitch [3]) have suggested that the Demotic is derived from the Akkadian. Yaron [4]) is more reserved in his judgment: the Aramaic may have served as the model of the Demotic but, in the light of the slight chronological precedence of the Demotic over the Aramaic, the derivation of the latter from the former seems more likely.

In all of these historical discussions, the scholars have tacitly assumed that the functions of the Aramaic and Demotic terms overlap. However, such a functional equivalence—plausible as it may seem—has never actually been established on philological grounds. The object of the following section is to determine exactly what the meaning of the Demotic term is and to what degree it corresponds to the Aramaic.

A. *The Demotic dj.k-mtj ḥ3tj(.i) "You Have Satisfied My Heart" in the Law of Conveyance Documents*

The Demotic term of satisfaction *dj.k-mtj ḥ3tj(.i)* [5]) "you have satisfied

[1]) Cf. *ZVRW*, 27 (1912), p. 17; cf. the comments of Revillout in his *Les origines égyptiennes*, pp. 92-5.

[2]) Cf. *ÄRg*, pp. 41 and 71.

[3]) *BIE*, 18 (1936), p. 25.

[4]) *LAP*, pp. 123-4.

[5]) The translation "you have satisfied my heart" accepted by Malinine, Partsch-Sethe, Erichsen and others is somewhat misleading. It gives the impression that the root *mtj* has the basic meaning of "satisfied, content." If this were the case, one could logically assume that the Aramaic *ṭyb lbby* was a direct and literal loan-translation. However, the actual linguistic situation is more complicated than it seems at first glance. As far as can be ascertained from the dictionaries of older Egyptian, the root *mtr*—the older form of the Demotic *mtj*—never conveys the idea of satisfaction: its basic meaning is "to be straight, to be equal, equivalent to, to face, to opposite." This same meaning is preserved in all non-legal Demotic usages. It is only in the legal contexts that *mtj* takes on the meaning "to satisfy." Was this meaning determined by the context, or was it suggested from the Greek translations or the Aramaic analogues? Whatever the case may be, this meaning is somewhat unusual; it departs from the older meaning of the term as well as the common non-

my heart" is used most frequently in conveyances. Since the function of a term depends on its use within the larger context of the document, the schemata of the Demotic and Aramaic conveyances and their respective use of the satisfaction clauses will be presented for the sake of comparison.

The Early Demotic (Saitic-Persian) Scheme

Regular

Date: on that day, A said to B: "you have satisfied my heart [1]) with the money (equivalent to the price) of my field/house (exact amount never given). [2])

Boundaries sometimes described.

It is yours; (var. I have given it to you none but you shall exercise authority over it.)" [3])

Schlussklauseln

Irregular (Elephantine, 589 B.C.) [4])

Date: on that day, A said to B: "you have satisfied my heart with the money (equivalent to the price). I have sold it to you. You have given me its money (equivalent to its price). I have received it from your hand; my heart is satisfied with it. [5]) It is yours."

Schlussklauseln.

With certain additions, the irregular Saitic schema, becomes the common schema of the Ptolemaic and Roman periods.

---

legal Demotic usage (oral communication of Dr. Parker). What are the implications of this for the study of the Aramaic term ? First of all, since the root meaning of the Egyptian term has nothing to do with satisfaction, the assumption that the Aramaic was translated from the Demotic does not seem likely. Secondly, the deviation of the legal Demotic *mtj* from the normal Egyptian semantic range of the verb may be due to a certain accomodation to the Aramaic *hwṭbt lbby* "you have satisfied my heart" which may have served as the model of the Demotic term. The writer is no Demotic scholar; however, Dr. Parker agrees that the phenomenon is strange and is well worth an investigation by Demotic legal historians.

[1]) The oldest use of this terms is found in Papyrus Rylands 1 (circa 641 B.C.). Cf. *DJE* 2, p. 43.

[2]) According to Seidl (*ÄRg*, p. 41), the absence of the exact amount of money is an indication that early Demotic sale had transcended the principle of the necessary consideration.

[3]) Cf. P. BM 10117 (=*DJE* 2, p. 26) reads simply: "It is yours; none but you shall exercise authority." In P. Louvre E 9204 (*DJE* 2, p. 47), the formula is somewhat fuller: "It is yours; I have given it to you; none but you shall exercise authority." For the abbreviated formula: "It belongs to you," cf. P. Lilley 27 (*DJE* 2, p. 35). This Demotic clause is quite similar to the Aramaic *zylk hw ʾnt šlyṭ b/ lʾ yšlṭ b . . . lhn ʾnt* "It is yours; you shall exercise authority over . . . / none but you shall exercise authority over . . ."

[4]) For the translation and commentary, cf. P. Berlin 13571 (*DJE* 2, p. 55).

[5]) Demotic *ḥ3tj(.í) mtjw*; cf. the glossary at the end of *DJE* 2, p. 85.

Ptolemaic [1])

Date: on that day, A said to B: "You have satisfied my heart with the silver (equivalent to the price) no sum is specified. (Griffith translates the clauses differently: "You have caused my heart to agree to the silver")

Description of the condition of the land
I have given it to you; it is yours;
(Variant: you have contented my heart with the money) [2])
I have received its price in silver, complete without remainder; my heart is satisfied therewith."

Aramaic [3])

Date: on that day, A said to B: "I have sold and transferred my house to you (*zbn wyhbn*)"

Condition of the house
I have sold it to you; you have given me its price (amount specified) and my heart is satisfied therewith (var. in that none of the price is outstanding against you on my account).

Boundaries
I have sold it to you and removed myself from it. You may now exercise ownership over it (*šlyṭ*); it is yours (*zylk hw*).
Schlussklauseln

Structural Comparison. Since the function of individual terms are dependent on the role they play within specific contexts, a comparison of semantic ranges demands a prior comparison of contextual structure. The contextual structures in which the Aramaic and Demotic terms of satisfaction are employed are quite similar. Both deeds of sale begin with the same formula: Date; on that day, A said to B, followed by a subjectively formulated declaration. At this point the Aramaic and the Demotic part company. The Demotic has: "you have satisfied my heart," while the Aramaic has: "I have sold and transferred to you." However, the contrast is not as great as it seems; the first known Demotic conveyance—Papyrus Rylands 1—is similar to the Aramaic; it begins with the clause: "I have given to you." [4])

Both deeds continue with a description of the boundaries. The Aramaic also contains a description of the condition of the property which is

[1]) Cf. Griffith, *Catalogue of Demotic Papyri*, pp. 118-121 for the Ptolemaic schema. For a discussion of the underlying legal principles of this conveyance, cf. Seidl, *PRg*, pp. 116 ff.

[2]) For this variant, cf. Pestman, p. 19.

[3]) Cf. *BP* 3 or 12.

[4]) *DJE* 2, pp. 43 ff.

missing in the early Demotic deeds. Such descriptions do appear later in the conveyances of the Ptolemaic and Roman periods. [1]) The Aramaic conveyances continue with the satisfaction clause, always passively formulated, [2]) and the exact amount of money always stated. In the early Demotic deeds, the satisfaction clause is almost always found at the beginning of the deed and in the active voice. In this respect, the Demotic conveyance usage is identical with the Aramaic litigation (*mrḥq*) usage where the clause *hwṭbt lbby* "you have satisfied my heart" is always found at the beginning of the deed. However, in one early Demotic deed, [3]) the satisfaction clause appears twice: in the active voice at the beginning of the deed—like the regular Demotic usage—and again in the middle of the deed "I have received the money; my heart is satisfied with therewith"—like the Aramaic usage. This irregular early Demotic schema becomes normative in the Ptolemaic deeds.

Both deeds contain a transfer-investiture clause: "It is yours; none but you may exercise control/you may now exercise control." The Aramaic and Demotic transfer clauses of all periods are quite similar. [4]) Both sets of deeds end with *Schlussklauseln* which, although not identical in all respects, are quite similar. [5]) Above all, in the type of clauses used, in the general configuration of the deed, and especially in the overall subjective-first person formulation, the Aramaic and Demotic deeds have more in common with each other, than the former has with the cuneiform tradition, or the latter with the older Egyptian tradition.

However, there are differences between the Aramaic and the Demotic as well: neither can be considered as a literal copy of the other. The Demotic clause "you have satisfied my heart with the money" never specifies the exact amount paid out; the Aramaic, on the other hand, does. Furthermore, the term *rḥqt* "I have removed myself" is usually found in close association with the term *ṭyb lbby* "my heart is satisfied." This is not true of the parallel Demotic usage: in the earlier Demotic

---

[1]) Cf. Kutscher, *New Aramaic Texts*, p. 235 and Rabinowitz, *Legal History*, pp. 7 ff.

[2]) For some reason, the active form *hwṭbt lbby* "you have satisfied my heart" is only used in the *mrḥq* deeds—where the passive is never used. Is this contrast due simply to the hazards of excavation or does it reflect some inner differentiation in usage?

[3]) Cf. P. Berlin 13571, 589 B.C. (*DJE* 2, p. 55).

[4]) The Akkadian, Aramaic, and Demotic transfer clauses are so similar that they must be historically related. For the time being see Rabinowitz, *Jewish Law*, pp. 124-152. There can be no doubt in my mind that the Arsacid-Neo-Babylonian *lā išallaṭ* "he has no right" is the model of the Aramaic *lʾ yšlṭ* "he has no right"; furthermore, the Demotic term is almost identical with the Aramaic. The only way this relationship can be explained is to assume once more that the Aramaic served as the historical bridge between the cuneiform and the Demotic legal traditions.

[5]) Provisionally, cf. *LAP*, pp. 83-92.

praxis, the Egyptian term of removal is found only in deeds of litigation but not in sale. [1]) In the following periods, however, two separate documents were required for each sale transaction: (a) a deed of specie-payment whose main term is "you have satisfied my heart" [2]) and (b) a deed of renunciation of claim or non-ownership whose main term is "I have removed myself." [3]) Whatever the direction of reception, the dependent tradition did not merely copy the models before it, since each tradition exhibits its own peculiar characteristics The reception, therefore, was a creative process.

Functional Comparison. The Aramaic and the Demotic terms of satisfaction share not only a common root-metaphor, subjective formulation, and active-stative aspects, but also common syntactical structures. Furthermore, at least on superficial observation, the two terms seem to have identical juridical functions: they both seem to be the terminological expression of "*notwendige Entgeltlichkeit.*" Thus, the meaning established for the Akkadian *libbašu ṭāb/libbašu uṭīb* and for the Aramaic *ṭyb lbby/hwṭbt lbby* seems perfectly applicable to the Demotic *dj.k-mtj ḥ3tj(.ỉ)* "you have satisfied my heart." The term must mean: "You have tendered me complete and satisfactory payment; nothing more is demanded; I relinquish all claims; I am quit." The passive expression "my heart is satisfied" means: "having been tendered full and satisfactory payment, I am quit."

However, just at the point where the two terms seem to overlap in meaning as well as in general contextual structure, the equivalence seems to break down: the result of the Aramaic and Akkadian studies do not tally with the meaning attributed to the Egyptian term by most Demotic legal historians. Griffith by translating the clause "you have caused my heart to agree to the money" [4]) rather than "you have satisfied my

[1]) All of the so-called *Abstandsurkunden* of the early Demotic period are discussed by Seidl in *ÄRg*, p. 25. The oldest known examples of such a document are P. Rylands 4 (2 year of Amasis) and P. Loeb 43 (525 B.C.). The Egyptian terminology is virtually identical with the Aramaic: The Demotic *ỉw-y wy-k(wy)* "I am far" is usually followed by the prepositions *r* of the person concerned and *n* of the thing concerned, i.e., "I renounce claim upon (*r*) you in regard to (*n*) your house." (Cf. C. F. Nims, "The Term *HP*, 'Law, Right,' in Demotic," *JNES*, 7 [1948], p. 247, n. 39.) This syntactical usage is virtually identical with the Aramaic; cf. *AP* 25 : 4 *rḥqt mnkm mn byt yznyh* "I renounce claim upon you (*mnkm*) in regard to (*mn*) the house of Yezaniah."

[2]) For the latest discussion of this deed, cf. Pestman, p. 17, n. 6. For the practice of using two deeds to record one transaction, cf. Pestman, p. 19 and especially Seidl, *PRg*, p. 118. Cf. also Rabinowitz, *Jewish Law*, p. 22, n. 10.

[3]) Cf. Pestman, p. 17.

[4]) *Catalogue of Demotic Papyri*, p. 120. Similarly, the passive clause is rendered: "my heart is in agreement with it." In his commentary Griffith remarks: " 'It'

heart with the money" clearly understands the term to express the concepts of volition and agreement rather than receipt and payment. The volitional interpretation has been accepted more recently by Seidl in his study of the term. [1])

The Faulty Basis of the Volitional Interpretation. Seidl interprets the Demotic *dj.k-mtj ḥ3tj(.i)* as a term of volition for the following reasons: (a) since it is based on the same root-metaphor of satisfaction as the abnormal Hieratic *m-ib-hr* "with a satisfied heart, willingly," therefore it must have the same volitional function; [2]) (b) since, according to Seidl, *dj.k-mtj ḥ3tj(.i)* is based on the Akkadian *libbašu ṭāb* which is understood by him as a term of volition, the Demotic term must have the same meaning. [3])

On the basis of this interpretation, Seidl has the following to say about the contrast between the underlying legal principles of abnormal Hieratic and Demotic conveyance law: while abnormal Hieratic sale was based on the principle of volition (*m-ib-hr*) as well as necessary consideration ("I have received the money amount specified from you"), Demotic sale, by omitting the exact amount paid and by retaining the term of volition ("you have satisfied our heart"—or following Griffith—"you have made our heart agree to the money"), makes the agreement of the seller to the suggested sale-price the constitutive element in the transaction. [4]) Furthermore, according to Seidl, the same substitution of *Entgeltlichkeit* by the principle of consent is reflected in early OB conveyances where *libbašu ṭāb* is employed without the specific sum of money being mentioned. [5])

Each one of these arguments is open to serious criticism. First of all, the fact that *m-ib-hr* and *dj.k-mtj ḥ3tj(.i)* are based on the same root metaphor does not necessarily indicate that they fill the same juridical

here seems indefinite, meaning the arrangement generally rather than the price in particular." However, the Aramaic parallel *ṭyb lbby bgw dmyʾ zy yhbt ly* "my heart is satisfied with the money you have given me" clearly does not support Griffith's interpretation.

[1]) Cf. *ÄRg,* pp. 40 ff. where the principle of *notwendige Entgeltlichkeit* is discussed.

[2]) *Ibid.*

[3]) *Ibid.*

[4]) *Ibid.* The volitional-consensual interpretation has been defended most recently by R. H. Pierce in an unpublished dissertation *Three Demotic Papyri in the Brooklyn Museum* (Brown University, 1963), pp. 138 ff., 144 ff. (A copy of this thesis was made available to me by the kind efforts of Dr. Richard Parker of Brown University. Unfortunately, Pierce's study reached me after my own work was completed and therefore, I have only been able to cite page references without going into a detailed comment of his interpretations as they rightly deserve.)

[5]) *ÄRg,* p. 41, n. 10.

function. It was a similar methodological error which obscured the inner semantic contrast between the homonymous terms *ina ṭūb libbi* and *libbašu ṭāb*. However, further examination will demonstrate that *dj.k-mtj ḥ3tj(.i)* is used in contextual structures quite different from those in which *m-ib-hr* is employed.

Secondly, it was established above that the Akkadian *libbašu ṭāb* can only be interpreted as a term of quittance upon the tendering of full and satisfactory payment. If the Demotic term of satisfaction is derived from the Akkadian as Seidl suggests, it too must be a term of quittance rather than volition. I can see no other interpretation of the Demotic "you have satisfied my heart with the money amount not specified" than: "you have tendered me full and satisfactory payment; I am quit." There is no real functional difference, therefore, between the Egyptian usage where the money is not specified and the Aramaic usage where it is: both terms of satisfaction are the terminological expression of the *Entgeltlichkeit* principle. [1] It is therefore somewhat paradoxical that the centrality of the term *dj.k-mtj ḥ3tj(.i)* in the Demotic conveyances should have been cited as proof that these conveyances substituted volition for consideration as the underlying basis of the transaction.

Finally, a word concerning the early OB usage cited by Seidl. He quotes several early OB texts in which *libbašu ṭāb*—taken by Seidl as a term of volition—with the exact amount of the price being specified. Meanwhile, thanks to the publications of early Diyala conveyances, [2] the number of such examples has increased greatly. However, this evidence, which is similar to the Demotic usage, can be interpreted in an entirely different way. First of all, it should be noted that even though these deeds do not mention the specific amount of the sale-price, they clearly stress the principle of the necessary consideration ("as its full price, he weighed out the silver"). [3]

Furthermore, it is strange that Seidl should quote the early Old Babylonian usage in support of the volitional interpretation of the term, since it is precisely in these early deeds that the quittance-performance meaning of *libbam uṭīb-libbum ṭūb* is most clearly reflected. Finally, his arguments, both from the early OB and from the Demotic, are open

[1] A similar line of reasoning is implicit in all of Pestman's discussions of the necessary consideration; cf. Pestman, pp. 18 ff. and especially in his interpretation of the clause "you have satisfied my heart": "So it is quite clear that it is essential for the transfer of title that the seller has received the purchase-money completely and to his satisfaction" (p. 19).

[2] Cf. Harris, *Khafajah*, p. 93, Nos. 60 and 61 and *passim*.

[3] Cf. for example No. 75: (5) [*a-na ši*]-*mi*-[*im*] *ga-am-ri-im* (6) k ù . b a b b a r *iš*-[*qú-ul*] (7) *li-ba*-⌜*šu*⌝ *ṭú-ub*

to a serious logical objection. If Seidl were right in his interpretation, it would be somewhat difficult to assume that early OB and early Demotic had completely transcended the older principle of necessary consideration, and that for some unexplained reason, later OB and later Graeco-Egyptian praxis reinstituted it.

A Redefinition on Inner-Demotic Grounds. Purely on inner-Demotic grounds, *dj.k-mtj ḥ3tj(.i)* can only mean "you have tendered me full and satisfactory payment", not: "you have caused me to agree to the price." This interpretation is confirmed by the Ptolemaic Demotic usage of the term. In this later usage—derived from irregular early Demotic models—the term of satisfaction is used twice: (a) in the active form "you have satisfied ..." at the beginning of the deed; here, the term's meaning is ambiguous since it is not explicated by any complement; (b) at the end of the deed: "I have received its price in silver, without remainder; my heart is satisfied therewith." The close relationship between payment and satisfaction and the complement "without remainder" leave no doubt as to the receipt-quittance meaning of this passive formulation.

Furthermore, the active and passive forms of the term form a (broken) cluster "you have satisfied my heart . . . my heart is satisfied" which is structurally and functionally identical with the Old Assyrian *ušabbišu-šabû* "he satisfied him-he is satisfied" and the Aramaic *hwṭbtm lbbn* . . . *ṭyb lbbn* "you have satisfied our heart . . . our heart is satisfied" (*AP* 20). As Partsch-Sethe realized, the ambiguous active form "you have satisfied our heart" has to be interpreted in the light of the more explicated passive form: "Den Worten *dj-k* (hier wie so oft *tw-k* geschrieben) *mjt ḥ3tj-j* „du hast mein Hertz zufriedenstellt" usw. entspricht in den griechischen Paraphrasen ägyptischer Kaufverträge: πέπεικάς με τῇ τιμῇ oder ἀπηυδόκησάς με τῆς τιμῆς (Griff. Ryl. III 118 ff.). Der präpositionelle Ausdruck *n p3 ḥd n swn* „mit dem Silber des Wertes" (bzw. *n swn* „mit dem Werte") des verkauften Gegenstandes scheint dabei als Mittel oder Werkzeug der Befriedigung angesehen zu sein. Man könnte danach immer noch zweifeln, wie das Verbum *mtj* (ⲙⲁⲧⲉ) dabei eigentlich zu verstehen sei. Ob gemeint sei, dass das Herz des Verkäufers zur Einwilligung in das Geschäft, zum Einverständnis mit der Höhe des Kaufpreises oder zur Zufriedenheit mit der Zahlung, der Befriedigung, gebracht sei.

Dass der letztere Gedanke vorliegt, zeigt nun die synonyme Erklärung *ḥ3tj mtj.w im-f* „mein Herz is damit zufrieden" (ebenfalls durch ἀπηυδόκησάς με wiedergeben, Griff. a.a.O. 120, Nr. 7) der Kauf- und Eheverträge (Griff, a.a.O. 256, Nr. 7; 269, Nr. 13 = 135, Nr. 13) die auch bei uns nachher an ihrer gewohnten Stelle erscheint. Nachdem dort gesagt ist: „ich habe den Wert der verkauften Sache empfangen, vollzählig ohne Rest“ kann nun nicht mehr folgen: „Ich bin mit ihm einverstanden,“ finde ihn angemessen, sondern nur „ich bin mit ihm zufrieden“ im Sinne von „ich bin durch ihn, durch seine Zahlung, befreidigt.“ [1])

This interpretation is followed by Pestman in his study of Egyptian marriage law, who paraphrases the terms of satisfaction as follows: "So it is quite clear that it is essential for the transfer of title that the seller has received the purchase money completely and to his satisfaction." [2]) The interpretations of Partsch-Sethe and Pestman tally completely with the results of the Akkadian and Aramaic investigations.

B. *The Terms dj.k mtj ḥ3tj(.i) "you have satisfied my heart" and ḥ3tj(.i) mtj.w "my heart is satisfied" in Litigation Contexts*

One of the main uses of the Aramaic *hwṭbt lbby* "you have satisfied my heart" is in the *spr mrḥq* "the deed of removal". This type of document is quite similar in function to the Old Babylonian *ṭuppi lā ragāmim* "deed of no-contest": both documents record the cessation of litigation by an unsuccessful claimant and his relinquishment of all future claims to the property and person of the defendant. In Aramaic praxis, the reason for this relinquishment is a purgatory oath tendered by the defendant to the litigant. The litigant then declares: "you have satisfied my heart with the oath you have taken from me and I hereby remove myself from you, from this day, forever." Two things should be noted about this usage: (a) the defendant satisfies the claimant with the oath in the same manner as the buyer satisfies the seller with the sale price: the oath is therefore conceived as a kind of *Entgelt*-consideration, in return for which a right-holder (seller or claimant) relinquishes his right/claim; (b) in the Aramaic praxis, satisfaction (*hwṭbt lbby*) and relinquishment (*spr mrḥq*; *rḥqt mnk*) are organically connected.

This particular configuration of elements is distinctively Aramaic: even though the parallel Akkadian terms *libbašu uṭīb* and *libbašu ṭāb* are quite common in the OB *ṭuppi lā ragāmim*, the means of satisfaction, as far as I can tell, is always a sum of money; never an oath of purgation. I know of no case where the deed reads: "The defendent satisfied the heart of the claimant with the oath." Furthermore, although the Sippar *libbašu ṭāb* is replaced by the Susa *duppur* "removed" in division deeds, as far as I can tell, the contiguous and complementary usage of *libbašu*

---

[1]) Partsch-Sethe, p. 262.
[2]) Pestman, p. 19.

ṭāb "his heart is satisfied" and *duppur* "he has removed himself" as two different stages of a litigation transaction is nowhere attested to: the combination of elements is typically Aramaic.

Egyptian Deeds of No-Contest. Later Egyptian legal praxis (abnormal Hieratic and Demotic) also employs deed of no-contest, although they are not as commonly used as the Aramaic *spr mrḥq* or the Akkadian *ṭuppi lā ragāmim*. This contrasting distribution pattern may, however, be due to the hazards of excavation. The Hieratic deeds of no-contest are not known by any special name and do not employ "removal/distance" terminology. [1]) However, the main clause of one of these rare documents happend to be "you have satisfied my heart." Remarkably, the method of satisfaction is the oath of purgation, exactly like in the common Aramaic praxis.

Papyrus Louvre E. 7861 (Abnormal Hieratic, 566 B.C., Thebes) A has entrusted goods with B. When A demands his goods back, B claims that they were stolen. B then clears himself with the purgatory oath and A, the plaintiff, then declares before the court: [2])

(6) . . . "Je n'ai (7) (aucune) réclamation à te faire, à partir d'aujourd'hui, dorénavant. Je ne pourrai pas (8) laisser venir (pour faire une contestation) contre toi aucune personne au monde, que se soit: frère, soeur, (9) fils, fille, maître, maîtresse (ou) toute (autre) personne au monde entier—à leur suject. (10) Tu m'as contenté le coeur [*dj.k-mtj h3tj(.i)*] avec le serment devant (?) Khons- (11) à-Thèbes-Neferhotep, à partir d'aujourd'hui, dorénavant'."

Thus, the abnormal Hieratic usage overlaps the Aramaic in two significant respects: (a) it uses terms of satisfaction in deeds of litigation; (b) the means of satisfaction is not the payment of money but the oath of purgation conceived as an *Entgelt*-consideration, the tendering of which dislodges the claimant from his claim (or the seller from his property) and makes him quit from this time and forever. However, the abnormal Hieratic usage—if one can judge from a limited number of texts—does not know the organic link between satisfaction and removal that is so typical of the Aramaic praxis: in fact, it does not seem to employ removal terminology at all.

The Later Demotic Usage. Terms of removal, however, are known from the Demotic tradition, but significantly only from deeds of the late

[1]) Cf. Seidl, *ÄRg*, p. 24.

[2]) M. Malinine, "Deux documents égyptiens relatifs au dépôt," *MDAIK*, 16 (1958), p. 221-22.

Persian and Ptolemaic periods. These later Demotic deeds of no-contest are called *sẖ n wy*, literally "deeds of being far," usually translated as "deeds of cession," and more recently by Pestman as "deeds of renunciation" or "deeds of no-title." [1] The main term of this type of deed is the expression "I am far from you in respect to the property." [2] Functionally and etymologically the early Aramaic *spr mrḥq* "deed of being-far" and the expression *rḥqt mnk mn* "I have removed myself from you concerning (the property)" are identical, with the later Demotic *sẖ n wy* and the expression *iw.y wy.k(wy)*, "I am far."

The first example of such a deed is from the year 334 B.C. The schema of the deed is the following:

"I renounce claim (lit. I am far) to the right of the house/land concerning which I came against you . . .
There is not owing to me a right, a judgment, an oath or anything in the world from you, from today on." [3]

In a deed from Elephantine (245 B.C.), the following is added:

"You have done its (the contested good's) right, their judgment and their oath before Knum for me." [4]

Unlike the usage reflected in the earlier, Aramaic *spr mrḥq* where the reason for the renunciation is clearly spelled out ("you have taken the oath for me" or "you have satisfied my heart with the oath; I now remove myself from you"), the Demotic deeds are ambiguous; the meaning of the expression "you have done its right (*hp*) for me" is not in itself very clear. If it were not far the slightly more explicated Elephantine formulary which obliquely mentions an oath, the meaning of the term *hp* in this context might still be unknown.

It was pointed out above that the abnormal Hieratic deed of no-contest was similar to the Aramaic *spr mrḥq* in its use of the clause "you have satisfied my heart (i.e., you have induced me to relinquish my claim/right) with the oath you have taken for me." However, it differed from the Aramaic in that it did not employ the term of removal. The later Demotic deeds, on the other hand, use both the nominal and verbal terms of removal exactly as the early Aramaic, but do not employ, at

---

[1]) Cf. Pestman, p. 17, n. 6.

[2]) Cf. the discussion in Nims, "The Term *HP*, 'Law, Right,' in Demotic," *JNES*, 7 (1948), p. 247, n. 39.

[3]) *Ibid.*, pp. 248 ff: Corp. Papyrus 3: 1-2 (second year of Darius III—334 B.C.).

[4]) *Ibid.*, p. 249: Elephantine 12 (245 B.C.)

least as a general rule, the clause of satisfaction. However, there are at least two exceptions to this rule—P. BM 10526-7, 288 B.C. The schema of these documents reads:

"I renounce claim against you in regard to your house . . . concerning which I came against you, saying, 'It is mine.' (Now) you have done its right for me; my heart is satisfied therewith.

There is not owning to me a right, a judgment, or anything in the world from you in its name, from today onward." [1]

Here, the elements of removal and satisfaction are finally associated in the same context. However, it should be noted that this association is late and exceedingly rare in Demotic praxis, while it is early and common in the Aramaic tradition. Secondly, in the Demotic usage, the expression "I renounce claim" is the central term of the deed, is not the immediate result of the act of satisfaction, and in general, is not organically linked with it, while in the Aramaic usage, the term of satisfaction (*hwṭbt*) is the central term of the transaction and is organically linked to the following *wrḥqt mnk* "and I hereby remove myself from you" which is conceived as the reaction to the preceding satisfactory performance. Certainly, although the Aramaic and the Demotic deeds of no-contest employ the same linguistic elements, their deployment of these elements reflects contrasting legal conceptions. Finally, it should be noted that in terms of the general construction of the deed in which the term of satisfaction is used and in common use of the active voice, the Aramaic seems closer to the abnormal Hieratic than to the later Demotic, even though the Demotic shares with the Aramaic the association of satisfaction and removal.

By way of summary, the following can be said: the configuration "you have satisfied my heart with the oath; therefore, I remove myself from you" is an organic complex of legal and linguistic elements to be found only in the Aramaic. Parts of this complex are known from Egyptian sources but not the complex itself. Thus, the element "you have satisfied my heart with the oath"—without the association with the term of removal—is found in the abnormal Hieratic tradition; on the other hand, the association of satisfaction and removal, although rare and late, is known from the Demotic tradition. However, the complex (a) "you have satisfied my heart with the oath" (cf. "you have satisfied my heart with the price") and (b) "I therefore remove myself from you"—is only found in the Aramaic usage.

[1] *Ibid.*, p. 249.

One can only speculate concerning the historical relationship among these three traditions. The following alternatives should be considered:

(a) If it is assumed that the Aramaic is a reflection of the Egyptian legal tradition, then the following reconstruction may be posited: first of all, the Demotic association of satisfaction and removal, although attested to only sporadically in late deeds, must have been used in early Demotic deeds as yet undiscovered. (Such an assumption, however, seems unwarranted on the basis of present documentary evidence. New publications may yet uncover such usage.) Secondly, it must be assumed that the Aramaic scribes borrowed elements from both the abnormal Hieratic and the Demotic traditions and combined them into a new organic complex. The expression "you have satisfied my heart with the oath" was borrowed from the abnormal Hieratic tradition and the association of satisfaction with removal was borrowed from the Demotic. However, the order of these elements was changed: the relinquishment in Aramaic praxis was now organically linked to the satisfaction and conceived as its immediate result.

(b) The other alternative is simply to assume that the more complicated and organic complex reflected in the Aramaic is the end product of many inner-Assyriological developments and the amalgamation of many complex elements; hence the highly nuanced character of this formulary. In comparison, the newer Egyptian formularies are less complex in structure and underlying legal principles. In all probability, each of the newly created formularies borrowed only certain elements from the more complex Aramaic: the Hieratic borrowed "you have satisfied my heart with the oath;" the early Demotic borrowed "you have satisfied my heart with the price" in conveyances; at a later period it borrowed the removal terminology and employed it in litigation but not in sale; at an even later period it borrowed the configuration of removal and satisfaction elements from the Aramaic *spr mrḥq* and employed them in the *sẖ n wy* "deed of renunciation;" however, it did so only sporadically and without preserving the original organic and logical connection between satisfaction and the concommitant removal.

Either of these alternatives is logically possible; on historical, cultural grounds I am inclined to favor the second one. In any case, whatever the direction of reception, the three traditions are clearly related and somehow ultimately influenced by the cuneiform heritage.

C. *Demotic Terms of Satisfaction in Marriage Documents*

The fifth century Aramaic papyri from Elephantine often contain legal usages which, although unknown from contemporary Demotic sources, are quite common in the Demotic deeds of the Ptolemaic and later periods. Thus, for example, the association of satisfaction and removal terminology so typical of the Aramaic *spr mrḥq*, is attested to in Demotic sources only in deeds of the third century B.C. Similarly, the use of terms of satisfaction in marriage documents, so common in the Aramaic deeds of the fifth century, is known only from the Demotic deeds of the late Ptolemaic period.

Terms of satisfaction are used in two different contexts within the Aramaic marriage document: (a) upon the receipt of the brideprice (*mohar*) by the father, the groom declares: "you have received the *mohar* of your daughter and your heart is satisfied therewith"; in this context, the father is conceived as a right-holder who cedes his rights over his daughter in return for a satisfactory consideration which is structurally similar to the *Entgelt* tendered in sale transactions; (b) after the husband received his wife's dowry and counts each individual item to see that it tallies with the sum recorded in the deed, he declares: "This is the sum of the goods which you have brought into my house; I have received it and my heart is satisfied therewith." In this context, the husband is conceived as a consignee to whom goods have been entrusted and who obligates himself to return them at a given time in the future—in this case, his wife's divorce. Before accepting the obligation, the consignee has to be "satisfied" that the goods actually received tally with the goods recorded in the deed.

Although the receipt-quittance function of the term of satisfaction is not unknown in Egyptian legal sources, it is not to be found in Egyptian marriage contracts. In the abnormal Hieratic contract, the bride price is paid directly to the father of the bride as in the Aramaic praxis. [1]) Here, one would expect the idiom "my heart is satisfied therewith." However, the receipt-quittance usage of the term of satisfaction is not known from abnormal Hieratic sources: it is typical only of the Demotic praxis.

Yet, although the receipt-satisfaction of the Demotic term of satisfaction is known from conveyances, and, according to Pestman, the money paid by the husband to the wife was considered as a necessary consideration—something like the *Entgelt* in sale—, [2]) nevertheless,

[1]) Cf. Lüddeckens, Nos. 1-4.
[2]) Pestman, pp. 18 ff.

the receipt-quittance use of the term of satisfaction is not to be found in the Demotic marriage documents. Possibly, this had to do with the fact that the money was paid not to the father of the bride but to the bride herself, thus attenuating the structural similarity between sale and marriage: when the father cedes his daughter in return for a sum of money he personally receives, one can still feel the analogy between sale and marriage; however, when the bride herself receives the money —even though the money is still called a *šp* "consideration"—the transaction does not look like a self-sale but as something of an entirely different order: a transaction based on consent rather than consideration.

On the other hand, the second use of term of satisfaction—the obligation-creating function reflected in the husband's declaration upon the receipt of the dowry—is amply attested to in all types of Egyptian marriage settlements.

Two main types of Egyptian marriage are known: (a) one based on the payment of money (*šp* "consideration") by the husband to the wife: at times, this type of transaction also mentions a dowry brought by the wife into her husḅand's house; the husband has the right of usifruct but is obligated to return the dowry in case of divorce; [1]) (b) another type of marriage based on the payment made by the wife to the husband. The obligatory use of the Demotic term of satisfaction is to be found in both types of transaction. [2])

Marriage based on Payment by the Husband. From about the end of the third century B.C., marriage documents recording, among other things, the receipt of the wife's *Frauensachen* by the husband and his satisfaction therewith are attested to. The schema is the following: (in the German translation of Lüddeckens)

The list of the goods and their value; sum total;

"Wert deiner Frauensachen, die du gebrachst hast in mein Haus mit dir. Empfangen habe ich sie aus deiner Hand, indem sie vollständig sind ohne irgendeinen Rest. Mein Herz ist zufrieden mit ihnen.

Bist du drinnen, so bist du drinnen mit ihnen. Bist du draussen, so bist du draussen mit ihnen. Dein ist ihre Bestimmung, mein ist ihre Verwahrung.

Entlasse ich dich (als) Ehefrau, oder beliebst du zu gehen, (so werde) ich geben (dir) deine Frauensachen, welche oben (geschrieben) sind . . .

---

[1]) *Ibid.*, pp. 13-20.
[2]) *Ibid.*, pp. 21 ff.

Nicht soll ich (?) können (geben) einen Eid hinter dich (?) wegen deiner Frauensachen . . ." Lüddeckens 18, 226 B.C.); also Nos. 8 and 16.

The clause "I have received them without remainder; my heart is satisfied therewith" is virtually identical with the Ptolemaic conveyance formula recording the receipt of the sale-price. However, functionally, the two clauses, in spite of their formal identity, contrast with each other: in sale, the declaration of satisfaction announces the relinquishment of a right by an owner; in marriage, the declaration of satisfaction announces the acceptance of an obligation by a consignee (the husband). Significantly, the late Demotic dowry-receipt clause is functionally identical with the early Aramaic usage discussed above; furthermore, both use their respective satisfaction terms in an obligation-creating manner. Therefore, there can be little doubt that the two terms and their respective clauses and contextual structures are historically related. However, the direction of reception is difficult to establish. [1])

One can assume that the Egyptian usage is primary and that the Aramaic is derivative. However, to do so, one must make a further assumption: that the Demotic usage which is attested to only from a much later period than the Aramaic, was in common usage in Demotic documents of the sixth century, and that the Demotic prototype was not preserved, while the Aramaic adaptation was.

More probable is the assumption that the Aramaic usage, attested to several centuries before the Demotic is the original and that the later Demotic usage was patterned after it. There are just too many cases where the fifth century Aramaic anticipates the later Demotic usage to read the facts in any other way. Further discoveries of early Demotic deeds may, however, call for a re-evaluation of the evidence in favor of the first hypothesis. In the meanwhile, the fact that a significant number of early deeds are already known and that these deeds do not contain signs of the later Demotic usage seems to confirm the second suggestion. Furthermore, as a general rule, one can say that the later the Egyptian document, the greater the Aramaic (read: cuneiform) influence. This judgment is confirmed by the investigations of Taubenschlag concerning the influence of cuneiform law on the Egyptian legal praxis of the Ptole-

---

[1]) According to Möller, *Eheverträge*, p. 21, n. 2, the Egyptian practice is derived from the (Elephantine) Aramaic, which in itself is based on cuneiform prototypes. Cf. also the discussion of Wahrmund, *Ehe*, pp. 83 ff. Pestman, p. 101, admits the possibility of an Aramaic derivation, even though he considers it more likely that the practice was an inner-Egyptian development.

maic and Roman periods. [1]) A similar pattern—the revival of ancient legal elements in the youngest layer of legal tradition—is also typical of the inner rhythm of the cuneiform tradition. The explanation for this significant phenomenon has yet to be offered.

Marriage Based on the Payment of the Wife. The exact legal nature of this second type of Egyptian marriage has been the subject of much scholarly discussion; [2]) all that can reasonably be said without relying on conjecture is that this type of marriage is based on a payment of money tendered by the wife to the husband rather than on the *šp* "consideration" paid by the husband to the wife. Furthermore, two subcategories of this type of marriage can be distinguished: (a) a deed mentioning a *ḥd n ỉr ḥm.t* "money of becoming a wife" (Pestman, type B); [3]) (b) a deed mentioning a *s'nḫ* "(money) which causes her to live" (Pestman, type C). [4]) In both of these transactions terms of satisfaction play a significant—although as yet unclarified—role. The deed mentioning the "money of becoming a wife" has the following schema:

The woman pays the money to the man who then declares:

"You have given me x amount of money—your money to become a wife. I have received it from your hand; my heart is content with it, (for) it is complete without remainder."
The deed continues with the obligations the man assumes to perform for the woman: to provide her with an annual amount of food and clothing; to deliver the sum of money in full in case of divorce; the placing of all his property, present and future, as the security for the payment of this money. [5])

The schema for the deed of *s'nḫ* is as follows:

The husband declares:

"You have given me x amount of money as your *s'nḫ*."

The deed continues with the husband's promise to provide an annual allowance; stipulations concerning the inheritance rights of her children; a promise to pay any arrears on her maintenance and the final clause: "I shall not be able to say to you: 'receive your *s'nḫ* (back).' (However),

---

[1]) R. Taubenschlag, "Das babylonische Recht in den griechischen Papyri," *JJP*, 7/8 (1953/54), pp. 169-185.

[2]) For the latest discussion of the problem and a full bibliography, cf. Pestman, pp. 21 ff.

[3]) *Ibid.*, pp. 32 ff.

[4]) *Ibid.*, pp. 37 ff.

[5]) *Ibid.*, pp. 33-4.

on your day that you want to receive it back, I shall give it to you thereon." [1])

In this second type of transaction, the following deed of specie-payment is added:

"You have contented my heart with the money for all and everything that I possess and that I shall acquire . . . It belongs, to you from this above mentioned date." [2])

The active form "you have satisfied my heart" used in the deed of specie-payment accompanying the *sʿnḫ*, and the passive from "my heart is satisfied" used in "the deed of becoming a wife" are clearly related to each other. Unfortunately, since the meaning of the individual terms is dependent on the interpretation of the deeds as a whole, and especially on the legal nature of the payments—a matter in which there is little or no scholarly consensus—the exact legal functions of the terms are still unclear.

Clauses of satisfaction can be used in three different ways; which of these three logical possibilities fits the documents under discussion?

(a) The clause of satisfaction records the receipt of a consideration by a right-holder in return for a consideration and his concommitant relinquishment of rights; this is the use attested to in the conveyance formula: "I have received the money completely, without remainder; my heart is satisfied therewith."

(b) It also records the receipt of wages by someone with services to offer (cf. the shepherd in *CH* 264 and the person who hires out his slaves in older Egyptian law); once the hirer receives his *Entgelt*-wages and is quit therewith, he is immediately obligated to perform in full measure; the declaration of satisfaction triggers the obligation.

(c) In other contexts, even though the money received is not an *Entgelt*-wage, the receipt of goods and the satisfaction therewith still triggers an obligation. Cf. the Aramaic deed of consignment (*AP* 2) and the Aramaic and Demotic receipt of the dowry-*Frauensachen*: "I have received the goods completely, without remainder; my heart is satisfied therewith" = "I obligate myself to return the goods in full."

In which of these three ways is the declaration of satisfaction in this second type of Egyptian marriage used? When the husband receives the money tendered by the wife and declares that he is satisfied therewith does he do so (a) as a right-holder who cedes his rights in return for a

[1]) *Ibid.*, p. 38.
[2]) *Ibid.*, p. 40.

"consideration"; (b) as a depositee who has received a deposit of a consignment and obligates himself to return it on a future date; (c) as a hired hand who, upon the receipt of his *Entgelt*-wage, becomes obligated to perform in full?

Since structurally the money paid by the wife to the husband in the second type of marriage is identical with the Frauensachen delivered by the wife to the husband in the first type of marriage, one could argue that the receipt of the money and the concommitant satisfaction are functionally identical in both cases: an acceptance of obligation to return the money in full on some later date (divorce). However, there is a significant difference between the receipt of the dowry and the receipt of the wife's payment in the second type of marriage: in the first case, the delivery of goods does not constitute marriage; it is merely a supplementary performance; in the second type of marriage, on the other hand, it is the only performance which constitutes marriage. The payment is now a consideration; it is "money of becoming a wife" whose acceptance on the part of the husband is the formal acknowledgemnt of the new tie. However, it should be noted that to call this sum a consideration does not deny that, on another level, it also functions as a deposit.

What kind of a consideration is this payment? Is it like the payment of the bride-price in normal Aramaic marriage? Can the husband be conceived as a right-holder who cedes his rights upon the receipt of the consideration after the manner of the father of the bride who relinquishes control over his daughter upon the receipt of the *mohar-Entgelt*? Since the husband in this type of marriage does not have any rights which he cedes—he only has responsibilities to feed his wife and clothe her, etc.—such an interpretation is plainly untenable. Furthermore, the money itself cannot be the consideration since he does not really own the money but simply enjoys its usifruct as in a loan. However, the transaction is not a loan since the money is called "money of becoming a wife" and, furthermore, there is no time stipulation when it has to be paid back. [1])

In these circumstances, I would suggest the following interpretation: the money received by the husband in this second type of marriage has to be seen under several aspects simultaneously: (a) structurally, it is like the dowry of normal marriage entrusted to the husband who obligates himself to return it on some future date; the declaration: "I have received it in full; my heart is satisfied therewith" is a declaration of obligation; (b) however, this sum of money also plays a constitutive role in the transaction; in one case at least—it is the "money of becoming a wife."

---

[1]) *Ibid.*, pp. 41 ff.

It is a type of consideration. Its receipt by the husband constitutes the marriage. However, since the husband does not really own this sum but only enjoys its usifruct one must say that it is the use of the money rather than the money itself which is the consideration in this transaction. However, when the husband receives this money and says "my heart is satisfied therewith" or "you have satisfied my heart," he does not do so as a right-holder who relinquishes his rights in return for an Entgelt but rather as a person with services to hire who obligates himself to perform upon the receipt of his *Entgelt*-wage. In a sense, the wife by tendering to the husband a sum of money which he can use as a loan for a period of time, buys for herself certain obligations on the part of the husband. When he receives the money and says "my heart is satisfied", he obligates himself to provide her with foods and clothing after the manner of the shepherd in *CH* 264 who upon the receipt of his wage obligates himself to take good care of the sheep. However, by the same declaration, the husband obligates himself to return the dowry-like sum of money with which he has been entrusted as a depositee.

D. *Demotic Terms of Satisfaction in the So-Called Adhesions*

It was pointed out above that in early Mesopotamian law, the sale of land was subject to many impediments: first of all, the owner was almost magically attached to his land; it was part of his past and he did not part with it readily; secondly, land was originally owned by the extended family; if the individual wanted to sell his share, he needed the consent of the other joint-owners or close relatives who had some claim to the property. The extra payments tendered to the family of the seller, his relatives and neighbors, in the early sale transactions of third millennium B.C. were all meant to "satisfy" these right-holders into relinquishing their claims. These extra payments were the forerunners of the later Ur III and OB *Schlussklauseln*. [1])

Evidently, the same mentality survived in other areas of cuneiform culture. Neo-Babylonian sale transactions also mention the tendering of extra payments of food, money and goods to the close relatives of the seller. Quite often, the conveyances state that the transaction took place *ina ašābi* "in the presence, i.e., with the consent" of the seller's wife. Since the wife had a claim on her husband's property—let us say in case of divorce—the transaction could not take place until she had relinquished her claim on the property of her husband. [2])

[1]) Cf. Chapter IV, p. 100 - 03 and 107 ff.

[2]) Cf. San Nicolò, "Zum *atru* and anderen Nebenleistungen des Käufers beim neubabylonischen Immobiliarkauf," *Or*, 16 (1947), pp. 272 ff.

A similar situation existed in Demotic legal practice. Since according to most Demotic marriage contracts, all of the husband's property was security for the payment of the wife's dowry (if the marriage was based on the consideration of the man) or her "money of becoming a wife" or *sʿnḫ* (if the marriage was based on the payment of the woman), the husband could not sell his property without the wife's consent, more specifically, her renunciation of all claims.

Furthermore, since most marriage contracts also contained stipulations concerning the inheritance rights of the wife's sons, [1]) the transfer of property often could not take place without the agreement of the heir. Such agreements—or more correctly, relinquishments of claims—are called "adhesions" by Demotic legal historians. [2]) The adhesions were separate documents, drawn up at the time of sale. There are cases, however, where the adhesion is incorporated into the deed of conveyance. Several formulations are known:

(a) The person who writes the adhesion—wife, son or relative—makes the following declaration: "Write and do all the words which (are) written above; my heart is satisfied with them (or: in agreement with them)." [3])

(b) "Receive the deed from the hand of A (the transferrer) . . . Let him do according to all the words specified above, concerning which he drew up the document for you . . . My heart is satisfied with them (or: in agreement with them)." [4])

(c) "Receive the deed . . . My heart is satisfied with them (or: in agreement with them). I am removed from you in respect to the property." [5])

Significantly, the clause "I am satisfied with them/in agreement with them" is the same, at least linguistically, as the one used in conveyances, [6]) litigation, and marriage. Here, however, there is some room for doubt concerning the meaning of the term. At first glance, the term seems to be one of volition rather than of quittance. If this interpretation

1) Cf. Pestman, pp. 38 and *passim*.

2) Cf. Partsch-Sethe, pp. 683 ff. For the term "adhesion", cf. *DJE* 2, p. 27 and *passim*. Similar adhesions are also found in the Jewish documents from Wadi Murabbaʿat (cf., for example, *Les grottes de Murabbaʿat*, No. 30: 25 ff. and the deed published by Abramson and Ginsberg in *BASOR*, 136 (1954), pp. 17-19). Cf. J. J. Rabinowitz; *BASOR*, 154 (1957), p. 16 for Talmudic parallels.

3) Partsch-Sethe, p. 685 (P. BM 10177).

4) P. Louvre 2438 (245 B.C.); cf. Partsch-Sethe, p. 694.

5) P. Berlin 3089 (231 B.C.); cf. Partsch-Sethe, p. 695.

6) Partsch-Sethe, p. 263.

is correct, adhesions are the only Demotic context I know of where the volitional interpretation of the term of satisfaction makes sense.

One thing is clear: the expression "my heart is satisfied with the words. conditions" does not express the receipt of an *Entgelt* by a right-holder and his concommitant consideration. Nevertheless, even though there is no consideration and no receipt, there is the relinquishment of rights on the part of a right-holder. It is quite possible, therefore, that the term of satisfaction has an extended use in this context which is somewhat different from that which it has in its original *Sitz im Leben*. Here, the right-holder declares that he has no opposition to the transfer of the property recorded in the deed and its stipulations; he does so even though he receives no consideration. The quittance meaning of the term is confirmed by the explicative used in formulation c: "I am removed from you . . ."

If this interpretation, necessarily conjectural, is correct, it may be assumed that the term of satisfaction, besides its original use as a term of receipt-quittance, was used in several *nachgeformte Rechtsgeschäften*: (a) even though no consideration was tendered, a right holder relinquishes his rights by the declaration: "My heart is satisfied." (b) even though the goods received are not a consideration, depositees who receive a deposit or a consignment, obligate themselves to deliver the goods by declaring: "my heart is satisfied."

To sum up: the Aramaic and Demotic terms of satisfaction share so many features that some historical relationship may be presumed to have existed between them. First of all, while all Akkadian formulations of the term of satisfaction—except one—are formulated objectively, both the Aramaic and the Demotic terms are formulated subjectively in the first person. Secondly, the Aramaic and the Demotic share a common semantic range that includes the ideas of quittance upon the receipt of a consideration and the acceptance of an obligation to deliver upon the receipt of a consignment. The first usage is commonly attested to in Aramaic and Demotic conveyances, while the second usage is reflected in many Aramaic and Demotic marriage documents. The husband's declaration upon the receipt of the *Frauensachen/tkwnh* that "his heart is satisfied with the goods" signals his acceptance of the obligation to return the goods in full in case of divorce. Significantly, although the quittance usage of the term of satisfaction is known from cuneiform sources, the obligatory usage—especially in the receipt of the *Frauensachen/tkwnh*—is not.

Within this general pattern of agreement, the Aramaic and the Demotic each retain their own specific characteristics. Thus, for example, terms of satisfaction are found in many Aramaic deeds of no-contest—as they are also in the parallel Akkadian instrument, the *ṭuppi lā ragāmim*; their use, however, in Egyptian sources is both sporadic and late. Furthermore, while the obligatory use of the term of satisfaction is reflected both in the Demotic and the Aramaic usage, its use in the former is limited to marriage documents, while Aramaic praxis extends it to deeds of consignment as well. On the other hand, there are cases where the Demotic usage is more inclusive than the Aramaic. Thus, for example, terms of satisfaction are employed in marriages based on the payment of the wife and in adhesions—both instruments unknown to Aramaic praxis.

The similarities—which have not always been noted by the Demotic scholars—are a clear indication that the Aramaic and Demotic formularies came into being in a common legal milieu. On the other hand, the peculiarities of each tradition indicate that, no matter what the direction of the reception may have been, the process of assimilating foreign elements was certainly a creative one. Thus, if the Aramaic scribes accepted Egyptian legal elements, they incorporated them into a legal tradition that was essentially cuneiform in origin. And if the Demotic scribes accepted Near Eastern elements through an Aramaic medium, they incorporated them into a structure that was clearly Egyptian. It is, therefore, unfortunate that Rabinowitz in his attempt to discover Jewish influences in most unlikely places only confirmed the tendency of Egyptologists to disregard the significance of the Aramaic legal papyri as a possible medium of Near Eastern influences. A re-examination of the whole problem is certainly in order.

CHAPTER SEVEN

CONCLUSION

1. The Coordination of the Akkadian, Aramaic, and Demotic Terms

The fact that the three terms of satisfaction agree with each other in terms of meaning and legal function may be dismissed by some as coincidence or as the result of parallel development. [1]) However, the fact that in respect to common etyma, [2]) root metaphor, [3]) complements,[4]) and contextual range, [5]) *ṭyb lbby* is virtually identical with *libbašu ṭāb*, while in terms of over-all structure and formulation of the deeds in which the term of satisfaction is used *ṭyb lbby* is practically identical with the Demotic *dj.k-mtj ḥ3tj(.i)* [6])—can only mean one thing: the Aramaic formulary, and specifically the term *ṭyb lbby*, have definite historical connections with both the cuneiform and the Demotic legal traditions.

Furthermore, if one assumes with Seidl that the Demotic term may be derived from the Akkadian, [7]) the fact that (a) the Aramaic is often closer to the Akkadian than the Demotic is—the former still bearing "tracers" of its cuneiform origins not found in the Demotic [8])—and that (b) the Aramaic often anticipates the later Demotic usage by several centuries, [9]) one can argue with some cogency that it was the Aramaic that served as

---

[1]) Cf. the discussion of the individual terms in their respective chapters.

[2]) Both the Akkadian and the Aramaic are based on the root *ṭ-y-b*. It is inconceivable that if the Aramaic were translated from the Demotic, the Aramaic and the Akkadian would correspond so closely.

[3]) The basic meaning of the Egyptian root *mtr/j* is "to be straight," not "to be satisfied"; cf. the discussion above p. 150, n. 5.

[4]) The Akkadian *maḫir libbašu ṭāb* "(the money) was received; his heart is satisfied" = Ar. *ʿl ʿlyk ṭyb lbbk* "(the money) was received by you, your heart is satisfied"; Akkadian *šiqlu lā rēḫe* "no money is outstanding" = Ar. *zy lʾ ʾštʾr* "in that no money is outstanding." For other examples, cf. the respective sections on the complements of *libbašu ṭāb* and *ṭyb lbby*.

[5]) All three terms are common in sale. However, only the Akkadian and the Aramaic use terms of satisfaction to record the receipt of the bride-price. Furthermore, both Akkadian and Aramaic use the term in deeds of no-contest. Only two examples of such a usage are known from very late Egyptian sources.

[6]) See Chapter VI.

[7]) *ÄRg*, p. 41.

[8]) Cf. above, n. 4.

[9]) Cf. the many examples cited in Chapter VI.

the historic bridge between the Akkadian *libbašu ṭāb* and the Demotic *dj.k-mtj ḥ3tj(.ỉ)*.

There are, however, many cases where the Demotic and the Aramaic agree with each other against the Akkadian. Thus, for example, the Aramaic and the Demotic share (a) a common subjective, first-person formulation; [1]) (b) a common association of the term of satisfaction with removal and transfer clauses; [2]) (c) and a common opening clause, "Date: on that day, A said to B: 'I have sold/given/taken as wife . . .' " [3]) Therefore, even though a given Aramaic term may read like a reflex of the Akkadian, the deed as a whole in its over-all subjective formulation and in the order of its clauses reads very much like a contemporary Demotic document. In general, the Aramaic and the Demotic deeds share an expansiveness of formulation that often borders on the narrative, a characteristic that contrasts markedly with the laconic style of the cuneiform legal document. [4])

What is the origin of these common Aramaic-Demotic* elements? The Assyriologist may be tempted to see in them the reflex of a common cuneiform model still to be unearthed. Such an assumption would be a natural extension of the Assyriological thesis that most of the innovations in the Demotic are based on Near Eastern prototypes. As we have seen, such assumptions are not foreign to Demoticists either. Their only reservation is that the Demotic reception of cuneiform elements did not take place through an Aramaic medium. [5])

The more conservative Demoticist, and even a comparative legal historian like Yaron, may claim that since the Demotic deeds are slightly older than the Aramaic, the fifth-century Aramaic deeds are in some respects the partial reflex of Demotic innovations. [6]) Logical and historical considerations certainly do not preclude such a possibility.

Kutscher would argue that if the Aramaic and the Demotic share common features, attested to neither in the earlier Egyptian or cuneiform traditions, these features must be considered as innovations by Aramaic

---

[1]) "You have satisfied my heart" as against the Akkadian "he satisfied his heart."

[2]) Cf. p. 151 ff.

[3]) Cf. above, p. 151. There is also a certain degree of contextual overlap between the Demotic and the Aramaic in which both contrast with the Akkadian. For example, only the Aramaic and the Demotic record the receipt of the *tkwnh*/ "Frauensachen" by the term "my heart is satisfied" which, in this context, carries an obligatory rather than a quittance function.

[4]) The fact that both the Aramaic and the Egyptian documents were written on papyrus rather than clay may perhaps account for the difference.

[5]) Seidl, *ÄRg*, p. 73.

[6]) *LAP*, p. 123 f.

scribes. Kutscher places great emphasis on the creative role of the Aramaic scribes who originated the Aramaic formulary. They were not slavish imitators of a particular cuneiform formulary but innovators of the highest degree who fused bits and pieces of cuneiform, West Semitic, and indigenous Aramaic legal traditions into a structure whose whole was quite different from the sum of its individual parts. [1]

Logically, one must admit that each one of these theories has much cogency to it. Furthermore, these interpretations are not mutually exclusive. Therefore, each case of Aramaic-Demotic overlap must be judged entirely on its own merits.

Subjective Formulation. The Aramaic and the Demotic share a common, first-person, subjective formulation ("you have satisfied my heart") which contrasts with the third-person, objective formulation of the Akkadian ("his heart is satisfied"). Since the only type of formulation ever used in Egyptian legal documents was the first-person, subjective formulation, [2] it stands to reason that once the cuneiform term was transferred to Egypt it was recast into the subjective structure common in the local tradition.

However, another alternative should be considered. Even though third-person formulations seem to be more common in the cuneiform praxis, it should not be forgotten that the Old Akkadian [3] tradition also used subjective formulations, and that this type of formulation was preserved in the fringe areas of Susa, [4] Kültepe, [5] Nuzi, [6] Alalakh, [7] Ras Shamra, [8] and in the form of the dialogue-document in Neo-Babylonian [9] and Arsacid[10] deeds. Furthermore, it was just in such areas that *libbašu ṭāb* was used and likely to have survived.[11] Thus, the use of the Akkadian term of satisfaction in a subjectively deed from Syria-

---

[1] Kutscher, *New Aramaic Texts*, p. 246.

[2] Cf. the deeds of the archaic periods published by Pirenne and Van de Walle in *DJE* I.

[3] Cf. Gelb, *Akkadian Inscriptions*, Nos. 8, 10, 11, 21. Cf. above, p. 91, n. 8.

[4] Cf. *MDP* XXIII 317. Like the later Nuzi *lišānšu* document, this deed begins with a list of witnesses before whom the declaration was made.

[5] Cf. *EL* III-IV, pp. 1 ff., especially the deeds listed as "Urkunden in Form gewöhnlicher Protokolle."

[6] Cf. Koschaker, *NKRA*, p. 23, n. 6.

[7] Cf. AT *11 (Old Babylonian; a will).

[8] Cf. Thureau-Dangin, "Trois contrats de Ras Shamra," *Syria*, 18 (1937), p. 245 (=*RS* 8.145) is formulated completely in the first person. Many of the objectively formulated deeds contain subjective sections. Cf., for example, *PRU* III 16.250 (pp. 85-86), *RS* 8.208 (*ibid.*, p. 110), *PRU* III 15.86 (p. 51), and 16.143 (p. 81).

[9] Cf. San Nicolò, *Beiträge*, pp. 152 ff.

[10] Cf. Krückmann, *BRVU*, pp. 63 ff.

[11] Cf. Chapter VI, p. 80.

Palestine—an area in close contact with Egypt—is certainly not beyond the limits of probability. In fact, exactly such a usage can be isolated in a subjectively formulated OB deed from Sippar (*CT* IV 7a = Schorr 310; Apil-Sîn).

The deed—very similar to a Nuzi *lišānšu* document in its over-all construction—is formulated as an oral declaration* before many witnesses, who are listed at the beginning of the deed:

(25) *kaspam ši-im bi-ti-ya* (26) *ga-am-ra-am ù bi-tam ki-ma bi-tim* (27) *[I][I-b]i-[d]Nin-šubur i-din-nam* (28) *li-[i]b-bi ṭāb[ab]* (29) *bi-tam ša ki-ma bi-tim* (30) *id-di-nam a-šar e-li-ya ṭābu[bu]* (31) *a-na-ad-di-in mi-nam* (32) *e-li-ia ti-šu* (33) *li-ib-bi tu-uṭ-ṭé-ib* (34) *ki-a-am [d]Sîn-ub-lam* (35) *I-bi-[d]Nin-šubur i-pu-ul*

("Sîn-ublam made the following declaration before witnesses): (25-8) 'My heart is satisfied with the complete price of my house and with the house that Ibbi-Ninšubur gave me in exchange for [my] house (29-32) He gave me house for house. (Now) I can give it to whomever I want. [1]) Do you have any claim (outstanding) against me?' Thus Sîn-ublam replied to Ibbi-Ninšubur: 'You have satisfied my heart.' " [2])

Thus, it is quite possible to attribute the first-person, subjective formulation of the Aramaic term to a rare cuneiform prototype rather than to the influence of Egyptian scribal praxis. However, caution is still called for. As close as the cuneiform *lišānšu* and the Egyptian *Sprechurkunde* may be, they are not identical. [3]) Therefore, one can assume that even though the Aramaic term owed its first-person formulation to its Akkadian model, nevertheless its particular first-person formulation is probably the result of some accommodation to the local Egyptian scribal praxis.

Particular Association of Clauses. There are many terms used in common by the Aramaic and Demotic deeds whose cuneiform origins are beyond any reasonable doubt, yet whose specific usage within the Aramaic or Demotic deed has no known cuneiform antecedent. For example, in the Aramaic conveyance the terms *ṭyb lbby* "my heart is satisfied," *rḥqt mnk* "I hereby remove myself from you," and *ʾnt šlyṭ bbytʾ* "you are now in

[1]) The Akkadian equivalent of the Aramaic transfer-investiture clause. Cf. especially the use of this clause in deeds of gift in *MDP* XXIV: 379 and 382. In the Susan and Aramaic usage, the old owner invests the new one, while in the text cited above, the owner "invests" himself.

[2]) I.e., "you have made me quit."

[3]) Cf. *NKRA*, p. 23, n. 6, for the comparison of the Egyptian deeds with the *lišānšu*.

sole control of the house" are used in an organic complex: the receipt of the satisfactory payment expressed by the first term precipitates the relinquishment reflected in the second term. Finally, the transfer and investiture of the new owner reflected in the third clause are the direct result of the old right-holder's relinquishment expressed by the second term. [1]) All three terms are cuneiform in origin: *ṭyb lbby* is the reflex of *libbašu ṭāb*; *rḥqt mnk* is the reflex of the Nuzi *irtēq* "he removed himself," [2]) and the last term *šlyṭ* is based on the NB/Arsacid *išallaṭ* "he has control over." [3])

Furthermore, each of these clauses has its Demotic analogue. [4]) Even though the parallel Egyptian clauses are not as organically interrelated as the Aramaic terms, [5]) the Egyptian usage of the terms in closely related contexts clearly indicates a common Aramaic-Demotic pattern.

What is the origin of these organic complexes of related terms? Is it possible that the terms are cuneiform in origin, yet their particular association patterns are Aramaic or possibly Demotic? Since the patterns of association are less articulated in the Demotic—and then usually only in the later Demotic—it would seem to follow that these innovations are the result of Aramaic scribal creativity, based on tendencies that are inherent in the older cuneiform.

Thus, for example, in their original cuneiform settings, *libbašu ṭāb, irtēq*, and *išallaṭ* had nothing to do with each other: the first term is OB, the second Nuzi, the third NA and NB. However, it will be remembered that the OB isogloss of *libbašu ṭāb* is the Susa term *duppur* "removed" and the NB isogloss is *eṭir* also "removed." Thus, there already existed an underlying inner-cuneiform affinity between terms of satisfaction and terms of removal.

In their original cuneiform setting, *rêqu* and *šalāṭu* seemed to have little to do with each other. On the other hand, their Aramaic cognates—*rḥq* and *šlṭ*—were closely related as antonyms: PN_1 relinquishes his rights/removes himself (*rḥq*); PN_2 is now master/is invested with rights (*šlṭ*). From a purely stylistic point of view, one would have expected the antonym of *rḥq* to have been *qrb* "to come close, to have a claim to."

---

[1]) Cf. above, Introduction, p. 27.
[2]) Cf. above, Chapter V, section 1. Cf. below, p. 178.
[3]) Provisionally, cf. above, p. 41 and p. 153, n. 4. Cf. also p. 134, n. 3.
[4]) The Egyptian analogues of *ṭyb lbby* are discussed in the Egyptian section; for the Egyptian analogues of *rḥq*, cf. above, p. 160. For the Egyptian analogue of *šlyṭ*, cf. "it is yours; none shall exercise authority over it except you, from this day forever" found in all Demotic conveyances (for example, P. Louvre E 7128 = Malinine, *Choix de textes*, p. 87). Cf. above, p. 152.
[5]) Cf. above, pp. 161 ff.

In fact, Rabinowitz correctly pointed out the legal and semantic affinity between the Nuzi usage *qerēbu* "to come close/to have a claim to" and the Aramaic *rḥq* "to remove oneself/to relinquish a claim" ("The Susa Tablets, the Bible and the Aramaic Papyri," *VT*, 11 (1961), pp. 74 f.). However, he was not able to demonstrate the presence of an Akkadian *rêqu* used in a manner identical with the Aramaic *rḥq*. Further investigation can now point out just such a usage. In a hitherto unnoticed Nuzi conveyance (*JEN* 221), it is said of the old right-holders that: (17) *la i!-qe-<ri>-bu ul-la-an* (18) *eqlēti*$^{meš.ti}$*-šu-nu ir-ti-e-qú* (17) "they shall not lay claim (to their property); (18) they have removed themselves from their fields." First of all, it should be noticed that here the Akkadian *rêqu** is functionally and semantically identical with the Aramaic *rḥq*: both record the relinquishment of property rights by former right-holders (contrast the other uses of *rêqu* cited above, Chapter V). Secondly, it should be noted that the Aramaic *šlṭ* and the Akkadian *qerēbu* are functional equivalents of each other, both being the antonyms of *rêqu/rḥq*. Is the functional equivalence of the Aramaic *šlṭ* with the older Akkadian *qerēbu* merely a late Aramaic development, or is it prefigured by an inner-Assyriological development whereby the older *qerēbu* "to lay claim to/to come near" was replaced by the younger *šalāṭu** "to exercise control over/lay claim to"? There is some new evidence that this was actually the case. In a Neo-Assyrian text from Nimrud, [1]) we read the following clause prohibiting all creditors from laying claim to a certain Milki-Ḫaya, a servant-girl of the king: (9) *la i-šal-liṭ ina muḫḫi*^{hi}*-šá* (10) *la iq-qa-rab* "(9) they shall not exercise control (10), they shall not lay claim/come near to her person." In later NA and NB documents *šalāṭu* completely replaces *qerēbu*; the same situation is also reflected in the Elephantine usage. Is it possible that the Aramaic *rḥq-šlṭ* was based on a hitherto undiscovered NA **rêqu-šalāṭu*, itself a late reflex of the older *rêqu-qerēbu*? Only further publications of NA deeds will tell. Evidently, the three terms *libbašu ṭāb*, *irtēq*, and *išallaṭ* were all used in the late cuneiform formulary that served as the model of the Aramaic formulary. It is quite possible that the Aramaic scribes* fused these three terms into new organic patterns and relationships on the basis of inner-Assyriological tendencies which were never realized by the cuneiform scribes themselves. Since the Aramaic scribes were breaking with tradition, they were freer than their cuneiform colleagues in the use of the old building blocks. [2])

---

[1]) B. Parker, "The Nimrud Tablets, 1952—Business Documents," *Iraq*, 16 (1954), p. 40. The text is *ND* 2316. Parker seems completely unaware of the relationship between the MA/Nuzi *qerēbu* and its Neo-Assyrian reflex.

[2]) Compare, for example, the common assumption that the alphabetical elements

It was the Aramaic scribes who by articulating the older cuneiform affinities, created new organic legal structures whose influence was felt far beyond the borders of Mesopotamia. The fact that the organic interrelationship of the satisfaction, removal, and transfer clauses is more articulated in the Aramaic than in the Demotic makes perfect sense once it is assumed that the Aramaic scribes were the innovators and the Demotic scribes, their students, who did not fully appreciate the logic inherent in the Aramaic formulations. Significantly, however, the later the Demotic deed, the more closely it conforms to the older Aramaic pattern. [1])

Introductory Stereotype. Aramaic and Demotic deeds begin with the clause: "Date; on that day, A said to B: 'I have given etc.... to you ...'." Since this clause has no real analogues in cuneiform legal documents and is a regular element of many archaic Egyptian documents, [2]) there is little doubt that this structure was inherited by the Demotic from the older indigenous tradition and later influenced the Aramaic deeds after their introduction to Egypt. The fact that this one Aramaic-Demotic feature is clearly of Egyptian origin probably indicates the presence of other such Egyptian elements in the Aramaic deeds. Thus, all previous arguments that common Aramaic-Demotic features may be cuneiform in origin are in constant need of qualification.

2. The Origins of Aramaic Common Law Formularies

The transformation of millennia-old cuneiform legal traditions into a new Aramaic garb was as significant an event in the subsequent cultural history of the Near East—and possibly of the West as well—as the Akkadian metamorphosis of Sumerian legal material was for an earlier period. Both are not isolated events in the history of scribal praxis but indices of profound social upheaval and of great cultural innovation. Thus, to understand a given Aramaic term is to search for the origins of the formulary in which it is but one part of an organic whole. However, any attempt to understand the genesis of the Aramaic common-law formulary cannot content itself with the identification of unrelated analogues or with problems of mere chronology. It is the given social-cultural matrix from which the new formulary emerged that has to be isolated; the place and time of its birth; the political role of the

---

inherent in older Egyptian writing were realized not by Egyptian scribes but rather by foreigners, not bound to the Egyptian scribal tradition.

[1]) For many examples of this phenomenon, cf. Chapter VI of this study.

[2]) *DJE* 1, pp. 17 ff. (P. Berlin 9784; 14th Century B.C.).

Arameans its innovators; and, above all, the proximate cuneiform model, if any, that may have served as the basis of the new scribal tradition. For it is inconceivable that the Aramaic formulary is simply the receptacle of organically unrelated pieces of cuneiform tradition that happen to converge over a long period of time. Only by isolating the particular historical roots of the formulary within the larger legal history of the Near East can the organic relationship between individual Aramaic terms and the larger structure of the formulary be determined.

It is exactly the lack of such a cultural-historical approach that vitiates the value of Yaron's studies. He often comes to conclusions which, although often quite correct from a purely descriptive point of view, are exactly the opposite of what would have been expected from historical induction. This is not to disparage accurate description or to substitute historical induction in its place: on the contrary, if anything, this study has sought to emphasize a precision in description. However, if the results of one's descriptive investigations conflict with the results of sound historical induction, either the theory is in need of revision or the description is faulty.

A case in point: According to Yaron, there is virtually no trace of Neo-Babylonian or Neo-Assyrian legal traditions in the Aramaic deeds; [1]) it is with the deeds of second millennium Syria-Palestine that the Aramaic legal papyri have the greatest affinity. [2]) Valid as these observations may have been on the basis of the then available material, two vital historical questions should have been raised: (a) Through what later medium did these early West Semitic traditions make their way into the Elephantine papyri? (b) How can the lack of NB or NA legal traditions be accounted for? It is just these documents—contemporary or slightly earlier than the Aramaic papyri—that should logically have served as their immediate prototype.

A. *The Aramaic Common Law Tradition and Neo-Assyrian Law*

The supposed lack of later cuneiform traditions is the key to the genesis of the Aramaic formulary. As will soon be pointed out, this lack is more apparent than real. Unfortunately, most of the Neo-Assyrian analogues could not have been isolated until recently, since most of the relevant material was published only after the appearance of Yaron's studies. In the course of this investigation, over ten terms were isolated whose cuneiform origins seemed quite certain. Many of them had functional

---

1) Cf. *LAP*, p. 122.
2) *Ibid.*, p. 115.

cuneiform analogues, and yet were based on root metaphors that differed from the Akkadian models. At first I considered these terms to be Aramaic innovations, free-renderings of older Akkadian models. However, the possibility was still allowed for that these Aramaic expressions might be reflexes of unknown cuneiform models. A series of hitherto unpublished Neo-Assyrian legal expressions recently edited by Deller [1]) has enabled me to confirm the cuneiform origin of these Aramaic terms. In almost all cases, the cuneiform tradition from which the Aramaic term was derived was Neo-Assyrian.

1) The Aramaic term to "forfeit" is *'bd* "to be lost" (cf. the expression *mhrh y'bd* "his *mohar* will be lost, forfeited," *AP* 15:27). [2]) Functionally, Akkadian expressed the same concept by *ina kasapšu illi/qāssu ina kasapšu illi* "he/his hand goes up (i.e., away) from his money." [3]) One would have expected the Akkadian analogue to have been based on the same metaphor of "being lost." Such an etymologically analogous model is found, however, in the Neo-Assyrian term *kasapšu ḫaliq** "his money is lost, forfeited." [4]) In turn, the Neo-Assyrian model of the Aramaic goes back to the Old Assyrian use of the terms *ḫalāqum*, *abātum*, and *ru'āqum* "to get lost," "to run away," "to absent oneself" used of capital investments which are lost/forfeited as the result of negligence. [5])

2) One of the complements of the Aramaic *ṭyb lbby* is the clause *zy l' 'št'r ln ʿlyk mn dmy'* "(my heart is satisfied) in that none of the price is outstanding against you on our account" (*BP* 12). The same complement is also found in the Gaonic formulary with the added elements *mšwy prwṭh wlʿl'* "from a penny's-worth and up." [6]) Classical Akkadian expresses the completeness of payment in a different way: *kaspam šīm bītišu gamram libbašu ṭūb* "his heart has been satisfied with the full money, the price of his field." The form *kaspu gammur* "complete money" is also common in NA documents. [7]) None of these expressions, however, can be

[1]) Deller, *Terminologie*, pp. 29 ff. Cf. above, p. 76, n. 2.

[2]) For this translation, cf. Ginsberg, *JAOS*, 74 (1954), p. 156; Cf. above, p. 59.

[3]) Cf. *CAD, E* p. 125. The isogloss of this term is *idāšunu ittaṣṣā* "their hands shall go away from, i.e., they shall forfeit" (cf. Peiser, *KB* IV, p. 14—from the time of Apil-Sîn) and the Alalakh expression *ina x-šu ittaṣṣi* "he shall go away from/forfeit his (property)"; cf. *AT* *55: 29 and *AT* *63: 11-12. The same expression is found in an Alalakh text published by Draffkorn, "Was King Abba-AN of Yamḫad a Vizier for the King of Ḫattuša," *JCS*, 13 (1959), p. 96, lines 50 and 57.

[4]) *ARU* 649: 10 = *ADD* 20: 10.

[5]) J. Lewy, "Grammatical and Lexicographical Studies," *Or*, 29 (1960), pp. 22-29.

[6]) Cf. Asaf, *Formulary*, p. 26. Cf. above p. 76.

[7]) Cf. *ARU*, Nos. 173, 175 and *passim*. The Aramaic *dmyn gmrn* "complete money" found in one of the Murabbaʿat conveyances (cf. Ginsberg and Abramson, "On the Aramaic Deed of Sale of the Third Year of the Second Jewish Revolt," *BASOR*, 136 [1954], p. 17) is clearly related to this NA term.

considered as the immediate prototype of the Aramaic clause in its Egyptian and Gaonic formulations. Deller, in his recent publication of hitherto unknown or rare Neo-Assyrian legal terms, has commented on the rare expression 1$^1/_2$ GÍN *lā rēḫe* "one skekel, $^1/_2$ shekel is not outstanding" and its equivalent *lā memēni* "nothing whatsoever." This clause is clearly the model of the Aramaic *l' 'št'r* "nothing is left over." The almost mathematical correspondence of the Assyrian "not even a shekel and a half" with the Gaonic "whether it be a penny's worth or higher" clinches the "join" beyond any reasonable doubt. [1])

3) The Aramaic marriage contract stipulates that the divorced wife shall take with her all of her property *mḥm w'd ḥwṭ* "be it straw or string" is functionally identical with the OB *ištu pê adi ḫurāṣim zīzū gamrū* "they divided (everything) completely, from straw to gold." [2]) Etymologically, however, the Aramaic and Akkadian expressions contrast. Speiser pointed out that the Akkadian expression *ḫāmu u ḫuṣābu* "straw or splinter" is almost completely identical etymologically with the Biblical expression *mḥwṭ w'd śrwk n'l* "be it string or shoe-latch (Gen 14:23) and with the Aramaic *mḥm w'd ḥwṭ* "be it straw or string." [3]) However, it should be noted that this etymologically identical expression was not known to have been employed in contextual structures identical with the OB *ištu pê adi ḫurāṣim zīzū gamrū* "they have divided completely, from straw to gold." Once again, the proximate antecedent of the Aramaic is found in the publication of Deller. The rare NA expression used in deeds of division is *lu ḫāmu lu ḫuṣābu ibtataq* "he divided (the property)—bis zum letzten Strohhalm und Holtzsplitter" (so Deller). [4])

4) The Aramaic expression *l' 'grnk dyn wdbb* "I will not sue you in a formal suit" is partially identical with the OB Alalakh expression *dīnam gerû* "to sue someone in a suit" and is totally identical with the NA *ša dēnu dabābu itti PN igarrûni* "whoever shall sue PN in a formal suit" [5])

5) The Aramaic expression *l' yklwn ynpqwn 'lyky spr ḥdt w'ṭyq bšm byt' znh . . . zy yhnpq kdb hw* "they will not be allowed to produce against you a new or old document in the matter of this house . . . the one (i.e., the deed) produced, is invalid" (*BP* 10: 15-16). The Aramaic expression "to produce a deed" is *yhnpq*, lit. "to cause to go out." [6]) The functional Akkadian equivalent is *ṭuppu ša eliam sar*

[1]) Cf. Deller, *Terminologie*, pp. 41 ff. Cf. above, p. 76.
[2]) Pick, *OLZ*, 11 (1908), p. 137.
[3]) *JAOS*, 54 (1934), pp. 100 ff.
[4]) Deller, *Terminologie*, p. 34. Cf. above, p. 59, n. 1.
[5]) For a discussion and citation of these texts, cf. above, p. 31, n. 2.
[6]) Cf. also *AP* 8: 27 *spr' zk hnpqy wlqblh dyn 'wry* "produce this deed and go to

"the deed which appears (lit. which comes up) is false/invalid." [1]) Even though there is little doubt that the two clauses are historically related—even within Akkadian itself *elû* "to go up" and *waṣû* "to go out" are often either synonyms or isoglosses— [2]) nevertheless one would have expected the Akkadian model of the Aramaic to have been *ušēṣṣi* [3]) "he will bring forth" or at least *uṣṣi* "it will come forth." However, exactly this expected usage is found in the Neo-Assyrian deeds: *šum-ma ina še-er-tú ina li-diš e-gér-tú . . . tu-ṣa-a šá ma-ra-qu ši-i* "If tomorrow or the day after a deed . . . appears, it is to be erased/i.e., it is not valid." [4])

6) The opening clause *ina šērtu ina lidiš* "(If) tomorrow (or) the day after (some illegal action should be taken) . . ." is the synonym of the more common *ina urkiš ina matēma* "in the future; at some time" and functionally is identical with the older Alalakh [5])/Ras Shamra [6])* OB *urram šēram,* [7]) probably "(next) day, the (following) dawn (,and so

---

court against him." For the Talmudic use of this term and its relationship to the Elephantine usage, cf. Kutscher, *Tarbiẓ*, 17 (1945), pp. 125 ff. The same term is also attested to in Nabatean deeds; cf. Cantineau, *Le Nabateen,* II, p. 121. Cf. below, p. 187, n. 4.

[1]) Cf. *CAD, E,* p. 122.

[2]) Cf. above, p. 181, n. 3, where the expressions *ina x-šu elû* and *ina x-šu waṣû*—both meaning "to forfeit"—were equated. Cf. also Koschaker, *Göttliches Recht,* p. 44, where the Susa expressions *ina awat ili u šarri līli/līṣi* "he shall forfeit the protection of god and king" are discussed.

[3]) Mendelsohn, "On Slavery in Alalakh," *IEJ*, 5 (1955), p. 68, n. 28, cites *AT* 67: 9-10 *šum-ma bēlu ú-še-la šu-nu-ma ú-za-ku* "should (another) owner raise (a claim), they (the sellers) shall clear (the slave)." If this interpretation is correct—the clause is ambiguous, to say the least—the Alalakh use of the Š-form of the verb *elû* is parallel to the Aramaic use of the Haphel of the root *npq*. (For a contrasting, and more convincing, interpretation of the Alalakh clause, cf. *CAD, E,* p. 128.)

[4]) Cf. Deller, *Terminologie,* p. 37. The text cited is *MCS* 2, 19, 10-12.

[5]) Cf. Speiser, "The Alalakh Tablets," *JAOS,* 74 (1954), p. 23, for the text and suggested etymologies of the term.

[6]) Cf. *PRU* III 16.200 (p. 64) and *passim* in these texts.

[7]) Cf. Szlechter, *Tablettes juridiques* p. xi. The term is found in 16.524 of his collection which is probably from Dilbat (*ibid.*, p. viii). The term is thus probably of Semitic rather than Hurrian origin (so also Speiser, *JAOS,* 14 (1954), p. 23) as so often assumed. The element *šēram* is probably the regular word for "dawn" (Speiser, *ibid.*). I am almost certain that the common Susa expression *ana dūr u pala ana šēršerri/šēršēri* (cf., for example, *MDP* XXIII 200: 10; 201: 9; 228: 8; XVIII 215: 10; XXII 77: 9; XXIV 347: 10 and *passim*) is not to be translated "pour toujours et jamais, pour la postérité," (following Scheil) but "forever, for all reign(s), on the morrow of the morrow." *Šēršēri* is probably simply a reduplication of *šērum* "morrow" rather than of *šerrum* "brood, progeny." It means "any time in the future". [For the reduplicated form, cf. *matmati-ma* in *ARM* VIII 10: 7; for a similar interpretation of *šēršēri*, cf. de Meyer, *L'accadien des contrats de Suse* (Leiden, 1962), p. 71.] The Neo-Assyrian use of *šērtam* in the sense of *urkiš* "in the future" or *matēma* "whenever" seems to be a late reflex of (*urram*) *šēram* and possibly of *šēršēri*.*

forth)." [1] There can be little doubt that the common Aramaic expression *mḥr ʾw ywm ʾḥrn* "(If) tomorrow or the day after PN should undertake some illegal action) . . ." is derived directly from *ina šērtu ina lidiš*.

7) In his review of the Aramaic deeds, H. L. Ginsberg noted that after the list of dowry-items in which each entry is evaluated separately, and after the sum total of goods brought by the wife into her husband's house, a small number of goods—usually insignificant amounts of oil and cosmetics—are mentioned without any monetary evaluation. [2] A similar practice is known from Neo-Assyrian times. [3]

8) Aramaic deeds of loan often contain the stipulation that if the money is not paid back on time, then *yʿqp kspk wmrbyth zy yštʾr ʿly* "your money and its interest that is outstanding against me shall *yʿqp* (*AP* 11:8-9)." The meaning of the term has been open to question. Cowley—I think correctly—has interpreted the term to mean "it shall be doubled." [4] This interpretation, which seems demanded from the context, is confirmed by the mention of interest on the interest in contemporary Demotic deeds. [5] However, the origin of the term is yet to be determined. Scholars have related the root *ʿqp* to the Arabic *ḍʿf* and the later Aramaic *ʾʿp/ʿpp* "to be doubled." [6] The Akkadian equivalent is clearly *eṣēpu* "to be doubled." [7] Although *CAD* does not give any examples of *eṣēpu* in legal documents, Von Soden [8] and Deller have pointed out a number of examples where the idiom *kaspu eṣip iddan* "he will pay the money in double" is used in Neo-Assyrian legal documents: [9]

---

[1] Cf. Heb. *ʾeṯmōl šilšōm* "yesterday, the third day (back)," i.e., in the past.

[2] H. L. Ginsberg, "The Brooklyn Museum Aramaic Papyri," *JAOS*, 74 (1954), p. 156, n. 4. These would correspond to the Nuzi *sikiltu*, for which cf. Speiser, *Or*, 25 (1956), pp. 1 ff.

[3] Parker, *Iraq*, 16 (1954), pp. 37-39, *ND* 2307-46. Lines 35-38 list foods and cosmetics whose value is not given.

[4] Cf. *AP*, p. 35, where the Aramaic term is compared with the Arabic. The correspondence between the Arabic and the Old-Aramaic *q* and the later Aramaic ʿ is well known. In Hebrew and Akkadian the same phoneme becomes an *ṣ*.

[5] Cf. the Demotic deed of loan, P. Louvre E 9293 (499 B.C.) edited by Malinine in *Choix de textes*, pp. 20 ff. The debtor promises to return the money on a given day; if he does not return the money on time, it will be returned "à additioner (également) les intérêts des intérêts—jusqu'à ce qu'ils parviennent à l'égaler (le capital ?)."

[6] Cf. Von Soden, *AHw*, under "*eṣēpu*."

[7] The equivalence of Aramaic *ʿqp* with Akkadian *eṣēpu* is suggested but with much reservation by J. C. Greenfield in "Studies in Aramaic Lexicography I," *JAOS*, 82 (1962), p. 291, n. 14. It was correctly recognized many years ago by J. Halevy in a note to Barth's article, "Bemerkungen zu den aramäischen Papyri von Assuan," *Revue sémitique*, 15 (1907), p. 524, n. 1.

[8] Under "*eṣēpu*."

[9] Deller, *Terminologie*, p. 37. The term is used in a variety of transactions: sale, delivery, work-contracts, and litigation (?). Although so far it has not been

the doubling of the money is a type of fine. While it is impossible to preclude the possibility that the equation *eṣip*=*ʿqp* is simply a chance etymological convergence, the contextual and functional equivalence of the terms argues in favor of some historical relationship.

10) The Aramaic expressions *ʾ/yhk bdyn wlʾ ʾ/yṣdq* "though I/he go to trial, I/he shall not win" (*AP* 8:22 and *passim*), *lʾ yštmʿ lh* "no heed shall be paid to him/her, i.e., let his/her argument not be accepted" (*AP* 18:4) are probably based on the common NA *ina dēnišu idabbubma lā ilaqqi/ dayānu lā išammû** "let him argue in his suit and not receive (anything)/let the judge not listen to him, i.e., let the judge not accept (his arguments and claims)." The equivalence—functional, etymological, and metrical—between the Aramaic and the Assyrian can only be accounted for by assuming that the former was derived from the latter. [1])

11) The Aramaic expression *ʿšt lk . . . wyhbt lk brḥmn* "I have turned my thoughts to you . . . and have given you in affection" has its ultimate roots in the ninth century Babylonian *kuddurru* usage PN_1 PN_2 *ḫadīš ippalis . . . arassu* (i.e., PN_2) *irīm* "PN_1 looked joyfully (= willingly) at PN_2 . . . and granted his servant (a gift)." In this context, *ippalis* means "to think kindly about someone" and is the semantic parallel of the Aramaic *ʿšt* "to think about, to turn one's thoughts to." However, the Aramaic term is not derived from the earlier Babylonian usage but from the NA. The NA equivalent of the MB usage is *īnā attašu aḫsus* "I lifted up my eyes (and) thought about (PN, the recipient of a royal grant)." [2])

11) The Elephantine Aramaic term "shall bear interest" is *yrbh* (cf. *AP* 11 : 5). The term is related to the Neo-Assyrian *kaspu ana 4-tú-šu irabbi* "the money bears interest at 1/4 of its value." [3]) [Compare also the use of *irabbi* with a similar meaning in NB sources: San Nicolò-Ungnad, *NKVU*, *Glossar*, under *rabû*.] The historic bridge between the Neo-Assyrian formula and the Aramaic papyri is an Aramaic deed from Assyria written on clay and edited by Lidzbarski. [4]) The relevant line of this deed of loan is *brbʿ yrby* "the money bears interest at 1/4 of its value." [5])

---

found in a loan of money, it does appear in a loan of goods (*VAT* 8657): if the goods are not paid on time, *eṣip iddan*!

[1]) The equivalence of the Aramaic and Neo-Assyrian terms was independently arrived at by Ungnad, *Aramäische Papyrus*, p. 47. Cf. above, p. 43, n. 2 for some Demotic parallels. [Yaron (*Biblica*, 41 [1960], p. 391, n. 1), has pointed out the use of a similar clause in earlier Egyptian documents: The Karnak stela and the Will of Naunakhte. Further study is therefore in order.]

[2]) *ARU* No. 16 = *ADD* 646 : 19. For a fuller discussion, cf. above, pp. 134 ff.

[3]) Cf. *ARU* No. 267 = *ADD* 24 : 6-7 and *passim*.

[4]) Cf. Lidzbarski, *Altaramäische Urkunden*, Nos 4 and 6.

[5]) Lidzbarski, *Altaramäische Urkunden*, p. 19.

12) One rather striking NA-Aramaic correspondence that had been recognized many years ago is the term *nᵉḇaz* found in *AP* 11:6. In that context, the term can only mean "a receipt for partial repayment of a loan." Cowley in his discussion of the term (*AP*, p. 34) cites the note of C. H. W. Johns, one of the early pioneers in NA law, in *PSBA*, 1905, p. 187. Johns had correctly recognized the NA model of the Aramaic term in Harper's *Assyrian and Babylonian Letters*, Part VI, No. 633: 13-14. The text in translation reads: "The father of the king, my Lord, had the money due from the shepherds written in an Assyrian *nibzu* and in an Aramaic *nibzu*." Just such an Aramaic *nibzu* is cited in *AP* 11:6. The passage under discussion can now be studied in the edition of L. Waterman, *Royal Correspondence of the Assyrian Empire*, Vol. I (Ann Arbor, 1930), p. 443. In his glossary, Waterman lists several other uses of the term; its general meaning is receipt/deed of indebtedness." It should be noted in passing that Neo-Assyrianisms often occur in clusters; *AP* 11 has three such terms: *nᵉḇaz*, the expression *y'qp kspk* (l. 8) "your money shall be doubled" and *yrbh* (l. 5) "(the money) will bear interest."

[For a discussion of the Aramaic *nibzu* mentioned in Assyrian sources, cf. Landsberger's comments *apud* Altheim-Stiehl, *Die aramäische Sprache*, p. 102, and the literature he cites there, especially R. P. Dougherty, "Writing upon Parchment and Papyrus among the Babylonians and Assyrians," *JAOS*, 48 (1928), pp. 109-135 and E. Klauber, *Assyrisches Beamtentum* (Leipzig, 1910), pp. 84, 85, n. 2. Cf. also Lidzbarski, *Ephemeris* II, p. 226, n. 1, where Andreas called attention to a *nubazu* found in a NB deed from the time of Nebuchadnezzar.]

The Fringe Tradition, NA Law, and the Aramaic Papyri. In all probability, it was from Neo-Assyrian models that the Aramaic formulary was derived. Furthermore, it seems that the Neo-Assyrian formulary was in many ways the culmination of the peripheral tradition of cuneiform law. [1] The archaic norms first reflected in the Old Akkadian documents of the Sargonic period, preserved in the provincial formularies of Susa, Kültepe, the Diyala region, Alalakh, and Ras Shamra during the second millennium, are often preserved in the Neo-Assyrian formulary of the first millennium. [2] It was through this historic medium that the archaic

[1] Cf. above, Introduction, n. 99. Cf. also Chapter IV, section 5, nn. 69-85.

[2] For example, the Ras Shamra/Alalakh *urram šēram*=NA *ina šērtu ina lidiš* Cassite *ippalis* "consider" = NA *aḫsus*. All these examples are cases where the Akkadian reflex of older cuneiform traditions is incorporated in the Aramaic. However, there are many other examples of this marked connection of the NA formulary with the older fringe traditions where the term is not incorporated into the Aramaic. Compare, for example, the common use of the idiom "the tablet

norms of the third millennium and the legal practices of Ras Shamra and Alalakh made their way into the Aramaic formulary of the fifth century.

B. *The Aramaic Formulary and the Neo-Assyrian Dockets*

The Neo-Assyrian character of much of the Aramaic law would in itself be sufficient to establish the Assyrian provenience of the formulary. However, it would be paradoxical if the only example of an Aramaic formulary based on Neo-Assyrian models and containing few or no NB affinities happened to be found in Egypt rather than in Assyria proper. It would certainly be desirable to have actual examples of an Aramaic formulary from Mesopotamian—and more specifically—from Assyrian soil, and to compare them with the supposed Neo-Assyrian Aramaic deeds of Elephantine. It so happens that such Mesopotamian attempts at the creation of an Aramaic formulary based on cuneiform models do actually exist. For some reason, previous investigators of the Aramaic legal papyri have not coordinated the Mesopotamian and Egyptian Aramaic legal traditions. The fact is that from the ninth century on, many Neo-Assyrian deeds are provided with short Aramaic summaries or dockets. [1]) Many of these dockets are introduced by the word *dnt** (which is a loan-translation from the Assyrian *dannatu/dannitu* "valid deed") followed by a short description of the transaction recorded in the deed: thus, *dnt.'lmlk.zy.'rq.ḥm'* "the deed of Elmalaku concerning the land of Ḫama"; [2]) *dnt 'mt' ḥbš zy lqḥ* . . . "the deed (concerning) the slave girl Hambusu whom Luqu . . ."; [3]) or by the word *'grt* as in the clause *'grt ksp zy 'l zbn* "the deed of (= concerning) the money which Zabinu owes" [4]) The terminology used in these documents is based on

which appears *ana ḫepî nadi/ana ḫīpi nadāt* is to be destroyed" in the OB deeds from Susa and in NA documents (cf. *CAD, E*, p. 122) as contrasted with regular cuneiform *ṭuppu ša eliam sar*.]

[1]) For a convenient collection of these dockets, cf. Delaporte, *Épigraphes araméens*. For a study of the role of Aramaic in antiquity, and a history of the first attempts to create an Aramaic formulary, cf. Bowman, "Arameans, Aramaic, and the Bible," *JNES*, 7 (1948), pp. 65 ff. and especially pp. 71 ff., where most of the material relating to the dockets is cited and discussed. Cf. also San Nicolò, *Beiträge*, pp. 130 ff. and Lidzbarski, *Ephemeris* III, pp. 12-19.

[2]) Delaporte, *Épigraphes araméens*, p. 32.

[3]) *Ibid.*, p. 33.

[4]) *Ibid.*, p. 38. The word *'grt*=the Assyrian *egertu* "document" is used less frequently than *dnt/dannitu*, there being only one case of it in Delaporte's collection. It is quite possible that this term is originally Aramaic and that it is an Aramaic loan word in Assyrian (orally, Moshe Held). If this is so, there is an indication that the Aramaic scribes did not merely translate Assyrian models but at times used their own Aramaic legal vocabulary. In course of time, these Aramaic legal terms replaced older Assyrian ones in the cuneiform texts themselves. There is a good

Neo-Assyrian models or, in a few cases, on indigenous Aramaic legal traditions. [1]) Within several generations, the dockets develop into independent Aramaic documents written mostly on clay. [2]) Aramaic dockets are also attested from the Neo-Babylonian period. [3]) Furthermore, the only extant Aramaic legal document from Mesopotamia comes from this period.* [4]) Unlike the Neo-Assyrian dockets, the Neo-Babylonian ones are introduced by the word *šṭr* (from the Babylonian *šaṭāru* "document"). [5]) The significance of this dialectal difference between *šṭr* and *dnt* for the historical evaluation of the Elephantine deeds will soon be apparent.

It stands to reason that the Elephantine formulary with its Neo-Assyrian affinities is but a reflex of the docket tradition. Although the Elephantine formulary later assimilated Egyptian, Babylonian, and Persian elements, it still retained traces of its docket origins. Thus, for example, the short summaries found at the end of many Elephantine deeds—summaries that are not found in contemporary Egyptian deeds—are none other than the local version of the Mesopotamian dockets. For example, *spr* mrḥq zy ktb [drgmn] br ḥršyn l mḥsyh* "A deed of removal that [Dargaman] bar Ḫarshin wrote for Maḥseiah"; [6]) *spr by [1 zy yhb] mḥsh br ydn[yh] lmbṭḥ br mḥsh* "A deed to a house that Maḥseh son of Yedoniah gave to Mibṭaḥ daughter Maḥseh"; [7]) *spr plgn ʿbd* "A deed of assignment of a

chance that the term *murruqu* "to purify" which takes the place of the older *zukkû* in the *Reinigungsklauseln* of the late Neo-Babylonian period, is a loan word from the Aramaic. (For a discussion of this term, cf. Petschow, *Kaufformulare*, pp. 62 and 67; for a fuller discussion where the opinions of Meissner, Clay, San Nicolò, and Landsberger are cited, cf. Krückmann, *BRVU*, p. 29, n. 4.) For another example, cf. the use of the late Akkadian term *ḫarḫara* (*CAD*, under *ḫarḫar*) "to contest," which is clearly a loan word from the Aramaic *ʿrr*/*ʿrʿr* "to contest, to raise a claim," and is probably attested already in the *AP* 8: 27 *lqblh dyn ʿwry* "contest against him in court." (Is the Aramaic *ʿrr* lit. "to stir up, to cause to move" in itself a loan translation from the Ras Shamra *dīnam nummušu* "to stir up a litigation, to institute legal proceedings against" [*PRU* III, 16.205+192: 17-18] ?) Cf. also the late Akkadian *yāritu* "heir" from the Aramaic *yrt* (*CAD*, *I/J*, p. 235). [For a systematic study of Aramaic loan words in *NA* and *NB* sources, cf. Von Soden, "Aramäische Wörter in neuassyrischen und neu- und spätbabylonischen Texten. Ein Vorbericht. I (*agâ-*mūš*)," *Or*, 35 (1966), pp. 1 ff.]

[1]) The Assyriologically oriented legal investigation of the dockets is a desideratum of Aramaic studies. For some suggestive remarks, cf. Delaporte, *Épigraphes araméens*, p. 13, particularly his comment on the equivalence of *ʿl* with the Assyrian *ina pān*.

[2]) Cf. the examples studied by Lidzbarski in his *Altaramäische Urkunden*.

[3]) Cf. the second section of Delaporte, *Épigraphes araméens*.

[4]) Cf. Starcky, "Une tablette araméenne de l'an 34 de Nabuchodonosor (AO, 21.063)," *Syria*, 37 (1960), pp. 99 ff.

[5]) Cf. Delaporte, *Épigraphes araméens*, p. 56 (Nos. 48-50 and *passim*).

[6]) *AP* 6: 22.

[7]) *Ibid.*, No. 8: 35.

slave"; [1]) *spr zy zbn bgzšt wybl lʿnnyh* "A deed concerning that which Bagazušt and Ubil sold to Ananiah." [2])

The most conclusive proof of the historic link between the docket tradition and the Elephantine papyri is found in the docket of *AP* 10:23. It reads as follows: *spr ksp dnh zy ktbt yhwḥn brt mšlk* "Deed of money —a *dnh* [= *dannitu*] that Yehoḥan daughter of Meshullak wrote . . ." [3]) The presence of the Assyrian loan word *dnt/dannitu* in the fifth century Elephantine papyri is clear proof of the Neo-Assyrian provenience of the deeds.

C. *The Aramaic-Assyrian Symbiosis*

Standard Aramaic [4]) is the linguistic vehicle of the new Aramaic formulary. It can safely be assumed that wherever standard Aramaic was employed, the common law formulary written in it must have been known. Since standard Aramaic was employed all through the Assyrian Empire and is attested from the borders of Egypt to the borders of India,[5]) the wide diffusion of the Aramaic formulary and its potential influence on many different legal traditions cannot be overestimated. [6])

By the middle of the eighth century B.C., standard Aramaic replaced the local Syrian dialects. [7]) With standard Aramaic came Aramaic common law reflected in the dockets of Tell Halaf. [8]) By the time of Hezekiah (*ca.* 700 B.C.), Aramaic was known by Judaean government officials, even though the common folk were still ignorant of it. [9]) By 600, standard Aramaic was the language of diplomatic correspondence between a Canaanite king and the Egyptian court. [10]) The status of Aramaic in this area was probably akin to that of Akkadian in the Amarna

---

[1]) *Ibid.*, No. 28: 17.

[2]) *BP* 3: 25.

[3]) *AP* 10: 23.

[4]) Called "Reichsaramäisch" in Rosenthal's classic study, *Aramaistische Forschung*, pp. 24 ff., and "official" Aramaic by Ginsberg in "Aramaic Studies Today," *JAOS*, 62 (1942), p. 223. The term "standard" Aramaic is used by Kraeling, *BP*, p. 6.

[5]) Cf. the Taxila inscription of king Aśoka of India recently reproduced in Koopmans, *Aramäische Chrestomathie*, Vol. I, p. 178; cf. especially the rich bibliography cited there. [For a comprehensive investigation of the role that Aramaic played under the Achaimenids, cf. Altheim-Stiehl, *Die aramäische Sprache* and *Supplementum Aramaicum*.]

[6]) Cf. especially Kutscher, *New Aramaic Texts*, 74 (1954), pp. 244 ff.

[7]) Cf. H. L. Ginsberg, "Aramaic Dialect Problems," *AJSL*, 50 (1933), pp. 4 ff.

[8]) Cf. Friedrich, Ungnad, Meyer, and Weidner, *Die Inschriften von Tell Halaf*, Berlin, 1940 (= *AfO, Beiheft* 6).

[9]) Cf. II Kings, 18: 26 ff.

[10]) Cf. Ginsberg, "An Aramaic Contemporary of the Lachish Letters," *BASOR*, 111 (1948), pp. 24-27 and the literature cited there.

period. It was the language of diplomacy par excellence. The close relationship between diplomacy, bureaucracy, and law is well known to all.

Aramaeans and Assyrians in Egypt. Unlike Mesopotamia, Egypt lived her cultural life in relative isolation from the rest of the world. [1]) Its population was more or less homogeneous, its borders relatively secure from invasion, and its attitude isolationist. Yet even during these early periods, Egypt did experience the Hyksos invasion. Semitic loan words were incorporated into Egypt, and Western gods were not unknown in the land. [2])

During the Saitic period, these outside influences increased. The borders of Egypt were opened up—first by traders, [3]) mercenaries, [4]) and political refugees, [5]) and then, forcibly, by Assyrian conquest. [6]) According to some scholars, one of the main reasons for Assyrian expansionism was the desire for increased trade and new markets. [7]) Thus, if Near Eastern traders—probably Aramaic-speaking or at least Aramaic-writing—flocked to Egypt from the eighth century on, this independent trading activity was but a prelude to the subsequent Assyrian conquest. The flag followed trade. Assyria and Egypt may have been political rivals, but in all ages political rivalry never precluded cultural and economic intercourse. [8])

---

[1]) Once the early Near Eastern influences were assimilated, Egypt went on its own unique path. Cf. Frankfort, *Birth of Civilization*, pp. 90 ff.

[2]) For a comprehensive study of the Egyptian contacts with the Near East during the third and second millennia, cf. Helck, *Die Beziehungen.**

[3]) Cf. the discussion of Griffith in the *Catalogue of Demotic Papyri*, pp. 22 ff.

[4]) Cf. the literature cited by Moshe Greenberg, "Ezekiel 17 and the Policy of Psammetichus II," *JBL*, 76 (1957), p. 307. Cf. also Slouschz, *Thesaurus*, p. 62.

[5]) Cf. I Kings 11: 17 (Edomites); Jer 26: 20 ff. (a Judean prophet); Jer 44 (the murderers of Gedaliah ben Ahiqam and the prophet Jeremiah himself). [Cf. A. Verger, *Ricerche giuridiche sui papiri aramaici di Elefantina*, Rome, 1965, pp. 37-50 for a summary of the Aramaic and other West-Semitic communities in Egypt.]*

[6]) For details, cf. Schmökel, *Geschichte*, pp. 276 ff. [For the whole period, cf. Kienitz.]

[7]) This interpretation of Assyrian expansionism, and especially Assyrian interest in Egypt, is stated quite strongly by many of the participants of the symposium recorded in *The City Invincible*, especially Goetze (p. 172), Oppenheim (p. 173) and Cameron (p. 176). Cf. also Oppenheim in *Economic History*, pp. 34-36. [The mercantile role of the Assyrians was well known to their contemporaries: cf. Nahum 3: 16. This passage was discussed independently and in a similar context by H. Lewy, *JNES*, 26 (1967), p. 140.]

[8]) The Romans traded with the Persians their enemies. Likewise, Byzantium engaged in the liveliest of trade relationships with both Persians and Arabs. During the Civil War, the cotton trade between the North and South never stopped. (For the details of the silk trade between Rome and Persia, cf. J. Neusner, "Some Aspects of the Economic and Political Life of Babylonian Jewry, Ca. 160-220 C.E.," *PAAJR*, 31 (1963), pp. 165 ff.)

This general trend is nicely illustrated by an Assyrian text from the time of Sargon. After the Assyrian king conquered Rafia, south of the "Brook of Egypt." he built an Assyrian settlement there. [1]) What is even more significant is the following:

(46) *[ka]r-ri kur Mu-ṣur kan-gu ap-te-e-ma* (47) [UN].MEŠ KUR *Aš+šur ù* KUR *Mu-ṣur* (48) *[it-ti] a-ḫa-meš ab-lul-ma* (49) *[ú-še-p]i-ša ma-ḫi-ru*[2])

(46) "I opened the sealed [harbo]ur of Egypt. (47) The Assyrians and the Egyptians (48) I mingled [to]gether and (49) made them trade [with each other]" (Nimrud Prism, Fragment D, Col. IV).

There can be little doubt that no matter what language the pre-Sargonic traders did their business in, from the time of the "Sargonic opening of the sealed borders," the language of commerce between Egypt and the East was certainly Aramaic. In less than a century Egypt was conquered by Assyria, and Neo-Assyrian legal influence in Aramaic garb could only have increased.

Wherever and whenever the Jewish settlers of Elephantine came from, [3]) some version of the Aramaic common law formulary must have been known. If they came from Mesopotamia, they would have adopted the formulary in the land of its birth. Even if they came from Palestine, there is some evidence that a version of this common law was not unknown in that land. Jeremiah, after all, uses a type of conveyance—the so-called *Doppelurkunde* [4])—which is of clear cuneiform provenience [5]) and

---

[1]) Cf. H. Tadmor, "The Campaigns of Sargon II of Assur: A Chronological-Historical Study," *JCS*, 12 (1958), p. 34.

[2]) *Ibid.* [According to H. L. Ginsberg (in his forthcoming commentary to Isaiah), the road uniting Egypt and Assyria mentioned in Is 19 : 23 is but a contemporary reaction to this Sargonic conquest. Is 19 : 24 is the prophet's religious interpretation of the same event.]*

[3]) For a discussion of the various opinions, cf. *BP*, Chapter IV: "Nature and Origin of the Jewish Colony," pp. 41 ff.

[4]) Cf. Jer 32 : 11. [Quoted by San Nicolò, *Beiträge*, p. 128. The correct identification of the biblical deed with cuneiform models, with Egyptian and Greek documents from Egypt, and with the rabbinic *geṭ mᵉquššar*, was first made by L. Fischer, *ZAW*, 30 (1910), pp. 136-142. The most recent discussion is that of Verger, *Recerche*, p. 83 and of E. Volterra, "Sulla redazione dei contratti nell'antico diritto ebraico," in *Synteleïa Vincenzo Arangio Ruiz*, Naples, 1964, pp. 1190-97 (unavailable to me).]*

[5]) San Nicolò, *Beiträge*, pp. 128 ff. [San Nicolò notes that the biblical deed must be a reflex of NA rather than NB usage, since it was only the NA scribes who still continued the ancient practise of writing the deed a second time on the outer envelope. The NA background of the biblical double-document was also discussed by E. Hammershaimb, "Some Observations on the Aramaic Elephantine Papyri," *VT*, 7 (1957), pp. 24-27. He also points out the importance of the Assyrian sale documents discovered at Gezer (651 and 649 B.C.) for the understanding of the Assyrian influence on Biblical legal praxis.]*

is attested later in Egypt, Naḥal Ḥever, and the Talmud. [1]) San Nicolò even suggested (incorrectly) that it was the Jewish settlers who brought this adaptation of the cuneiform deed to Egypt. [2]) However, wherever the Jewish colonists came from, the Aramaic common law formulary had probably been used there before their arrival by other Asiatics who had come there during the rise of Assyrian power.

D. *Later Reflexes of the Aramaic Formulary*

Aramaic common law must have played the same role in later antiquity that cuneiform law played in early Mesopotamia. It could be used by all who knew Aramaic as a written language, regardless of nationality. There is the distinct possibility that it influenced Demotic law. [3]) If this thesis holds true, much of Graeco-Egyptian law can be ultimately derived from Aramaic-cuneiform prototypes. [4]) However, this is a matter for Demotic and Greek legal historians to determine.

The later history of Aramaic common law in Mesopotamia is much less a matter of conjecture. Recently, a collection of Aramaic legal documents was discovered in Samaria. [5]) They were written some time during the second half of the third century B.C. [6]) It may be expected that the formulary used in these deeds will exhibit characteristics to be found in the Aramaic dockets and especially in the Elephantine papyri. In fact, one bit of evidence is already available. A date formula in one of the fragments published by Cross reads as follows: *b*20 *l'dr šnt* 2 *r'š mlkwt* [*d*]*ryhwš mlk' bšmry*[*n* . . .] "On the twentieth day of Adar, year 2 (the same year being) the accession year [7]) of Darius the king, in Samaria . . ." [8]) H. L. Ginsberg (oral communication) has compared this formula with the Elephantine *b*18 *lkslw* . . . *šnt* 21 *r'š mlwkt' kzy 'rtḥšsš mlk' ytb bkrs'h* "On the eighteenth of Kislew . . ., year 21, the *reš šarrūti*, when king Artaxerxes sat on his throne. . . " (*AP* 6:1-2). Only further

[1]) Cf. San Nicolò, *Beiträge*, pp. 126, n. 2 and 128 ff.; cf. the literature quoted in note 2 above. For Naḥal Ḥever, cf. Yadin, *BIES*, 26 (1962), p. 214, n. 10 (quoting Saul Lieberman).

[2]) [San Nicolò, *Beiträge*, p. 128, incorrectly assuming that the Aramaic endorsements were residual *Doppelurkunden* rather than reflexes of the docket tradition. Cf. now, Verger, *Recerche*, p. 83, n. 11.]

[3]) See the discussion at the beginning of this chapter.

[4]) The relationship between Demotic and Greek sale law was the subject of a recent dissertation at Brown University by Richard H. Pierce, 1963. For the time being, cf. the parallels cited by Griffith, *Catalogue of Demotic Papyri*, pp. 117 ff.

[5]) F. M. Cross, "The Discovery of the Samaria Papyri," *BA*, 26 (1963), pp. 110 ff.

[6]) *Ibid.*, p. 112.

[7]) The period after the dead of the old king and before the formal corronation of the new one=the Akkadian *rēš šarrūti*.

[8]) Cross, *BA*, 26 (1963), p. 113.

publication of this precious material will tell how close the two Aramaic traditions actually were.

Furthermore, there can be little doubt that subsequent Near Eastern legal documents written in Aramaic, Syriac, or Hebrew are all reflexes of the older Aramaic common-law tradition represented by the Assyrian and Babylonian dockets and by the Elephantine papyri. This important fact of Near Eastern legal history was recognized many years ago by Lidzbarski, [1]) was reiterated by Kutscher [2]) on the basis of later discoveries, and can now be amply confirmed on the basis of even more substantial documentary evidence. [3]) Furthermore, the fragments of deeds preserved in the Talmud are also part of the Aramaic common-law tradition. [4]) In calling these deeds *lešōn hedyōṭ* or "layman's formulary" (*TB*, *Bāḇā Meṣīʿā* 104a-b), the Rabbis tacitly admitted the non-rabbinic provenience of the documents. Furthermore, many of the stipulations used in the deeds, being reflexes of non-Jewish traditions, were not always in accord with formal Rabbinic jurisprudence. Nevertheless, aided by a realistic use of legal fiction, the Rabbis often accepted such conditions as valid. [5]) What is urgently needed is the coordination of all

---

[1]) Cf. above, Introduction, pp. 6-7.

[2]) In his study of Talmudic legal terminology in *Tarbiẕ*, 17 (1945), pp. 125 ff., and especially in his review of the Aramaic papyri in *New Aramaic Texts*.

[3]) Even a cursory study of the Nabatean grave inscriptions (many of which are actual conveyances—cf. H. L. Ginsberg, *Tarbiẕ*, 7 (1935/6), pp. 223-226),* the documents of Wadi Murabbaʿat and Naḥal Ḥever (cf. most recently, Y. Yadin, "Expedition D — the Cave of the Documents," *BIES*, 26 (1962), pp. 204-236), the Dura slave sale [cf. J. Goldstein, *JNES*, 25 (1966), pp. 1-16], and the Gaonic deeds, is sufficient proof of their historical interdependence. This fact has been recognized by the philologians who have studied the deeds, especially by Kutscher and Milik, yet for some reason, has been treated with scepticism by a legal historian like Yaron (cf. the last pages of *LAP*). In a future study, I hope to point out why such scepticism is not in order.

[4]) [Cf. for the time being, the various studies of J. J. Rabinowitz, especially *Jewish Elements*, where the relationship between the Jewish marriage-contract and the NB dialogue-document is discussed. Cf. also the various studies of Yaron, especially his article in *BiOr*, 15 (1958), pp. 15-22, where the cuneiform origins of the Talmudic *Reinigungsklausel* are studied. Cf. also his review of *Les grottes de Murabbaʿât* in *JJS*, 11 (1960), pp. 157-171, where the origins of the Mishnaic-Murabbaʿat sale-clause "more or less" are discussed; cf. also J. Goldstein, *JNES*, 25 (1966), p. 11. It should be noted in passing that cuneiform influence is to be directed not only in rabbinic deeds—whose non-Jewish origins the Rabbis would have admitted themselves—but also in the official corpora as well: cf. A. L. Oppenheim, "A Note on *Ṣôn Barzel*," *IEJ*, 5 (1955), pp. 89-92.]

[5]) Cf. for example the *tenai māmōn* mentioned in *TP*, *Keṯubbōṯ*, Chapter V, Law 10 and *TP*, *Bāḇā Baṯrā*, Chapter V, Law 9. Although formal Talmudic law did not allow the wife to repudiate her husband—a wife who did so was considered a *moredeth* "a rebellious one" and gradually lost her *keṯubbā*—there were some Jews who would enter the following monetary (or secular) condition into their marriage contracts: *ʾyn snʾ ʾyn snt* "If he repudiates; if she repudiates." In this case, the wife

of this material into a history of Aramaic common-law, its origins and developments. [1] The value of such a study for all concerned with Near Eastern culture needs no further justification.

---

was not treated as a *moredeth*: she could divorce her husband and settled her *k^e^ṯubbā* according to stipulation. Although the practice was not at all in accord with normal rabbinic jurisprudence, the condition was considered valid. Such conditions were even known from medieval times (Asaf, *Formulary*, p. 56). [Cf. the discussion of S. Lieberman, *Hilkhoth Ha-Yerushalmi* (The Laws of *the Palestinian Talmud*) *of Rabbi Moses Ben Maimon*, New York, 1947, p. 61.] This tradition is clearly anticipated by the praxis of the Elephantine papyri, as J. N. Epstein, *JJLG*, 6 (1908/09), p. 369, had already seen, which in itself is derived from cuneiform legal traditions going back as far as Kültepe (cf. B. Hrozný, *Symbolae Koschaker*, pp. 108-111) and OB Alalakh (cf. I. Mendelsohn, *On Marriage in Alalakh*).

[1]) Cf. The author's paper on the subject, *American Academy of Jewish Research*, December, 1964. Among the cuneiform-rabbinic parallels discussed was the virtual identity of the Alalakh punishment *abāram ana pīšu išappakū* "They shall pour (hot) lead down down his (i.e., the criminal's) throat" (cf. above, p. 45, n. 1) with the mishnaic punishment recorded in *Mishnah Sanhedrin*, 7 : 2.*

ADDENDA ET CORRIGENDA

P. 1, n. 1. Cf. A. Verger, *Ricerche giuridiche sui papiri aramaici di Elefantina* (*Studi Semitici* 16; Rome, 1965), pp. 73-75.

P. 3. For the woman's right to divorce in OB documents, cf. W. W. Hallo, "The Slandered Bride," *Studies Presented to A. Leo Oppenheim* (Chicago, 1964), pp. 95-105.

P. 4, n. 2. For recent presentations of biblical law, cf. R. de Vaux, *Ancient Israel. Its Life and Institutions* (New York-Toronto-London, 1961) and Z. W. Falk, *Hebrew Law in Biblical Times. An Introduction* (Jerusalem, 1964). The bibliographical sections of *Biblica* and the *Revue historique de droit français et étranger* are particularly thorough in their documentation of recent studies in this area.

P. 7, n. 12. Cf. G. Cardascia, "Les droits cunéiformes," in R. Mounier, G. Cardascia, J. Imbert, *Histoire des institutions et des faits sociaux des orignes à l'aube du moyen age* (Paris, 1956). More recently, cf. V. Korošec, "Keilschriftrecht," in *Orientalisches Recht*, ed. B. Spuler (*Handbuch der Orientalistik*, Erste Abteilung, Ergänzungsband III; Leiden/Köln, 1964); R. Haase, *Einführung in das Studium keilschriftlicher Rechtsquellen* (Wiesbaden, 1965); H. Petschow and V. Korošec, "Gesetze," *RLA*, III, pp. 243-297; P. Artzi, "Law," *Lexicon Biblicum*, II (Tel Aviv, 1965), pp. 581-610 (in Hebrew).

P. 8. For more recent studies in Egyptian law, cf. E. Seidl, "Altägyptisches Recht," in *Orientalisches Recht*, ed. B. Spuler (Leiden/Köln, 1964), pp. 1-48. Cf. also the literature cited in the addendum to p. 143.

P. 15, n. 3. For the preservation of archaic Akkadian legal norms in Susa, cf. Koschaker, "Keilschriftrecht," *ZDMG*, 89 (1935), p. 11. Speiser applied a similar principle to explain the contrast between the laws of the peripheral areas (especially Nuzi and Assyria) and those of central Mesopotamia (OB). Cf. also T. Jacobsen, *Notes on Eshnunna*, pp. 29-35 and J. Lewy, *ZA*, 36 (1924), pp. 160 f.

While this seems to be still the most reasonable thesis suggested so far, it is not without its own difficulties. The contrasts are often not as definitive as one might assume. Central Mesopotamian documents often contain "peripheral" elements: are these Old Akkadian remnants, indices of external influence, or something entirely different? Furthermore, although I assume that much of the cuneiform law found in the deeds of Alalakh and Ras Shamra is of an archaic Mesopotamian background (cf. p. 31, end of the first note), nevertheless, one cannot preclude the possibility that these documents do reflect an indigenous Western ("Amorite") legal tradition (cf. the term *ṣamid/t*, above, p. 20). Thus, not all peripheral law is necessarily Old Akkadian. Finally, the very assumption of a contrast between Sumerian and Akkadian law is now open to question (cf. the discussion, above, pp. 90-95). The whole problem of the traditions of cuneiform law deserves a systematic investigation.

P. 19, n. 3. For Cassite analogues of the *ṭuppu dannatu*, cf. L. Oppenheim, "Ein Beitrag zum Kassitenproblem," *Analecta Orientalia*, 12 (1935), pp. 266 ff.

P. 21. To the transfer clauses cited above, add the following: *eqlu e-el ša-mu ba-a-lu* "the field is clear (of claims), it is bought and taken into possession" in Harris, *Khafajah* 82:17. This clause should be compared with the Susa transfer clause: *eqlu ša-i-im* [*u kaspu li-qi*] "the field is bought [and the money has been received]" in *MDP* XXIII 206:30; cf. also *MDP* XXIII 208:21 and 209:8-9. (For other connections between Susa and Khafajah, cf. above, p. 100, n. 4). The parallel between OB *el*, MA *uppû* and NA *ṣarip* should also be noted.

P. 23n. My investigations into the NA background of many terms and clauses used in the deeds (cf., above, pp. 179-192) has to be coordinated with Kutscher's studies concerning the syntactical orientation of the language of the deeds. While the *content* of the deeds points, at least in part, to a NA (political) milieu, the *language* of the deeds points to a Western milieu. I would suggest the following tentative synthesis of these two points of view.

The indigenous legal traditions of second millennium Syria-Palestine (reflected in the deeds of Ras Shamra and Alalakh, and in contemporary West-Semitic legal loan words into Egyptian) were taken over by the first millennium Aramean dynasties of the West. (Note the continuity of the West-Semitic term *spr* "deed/inscription" from Ras Shamra to Sefîre). As Mazar (*The Biblical Archaeologist Reader* II, ed. E. F. Campbell and D. N. Freedman [New York, 1964], pp. 145 ff.) has pointed out, these kingdoms with their expanding mercantile and administrative activities, could not have functioned efficiently without some sort of a legal formulary written, without a doubt, in Old Aramaic. One would naturally expect that the verbs in this formulary would be placed at the beginning of the sentence, following Western linguistic patterns. Thus, the Elephantine formulary, with its Western linguistic orientation, must be, at least in part, a reflex of this Old Aramaic formulary. These, then, are some of the historical implications of Kutscher's grammatical investigations.

However, the strong NA component in the Elephantine formulary clearly indicates that this formulary is not simply a direct scion of the Old Aramaic one. Before it made its way to Egypt, it must have undergone a strong "Assyrianization," comparable to that which the local Aramaic dialects of the West experienced when they gave way to the (Eastern-based) *Reichsaramäisch*, introduced by the Assyrians when they conquered the area. Although NB, Egyptian and Persian elements were subsequently assimilated, the Elephantine formulary represents, in essence, a fusion of the Old Aramaic formulary, based on Western cuneiform traditions, with the *Reichsaramäisch* formulary, based on Assyrian ones.

P. 31, end of first note. Cf. S. Loewenstamm, "From This Time and Forevermore," *Tarbiẕ*, 32 (1963), pp. 313-316.

P. 31, n. 2. In order to determine more exactly the proximate model of the clause *lʾ ʾgrnk dyn wdbb*, it will be useful to break it down into its various linguistic components. First of all, *grh* is not used absolutely (like the OB *lā igerri*), but with an object (*ʾgrh dyn* not *ʾgrh*). Secondly, this object is complex rather than simple; in this case, a hendiadys (*'grh dyn wdbb* not *'grh dyn*). Thirdly, this object is direct, not indirect (*'grh dyn* = Akkadian *dīnam igerri* not *'grh bdyn* = Akkadian *ina/ana dīnim igerri*). Finally, *grh* takes a second object as well—personal and direct (*'grnk* = Akkadian PN PN_2 *igerri* not *'grh ʿmk* = Akkadian PN *itti* PN_2 *igerri*). Thus, the theoretical model of the Aramaic clause would read something like this: PN (subject) PN_2 (object) *dīnam (u) dabābam lā igerri*. While the NA clause *ša . . . dēnu dabābu itti* PN *igarrûni* is identical with the Aramaic in most respects (use of composite impersonal object), its personal object is indirect (*itti* PN *igarrûni*), rather than direct (PN *igarrûni*). Closer to the Aramaic in this one respect is the late NB expression: PN (subject) PN_2 (object) *dīna igri* (cf. *CAD, G*, p. 62a, s.v. *gerû* 3'). To stress only the NA background of this particular clause—and of the formulary in general—is therefore a bit onesided. As we have just seen, the formulary may have a (late) NB component as well. For the time being, cf. the discussion of the NB-Arsacid background of the Elephantine transfer clause (above, pp. 41n and 134n).

A few words about the cuneiform background of *ršh* are in order. While the idiom *dīnam gerû* is well attested in Akkadian, I am less certain about the presence of a *dīnam rašû*. Linguistically, such a combination would be functionally equivalent to *dīnam ṣabātu* or *dīnam aḫāzu*. [Cf. F. R. Kraus, "Ein mittelbabylonischer Rechtsterminus," *Symbolae . . . Martino David* II (Leiden, 1968), p. 10.]

P. 33n. My translations of *tarteši* and *ša ibašši ana yāši* differ from those of Thureau-Dangin who takes the forms as perfect ("she acquired") and present ("I have") respectively. There is some reason, however, to believe that these forms may be Canaanisms reflecting West-Semitic imperfects.

First of all, standard Akkadian for "I have" is *ša ittiya ibašši* not *ša ibašši ana yāši*. The element *ana yāši* seems to be a clear index of the West-Semitic background of the idiom: cf. *EA* 116:48-49 *damiq ana yāši u i-ba-ša-ti ittika* "it would be good for me if I were with you" (Hebrew *ṭōḇ lī (wᵉ)hāyīṯi ʿimmāk*) I think there is a good possibility that RS *ibašši* is the equivalent of Hebrew *yihyeh (lī)* or Aramaic *yhwh ly* ("will accrue unto me") rather than of Hebrew *yēš*. (Alternately, understand *ibašši* as *ibbašši* (N), as in the expression *nēmel ibbašši* "the profit that accrues"; for the difficulty of distinguishing between the two forms, cf. *CAD, B*, p. 161a).

Secondly, *ta-ar-te-ši* seems somewhat unusual for the perfect of *rašû*. Contextually, an imperfect seems to be needed. Compare *RS* 15.168:8-10 (= *PRU* III, p. 137) *ù inanna* ᶠPN *ti-ir-ta-ṣí-ip bīta ann[â]*, where *ti-ir-ta-ṣí-ip* after *inanna* "now" must be translated as "she shall build." Both *ti-ir-ta-ṣí-ip* and *ta-ar-te-ši* do not reflect the normal vowel patterns of the perfect and, in spite of their t-infix, seem to function as imperfects. The whole problem is in need of further investigation.

P. 36, line 8. Delete *brḥmn* after *bḥyy* and place it after *bmwty*. In line 9, delete "in affection" after "my life" and place it in line 10, after "upon my death."

P. 36, n. 2. The idiomatic use of *lʾ tkhl* "you are not able" = "you are not allowed" is not a Hebraism since it is already found in the Old Aramaic inscription of Sefire. Sefîre I B 25 *wlykhl bry* [*l*]*yšlḥ yd bbr*[*k*] is to be translated "nor will my son be *allowed* to raise a hand against [your] son." Cf. also I B 34; II B 6. As far as I can tell, this nuance has not been noticed by previous interpreters of the texts.

P. 37, n. 3. The documents edited by Milik in *Biblica*, 38 (1957), pp. 245-68 are from Wadi Seiyāl not from Wadi Murabbaʿat.

P. 38, n. 3. For a detailed study of the Akkadian clause and its Aramaic reflex at Sefîre, cf. K. R. Veenhof, "An Aramaic Curse with a Sumero-Akkadian Prototype," *BiOr*, 20 (1963), 142-44.

P. 39, n. 1. For *ʿšt* in Hebrew and Aramaic, cf. H. L. Ginsberg, "Lexicographical Notes," in *Hebräische Wortforschung. Festschrift zum 80. Geburtstag von Walter Baumgartner* (Leiden, 1967), pp. 81 f.

P. 39, n. 4. Although some of my colleagues insist that *nāśāʾ* "to provide" is reflected in Is 46:4, I am still convinced that this is not so. In this context, "carry" is what is demanded. The gods of the nations cannot carry their load (i.e., the people who trust in them); they grow weak and fall. The God of Israel, on the other hand, never tires: He can *carry* from childhood to old age (so C. C. Torrey, *The Second Isaiah*, p. 364). Aramaic *sbl*, on the other hand, like the Akkadian *našû* and *abālu* (cf. *CAD*, *A*[1], p. 23) does mean "to provide." Cf. E. Bresciani and M. Kamil, *Le lettere aramaiche di Hermopoli* (Rome, 1966), No. 1:5; cf. also *sbl*/*sbwl* "food" in Aḥiqar 74 and 205 (pointed out to me by H. L. Ginsberg). Note also the Syriac *sybrtʾ* "food, provisions."

P. 45, n. 1. I argued that *ṭyb lbby* was used to strengthen the relatively "weak" character of the Elephantine conveyance (which did not employ the oath or threat of physical punishments). Since OB conveyances which use the oath, and Alalakh conveyances which use physical punishments, also employ *libbašu ṭāb*, my argument is without foundation.

P. 55. For a discussion of *patria potestas*, cf. Haase, *Einführung*, pp. 70 ff. and the literature cited there.

P. 60, n. 2. For the background of this divorce, cf. W. L. Moran, "The Scandal of the 'Great Sin' at Ugarit," *JNES*, 18 (1958), pp. 280 f.

P. 61, second paragraph of notes. I now consider Yaron's interpretation of *i-na-ki-ru* as philologically incorrect. The initial *i* of *i-na-ki-ru* is influenced by the final vowel of Ammistamri. The underlying form, therefore, is *unakkiru*.

P. 64. For *bukannu šūtuq* read *bukānam šūtuq*. Cf. *CAD* and Von Soden, *AHw*, s.v., *bukānu*. For the use of a wooden stick in conjunction with the completion of sale transactions (inim.bi al.til) in Ur III documents, cf. D. O. Edzard's review of Hackman, *BIN* VIII, in *ZANF* 22 (1964), p. 277.

P. 66. According to Simmons (*JCS*, 13 [1959], p. 90., šà.ga.ni al.dùg should always be understood as the active form. If Simmons is right, may we assume that the ì.dug form represents the stative *libbašu ṭāb*? Poebel, *Grundzüge der Sumerischen Grammatik* (Rostock, 1928), p. 233 posits a different contrast. According to Poebel, the al.dùg form is to be translated "sein Herz ist befriedigt;" the ì.dùg form, as "sein Herz ist zufrieden (als Tätigkeit)."

If I understand Poebel correctly, the first form represents *libbašu ṭūb* "his heart has been satisfied (by some previous action)," while the latter form represents *libbašu ṭāb* "his heart is satisfied." Cf. Poebel's comments on p. 232.

P. 76, second paragraph. The clause *dmy zbyny ʾylyn* should not be translated "this price" as I did above. Although *zᵉḇīn(ē)* can mean "sale-price" (Onqelos to Lev 25:16), used with *dmy* "money/price," it must have some other nuance, either that of "sale transaction" (Onqelos to Deut 18:8) or "salable property" (Targum to Ez 7:13—*mimkār* = *zᵉḇīn*; for the plural *zᵉḇīnē* as a collective, cf. Onqelos to Lev 25:14). The clause *dmy zbyny ʾylyn* should probably be rendered: "the price of this property." It is significant that both Aramaic *zᵉḇīn* and Akkadian *šīmu* share the semantic range: sale transaction, sale-price, salable goods. Furthermore, both often appear as a plurale tantum. For the range of *šīmu*, cf. Kraus, *Ammi-ṣaduqa*, p. 75; [Add *ly* after *ʾštyyr*.]

P. 80. The term *libbašu ṭāb* is found sporadically in OB letters. Cf., P. Kraus, *Altbabylonische Briefe* (= *MVAG* 36 [1932]), where examples of the term are found in the following texts from *VS* XVI—77:8 (after *apālu*); 126:17 (after *šīmam maḫrāku*) and 21 (in the D form); 174:27. Cf. also F. R. Kraus, *Briefe aus dem British Museum* (Leiden, 1964), 31:15 (*libbu ṭāb*); 68:18 (*libbaki u[ṭâb]*); 139:7' (*maḫir libbašu ṭāb*). Cf. also R. Frankena, *Briefe aus dem British Museum* (Leiden, 1966), 164:12-13 (*libbaka uṭâb*). In all of these cases, the meaning of the term is identical with that established for the legal documents: *libbašu uṭâb* "he will satisfy his heart (with full payment);" *libbašu ṭāb* "his heart is satisfied (upon the receipt of full payment)."

P. 81. The affinity between "satisfaction" and a predisposition against "fighting" is nicely illustrated in a nonlegal passage from Mari: *Ḫanû išabbīma ša-bi-ḫu-um ge-re-em ul īšû* "The Hana people will be satisfied, and a satisfied man has no (desire to) fight" (*ARM* II 37:18).

P. 97. *MDP* XXII 83:3' has to be added as another example of *libbašu ṭāb* from Susa (a sale transaction).

P. 99, n. 3. For a recent discussion of this rare legal genre, cf. R. Harris, "Old Babylonian Temple Loans," *JCS*, 14 (1960), pp. 133-137.

P. 100, n. 4. Harris emended the idiom *qaqqassunu šamna pašiš* to the singular *šamna qaqqassu pašiš*. In the light of the praxis reflected in *ARM* VIII 13:13'-14' (cited above, p. 137) where both buyer and seller annoint themselves (*iptaššū*), the emendation is unnecessary. Cf. also K. R. Veenhof's review of E. Kutsch, *Salbung als Rechtsakt im Alten Testament und in Alten Orient* (Berlin, 1963) in *BiOr*, 23 (1966), 308-313.

P. 103. For the Sumerianizing tendency of the scribes of Alalakh Level IV, cf. Barry L. Eichler, *Nuzi Personal Ditennūtu Transactions and their Mesopotamian Analogues* (unpublished dissertation, University of Pennsylvania, 1967), p. 235, n. 50.

P. 106. For an interpretation of cuneiform sale which does not place sufficient emphasis either on the role of the seller, or on the transfer-investiture aspect of the transaction, cf. Haase, *Einführung*, pp. 90-95. His generalizations, while correct for the OB material from central Mesopotamia, do not adequately explain the frequency of seller oriented transactions in the more archaic or provincial formularies.

P. 107, n. 4. The word for "price" in the expression *ana šīmim nadānum* was written logographically in Old Akkadian as ŠÁM or NÍG.ŠÁM, or with syllabic indicators, showing the Akkadian to be a plurale tantum—*šīmū* or *šiʾmū* (Gelb, *MAD* III, p. 259). Significantly, the same expression, written logographically with plural indicators, is found in MB conveyances from Alalakh. Cf. *AT* 71:3-4 *ana* PN ŠIM.MEŠ-*šu* [*iddin*] *aplū*.

For the same expression without plural indicator, cf. *AT* 75:4 (MB). This is not the only archaic usage preserved in these relatively late documents. The grid *ana šīmim iddin aplū* is virtually identical with the Old Akkadian Susa *i-ti-in* ... šu.ti.a in *MDP* XXIV 361:2-6, cited above, p. 107, n. 4.

P. 113 ff. For a discussion of collective versus private property in cuneiform law, cf. Haase, *Einführung*, pp. 78 ff.

P. 116, n. 2. For an illustration of interdialectal distribution by Landsberger himself, cf. "Tin and Lead: The Adventures of Two Vocables," *JNES*, 24 (1965), pp. 285-296. It should be noted that although functional equivalence is the guiding principle in Landsberger's study, he still considers etymology a valuable philological tool (cf. the last paragraph of the article).

P. 116, n. 3. For *ʾalōṯ habbᵉrīṯ* = *adê māmīt ilāni*, cf. E. A. Speiser, "An Angelic 'Curse:' Exodus 14:20," *JAOS*, 80 (1960), p. 198.

P. 117. de Meyer, *L'accadien des contrats de Suse* (Leiden, 1962) translates *duppur* either as "terminer" (pp. 5 and 179) or as "satisfait" (pp. 121 and 123).

P. 117. The equivalence of *mesû* with *gamāru* was suggested to me by the parallelism between OB *zīzū gamrū* (*libbašunu ṭāb*) and Susa *zīzū gamrū* (*duppurū*). Speiser agreed with this equation and was of the opinion that Susa *mesû* "to terminate" was to be separated from *mesû* "to wash." (Contrast Koschaker, *OLZ*, 35, p. 321; *CAD*, s.v. *dapāru*; E. Salonen, *Studia Orientalia*, XXVII/1, pp. 127 and 159—all of whom derive Susa *mesû* from the metaphor of "purity;" compare *el*, *eb*, *zakû*, etc.).

Even before Speiser, the existence of a root *mesû* "to decide, determine, distinguish"—separate from the regular *mesû* "to wash"—had been recognized by Jensen (*apud* Baumgartner, *ZA*, 2 (1925), p. 31n). He interpreted the expression *dīnam mussû* in the Hymn to Shamash (cf. Lambert, *BWL*, p. 134:127) as "to determine a law suit." His interpretation was followed by many: Baumgartner, *ZA*, 2 (1925), p. 31n; Bauer, *Akkadische Lesestücke*, II, p. 46; Falkenstein, *Literarische Keilschrifttexte aus Uruk* (Berlin, 1931), p. 13; Landsberger (*apud* Falkenstein) who cites *KAH* 2 122:38 *aššu qaqqar āli šuʾāti* [*lā mussî*] "damit die Stelle jener Stadt nich mehr unterschieden werde." Although Lambert (*BWL*, pp. 134 and 322) follows Jensen's translation of *dīnam mussû* "to determine a law suit," he is still of the opinion that *mussû* "is no doubt the same root as *mesû* 'to wash,' a metaphor arising from the water ordeal" (p. 322).

The expression *dīnam mussû*—with a similar but not identical meaning—is found in several NB texts: *RA* 12 6:11 and *ZA* 3 228:5 (cited by *CAD*, *D*, p. 10a).

P. 119. For more on *nasiḫ* in the deeds of Susa, cf. de Meyer, p. 127.

P. 120. For additional material on *šabû*, cf. L. Oppenheim, *AfO*, 12, pp. 357 and 360. Cf. also B. Kienast, *Altassyrische Texte des orientalischen Seminars der Universität Heidelberg* ... (Berlin, 1960), p. 7; cf. also the texts cited by *CAD*, *H*, p. 6b.

P. 122. For *ḫabālu* in the deeds of Kültepe, cf. *CAD*, *Ḫ*, pp. 6 ff.

P. 122, n. 1. The clause has been rendered recently as "its *nisḫātu*-tax added, its *šaddu'utu*-tax paid for." Cf. M. T. Larsen, *Old Assyrian Caravan Procedures* (Istanbul, 1967), p. 8 and *passim*. Usually, the subject of *šabû* is a *person* who is "satisfied" with money, i.e. paid off. The root-metaphor of satisfaction would seem to demand that the subject always be personal. Yet, such is not always the case: the *šaddu'utu*-tax is paid for impersonally. In all probability, this impersonal use of *šabû* is a secondary development derived from a previous clause "PN is *šabû* with his *šaddu'utu*-tax" > "(PN is) *šabû* with the *š*." > "the *š*. is *šabû*." As far as I can tell, *libbašu ṭāb* did not undergo a similar secondary development.

P. 123. The functional equivalence of OB *libbašu ṭāb* with MB *zakû* was also seen by Haase, *Einführung*, p. 92.

P. 123, last line. For "dialectical change" read "dialectal change."

P. 126, n. 2. The rare Aramaic *ʿṭr* (= Akkadian *eṭēru*) is reflected in the Targum's rendering of the biblical stereotype *wᵉhabbāmōṯ lōʾ sārū* "nevertheless the high-places were not removed" (I Kings 15:4 and *passim*) as *wbmtʾ lʾ ʿṭrʾ*. Furthermore, according to the *Aruk*, s.v. *ʿaṭīrāh*, the rabbinic editorial term *ʿiṭṭūr sōfᵉrīm* is to be interpreted in the light of the same root as "the scribal removal (of extra *waws*)."

P. 127. Although the OB *libbašu ṭāb* and the Aramaic agree with each other so closely, both in form and function, that some historical relationship between them must be posited, it is still impossible to determine the proximate cuneiform model from which the Aramaic term was derived. As we have seen, *libbašu ṭāb* gave way to the MB *zakû*, which was ultimately replaced by *eṭir* at about the same time that *ṭyb lbby* and its Demotic analogues appear in Egypt. Did *libbašu ṭāb* survive in some isolated cultural island to be revived, by conscious or unconscious archaizing, during the late NB period? One can only conjecture about such matters. However, the reappearance of archaic material in the Arsacid-Seleucid formulary would provide a suggestive parallel to the assumed revival of "satisfaction" terminology. The revival of early legal material in the latest documents of cuneiform legal culture may also be compared to the archaizing tendencies in both Egypt and Mesopotamia during the late NB period. The problem deserves a systematic investigation.

P. 127. Above, I argued that while the subject of *šabû* is a right-holder who relinquishes rights upon the receipt of payment, the subject of *zakû* is a person under obligation (slave, debtor, etc.) who is freed from his obligation. This generalization is in need of qualification. *CAD*, *E*, p. 131b cites *BIN* IV 147:15 and 19 where the subject of *šabbû* is not a former right-holder, but a person under obligation; in this context *šabbû* seems to mean "free of obligation" (= *zakû*), not "quit after receipt of payment." *CAD* translates the passage as: "If he produces a tablet or witnesses, PN has been discharged (*šabbû*) of (the obligation to pay) the silver." May we assume then that *šabû* is not to be derived from the metaphor of satisfaction? Although possible, this seems unlikely. It seems more probable to assume that a term which originally described the satisfaction of a right-holder with an *Entgelt*, and his concomitant relinquishment of ownership, came to describe the freedom of a person under obligation from that obligation. The term *zakû/uzakki* underwent a similar development in the opposite direction. The term, which described the freedom of the person under obligation from that obligation, was later applied to the "freedom" (= relinquishment) of a right-holder from his property upon the receipt of payment (cf. *apil zakû*).

P. 129, last paragraph. The oldest known use of the term *ina ḫūd libbišu* is found at Ras Shamra. It is *RS* 8.333:11 (*PRU* III, p. 7). The text cited at the bottom of p. 129 is not from Ras Shamra at all: it is the NB text *BE* VIII 106:11.

P. 130. CAD, *I*, p. 155a, translates *BBSt* 36, IV 42 ff. as follows: "he (the king) looked upon him with benevolence [*ḫadîš*], his countenance bright, his features ruddy, his eyes kindly."

P. 131, n. 1. The expression *kīniš naplusu* (a reflex of the Sumerian igi-zi(d) bar) overlaps to a very great degree with *ḫadīš naplusu*. Thus, the stereotype *ina būnīšu namrūti kīniš ippalis* is virtually identical in function, both in royal donations and in prayers, with *ina būnīšu namrūti ḫadīš ippalis* (for a wide range of examples, cf. *CAD*, s.v. *būnu*). While *kīniš* describes the *steadfastness* of the divine intention, and *ḫadīš* describes the *joy/willingness* of the divine intention, both are expressions of the *kind* disposition of the deity. Significantly, Poebel renders igi-zi(d) bar according to sense as "er blickte *freundlich*" (*Grundzüge der Sumerischen Grammatik*, p. 203). The expression *kīniš naplusu* is most probably derived from Sumerian models. The derivation of *ḫadīš naplusu* is less certain. It is already attested to from the time of Ḫammurabi (cf. Gelb, *JNES*, 7 (1948), p. 208). However, the metaphorical use of "joy" as an expression of willingness, although widespread in Akkadian, does not *seem* to have been employed in earlier Sumerian sources. Professor Jacobsen has kindly called my attention to King, *Letters and Inscriptions of Hammurabi*, No. 99:1-10 (= *VS* I 33:1 ff.) igi ḫul-la-ne-ne-a in-ši-in-bar-re-eš-a = *i-nu ḫa-di-iš ip-pa-al-su-šum*. Jacobsen is of the opinion that the Akkadian formulation is primary; the Sumerian, a secondary adaptation.

P. 132, n. 1. For more examples of *ezziš nekelmû*, cf. *CAD*, *E*, p. 432.

P. 133, n. 5. My attempt to interpret the abnormal form *rḥmt* (instead of the anticipated absolute *rḥmh*) as a calque from the Akkadian *rēmūtu* is not without parallels. In *AP* 11:5, we find the form *mrbyt* "interest" where the absolute *mrby* is required (cf. *AP* 11:7); similarly, the form *ʾgrt* "letter" is found (*AP* 30:7; 31:6; 38:10; 41:5) instead of the normal *ʾgrh*. While Lidzbarski (*Ephemeris*, III, p. 82) considered *ʾgrt* and *mrbyt* as Hebraisms, Ungnad (cited by Leander, p. 112) took *ʾgrt* as a calque from the Babylonian. I follow the same method in regard to *rḥmt*.

The presence of cuneiform calques in Egyptian Aramaic is confirmed from an independent, but related source. H. L. Ginsberg (Annual Meeting of the American Oriental Society, New Haven, 1967) has shown that the expression *nšy bytn/byth* mentioned several times in Driver, *Aramaic Documents of the Fifth Century B.C.*, No. 8, cannot mean "the women of our/his house," but must be rendered according to the context as: "the slaves/personnel of our/his household." It seems most likely to me that *nšy byt*ʾ—impossible as an Aramaic form—is simply a calque from the common NB *nišē bīti* "slaves, personnel" (cf. *VS* IV 46:9 = *NRVU* 301; *VS* VI 84:11 = *NRVU* 626; *VS* VI 86:2 = *NRVU* 668). Ginsberg is in agreement with me concerning the NB derivation of the term. [Cf. also *amēlūtu* 'personnel'].

Pp. 134-135. For *bēl dēqti* = *bēl damiqti*, cf. *CAD, D*, p. 67a. My translation of *ARU* 16:14-16 differs somewhat from that of Kohler-Ungnad in that I read *ittallaku šalmeš* together with *qirib ekalliya* as one clause, coordinate with *ina kīnāti izzizuma*: "(who) served me faithfully and loyally performed his duties in my palace." Both *uzzuzu maḫar* RN and *alāku* in the *tan*-form are expressions of service and performance of duty. (The former corresponds to the Hebrew *ʿāmaḏ lifnê* "to be in the service of;" the latter, to Hebrew *hiṯhallēḵ lifnê*; cf. II Kings 20:3 and E. A. Speiser, "The Durative Hithpaʿel: a *tan* Form," *JAOS* (1955), pp. 118-121. Cf. also the expression *hālaḵ lifnê* in I Kings 3:6; 8:25; 9:4. The complement *ina kīnāti* "in truth" used with *uzzuzu maḫar* is identical with the complement *beʾemeṯ* "in truth" used with *hālaḵ lifnê* in I Kings 3:6).

Just as *ina kīnāti* describes the faithfulness of the service, so *šalmeš* must somehow describe the loyalty, more specifically, the fullness and exactitude with which the courtier performed his duties. The complement *šalmeš*, therefore, does not describe the contented/successful life of the courtier in the palace, as Kohler-Ungnad would have it ("wohlbehalten"), even though *šalmeš atalluku* can have this meaning in other contexts (cf. *littallak šalmeš* "let him live contentedly" in *KAR* 105:2'; *CAD* A[1], p. 326a).

According to *CAD*, the same idiom is found in a NB copy of a donation of the Cassite period. *RA* 19 86:10 (cited by *CAD*, *A*[1], p. 326a) reads as follows: *ana urruk umēšu šalām zērišu u šalmeš* DU.MEŠ *maḫar* RN "(the official donated the seal to the goddess) for the lengthening of his days, (for) the welfare of his seed and . . ." While Thureau-Dangin, the editor of the text, took *šalmeš atalluki* as "pour passe son existence sain et sauf," *CAD* renders it "for his serving the king properly." "Properly" in this context means: without the type of faults which precipitate royal anger and shorten the days of imperfect courtiers.

The idiom *šalmeš atalluku* is found in another text cited by CAD, in which the meaning "to perform one's duties perfectly/faithfully" seems to be the one demanded by the context. In Pinches, *Texts in Babylonian Wedge-Writing*, p. 16:9' (cited by *CAD*, *A*[1], p. 325b), it is said of a temple official that *qirbi ekurrātišu šalmeš littallakuma lišallimma parṣīšu*. While CAD renders the clause as "let him move about undisturbed in his sanctuaries and duly perform his rites," I would suggest the alternate translation: "let him serve perfectly/correctly in his sanctuaries and duly perform his rites." This description corresponds exactly, both in sentiment and terminology, with that of the ideal priest in Malachi 2:6—*bešālōm ubmīšōr hālaḵ ittī* "he served me with integrity and equity." Hebrew *hālak̲* (*ittī*) = Akkadian *atalluku*; Hebrew *b^eš ālōm* = Akkadian *šalmeš*. For *šālōm* with the meaning of "integrity," cf. Ps 37:37 where it is parallel to *tom* and *yóšer* (pointed out to me by H. L. Ginsberg). The usual complements of *hālak̲ lifnê* DN are *ʾemet̲, yišrat̲ lēk̲āb̲* (I Kings 3:6) or *tom lēb̲āb̲* and *yóšer* (I Kings 9:4).

The root *šlm* conveys the idea of perfection: in the cultic sphere, it indicates the correct performance of rites; in the moral sphere, it indicates integrity and goodness. For the former, cf. Delitzsch, *AHw*, p. 664a: sacrifices are offered *ki šalmu* "wie est recht ist." For the latter, cf. the idiom *lā šalmāti* "(words) that are improper/evil" found so often in Babylonian confessions of sin (cf. M. Weir, *Lexicon of Akkadian Prayers*, p. 321).

P. 134, n. 3. For the relationship between Aramaic *šlṭ* and NB *šalāṭu*, cf. J. J. Rabinowitz, "Neo-Babylonian Legal Documents and Jewish Law," *JJP*, 13, pp. 150 ff.

P. 136, n. 1. Just as the rabbinic *b^eṭōb̲āṭō* "willingly" is derived from the metaphor of joy, so its antonym *b^eʿal korḥō* "unwillingly" is probably derived from the metaphor of sadness or sickness. The root of *korḥō* is probably identical with the Syriac *kurhānā* "sickness;" cf. also the Arabic expression *ʿalā karāhiyatihī* "unwillingly"—from *kariha* "to dislike."

P. 137. The difficult expression in *ARM* VIII 13—*kāram īkulū* is rendered by *CAD* (*A*, p. 247a) as: "they have eaten from the (same) plate (?)." For the rare term *zaqādu*, cf. *CAD*, *Z*, p. 50. *CAD* reads the verb as I/2 and translates: "(the houses) were exchanged (?) voluntarily, PN and PN_2 were present when they exchanged (?) (or: when the houses were exchanged (?)).

P. 138, n. 3. A systematic presentation of the cuneiform-Aramaic background of the Arabic legal papyri is now in order. Any such study will have to consider the role of the Nabateans in this process of transmission.

P. 139. For the date of the Mâlamir texts, cf. E. Salonen, *Studia Orientalia*, XXVII/1, p. 23.

P. 139, n. 2. Cf. de Meyer, p. 5 and p. 54 for the meaning and grammatical structure of *ina nar'amātišu*.

P. 141. The expression PN *libbi* PN_2 *uṭâb* is found in several OB contexts that have nothing to do with receipt and payment. Thus, for example, a widow may leave her property to *ša elīša ṭābu* "whomever is pleasing to her" (Schorr, *Urkunden*, 204:20 and *passim*) or *ana ša ipallaḫuši u libbaša uṭabbu* "whoever serves her and satisfies her heart" (Schorr, *Urkunden*, 202:18-19). Clearly, the implications of *libbi* PN *uṭâb* are spelled out by the complement *palāḫu* "to serve." Translated as a hendiadys, the clause would read: "whoever serves her to her satisfaction." At Susa, the parallel clause was *māru ša palāḫša īpušu maḫriša uššab* "the son who serves her shall live in her house" (*MDP* XXIV 379:19). At Ras Shamra, the same idea was expressed by the clause *ša ukabbit* "whoever honors" and its antonym *ša uqallil* "whoever dishonors" (*Syria*, 18 [1937], p. 250; the text is *RS* 8.145:24-25 and 19; the terms are of course the models of the biblical *kibbēd* and *qillēl*).

As far as the idiom PN *libbi* PN_2 *uṭâb* is concerned, in inheritance contexts it simply means: "to perform service to one's satisfaction." Such an interpretation would also apply to the law of the *nadītu*, who may give her property to anyone she sees fit, if her brothers *libbaša lā uṭibbū* (*CH* 178). The expression can only mean: "if they do not serve her to her satisfaction (by the proper handling of her affairs)."

Above, I suggested that the epithet *muṭīb libbi Marduk* applied to Ḫammurabi, may have something to do with his pious deeds. The specific legal usage just cited would seem to fit this royal context. Ḫammurabi performs the tasks assigned to him by Marduk to perfection, i.e., to the satisfaction of Marduk, his lord. Such an interpretation would also seem to be reflected in Kraus' translation of the clause: "Ich, der für das Wohlbefinden seines Herrn Marduk sorgt" (cf. *Könige, die in Zelten Wohnten* [Amsterdam, 1965], p. 8, n. 47).

P. 142, n. 1. West-Semitic legal loan-words are found in Egypt before the Saitic period. For *brt* (= *b^erīṯ* "covenant"), cf. the literature cited by D. J. McCarthy, S. J., *Treaty and Covenant* (*Analecta Biblica* 21; Rome, 1963), p. 105, n. 26 (the term appears in a text from the time of Ramesses III). For *sfr* (= *spr*) with the specific meaning of "dowry(-document"), cf. the literature cited by Pestman, p. 153, n. 8 and J. J. Rabinowitz, *JNES*, 17 (1958), p. 146, n. 15. For *ʿdt* (= *ʿēḏūṯ*), cf. the discussion of K. A. Kitchen, *Ancient Orient and Old Testament* (London, 1966), p. 108, n. 84. This information forces us to revise our ideas concerning the process by which Western cuneiform legal elements were transmitted to Egypt: it was much earlier than previously assumed, and not necessarily through an Aramaic medium alone. Further study of the problem is in order.

P. 143. For an approach which places greater emphasis on the centrality of law in Egypt, cf. A. Théoridides, "À propos de la loi dans l'Égypte pharaonique," *RIDA*, 3e série, 15 (1967), pp. 107-152 and the literature cited there. I presently feel that some lacuna in the preservation and discovery of legal documents accounts for the comparative absence of this particular genre in Egypt. Contrasts between societal patterns, although suggestive and important, must always be tempered by a more sceptical or "positivistic" attitude.

P. 143. For some recent studies in Egyptian law, cf. S. Allam, "Zwei Schlussklauseln zur Übertragung eines Rechts im Alten Ägypten," *BiOr*, 24 (1967), pp. 14-20; Among the studies cited there are W. Helck, *Materialien zur Wirtschaftsgeschichte des Neuen Reiches*, III (Mainz, 1963) and I. M. Lurje, *Studies in Ancient Egyptian Law* (Leningrad, 1960) (in Russian).

P. 174. The modes of cultural exchange between Egyptians and Arameans (and West-Semites) are many and varied. Thus, the exchange took place in religion as well as in law; cf. R. A. Bowman, "An Aramaic Religious Text in Demotic Script," *JNES*, 3 (1944), pp. 219-231. Furthermore, the Egyptians were not always the passive party: cf. the Aramaic subscription to a Demotic legal document that follows the Egyptian rather than the Aramaic pattern, M. Noël Aimé-Giron, *Textes araméens d'Égypte* (Cairo, 1931), pp. 67 ff. Nor does the contact necessarily take place in Egypt proper: cf. S. Yeivin, "A Hieratic Ostracon from Tel Arad," *IEJ*, 16 (1966), pp. 153-59. Egyptian mercenaries, employing a Hieratic administrative tradition, were in the service of the Judean government of the late seventh century B.C. According to Y. Aharoni, "The Use of Hieratic Numbers in Hebrew Ostraca and Shekel Weights," *BASOR*, 184 (1966), pp. 13-19, hieratic numbers were employed by Israelite merchants and scribes. The Israelite merchants did not simply read the Egyptian symbols in terms of their own needs, such as would be the case if the hieratic number ten were inscribed on an eight-shekel weight and simply read as eight, but seem to have read them at face value. Cf. I. T. Kaufman, "New Evidence for Hieratic Numerals on Hebrew Weights," *BASOR*, 188 (1967), pp. 39-41.

P. 176. For subjectively formulated declarations before witness from central Mesopotamia (OB), cf. *TCL* I 184 (= *HG* 1100) and *TCL* X 38 (cited by Lautner, *Symbolae Koschaker*, p. 92; cf. also J. Van Dijk, *Cuneiform Texts. Old Babylonian Contracts and Juridical Texts* (*Texts in the Iraq Museum* IV; Wiesbaden, 1967), Texts 38 and following, described as "Declarations Before Witnesses." The relationship between such declarations and the Nuzi *lišānšu* has yet to be determined.

P. 178. The NB/NA *lā išallaṭ* is to be compared not only with Hebrew *lōʾ yimšol* in Ex 21:8 (so Kutscher, *New Aramaic Texts*, p. 239), but also with the rare Ras Shamra *lā imallik* "he shall not exercise authority (over)" (*RS* 16.250:19 = *PRU* III, p. 135) where it is the virtual isogloss of the more common *lā iqerrib* (cf. p. 86). This is a West-Semitism (related to the common Arabic *mulk* "property" and *malaka* "to take possession of") as was correctly seen by Von Soden, *AHw*, s.v., *malāku* III.

P. 178. For the creative role of the Arameans, cf. A. L. Oppenheim, *Letters From Mesopotamia* (Chicago, 1967), p. 43: "In certain respects, this phase [that of the first millennium] represents the climax of an evolution in which a number of major Mesopotamian intellectual achievements were cast into forms readily acceptable by Babylonia's neighbors to the west and to the east, thus producing a cultural legacy whose effects were far-reaching and are in evidence even today."

P. 178. The expression *ellān rêqu* is also found with the meaning "defect from" in *RS* 17.335 + 379 + 381 + 235:6-7 = *PRU* IV, p. 72. The expression is identical in both form and function with Jer 2:5 *rāḥᵃqū mēʿālay* "they defected from me."

P. 181. For the equivalence of West-Semitic *ʾbd* "to be lost" with Akkadian *ḫalāqu*, cf. *EA* 288:52 (Moshe Held).

P. 183. The Aramaic *mḥr ʾw ywm ʾḥrn* is merely the last in a long line of idioms—the RS/Alalakh *urram šēram*, the Ugaritic *śḥr ʿlmt*, the NA *ina šērtu ina lidiš*—which express the idea of "(if), some time in the future." It should be noted that no idiom is a literal translation of any other, even though it is quite clear that *śḥr ʿlmt* is the direct reflex of RS *urram šēram* (Nougayrol, *PRU* II, p. 22). Thus, the more distant time in the future, represented by the Akkadian *šēram*, is reflected not in the Ugaritic *śḥr*, as one would have expected, but in the Ugaritic *ʿlmt*. Yet, the use of the cognate *śḥr*, instead of some other word for the near future, is not without significance. Similarly, the Aramaic *ywm ʾḥrn* is not the exact translation of either *lidiš* "the day after tomorrow" (in the idiom *šērtam lidiš*) or of *šēram* "the morning (after tomorrow) (in the idiom *urram šēram*). Whether the Aramaic is based on *urram šēram* or *ina šērtam ina lidiš*, the Aramaic scribes remained loyal to the older concept, but exercised their freedom of formulation. Anyone acquainted with Akkadian loan translations from the Sumerian will realize that a reworking of older elements into a new language need not to be literal to qualify as a translation. Compare for example the relationship between the Sumerian *igi-zi(d) bar* "he opened a steadfast eye" and the Akkadian *kīniš ippalis* "he looked steadfastly."

P. 183, n. 7. For the expression *ana dūr u pala ana šēršerri*, cf. *CAD, D*, p. 198 where *ana dūr u pala* is rendered "for continuation or change."

If *šēršēri* is interpreted as a reduplication of *šērum* "dawn," the final consonant in the form *šēršerri* is probably a reflection of the doubling of final consonants that often replaces penultimate long vowels in Susa Akkadian. Cf. *zīzakku* for *zīzāku*; *parkuttu* for *parkūtu*; *rugimanni* for *rugimāni* (cited by Salonen, *Studia Orientalia* XXVII/1, pp. 40 and 90). For doubling as the equivalent of tone length, cf. E. Reiner, *A Linguistic Analysis of Akkadian* (1966), pp. 45 ff.

P. 185, 1. 9. For *dayānu lā išammû* read *dēnšu dayānu lā išammû*.

P. 187. The Aramaic-Persian Wordbook still preserves reflexes of the various Akkadian terms for "deed"—*ṭuppu, dannitu, šaṭāru* and *giṭṭu*; cf. Ebeling, *Glossar*, p. 34.

P. 188. For the process by which Akkadian names for clay tablets were later applied to deeds written on parchment, cf. the term kušGÍD.DA "Pergamenturkunde" in *VS* XV 34, 21 cited by Von Soden, *AHw*, s.v., *giṭṭu*.

P. 188. The regular West-Semitic term for "document" is *spr*. It first appears in Ugaritic with this meaning (cf. *PRU* II, 5:9, 13). Soon thereafter it appears as a loan-word in Egyptian with the meaning "dowry(-document)" (cf. Pestman, p. 153, n. 8 and the literature cited there). The same term is found later in the Old Aramaic of Sefîre with the meaning "written inscription" (cf. Sefîre I B 28 and *passim*); in the Bible with the meaning "inscription" (Is 30:8) and "document" (Deuteronomy 24:1); in Elephantine Aramaic with the meaning "document."

The commonly accepted derivation of this West-Semitic term from Akkadian *šipru* seems unjustified. Akkadian has many words for "document"—*ṭuppu, dannatu, šaṭāru, giṭṭu*, etc. As far as I can tell, *šipru* is not one of them. It simply means "(written) message." Nor is the picture any different at Ras Shamra, an ideal locus for the transmission of cuneiform terms to early Canaanite: there, the regular word for deed is *ṭuppu*. The idea that West-Semitic scribes borrowed *spr* from a Ras Shamra **šipru* "document" is without basis in fact. RS *spr* renders *ṭuppu*, nothing else.

Similarly, Aramaic/Hebrew *spr*/*sōfēr* "scribe" is not to be derived from Akkadian *šāpiru*, as so commonly assumed. The term *šāpiru* simply does not mean "scribe" (cf. J. Lewy, "Section 70 of the Bisutun Inscription," *HUCA*, 25 [1954], pp. 191 ff.). West-Semitic did not derive its word for "scribe" from an Akkadian word that never had such a meaning. On the contrary, it was Akkadian that borrowed the term *sipirru* "scribe" from West-Semitic (cf. Landsberger *apud* H. H. Schaeder, *Esra der Schreiber* [Tübingen, 1930], p. 39, n. 2).

P. 190, n. 2. For Canaanite gods in Egypt, cf. R. Stadelmann, *Syrisch palästinensische Gottheiten in Ägypten* (*Probleme der Ägyptologie* 5; Leiden, 1967).

P. 190, n. 5. Cf. also M. Noël Aimé-Giron, *Textes araméens d'Égypte*, pp. 54-63; G. Posener, *La première domination perse en Égypte* (Cairo, 1936); E. Bresciani, "Ägypten und das Perserreich," in *Fischer Weltgeschichte*, V, pp. 311 ff.; E. Bresciani and M. Kamil, *Le lettere aramaiche di Hermopoli* (Rome, 1966).

P. 191, n. 2. Cf. H. L. Ginsberg, "Isaiah in the Light of History," *Conservative Judaism* [The Jewish Theological Seminary, New York City], 22 (1967), p. 16.

P. 191, n. 4. The NA background of the biblical double document is paralleled by possible NA influences on the covenant-form of the Deuteronomist. Cf. M. Weinfeld, "Traces of Assyrian Treaty Formulae in Deuteronomy," *Biblica*, 46 (1965), pp. 417 ff. Cf. also R. Frankena, "The Vassal-Treaties of Esarhaddon," *Oudtestamentische Studiën*, XIV, pp. 140-150.

P. 191, n. 5. Cf. Elisabeth Koffmahn, *Die Doppelurkunden aus der Wüste Juda* (Leiden, 1968), pp. 10-30 for a discussion of the nature and possible origins of this type of deed. The cuneiform background of the biblical double document is rejected without any serious discussion of the problem.

P. 193, n. 3. Ginsberg's interpretation of the Nabatean grave inscriptions as legal documents is independently confirmed by a study of their main operative clause: "PN (the donee) or no other man shall be allowed (*ršy* = Elephantine *šlyṭ*) to sell this tomb or to write a deed of gift, or anything else, to any man except that one of them write for his wife, or for his daughters . . ." (Cooke, *A Text-Book of North-Semitic Inscriptions*, No. 89 and *passim*). The virtual identity of this clause with the Elephantine and Arsacid transfer clause (cf. above, pp. 41n and 134n), and with similar clauses found in Dead Sea documents (cf. Milik, *Biblica*, 38 [1957], p. 259 and *Les grottes de Murabbaʿat* 30:22-23) is unmistakable. For the use of *ršh* as an equivalent of *mlk/šlṭ* in Old Aramaic, cf. Sefîre III 9 (already recognized by J. A. Fitzmyer, *The Aramaic Inscriptions of Sefîre* [Rome, 1967], p. 112). The verb *ršh* with the meaning "to have authority over" is employed in synonymous parallelism with *šlṭ* in one of the apocryphal psalms of Qumran: *ʾl tšlṭ by śṭn wrwḥ ṭmʾh mkʾwb wyṣr rʿ ʾl yršw bʿṣmy* "Let not Satan rule over me nor an unclean spirit; neither let pain nor the evil inclination rule my limbs" (cf. J. A. Sanders, *The Psalms Scroll of Qumran Cave* 11 [Oxford, 1965], p. 40, lines 15-16 and p. 77, lines 15-16). Although Sanders evidently took *yršw* from *yrš* "to inherit," A. Bendavid, *Biblical Hebrew and Mishnaic Hebrew* (Devir; Tel-Aviv, 1967), p. 85 (in Hebrew) and J. Goldstein, *JNES* (1967), p. 301, are certainly correct in deriving the word from *ršh*.

For other cuneiform-Nabatean affinities, note *tqp* "a valid document" (Cooke, 79:3), probably a loan-translation from the NA *dannitu* (so also, J. Greenfield, independently).

P. 194n. For the idiom *abāram ana pīšu išappakū*, cf. the Alalakh texts cited in *CAD*, *A*, p. 36b.

BIBLIOGRAPHY AND ABBREVATIONS

AASOR: *The Annual of the American Schools of Oriental Research.*
ABAW: *Abhandlungen der Bayerischen Akademie der Wissenschaften.*
ADD: Johns, C. H. W., *Assyrian Deeds and Documents.* Four Vols. Cambridge, 1898-1923.
AfO: *Archiv für Orientforschung.*
AHDO: *Archives d'Histoire du Droit Oriental.*
AHw: Von Soden, W., *Akkadisches Handwörterbuch.*
AJSL: *American Journal of Semitic Languages and Literatures.*
Alexander, *BIN* VII: Alexander, J. B., *Early Babylonian Letters and Economic Texts.* New Haven, 1943.
Alt, *Kleine Schriften*: Alt, A., *Kleine Schriften zur Geschichte des Volkes Israels.* Three Vols. Munich, 1953-1959.
Altheim-Stiehl, *Die aramäische Sprache*: Altheim, F. and Stiehl, R. *Die aramäische Sprache unter den Achaimeniden.* Frankfurt am Main, 1963.
Altheim-Stiehl, *Supplementum Aramaicum*: Altheim, F. and Stiehl, R., *Supplementum Aramäicum. Aramäisches aus Iran.* Baden-Baden, 1963.
ANET: *Ancient Near Eastern Texts Relating to the Old Testament,* ed. J. Pritchard. Second edition. Princeton, 1955.
AO: Inventory mark of a Louvre collection of cuneiform tablets.
AOS: *American Oriental Society.*
AP: Cowley, A., *The Aramaic Papyri of the Fifth Century B.C.* Oxford, 1923.
APAW: *Abhandlungen der Preussischen Akademie der Wissenschaften.*
ÄRg: Seidl, *Ägyptische Rechtsgeschichte.*
ARM: *Archives Royales de Mari.*
ARN: Çiğ, M.; Kizilyay, H.; and Kraus, F. R., *Altbabylonische Rechtsurkunden aus Nippur.* Istanbul, 1952 (in Turkish).
Aro, *Glossar*: Aro, J., *Glossar zu den mittelbabylonischen Briefen.* Helsinki, 1957 (= *Studia Orientalia* 22).
ArOr: *Archiv Orientální.*
ARU: Kohler, J., and Ungnad, A., *Assyrische Rechtsurkunden in Umschrift und Uebersetzung nebst einem index der Personen-Namen und Rechtserlaüterungen.* Leipzig, 1913.
Aruk: *Aruch Completum,* ed. A. Kohut. New York, 1955 (reprint).
Asaf, *Formulary*: *The Formulary of Hai Gaon,* ed. S. Asaf in the Supplement to *Tarbiz,* 1 (1930) (in Hebrew).
ASAW: *Abhandlungen der Sächsischen Akademie der Wissenschaften.*
AT: *Alalakh Tablets.*
Augapfel, *Babylonische Rechtsurkunden*: Augapfel, J., *Babylonische Rechtsurkunden aus der Regierungszeit Artaxerxes I. und Darius II.* Wien, 1917 (= *Denkschriften der Kaiserlichen Akademie der Wissenschaften in Wien,* 59).

BA: *The Biblical Archaologist.*
Barth, J., "Babyl.-assyr., *ra-a-mu* ,lieben' ", *ZA*, 22 (1909), pp. 1-5.
——, "Bemerkungen zu den aramaeischen Papyri von Assuan," *Revue Sémitique,* 15 (1907), pp. 522-524.
BASOR: *Bulletin of the American Schools of Oriental Research.*
Bauer, H., and Meissner, B., "Ein aramäischer Pachtvertrag aus dem 7. Jahre Darius' I.," *SPAW*, 1936, pp. 414-424.
Bauer, W., Die Frühgeschichte des Eigentums in China," *ZVRW*, 63 (1961), pp. 118-184.

BE: *The Babylonian Expedition of the University of Pennsylvania*, Series A.
Belser, *Kudurru-Inschriften*: Belser, C. W., "Babylonische *Kudurru*-Inschriften," *Beiträge zur Assyriologie*, 2 (1894), pp. 111-203.
Ben-Ḥayyim, *Documents*: Ben-Ḥayyim, Z., "The Documents of Elephantine," in the *Encyclopaedia Biblica* (in Hebrew), III. Jerusalem, 1958, pp. 425-439.
Benoit P., Milik J. T., and de Vaux R.; cf. *Les grottes de Murabbaʿât*.
Ben Yehuda: *A Complete Dictionary of Ancient and Modern Hebrew by Eliezer Ben Yehuda*. Tel-Aviv, 1950.
Benveniste, É., "Élémentes perses en araméen d'Égypte," *JA* 242 (1954), pp. 297-310.
Bickerman, E. J., "Two Legal Interpretations of the Septuagint," *RIDA*, 3e série, 3 (1956), pp. 81-104.
BIE: *Bulletin de l'Institut de l'Égypte*.
BIES: *Bulletin of the Israel Exploration Society* (Hebrew) (= *Yediot*).
BIN: *Babylonian Inscriptions in the Collection of James B. Nies*, Yale University.
BiOr: *Bibliotheca Orientalis*.
Blau, L., "The Aramaic Papyri of Assuan in the Light of the Talmud," *Magyar-Zsidó Szemle*, 24 (1907), pp. 222-38; *ibid.*, 25 (1908), pp. 236-261; *ibid*, 29 (1912), pp. 41-67.
Blau, *Judaica*: Blau, L., "Zur demotischen und griechischen Papyrusurkunde," *Judaica*: *Festschrift zu Hermann Cohens siebzigstem Geburtstage*. Berlin, 1912, pp. 207-226.
Blau, L., "More New Papyri from Assuan," *Magyar-Zsidó Szemle*, 29 (1912), pp. 41-63 (in Hungarian).
Bloomfield, *Language*: Bloomfield, L., *Language*. New York, 1956.
BM: British Museum.
Böllenrücher, *Gebete*: Böllenrücher, J., *Gebete und Hymnen an Nergal*. Leipzig, 1904 (= *LSS* 1/6).
Bottero-Finet, *ARM*, XV: Bottero, J., and Finet, A., *ARM* XV: *Répertoire analytique des tomes I à V*. Paris, 1954.
Bowman, R. A., "Arameans, Aramaic, and the Bible," *JNES*, 7 (1948), pp. 65-90.
Boyer, *ARM* VIII: Boyer, G., *Archives royales de Mari* VIII: *Textes juridiques*. Paris, 1958.
Boyer, *Contribution*: Boyer, G., *Contribution à l'histoire juridique de la Ire dynastie babylonienne*. Paris, 1928.
Boyer, *Emplois de fiction*: Boyer, G., "Sur quelques emplois de la fiction dans l'ancien droit oriental," *RIDA*, 3e série, 1 (1954), pp. 73-100.
Boyer, *Formation de vente*: Boyer, G., "Nature et formation de la vente dans l'ancien droit babylonien," *AHDO+RIDA*, 2 (1953), pp. 45-85.
Boyer, G., "Introduction bibliographique à l'histoire du droit suméro-akkadien", *AHDO*, 2 (1938), pp. 63-110.
——, "Introduction bibliographique à l'histoire du droit suméro-akkadien II (1939-1955)," *RIDA*, 3e série, 3 (1956), pp. 41-79.
BP: Kraeling, E., *The Brooklyn Museum Aramaic Papyri*. New Haven, 1953 (often abbreviated in other works as *BMAP*).
BRM: *Babylonian Records in the Library of J. P. Morgan*.
Buhl, F., "Remarques sur les papyrus juifs d'Éléphantine," *Danske Videnskabernes Selskabs, Forhandlinger*, 1908, No. 2, pp. 37-64.

CAD: *Chicago Assyrian Dictionary*.
Cardascia, *Les Archives des Murašû*: Cardascia, G., *Les archives des Murašû. Une famille d'hommes d'affaires babyloniens à l'époque perse* (455-403 *av. J.-C.*). Paris, 1951.
Cardascia, *Propriété*: Cardascia, G., "Le concept babylonien de la propriété," *RIDA*, 3e série, 6 (1959), pp. 19-32.

Cassin, *Adoption*: Cassin, E. M., *L'adoption à Nuzi*. Paris, 1938.

Cassin, *Symboles de cession*: Cassin, E. M., "Symboles de cession immobilière dans l'ancien droit mésopotamien," *Année Sociologique*, 1952 (appeared in 1955), pp. 107-161.

Cassuto, U., "Biblical and Canaanite Literature," *Tarbiẓ*, 13 (1941), pp. 197-212; *ibid.*, 14 (1942), pp. 1-10 (in Hebrew).

Cazelles, H., "Nouveaux documents araméens d'Égypte," *Syria*, 32 (1955), pp. 75-100.

CBS: Tablets in the Collections of the University Museum of the University of Pennsylvania.

CH: *The Code of Hammurabi*.

Chiera, *UM* VIII/2: Chiera, E., *Old Babylonian Contracts*, Philadelphia, 1922.

Çiğ, M.; Kizilyay, H.; and Falkenstein, A., "Neue Rechts- und Gerichtsurkunden der Ur III-Zeit aus Lagaš aus den Sammlungen der Istanbuler Archäologischen Museen," *ZA*, 19 (1959), pp. 51-92.

Çiğ, M.; Kizilyay, H.; and Kraus, F. R., *Altbabylonische Rechtsurkunden aus Nippur*. Istanbul, 1952 (= *ARN*).

The City Invincible: *The City Invincible. A Symposium on Urbanization and Cultural Development in the Ancient Near East Held at the Oriental Institute of the University of Chicago, December 4-7, 1958*, ed. C. H. Kraeling and R. M. Adams. Chicago, 1960.

Clermont-Ganneau, Ch., *Revue Critique d'Histoire*, 1906, p. 341.

Como: F. Ballerini, "Antichità assiro-babilonesi nel Museo Civico di Como," *Rivista degli Studi Orientali*, 1909, pp. 539 ff.

Couroyer, B., "Termes égyptiens dans les papyri araméens du musée de Brooklyn," *RB*, 61 (1954), pp. 554-559.

Cowley, *AP*: Cowley, A., *The Aramaic Papyri of the Fifth Century B.C.* Oxford, 1923.

Cross, F. M., "The Discovery of the Samaria Papyri," *BA*, 26 (1963), pp. 110-120.

CT: *Cuneiform Texts from Babylonian Tablets in the British Museum*.

Cuq, E., "Les actes juridiques susiens," *RA*, 28 (1931), pp. 47-71.

——, "Commentaire juridique d'un jugement sous Ammi-ditana," *RA*, 7 (1908/10), pp. 129-138.

——, "Le droit élamite d'après les actes juridiques de Suse," *RA*, 29 (1932), pp. 149-182.

Cuq, *Études*: *Études sur le droit babylonien, les lois assyriennes et les lois hittites*. Paris, 1929.

Daube, D., review of Rabinowitz, *Jewish Law* in *JSS*, 2 (1957), pp. 407-408.

David, *Adoption*: David, M., *Die Adoption im altbabylonischen Recht*. Leipzig, 1927 (= *LRS* 23).

David, M., and Ebeling, E., *Assyrische Rechtsurkunden*. Stuttgart, 1929.

Deimel, *Fara*: Deimel, A., *Wirtschaftstexte aus Fara*. Leipzig, 1924 (= *WVDOG* 45).

Deimel, *Grammatik*: Deimel, P. A., *Šumerische Grammatik mit Übungsstücken und zwei Anhängen*. Second edition. Rome, 1939.

Delaporte, *Épigraphes araméens*: Delaporte, L., *Épigraphes araméens. Étude des textes araméens gravés ou écrits sur des tablettes cunéiformes*. Paris, 1912.

Deller, *Terminologie*: Deller, K., "Zur Terminologie neuassyrischer Urkunden," *WZKM*, 57 (1961), pp. 29-42.

Derret, J. D. M., "The Development of the Concept of Property in India c. A.D. 800-1800," *ZVRG*, 64 (1962), pp. 15-130.

Dhorme, P., "L'emploi métaphorique des noms de parties du corps en hébreu et en akkadien," *RB*, 29 (1920), pp. 465-506; *ibid.*, 30 (1921), pp. 374-399; *ibid.*, pp. 517-540; *ibid.*, 31 (1922), pp. 215-223; *ibid.*, pp. 240-517; *ibid.*, 32 (1923), pp. 185-212.

Djakonov, I. M., "Sale of Land in the Most Ancient Sumer and the Problem of the Sumerian Rural Community," *Vestnik Drevney Istorii*, 1951/2-1954/6, pp. 10-40.

DJE 1: Pirenne, J., and Van de Walle, B., "Documents juridiques égyptiens I. vente et louage de services," *AHDO*, 1 (1937), pp. 3-86.

DJE 2: Malinine, M., and Pirenne, J., "Documents juridiques égyptiens (deuxième série)," *AHDO*, 5 (1950), pp. 11-91.

DLZ: *Deutsche Literaturzeitung*.

Doresse, J., *The Secret Books of the Egyptian Gnostics*, trans. P. Mariet. New York, 1960.

Dossin, G., "L'article 142/143 du code de Hammurabi," *RA*, 42 (1948), pp. 113-124.

DP: Allotte de la Füye, M. F., *Documents présargoniques*. Paris, 1908.

Draffkorn, A., "Was King Abba-AN of Yamḫad a Vizier for the King of Ḫattuša?," *JCS*, 13 (1959), pp. 94-97.

Driver, *Aramaic Documents*: Driver, G. R., *Aramaic Documents of the Fifth Century B.C.* Oxford, 1957.

Driver, G. R., "The Aramaic *Papyri* from Egypt: Notes on Obscure Passages," *JRAS*, 1932, pp. 77-90.

——, review of Kraeling, *BP* in *PEQ*, 87 (1955), pp. 91-94.

——, and Miles, J. C., *The Babylonian Laws*. Two Vols. Oxford, 1935-1952.

Driver, *Tenses*: Driver, S. R., *A Treatise on the Use of the Tenses in Hebrew And Some Other Syntactical Questions*. Third edition, revised. Oxford, 1892.

Dupont-Sommer, A., "Un contrat de métayage égypto-arameén de l'an 7 de Darius Ier," *MAT*, 14^2 (1944), pp. 1-46.

——,"Un papyrus araméen d'époque Saïte découvert à Saqqarah," *Semitica*, 1 (1948), pp. 43-69.

Durrell, L., *Bitter Lemons*. New York, 1957.

Ebeling, *Glossar*: Ebeling, E., *Das aramäisch-mittelpersische Glossar Frahang-i-Pahlavik im Lichte der assyriologische Forschung*. Leipzig, 1941 (= *MAOG* 14).

Ebeling, *Kaufurkunden*: Ebeling, E., *Urkunden des Archivs von Assur aus mittelassyrischer Zeit. III. Assyrische Kauf-, Zessions- und Schenkungsurkunden*. Leipzig, 1933 (= *MAOG* 7).

Ebeling, E., and Korošec, V., "Ehe," in *RLA*, II, pp. 281-299.

Edzard, D. O., "Sumerer und Semiten in der frühen Geschichte Mesopotamiens," *Genava*, 8 (1960), pp. 241-258.

Edzard, *ZZB*: Edzard, D. O., *Die „zweite Zwischenzeit" Babyloniens*. Wiesbaden, 1957.

Ehrlich, *Randglossen*: Ehrlich, A., *Randglossen zur hebräischen Bibel*. Seven Vols. Berlin, 1908-1914.

Eilers, *Gesellschaft*: Eilers, W., *Gesellschaftsformen im altbabylonischen Recht*. Leipzig, 1931 (= *LRS* 65).

EL: Eisser, G., and Lewy, J., *Die altassyrischen Rechtsurkunden vom Kültepe*. Four Vols. Leipzig, 1930-1935 (= *MVAG* 33 and 35).

ENAN: *Enannatum*.

Epstein, J. N., "Notizen zu den jüdisch-aramäischen Papyri von Assuan," *JJLG*, 6 (1908/09), pp. 359-373.

Epstein, *Jewish Marriage Contract*: Epstein, L. M., *The Jewish Marriage Contract: A Study in the Status of the Woman in Jewish Law*. New York, 1927.

Euting, J., "Notice sur un papyrus égypto-araméen de la Bibliothèque Impériale de Strasbourg," *MAI*, 11 (1903), pp. 297-311.

Falkenstein, A., "La cité-temple sumérienne," *Cahiers d'Histoire Mondiale*, 1 (1954), pp. 784-814.

Falkenstein, *Grammatik*: Falkenstein, A., *Grammatik der Sprache Gudeas*. Two Vols. Rome, 1949-50 (= *Analecta Orientalia* 28-29).

Falkenstein, A., "Kontakte zwischen Sumerern und Akkadern auf sprachlichem Gebiet", *Genava*, 8 (1960), pp. 301-314.
——, *Die neusumerischen Gerichtsurkunden*. Three Vols. Munich, 1956-57 (= *ABAW* 39, 40, and 44).
——, "Zum sumerischen Tempussystem," *OLZ*, 34 (1931), pp. 791-794.
Faust, *YBT* 8: Faust, D. E., *Contracts from Larsa Dated in the Reign of Rîm-Sin*. New Haven, 1941.
Figulla-Martin, *UET* 5: Figulla, H. H., and Martin, W. J., *Letters and Documents of the Old-Babylonian Period*. London, 1953 (= *Publications of the Joint Expedition of the British Museum and of the University Museum, University of Pennsylvania, Philadelphia, to Mesopotamia*).
Finkelstein, J. J., "Ammiṣaduqa's Edict and the Babylonian 'Law Codes'," *JCS*, 15 (1961), pp. 91-104.
Fischer, L., "Glossen zu den jüdisch-aramäischen Papyri von Assuan," *JJLG*, 8 (1910/11), pp. 371-377.
——, "Die Urkunden im Talmud, zusammengestellt, erklärt und mit den Ausgrabungen verglichen," *JJLG*, 9 (1911/12), pp. 45-197; *ibid.*, 13 (1920), pp. 1-54; *ibid.*, 19 (1928), pp. 113-194; *ibid.*, 20 (1929), pp. 71-97.
Frankfort, *Birth of Civilization*: Frankfort, H., *The Birth of Civilization in the Near East*. New York, 1956.
Freund, L., "Bemerkungen zu Papyrus G. des Fundes von Assuan," *WZKM*, 21 (1907), pp. 169-177.
——, *Zur Geschichte des Ehegüterrechtes bei den Semiten*. Vienna, 1909 (= *Sitzungsberichte der Kaiserlichen Akademie der Wissenschaften*, 162/1).
——, "Zum semitischen Ehegüterrecht bei Auflösung der Ehe," *WZKM*, 30 (1917/18), pp. 163-176.
Friedrich, J.; Meier, G. R.; Ungnad, A.; Weidner, E. F., *Die Inschriften von Tell Halaf. Keilschrifttexte und aramäische Urkunden aus einer assyrischen Provinzhauptstadt*. Berlin, 1940 (= *AfO, Beiheft* 6).

Gautier, *Archives de Dilbat*: Gautier, M., *Archives d'une famille de Dilbat au temps de la première dynastie de Babylone*. Cairo, 1908 (= *Mémoires publiés par les membres de l'Institut Français d'Archéologie Orientale du Caire*, 26).
Gelb, *Akkadian Inscriptions*: Gelb, I. J., *Old Akkadian Inscriptions in the Chicago Natural History Museum. Texts of Legal and Business Interest*. Chicago, 1955 (= *Fieldiana: Anthropology* 44/2).
Gelb, *MAD* I: Gelb, I. J., *Sargonic Texts from the Diyala Region*. Chicago, 1952.
Gelb, *MAD* II: Gelb, I. J., *Old Akkadian Writing and Grammar*. Chicago, 1952.
Gelb, *MAD* III: Gelb, I. J., *Glossary of Old Akkadian*. Chicago, 1957.
Gelb, I. J., "Social Stratification in the Old Akkadian Period," *Proceedings of the International Congress of Orientalists*. Moscow, 1962, pp. 225-226.
——, "Sumerians and Akkadians in their Ethno-Linguistic Relationship," *Genava*, 8 (1960), pp. 258-271.
Gershevitch, I., "A Parthian Title in the Hymn of the Soul," *JRAS*, 1954, pp. 124-126.
Ginsberg, H. L., "An Aramaic Contemporary of the Lachish Letters," *BASOR*, 111 (1948), pp. 24-27.
——, "Aramaic Dialect Problems," *AJSL*, 50 (1933), pp. 1-9.
——, "Aramaic Dialect Problems: II," *AJSL*, 52 (1936), pp. 95-103.
——, "Aramaic Studies Today," *JAOS*, 62 (1942), pp. 229-238.
——, "The Brooklyn Museum Aramaic Papyri," *JAOS*, 74 (1954), pp. 153-162.
——, *Koheleth*. Tel Aviv-Jerusalem, 1961 (in Hebrew).
——, and Abramson, S., "On the Aramaic Deed of Sale of the Third Year of the Second Jewish Revolt," *BASOR*, 136 (1954), pp. 17-19.

Goetze, *Hethiter*: Götze, A., *Hethiter, Churriter und Assyrer. Hauptlinien der vorderasiatischen Kulturentwicklung im II. Jahrtausend v. Chr. Geb.* Oslo, 1938.

Goetze, *Kleinasien*: Goetze, A., *Kleinasien*. Second edition. Munich, 1957 (= *Kulturgeschichte des Alten Orients* 3/1).

Gordon, *Smith College Tablets*: Gordon, C., *Smith College Tablets. 110 Cuneiform Texts Selected from the College Collection.* Northhampton, Mass., 1952 (= *Smith College Studies in History* 38).

Greenberg, M., "Ezekiel 17 and the Policy of Psammetichus II," *JBL*, 76 (1957), pp. 304-309.

Greenberg, *Postulates*: Greenberg, M., "Some Postulates of Biblical Criminal Law," *Kaufmann Jubilee Volume*, pp. 5-28.

Greenfield, J. C., "Studies in Aramaic Lexicography I," *JAOS*, 82 (1962), pp. 290-299.

Griffith, *Catalogue of Demotic Papyri*: Griffith, F. L., *Catalogue of the Demotic Papyri in the John Rylands Library*. London, 1909.

GRÖG: Cf. Koschaker.

Grohmann, A. *Arabic Papyri in the Egyptian Library*. Vol. I: *Protocols and Legal Texts*. Cairo, 1934.

Les grottes de Murabbaʿât: Benoit, P.; Milik, J. T.; de Vaux, R., *Les grottes de Murabbaʿât*. Oxford, 1961 (= *Discoveries in the Judean Desert* 2).

Gulak, A., "Deed of a Sale of a Slave in Talmudic Law," *Tarbiẓ*, 4 (1932), pp. 1-10 (in Hebrew).

Gulak, A., *The History of Jewish Law During the Talmudic Period. Part I: the Law of Immobilia*. Jerusalem, 1929 (in Hebrew).

Gulak, *Jewish Law*: Gulak, A., *The Principles of Jewish Law*. Four Vols. Berlin-Jerusalem, 1922 (in Hebrew).

Gulak, *Urkundenwesen*: Gulak, A., *Das Urkundenwesen im Talmud im Lichte der griechisch-aegyptischen Papyri und des griechischen und roemischen Rechts*. Jerusalem, 1935.

Gunkel, H., *Genesis*. Göttingen, 1901 (= *Handkommentar zum Alten Testament*, I. Abtheilung, 1 Band).

Hackman, *BIN* VIII: Hackman, G. G., *Sumerian and Akkadian Administrative Texts from Predynastic Times to the End of the Akkad Dynasty*. New Haven, 1958.

Harris, *Khafajah*: Harris, R., "The Archives of the Sin Temple in Khafajah (Tutub)," *JCS*, 9 (1955), pp. 31-120 (offprint).

Helck, *Die Beziehungen*: Helck, W., *Die Beziehungen Ägyptens zu Vorderasien im 3. und 2. Jahrtausend v. Chr.* Wiesbaden, 1962 (= *Ägyptische Abhandlungen* 5).

Held, M., "The Action-Result (Factitive-Passive) Sequence of Identical Verbs in Biblical Hebrew and Ugaritic," *JBL*, 84 (1965), pp. 272-282.

——, "*mḫṣ*/**mḫš* in Ugaritic and Other Semitic Languages (A Study in Comparative Lexicography)," *JAOS*, 79 (1959), pp. 169-176.

Henninger, J., "Das Eigentumsrecht bei den heutigen Beduinen Arabiens," *ZVRW*, 61 (1959), pp. 6-56.

Heubner, *Germanic Private Law*: Heubner, R., *A History of Germanic Private Law*, trans. F. S. Philbrick. Boston, 1918 (= *The Continental Legal History Series* 4).

HG: Kohler, J.; Peiser, F. E.; Ungnad, A.; and Koschaker, P., *Hammurabi's Gesetz*. Leipzig, 1909-1923. Otherwise quoted as *KU*.

Hilgers-Hesse, I., "Das Eigentumsrecht bei den Toba-Batak in Nord-Sumatria," *ZVRW*, 63 (1961), pp. 185-217.

Hinke, *Boundary Stone*: Hinke, W. J., *A New Boundary Stone of Nebuchadrezzar I. From Nippur*. Philadelphia, 1907 (= *BE*, Series D, 4).

HSM: Cuneiform tablets in the Harvard Semitic Museum.

Hoffmann, *Midrasch Tannaïm*: Hoffmann, D., *Midrasch Tannaïm zum Déuteronomium*. Berlin, 1908/09.

Honeyman, A. M., "*Merismus* in Biblical Hebrew," *JBL*, 71 (1952), pp. 11-18.

Honroth, W.; Rubensohn, O.; and Zucker, F., "Bericht über die Ausgrabungen auf Elephantine in den Jahren 1906-1908," *ZAS*, 46 (1909-10), pp. 14-61.
Hrozný, B., "Über eine unveröffentlichte Urkunde von Kültepe (ca. 2000 v. Chr.)," *Symbolae Koschaker*, pp. 108-111.
——, "Un nouveau texte juridique du Kultépé (environ 2000 avant J.-C.)," *AHDO*, 1 (1937), pp. 87-90.
HSS: *Harvard Semitic Series*.

IEJ: *Israel Exploration Journal*.
IURA. *Rivista Internazionale di Diritto Romano e Antico*.

JA: *Journal Asiatique*.
Jacobsen, T., "The Assumed Conflict Between Sumerians and Semites in Early Mesopotomian History," *JAOS*, 59 (1939), pp. 485-495.
——, "Introduction to Chicago Grammatical Texts," *MSL* IV, pp. 1*-50*.
Jacobsen, *Notes on Eshnunna*: Jacobsen, T., *Philological Notes on Eshnunna and Its Inscriptions*. Chicago, 1934 (= *OIAS* 6).
Jacobsen, T., "Sumerian Mythology: A Review Article," *JNES*, 5 (1946), pp. 128-152.
JAOS: *Journal of the American Oriental Society*.
JBL: *Journal of Biblical Literature*.
JCS: *Journal of Cuneiform Studies*.
JEA: *Journal of Egyptian Archaology*.
Jean, *Larsa*: Jean, C. F., *Larsa d'après les textes cunéiformes *2187 à *1901*. Paris, 1931.
JEN: *Joint Expedition with the Iraq Museum at Nuzi* (sometimes listed as *N*).
Jestin, *Verbe*: Jestin, R., *Le verbe sumérien, déterminations verbales et infixes*. Paris, 1943
JJLG: *Jahrbuch der Jüdisch-Literarischen Gesellschaft*.
JJP: *Journal of Juristic Papyrology*.
JJS: *Journal of Jewish Studies*.
JNES: *Journal of Near Eastern Studies*.
JRAS: *Journal of the Royal Asiatic Society*.
JSS: *Journal of Semitic Studies*.

KAJ: Ebeling, E., *Keilschrifttexte aus Assur juristischen Inhalts*. Leipzig, 1927 (= *WVDOG* 50).
Kaufmann Jubilee Volume: *The Yehezkel Kaufmann Jubilee Volume*, ed. M. Haran Jerusalem, 1960.
KB: *Keilinschriftliche Bibliothek*.
Kelm, H., "Die Eigentumsrechte auf Samoa (Polynesien)," *ZVRW*, 64 (1962), pp. 131-230.
Kienitz: Kienitz, F., K., *Die politische Geschichte Ägyptens vom 7. bis zum 4. Jahrhundert vor der Zeitwende*. Berlin, 1953.
King, *BBSt*: King, L. W., *Babylonian Boundary-Stones and Memorial-Tablets in the British Museum*. London, 1912.
Klíma, J., "Bibliographisches zum Keilschriftrecht," *JJP*, 6 (1952), pp. 153-184.
——, "Bibliographisches zum Keilschriftrecht II," *JJP*, 7/8 (1953-54), pp. 295 356.
——, "Bibliographisches zum Keilschriftrecht III," *JJP*, 9/10 (1955-56), pp. 431-475.
——, "Bibliographisches zum Keilschriftrecht IV," *JJP*, 11/12 (1957-58), pp. 195 ff.
——, "Bibliographisches zum Keilschriftrecht V," *JJP*, 13 (1961), pp. 269-290.
Klíma, *Donationes*: Klíma, J., "Donationes mortis causa nach den akkadischen Rechtsurkunden aus Susa," *Festschrift Johannes Friedrich*, Heidelberg, 1959, pp. 229-259.

Klíma, *Elamischen Erbrecht*: Klíma, J., "Untersuchungen zum elamischen Erbrecht," *ArOr*, 28 (1960), pp. 5-54.

Klíma, J., "Über neuere Studien auf dem Gebiete des Keilschriftrechtes," *ArOr*, 18^{1-2} (1950), pp. 525-538.

——, "Über neuere Studien auf dem Gebiete des Keilschriftrechtes II," *ArOr*, 18^{4} (1950), pp. 351-366.

——, "Über neuere Studien auf dem Gebiete des Keilschriftsrechtes III," *ArOr*, 20 (1952), pp. 539-571.

——, "Über neuere Studien auf dem Gebiete des Keilschriftsrechtes IV," *ArOr*, 21 (1953), pp. 604-640.

——, "Über neuere Studien auf dem Gebiete des Keilschriftsrechtes V," *ArOr*, 26 (1957), pp. 224-242.

Klíma, *Reglung des Kaufs*: Klíma, J., "Einige Bemerkungen zur Reglung des Kaufes nach den vorḫammurapischen Gesetzen," *AHDO + RIDA*, 2 (1953), pp. 87-108.

Klíma, J., *Untersuchungen*: *Untersuchungen zum altbabylonischen Erbrecht*. Prag, 1940 (= Monographien des *Archiv Orientální* 8).

Kohler-Ungnad, *ARU*: Kohler, J., and Ungnad, A., *Assyrische Rechtsurkunden in Umschrift und Uebersetzung nebst einem Index der Personen-Namen und Rechtserläuterungen*. Leipzig, 1913.

Koopmans, J. J., *Aramäische Chrestomathie. Ausgewählte Texte (Inschriften, Ostraca und Papyri) bis zum 3. Jahrhundert n. Chr.* Two Vols. Leiden, 1962 (= *Nederlands Instituut voor het Nabije Oosten*).

Korngreen, P., *Jewish Military Colonies in Antiquity*. Tel-Aviv, 1948 (in Hebrew).

Korošec, V., "Le Code de Ḫammurabi et les droits antérieurs," *RIDA*, 3e série, 8 (1961), pp. 11-27.

Korošec, *Keilschriftrecht*: Korošec, V., "Keilschriftrecht," *Orientalisches Recht*. Leiden-Köln, 1964 (= *Handbuch der Orientalistik*, ed. B. Spuler, Erste Abteilung, Ergangzungsband 3).

Koschaker, *Begriff des Kaufs*: Koschaker, P., "Begriff des Kaufs nach keilschriftlichen Rechtsurkunden des 3. Jahrtausends v. Chr.," *Jahrbuch der Preussischen Akademie der Wissenschaften*, 1941. Berlin, 1942, pp. 118-119.

Koschaker, *Bürgschaftsrecht*: Koschaker, P., *Babylonisch-assyrisches Bürgschaftsrecht*. Leipzig, 1911.

Koschaker, *Eheschliessung*: Koschaker, P., "Eheschliessung und Kauf nach alten Rechten, mit besonderer Berücksichtigung der älteren Keilschriftrechte," *ArOr*, 18^{3} (1950), pp. 210-216.

Koschaker, *Göttliches Recht*: Koschaker, P., "Göttliches und weltliches Recht nach den Urkunden aus Susa. Zugleich ein Beitrag zu ihrer Chronologie," *Or*, 4 (1935), pp. 38-80.

Koschaker, *GRÖG*: Koschaker, P., *Über einige griechische Rechtsurkunden aus den östlichen Randgebieten des Hellenismus*. Leipzig, 1931 (= *ASAW* 42).

——, "Zur Interpretation des Art. 59 des Codex Bilalama," *JCS*, 5 (1951), pp. 104-122.

Koschaker, *Keilschriftrecht*: Koschaker, P., "Keilschriftrecht," *ZDMG*, 89 (1935), pp. 1-39.

Koschaker, *NKRA*: Koschaker, P., *Neue keilschriftliche Rechtsurkunden aus der El-Amarna-Zeit*. Leipzig, 1928 (= *ASAW* 39).

Koschaker, *Randnotizen*: Koschaker, P., "Randnotizen zu neueren keilschriftlichen Rechtsurkunden," *ZA* 9 (1936), pp. 196-232.

Koschaker, *Rechtsvergleichende Studien*: Koschaker, P., *Rechtsvergleichende Studien zur Gesetzgebung Ḫammurapis Königs von Babylon*. Leipzig, 1917.

Koschaker, P., review of Scheil, *MDP* XXII in *OLZ* 35 (1932), pp. 318-321.

Kraeling, *BP*: Kraeling, E., *The Brooklyn Museum Aramaic Papyri*. New Haven, 1953.

Krall, J., "Zwei koptische Verkaufsurkunden," *WZKM*, 2 (1888), pp. 273-280.
Kramer, S. N., "Sumerian Historiography," *IEJ*, 3 (1953), pp. 217-232.
——, "Sumero-Akkadian Interconnections: Religious Ideas," *Genava*, 8 (1960), pp. 272-283.
Kraus, *Ammi-Ṣaduqa*: Kraus, F. R., *Ein Edikt des Königs Ammi-Ṣaduqa von Babylon*. Leiden, 1958 (= *Studia et Documenta* 5).
Kraus, F. R., "Ein zentrales Problem des altmesopotamischen Rechtes: Was ist der Codex Hammu-rabi?," *Genava*, 8 (1960), pp. 283-296.
——, "Neue Rechtsurkunden der altbabylonischen Zeit. Bemerkungen zu *Ur Excavation Texts* 5," *WO*, 2 (1955), pp. 120-136.
Kraus, *Nippur und Isin*: Kraus, F. R., *Nippur und Isin nach altbabylonischen Rechtsurkunden*. New Haven, 1951 (= *JCS*, 3 [1951]).
Krückmann, *BRVU*: Krückmann, O., *Babylonische Rechts- und Verwaltungs-Urkunden aus der Zeit Alexanders und der Diadochen*. Weimar, 1931.
KTS: Lewy, J., *Die altassyrischen Texte vom Kültepe*. Konstantinopel, 1926.
Kupper, *Les nomades*: Kupper, J. R., *Les nomades en Mésopotamie au temps des rois de Mari*. Paris, 1957.
Kutscher, Y., "Concerning the Terminology of Legal Documents in the Talmud and in Gaonic Literature," *Tarbiẕ*, 17 (1946), pp. 125-127; *ibid.*, 19 (1947/8), pp. 53-59; *ibid.*, pp. 125-128 (in Hebrew).
——, "Is Biblical Aramaic Eastern or Western Aramaic?,' *Lᵉšōnēnu*, 17 (1951), pp. 119-122 (in Hebrew).
Kutscher, *New Aramaic Texts*: Kutscher, Y., "New Aramaic Texts," *JAOS*, 74 (1954), pp. 233-248.
Kutscher, E. Y., review of Driver, G. R., *Aramaic Documents of the Fifth Century B.C.* in *JBL*, 76 (1957), pp. 336-338.
Kutscher, *Words*: Kutscher, Y., *Words and Their Development*. Jerusalem, 1961 (in Hebrew).

Lambert, M., "Les 'réformes' d'Urukagina," *RA*, 50 (1956), pp. 169-184.
——, "Textes commerciaux de Lagaš (III)," *ArOr*, 23 (1955), pp. 557-574.
Lambert, *Wisdom*: Lambert, W. G., *Babylonian Wisdom Literature*. Oxford, 1960.
Landsberger, *Dunkles Zeitalter*: Landsberger, B., "Assyrische Königsliste und ‚dunkles Zeitalter', " *JCS*, 8 (1954), pp. 31-73 and 106-133.
Landsberger, *Eigenbegrifflichkeit*: Landsberger, B., "Die Eigenbegrifflichkeit der babylonischen Welt," *Islamica*, 2 (1927), pp. 355-372.
Landsberger, *Gesetz und Recht*: Landsberger, B., "Die babylonischen Termini für Gesetz und Recht," *Symbolæ Koschaker*, pp. 219-234.
LAP: Yaron, R., *The Law of the Aramaic Papyri*. Oxford, 1961.
LAP (Hebrew): Yaron, R., *HaMišpāṭ BᵉMismᵉḵē Yēḇ* (The Law of the Elephantine Documents). Jerusalem, 1961.
Lautner, *Personenmiete*: Lautner, J. G., *Altbabylonische Personenmiete und Erntearbeiterverträge*. Leiden, 1936 (= *Studia et Documenta* 1).
Lautner, *Rechtsverhältnisse*: Lautner, J.G., "Rechtsverhältnisse an Grenzmauern. Studien zum Miteigentum im altbabylonischen Recht I," *Symbolae Koschaker*, pp. 76-95.
Lautner, *Streitbeendigung*: Lautner, J. G., *Die richterliche Entscheidung und die Streitbeendigung im altbabylonischen Prozessrechte*. Leipzig, 1922 (= *LRS* 3).
LE: *The Laws of Ešnunna*.
Leander: Leander, P., *Laut- und Formenlehre des Ägyptisch-Aramäischen*. Göteborg, 1928.
Leemans, *SLB* I/2: Leemans, W. F., *Legal and Economic Records from the Kingdom of Larsa*. Leiden, 1954 (= *SLB* I[/2]).
Leemans, W. F., review of Gelb, *MAD* I in *BiOr*, 12 (1955), pp. 75-77.

Leibovitch, J., "Quelques égyptianismes contenus dans les textes araméens d'Égypte," *BIE*, 18 (1936), pp. 19-29.

Lewy, H., "The Babylonian Background of the Kay Kâûs Legend," *ArOr*, 17^2 (1949), pp. 28-109.

Lewy, J., "The Biblical Institution of *D^e^rôr* in the Light of Akkadian Documents," *Eretz-Israel*, 5 (1958), pp. *21-31.

——, "Grammatical and Lexicographical Studies," *Or*, 29 (1960), pp. 20-45.

——, "Old Assyrian Documents from Asia Minor," *AHDO*, 1 (1937), pp. 91-108.

Lidzbarski, *Altaramäische Urkunden*: Lidzbarski, M., *Altaramäischen Urkunden aus Assur*. Leipzig, 1921 (= *WVDOG* 38).

Lidzbarski, *Ephemeris*: Lidzbarski, M., *Ephemeris für semitische Epigraphik*. Three Vols. Giessen, 1900-1919.

Lidzbarski, M., review of Sachau, E., *Aramäische Papyrus und Ostraka* . . ., in *DLZ*, 32 (1911), pp. 2966-1981.

——, review of Sachau, E., *Drei aramäische Papyrusurkunden aus Elephantine*, in *DLZ*, 28^2 (1907), pp. 3160-3163.

——, review of Sayce, A. H., and A. E. Cowley, *Aramaic Papyri Discovered at Assuan* in *DLZ*, 27^2 (1906), pp. 3205-3215.

Loewenstamm, S. E., "The Foundation of the Alalakh Dynasty", *BIES*, 20 (1956), pp. 13-16 (in Hebrew).

——, "Notes on the Alalakh Tablets," *IEJ*, 6 (1956), pp. 217-225.

Loretz, O., "Ugaritisches *ṣamātu* und hebräisches *ṣm(y)tt*," *Biblische Zeitschrift*, 6 (1962), pp. 269-279.

LRS: *Leipzig Rechtswissenschaftliche Studien.*

LSS: *Leipziger Semitische Studien.*

Lüddeckens: Lüddeckens, E., *Ägyptische Eheverträge*. Wiesbaden, 1960 (= *Ägyptische Abhandlungen* 1).

Lutz, *Ashjali*: Lutz, H. F., *Legal and Economic Documents from Ashjali*. Berkeley, California, 1931 (= *University of California Publications in Semitic Philology* 10).

M: Cf. Meissner, *Beiträge*.

MA: Middle Assyrian.

MAD: *Materials for the Assyrian Dictionary*; cf. Gelb.

MAH: tablets in the collection of the Musée d'Art et d'Histoire, Geneva.

MAI: *Mémoires présentés par Divers Savants à l'Académie des Inscriptions et Belles Lettres.*

Malinine, *Choix de textes*: Malinine, M., *Choix de textes juridiques en hiératique "anormal" et en démotique* (XXVe-XXVIIe *dynasties*). Première partie, Paris 1953.

Malinine, M., "Un contrat de vente d'emplacements à construire de l'époque du roi Achoris (Pap. Lille no. 26)," *Revue d'Égyptologie*, 7 (1950), pp. 107-120.

——, "Deux documents égyptiens relatifs au dépôt (P. Louvre E. 7861 et P. Caire 30657)," *MDAIK*, 16 (1958), pp. 219-229 (= *Junker Festschrift* II).

——, "Un jugement rendu à Thebes sous la XXVe dynastie," *Revue d'Égyptologie*, 6 (1957), pp. 157-178.

——, "Trois documents de l'époque d'Amasis relatifs au louage de terres," *Revue d'Égyptologie*, 8 (1951), pp. 127-150.

——, "Une vente d'esclave à l'époque de Psammétique Ier," *Revue d'Égyptologie*, 5 (1946), pp. 119-131.

——, and Pirenne, J., "Documents juridiques égyptiens (deuxième série)," *AHDO*, 5 (1950), pp. 11-91.

MAOG: *Mitteilungen der Altorientalischen Gesellschaft.*

Matouš, *Ausdrücken*: Matouš, L., "Zu den Ausdrücken für ‚Zugaben' in den vorsargonischen Grundstückkaufurkunden," *ArOr*, 22 (1954), pp. 434-443.

Matouš, L., "Zur Chronologie der Geschichte von Larsa bis zum Einfall der Elamiter," *ArOr*, 20 (1952), pp. 288-313.
Matouš, *Partage*: Matouš, L., "Les contrats de partage de Larsa provenant des archives d'Iddin-Amurrum," *ArOr*, 17² (1949), pp. 142-173.
Matouš, L., "Quelques remarques sur les récentes publications de textes cunéiformes économiques et juridiques," *ArOr*, 27 (1959), pp. 438-446.
——, "Some Remarks to the Economical Sources from Larsa (in Margine of Two Publications by W. F. Leemans)," *ArOr*, 23 (1955), pp. 465-474.
Matouš, *Vente*: Matouš, L., "Les contrats de vente d'immeubles provenant de Larsa," *ArOr*, 18⁴ (1950), pp. 11-67.
MB: Middle Babylonian.
MDAIK: *Mitteilungen des Deutschen Archäeologischen Instituts, Abteilung, Kairo.*
MDOG: *Mitteilungen der Deutschen Orientgesellschaft.*
MDP: *Mémoires de la Mission Archéologique de Perse* (= *Mémoires de la Délegation en Perse*).
Meek, T. J., translation of the Code of Hammurabi, *ANET*², pp. 163-180.
Meissner, *Beiträge*: Meissner, B., *Beiträge zum altbabylonischen Privatrecht.* Leipzig, 1893.
Melamed, *Break-up of Stereotype Phrases*: Melamed, E. Z., "Break-up of Stereotype Phrases as an Artistic Device in Biblical Poetry," *Studies in the Bible*, ed. H. Rabin. Jerusalem, 1961 (= *Scripta Hierosolymitana* 8), pp. 115-153.
Melamed, E. Z., "Comments on the Language of *Ābōth*," *Lešōnēnu*, 20 (1954), pp. 106-111 (in Hebrew).
——, "Hendiadys (ἓν διὰ δυοῖν) in the Bible," *Tarbiẕ*, 16 (1945), pp. 173-189 (in Hebrew).
de Menasce, J., "Mots d'emprunt et noms propres iraniens dans les nouveaux documents araméens," *BiOr*, 11 (1954), pp. 161-162.
Mendelsohn, *On Marriage in Alalakh*: Mendelsohn, I., "On Marriage in Alalakh," *Essays on Jewish Life and Thought Presented in Honor of S. W. Baron.* New York, 1959, pp. 351-357.
Mendelsohn, I., "On Slavery in Alalakh," *IEJ*, 5 (1955), pp. 65-72.
MGWG: *Monatschrift für Geschichte und Wissenschaft der Judentums.*
Milik, J. T., "Un contrat juif de l'an 134 après J.-C.," *RB*, 61 (1954), pp. 182-190.
——, "Deux documents inédits du désert de Juda," *Biblica*, 38 (1957), pp. 245-268.
——, review of Kraeling, *BP* in *RB*, 61 (1954), pp. 247-251.
Modrzejewski, J., review of Seidl, *ÄRg* in *BiOr*, 14 (1957), pp. 219-221.
Möller, *Eheverträge*: Möller, G., *Zwei ägyptische Ehevertrage aus vorsaïtischer Zeit.* Berlin, 1918. (=*APAW*, 3).
MSL: *Materialien zum Sumerischen Lexikon.*
MVAG: *Mitteilungen der Vorderasiatischen Gesellschaft.*

NA: Neo-Assyrian.
ND: tablets excavated at Nimrud (Kalhu).
Neufeld, E., "Socio-Economic Background of the Yōbēl and Šᵉmiṭṭā," *RSO*, 33 (1958), pp. 53-124.
Neusner, J., "Some Aspects of the Economic and Political Life of Babylonian Jewry, Ca. 160-220 C.E.," *PAAJR*, 31 (1963), pp. 165-196.
Nies, J. B., "A Pre-Sargonic Inscription on Limestone from Warka," *JAOS*, 38 (1918), pp. 188-196.
Nims, C. F., "The Term *HP*, 'Law, Right,' in Demotic," *JNES*, 7 (1948), pp. 243-260.
NKRA: Koschaker, P., *Neue keilschriftliche Rechtsurkunden aus der El-Amarna-Zeit.* Leipzig, 1928 (= *ASAW* 39).
Nöldeke, T., "Die aramäischen Papyri von Assuan," *ZA*, 20 (1907), pp. 130-150.
Nougayrol, J., "Guerre et paix à Ugarit," *Iraq*, 25 (1963), pp. 110-123.
——, *Le palais royal d'Ugarit* III. Paris, 1955 (= *MRS* 6).

——, *Le palais royal d'Ugarit* IV. Paris, 1956 (= *MRS* 9).
NRVU: Cf. San Nicolò and Ungnad.

OA: Old Akkadian.
OAs: Old Assyrian.
OB: Old Babylonian.
O'Callahghan, *Aram Naharaim*: O'Callaghan, R., *Aram Naharaim. A Contribution to the History of Upper Mesopotamia in the Second Millennium* B.C. Rome, 1948 (= *Analecta Orientalia* 26).
OIAS: *Oriental Institute (of the University of Chicago); Assyriological Studies.*
OLZ: *Orientalistiche Literaturzeitung.*
Oppenheim, L., "Ein Beitrag zum Kassitenproblem," *Analecta Orientalia*, 12 (1935), pp. 266-274.
Oppenheim, *Economic History*: Oppenheim, A. L., "A Bird's-Eye View of Mesopotamian Economic History," in *Trade and Market in the Early Empires*, ed. K. Polanyi, C. M. Arensberg, and H. W. Pearson. Glenco, Ill., 1957, pp. 27-37.
Oppenheim, *Der Eid*: Oppenheim, L., "Der Eid in den Rechtsurkunden aus Susa," *WZKM*, 43 (1936), pp. 242-262.
Oppenheim, A. L., "Idiomatic Akkadian (Lexicographical Researches)," *JAOS*, 61 (1941), pp. 251-271.
——, " 'Siege Documents' from Nippur," *Iraq*, 17 (1955), pp. 69-89.
Oppenheim, *Studien*: Oppenheim, L., "Studien zu den altbabylonischen Stadtrechten," *Or*, 4 (1935), pp. 145-174.
Or: *Orientalia.*

P: Poebel, A., *Babylonian Legal and Business Documents from the Time of the First Dynasty of Babylon.* Philadelphia, 1909 (= *BE* 6/2).
PAAJR: *Proceedings of the American Academy for Jewish Research.*
Parker, B., "The Nimrud Tablets, 1952—Business Documents," *Iraq*, 16 (1954), pp. 29-58.
Partsch-Sethe: Partsch, J., and Sethe, K., *Demotische Urkunden zum ägyptischen Bürgschaftsrechte vorzüglich der Ptolemäerzeit.* Leipzig, 1920 (= *ASAW* 32).
Pavlovský, V., review of Rabinowitz, J. J., *Jewish Law* in *Biblica*, 39 (1958), pp. 388-392.
Peiser, *KB* IV: Peiser, F. E., *Texte juristischen und geschäftlichen Inhalts.* Berlin, 1896.
Peiser, F. E., review of Staerk, W., *Die jüdisch-aramäischen Papyri von Assuan*, in *OLZ*, 10 (1907), pp. 622-627; *ibid.*; 11 (1908), pp. 24-26 and 73-79.
Peiser-Kohler, *Babylonischen Rechtsleben*: Peiser, F. E., and Kohler, J., *Aus dem Babylonischen Rechtsleben.* Four Vols. Leipzig, 1890-98.
Peiser-Kohler; cf. also HG.
PEQ: *Palestine Exploration Quarterly.*
Pestman: Pestman, P. W., *Marriage and Matrimonial Property in Ancient Egypt. A Contribution to establishing the legal position of the woman.* Leiden, 1961 (= *Papyrologica Lugduno-Batava* 9).
Petschow, *Kaufformulare*: Petschow, H., *Die neubabylonischen Kaufformulare.* Leipzig, 1939 (= *LRS* 118).
Petschow, *Pfandrecht*: Petschow, H., *Neubabylonisches Pfandrecht.* Berlin, 1956 (= *ASAW* 48/1).
Pick, H., "Drei neue Veröffentlichungen zu den Privaturkunden aus der Hammurabi-Zeit," *OLZ*, 11 (1908), pp. 315-318.
Pirenne, J., "Introduction à l'histoire du droit égyptien. Les trois cycles de l'histoire juridique et sociale de l'ancienne Égypte," *AHDO*, 2 (1938), pp. 11-62.
Pirenne, J., and Van de Walle, B., Cf. *DJE* 1.
Poebel, *Grammatik*: Poebel, A., *Grundzüge der sumerischen Grammatik.* Rostock, 1923.

Poebel, A., "The Tenses of the Intransitive Verb in Sumerian," *AJSL*, 50 (1934), pp. 143-170.
Pollock and Maitland: Pollock, F., and Maitland, F. W., *The History of English Law Before the Time of Edward I*. Second edition, Two Vols. Boston, 1899.
Porten: Porten, B., *Archives From Elephantine. The Life of an Ancient Jewish Military Colony*. To be published by the University of California Press, Spring, 1968.
Pringsheim, *Sale*: Pringsheim, F., *The Greek Law of Sale*. Weimar, 1950.
Pritsch, E., "Die aramäischen Urkunden," in the collective study "Zum gegenwärtigen Stand der juristischen Papyrusforschung," *ZVRW*, 60 (1958), pp. 99-117.
——, "Jüdische Rechtsurkunden aus Aegypten," *ZVRW*, 27 (1912), pp. 7-70.
PRU II: Virolleaud, C., *Le palais royal d'Ugarit*. Paris, 1957 (=*MRS* 7).
PRU III: Nougayrol, J., *Le palais royal d'Ugarit* III. Paris, 1955. (= *MRS* 6)
PRU IV: Nougayrol, J., *Le palais royal d'Ugarit* IV. Paris, 1956 (= *MRS* 9).
PSBA: *Proceedings of the Society of Biblical Archaeology*.

R: Ranke, H., *Babylonian Legal and Business Documents from the Time of the First Dynasty of Babylon chiefly from Sippar*. Philadelphia, 1906 (= *BE* 6/1).
RA: *Revue d'Assyriologie*.
Rabinowitz, J. J., "A Biblical Parallel to a Legal Formula from Ugarit", *VT*, 8 (1958), p. 95.
——, "A Clue to the Nabatean Contract from the Dead Sea Region", *BASOR*, 139 (1955), pp. 11-14.
Rabinowitz, *Jewish Elements*: Rabinowitz, J. J., "Jewish Elements in Babylonian Legal Formulae of the Persian Period," in *Sefer Asaf*, ed. U. Cassuto, J. Klausner, and J. Gutmann. Jerusalem, 1953, pp. 433-443 (in Hebrew).
Rabinowitz, *Jewish Law*: Rabinowitz, J. J., *Jewish Law: Its Influence on the Development of Legal Institutions*. New York, 1956.
Rabinowitz, *Legal History*: Rabinowitz, J. J., *Studies in Legal History*. Jerusalem, 1958.
Rabinowitz, J. J., "The Susa Tablets, the Bible and the Aramaic Papyri," *VT* 11 (1961), pp. 55-76.
Revillout, *Les origines égyptiennes*: Revillout, E., *Les origines égyptiennes du droit civil romain*. Paris, 1912.
Revillout, *Précis*: Revillout, E., *Précis du droit égyptien comparé aux autres droits de l'antiquité*. Two Vols. Paris, 1903.
Revillout, *Propriété*: Revillout, E., *La propriété ses démembrements, la possession et leurs transmissions en droits égyptien comparé aux autres droits de l'antiquité*. Paris, 1897.
RIDA: *Revue Internationale des Droits de l'Antiiquité*.
RIDA + AHDO: *Revue Internationale des Droits de l'Antiquité + Archives d'Histoire du Droit Oriental*.
Riftin: Riftin, A. P., *Staro-Vavilonski iuridicheski i administrativnye dokumenty v sobraniiakh*. Moscow, 1937.
RLA: *Reallexikon der Assyriologie*.
Rosenthal, *Aramaistische Forschung*: Rosenthal, F., *Die aramaistische Forschung seit Th. Nöldeke's Veröffentlichungen*. Leiden, 1939.
Rosenthal, *Concept of Freedom*: Rosenthal, F., *The Muslim Concept of Freedom Prior to the Nineteenth Century*. Leiden, 1960.
Rosenthal, *Grammar*: Rosenthal, F., *A Grammar of Biblical Aramaic*. Wiesbaden, 1961 (= *Porta Linguarum Orientalium* 5).
Rowton, *Permansive*: Rowton, M. B., "The Use of the Permansive in Classic Babylonian," *JNES*, 21 (1962), pp. 233-303.
RS: *Ras Shamra*.
RSO: *Rivista degli Studi Orientali*.

S: Texts from Sippar in the Constantinople Museum.

Sachau, E., *Aramäische Papyrus und Ostraka aus einer jüdischen Militär-Kolonie zu Elephantine. Altorientalische Sprachdenkmäler des 5. Jahrhunderts vor Chr.* Two Vols. Leipzig, 1911.

——, *Drei aramäische Papyrusurkunden aus Elephantine.* Berlin, 1907 (= *APAW*, 1907).

San Nicolò, M., "Zum *atru* und anderen Nebenleistungen des Käufers beim neubabylonischen Immobiliarkauf," *Or*, 16 (1947), pp. 273-302.

San Nicolò, *Beiträge*: San Nicolò, M., *Beiträge zur Rechtsgeschichte im Bereiche der keilschriftlichen Rechtsquellen.* Oslo, 1931 (= *Instituttet for sammenlignende Kulturforskning*, Serie A, 13).

San Nicolò, M., "Darlehen," in *RLA*, II, pp. 123-131.

——, "Eid," in *RLA*, II, pp. 305-315.

San Nicolò, *Schlussklauseln*: San Nicolò, M., *Die Schlussklauseln der altbabylonischen Kauf- und Tauschverträge. Ein Beitrag zur Geschichte des Barkaufes.* Munich, 1922 (= *Münchener Beiträge zur Papyrusforschung und antiken Rechtsgeschichte* 4).

San Nicolò-Petschow: San Nicolò, M., and Petschow, H., *Babylonische Rechtsurkunden aus dem 6. Jahrhundert v. Chr.* Munich, 1960 (= *ABAW* 51).

San Nicolò-Ungnad, *NRVU*: San Nicolò, M., and Ungnad, A., *Neubabylonische Rechts- und Verwaltungsurkunden.* Vol. I and Glossary. Leipzig, 1929-37.

Sayce, A. H., with the assistance of A. E., Cowley, *Aramaic Papyri Discovered at Assuan.* London, 1906.

SBAW: *Sitzungsberichte der Bayerischen Akademie der Wissenschaften.*

Scharff and Moortgart: Scharff, A., and Moortgart, A., *Ägypten und Vorderasien im Altertum.* Munich, 1950.

Scheil, V., *Actes juridiques susiens.* Three Vols. Paris, 1930-1933 (= *MDP* XXII, XXIII, XXIV).

——, "La promesse dans la prière babylonienne," *RA*, 12 (1915), pp. 65-72.

Slouschz, *Thesaurus*: Slouschz, N., *Thesaurus of Phoenician Inscriptions.* Tel-Aviv, 1942 (in Hebrew).

Schmökel, *Geschichte*: Schmökel, H., *Geschichte des alten Vorderasien.* Leiden, 1957 (= *Handbuch der Orientalistik* II/3).

Schorr, *Urkunden*: Schorr, M., *Urkunden des altbabylonischen Zivil- und Prozessrechts.* Leipzig, 1913 (= *VAB* 5).

Schott, R., "Die Eigentumsrechte der Buschmänner in Südafrika," *ZVRW*, 61 (1959), pp. 101-223.

Sedlàková, J., review of Rabinowitz, *Jewish Law*, in *BiOr*, 16 (1959), pp. 49-50.

Seidl, *ÄRg*: Seidl, E., *Ägyptische Rechtsgeschichte der Saitien- und Perserzeit.* Glückstadt-Hamburg-New York, 1956 (= *Ägyptologische Forschungen* 20).

Seidl, *Einführung*: Seidl, E., *Einführung in die ägyptische Rechtsgeschichte bis zum Ende des neuen Reiches. I. Juristischer Teil.* Third edition. Glückstadt-Hamburg-New York, 1956 (= *Ägyptologische Forschungen* 10).

Seidl, *PRg*: Seidl, E., *Ptolemäische Rechtsgeschichte.* Second, revised edition. Glückstadt-Hamburg-New York, 1962 (= *Ägyptologische Forschungen* 22).

Shore, A. F., and Smith, H. S., "Two Unpublished Demotic Documents from the Asyūṭ Archive," *JEA*, 45 (1959), pp. 52-60.

Simmons, S. D., "Early Old Babylonian Tablets from Ḥarmal and Elsewhere," *JCS*, 13 (1959), pp. 71-93 and 105-119; *ibid.* 14 (1960), pp. 23-32, pp. 49-55, and 75-87; *ibid.*, 15 (1961), pp. 49-58; *ibid.*, pp. 81-83.

Simmons, *Ḥarmal*: texts edited by Simmons in preceding entry.

SLB: *Studia ad tabulas cuneiformes collectas a F. M. Th. de Liagre Böhl pertinentia, Leiden.*

Sollberger, *Le système verbal*: Sollberger, E., *Le système verbal dans les inscriptions "royales" présargoniques de Lagaš.* Geneva, 1952.

SPAW: *Sitzungsberichte der Preussischen Akademie der Wissenschaften.*
Speiser, E. A., "Akkadian Documents from Ras Shamra," *JAOS*, 75 (1955), pp. 154-165.
——, "The Alalakh Tablets," *JAOS*, 74 (1954), pp. 18-25.
——, "The Case of the Obliging Servant," *JCS*, 8 (1954), pp. 98-105.
——, "Census and Ritual Expiation in Mari and Israel," *BASOR*, 149 (1958), pp. 17-25.
——, "Cultural Factors in Social Dynamics in the Near East," *Middle East Journal*, 7 (1953), pp. 133 ff.
——, "Cuneiform Law and the History of Civilization," *Proceedings of the American Philosophical Society*, 107 (1963), pp. 536-541.
——, "A Figurative Equivalent for Totality in Akkadian and West-Semitic," *JAOS*, 54 (1934), pp. 200-203.
——, "Leviticus and the Critics," *Kaufmann Jubilee Volume*, pp. 29-45.
——, *New Kirkuk Documents Relating to Family Laws*. New Haven, 1930 (=*AASOR* 10).
——, "Nuzi Marginalia," *Or*, 25 (1956), pp. 1-23.
——, "The Pitfalls of Polarity," *Language*, 14 (1938), pp. 187-202.
Speiser-Pfeiffer: Speiser, E. A., and Pfeiffer, R. H., *One Hundred New Selected Nuzi Texts*. New Haven, 1936 (= *AASOR* 16).
Staerk, W., *Alte und neue aramäische Papyri übersetzt und erklärt*. Bonn, 1912 (= *Lietzmann, Kleine Texte* 94).
——, *Aramäische Urkunden zur Geschichte des Judentums im* VI *und* V *Jahrhundert vor Chr., sprachlich und sachlich erklärt*. Bonn, 1908 (= *Lietzmann, Kleine Texte* 32).
——, *Die jüdisch-aramäischen Papyri von Assuan sprachlich und sachlich erklärt*. Bonn, 1907 (= *Lietzmann, Kleine Texte* 22/23).
Stamm, J. J., *Die akkadische Namengebung*. Leipzig, 1939 (= *MVAG* 44).
Starcky, J., "Une tablette araméene de l'an 34 de Nabuchodonosor (AO, 21.063)," *Syria*, 37 (1960), pp. 99-115.
Steele, F. R., *Nuzi Real Estate Transactions*. New Haven, 1943 (= *AOS* 25).
Steinmetzer, *Grenzsteine*: Steinmetzer, F. X., *Die babylonischen Kudurru (Grenzsteine) als Urkundenform*. Paderborn, 1922 (*Studien zur Geschichte und Kultur des Altertums* 11/4-5).
Steinmetzer, *Schenkungsurkunde*: Steinmetzer, F. X., "Eine Schenkungsurkunde des Konigs Melišichu," *Beiträge zur Assyriologie*, 8^2 (1910), pp. 1-38.
Steinwenter, *RKU*: Steinwenter, A., *Das Recht der koptischen Urkunden*. Munich, 1955 (= *Handbuch der Altertumwissenschaft*, Abteilung 10, 4/2).
Stephens, F. J., "Notes on Some Economic Texts of the Time of Urukagina," *RA*, 49 (1955), pp. 129-136.
Studia et Documenta: *Studia et documenta ad iura orientis antiqui pertinentia*. Brill, Leiden.
Symbolae Koschaker: *Symbolae ad iura orientis antiqui pertinentes Paulo Koschaker dedicatae*. Leiden, 1938 (= *Studia et Documenta* 2).
Szlechter, E., "Les tablettes juridiques datées du règne d'Abî-Ešuḫ conservées au Musée d'Art et d'Histoire de Genève," *JCS*, 7 (1953).
Szlechter, *Tablettes juridiques*: Szlechter, E., *Tablettes juridiques de la 1re dynastie de Babylonie conservées au Musée d'Art et d'Histoire de Genève*. Paris, 1958.

Tadmor, H., "The Campaigns of Sargon II of Assur: A Chronological-Historical Study," *JCS*, 12 (1958), pp. 22-40 and 77-100.
Talmon, *Synonymous Readings*: Talmon, S., "Synonymous Readings in the Textual Traditions of the Old Testament," *Studies in the Bible*, ed. H. Rabin. Jerusalem, 1961 (= *Scripta Hierosolymitana* 8), pp. 335-383.

Taubenschlag, R., "Das babylonische Recht in den griechischen Papyri," *JJP*, 7/8 (1953/54), pp. 169-185.
——, review of Rabinowitz, *Jewish Law* in *JJP*, 11 (1958), pp. 306 ff.
——, review of Rabinowitz, *Jewish Law* in *Kiryat Sefer*, 33 (1958), pp. 182-185.
TB: Babylonian Talmud.
TCL: *Textes Cunéiformes, Musée de Louvre*. Paris, 1910 ff.
TD: Thureau-Dangin, F., *Lettres et contrats de l'époque de la premiere dynastie babylonienne*. Paris, 1910.
Thureau-Dangin, F., "Un acte de donation de Marduk-zâkir-šumi," *RA*, 16 (1919), pp. 117-156.
——, "Trois contrats de Ras Shamra," *Syria*, 18 (1937), pp. 245-255.
The Torah: *The Five Books of Moses*, Jewish Publication Society. Philadelphia, 1962.
TP: Palestinian Talmud.
Tur-Sinai: Torczyner, N. H. (Tur-Sinai), *The Language and the Book*, Vol. I. Jerusalem, 1948 (in Hebrew).

UCP: *University of California Publications in Semitic Philology*.
UET: *Ur Excavation Texts*.
UM: *University of Pennsylvania, The University Museum, Publications of the Babylonian Section*.
Ungnad, *Aramäische Papyrus*: Ungnad, A., *Aramäische Papyrus aus Elephantine. Kleine Ausgabe unter Zugrundlegung von Eduard Sachau's Erstausgabe*. Leipzig, 1911 (= *Hilfsbücher zur Kunde des Alten Orients* 4).

VAB: *Vorderasiatische Bibliothek*.
Van Praag, *Droit matrimonial*: Van Praag, A., *Droit matrimonial assyro-babylonien*. Amsterdam, 1945 (= *Archaeologisch-historische Bijdragen, Allard Pierson Stichting* 12).
VAT: *Inventarbezeichnung der Tontafeln der Vorderasiatischen Abteilung der Staadlichen Museen zu Berlin*.
de Vaux, *Ancient Israel*: de Vaux, R., *Ancient Israel*. New York-Toronto-London, 1961.
Verger, A., "Note sul diritto dei papiri aramaici di elephantine," *Oriens Antiqua*, 3 (1964), pp. 47-59.
Vincent, *Religion*: Vincent, A., *La religion des judéo-araméens d'Éléphantine*. Paris, 1937.
Virolleaud, C., *Le palais royal d'Ugarit* II. Paris, 1957 (= *MRS* 7).
Volterra, E., "Lo affrancazione di schiavi nei documenti aramaici del V secoulo a. C.," *RSO*, 32 (1957), pp. 675-696 (= *Scritti in onore di Giuseppi Furlani* II).
——, *Diritto Romano e Diritti Orientali*. Bologna, 1937.
——, "Introduction à l'histoire du droit romain dans ses rapports avec l'orient," *AHDO*, 4 (1949), pp. 117-159.
——, "Osservazioni sul divorzio nei documenti aramaici," *Studi orientalistici in onore di Giorgio Levi Della Vida* II, pp. 586-600.
——, "Les rapports entre le droit romain et les droits de l'orient," *RIDA*, 2 (1955), pp. 135-155.
——, review of Kraeling, *BP* in *Iura*, 6 (1955), pp. 349-360.
——, review of Rabinowitz, *Jewish Law* in *Iura*, 8 (1957), pp. 546-558.
Von Soden, W., "Zum akkadischen Wörterbuch. 31-40," *Or*, 18 (1949), pp. 385-403.
Von Soden, *GaG*: Von Soden, W., *Grundriss der akkadischen Grammatik*. Rome, 1952 (= *Analecta Orientalia* 35).
Von Soden, W., review of *ARM* VI, XV and VIII in *Or*, 28 (1959), pp. 314-317.

——, review of Cardascia, G., *Les archives des Murašû* in *BiOr*, 11 (1954), pp. 205-207.
VS: *Vorderasiatische Schriftdenkmäler der Königlichen Museum zu Berlin.*
VT: *Vetus Testamentum.*

W: Waterman, L., *Business Documents of the Hammurabi Period from the British Museum.* London, 1916 (= *AJSL* 29 1913, pp. 145-204 and pp. 288-303; *ibid.*, 30 1913-14, pp. 48-73).
Wahrmund, *Ehe*: Wahrmund, L., *Das Institut der Ehe im Altertum.* Weimar, 1933.
Walther, *Gerichtswesen*: Walther, A., *Das altbabylonische Gerichtswesen.* Leipzig, 1917 (= *LSS* 4-6).
Weisman, *AT*: Weisman, D. J., *The Alalakh Tablets.* London, 1953 (= *Occasional Publications of the British Institute of Archaology at Ankara* 2).
WO: *Welt des Orients.*
WVDOG: *Wissenschaftliche Veröffentlichung der Deutschen Orient-Gesellschaft.*
WZKM: *Wiener Zeitschrift für die Kunde des Morgenlandes.*

Yadin, Y., "Expedition D — 'Cave of the Documents'," *BIES*, 26 (1962), pp. 204-236 (in Hebrew).
Yaron, R., "Aramaic Deeds of Conveyance," *Biblica*, 41 (1960), pp. 248-274 and 379-394.
——, "Aramaic Marriage Contracts from Elephantine," *JSS*, 3 (1958), pp. 1-39.
——, "Aramaic Marriage Contracts: Corrigenda and Addenda," *JSS*, 5 (1960), pp. 66-70.
——, "On Defension Clauses of some Oriental deeds of Sale and Lease, from Mesopotamia," *BiOr*, 15 (1958), pp. 15-22.
——, "On Divorce in Old Testament Times," *RIDA*, 4 (1957), pp. 117-128.
——, "Jewish Law and Other Legal Systems of Antiquity," *JSS*, 4 (1959), pp. 308-331.
——, "Notes on Aramaic Papyri," *RIDA*, 5 (1958), pp. 299-310.
——, "Notes on Aramaic Papyri II," *JNES*, 20 (1961), pp. 127-130.
LAP: Yaron, R., *The Law of the Aramaic Papyri.* Oxford, 1961.
LAP (Hebrew): Yaron, R., *HaMišpāṭ BᵉMismᵉḵeYēḇ* (The Law of the Elephantine Documents). Jerusalem, 1961.
——, review of *Les grottes de Murabbaʿât* in *JJS*, 11 (1960), pp. 157-171.
——, "A Royal Divorce at Ugarit," *Or*, 32 (1963), pp. 21-31.
——, "The Schema of the Aramaic Legal Documents," *JSS*, 2 (1957), pp. 33-61.
YBT: *Yale Oriental Series, Babylonian Texts.*

ZA: *Zeitschrift für Assyriologie.*
ZAS: *Zeitschrift für Ägyptische Sprache und Altertumskunde.*
ZDMG: *Zeitschrift der Deutschen Morgenländischen Gesellschaft.*
ZSS: *Zeitschrift der Savigny-Stiftung, romanistische Abteilung.*
ZVRW: *Zeitschrift für Vergleichende Rechtswissenschaft.*

GLOSSARIES

I. WEST-SEMITIC TERMS

(*asterisk indicates addendum*)

ʾb father, 55n
thk lbyt ʾbwh she shall go back to her father's house, 55n
ʾāḇ father, 55n
ʾbd to be lost, forfeit
mhrh yʾbd his bride-price shall be forfeit, 59, 181, 181*
ʾgrh deed, document, 187, 133 n5*
ʾdr month of Adar, 192
ʾăhūḇāh beloved (wife), 37n
ʾwṣr treasury, 52
ʾzt free (= Persian *azāta*)
ʾzt šbq to set free, 40n
ʾḥ brother
lʾ ʾyty ly . . . ʾḥ wʾḥh I have no (other) brother or sister (who is owner), 34n
ʾḥd to hold; to have
ʾḥd gšwrn fitted with beams, 34n
ʾnt šlṭ lmʾḥd you have the right to seize (wages), 56
ʾḥrn other, 34n
ywm ʾḥrn (tomorrow or) another day, 23n, 31n, 59, 184
ʾyš man, person, 33 f.
ʾyty there is
lʾ ʾyty ly I do not have (anyone who is owner of this land but you), 34n
ʾālāh oath containing imprecations
ʾalōṯ habbᵉrīṯ oaths containing imprecations that seal a covenant, 116n, 116 n3*
ʾlhtʾ the goddess, 32, 61
ʾm moreover, surely, 36
ʾmh slave-girl, 187
ʾmr to say; to command, 23n, 38, 43, 59
ʾmr npš ʾḥryt to command another person (to perform an illegal act), 38
wyʾmr lʾ yhbt lk and will say: 'I did not give it to you,' 23n
ʾmrn lh mṣryt it is called in Egyptian, 133n
ʾᵉmeṯ truth, faithfulness
beʾᵉmeṯ faithfully, 134*
ʾns force, coercion
bʾns by force, 138n
ʾnth wife, 34n, 59
ʾntw wifehood, marriage, 6, 133n
ʾāsūr forbidden, 37n
ʾʿp to be doubled, 184
ʾrʿ (unbuilt) land, 34n
ʾrq (a plot of) land, 34n

badanu body (Arabic)
fī ṣiḥḥah min ʿaqlihī wa-badanihī being of sound mind and body, 138n
by house, 34, 36 f., 55n, 56, 154n, 182
byt mlkʾ Government House, 56
thk lbyt ʾbwh she shall go back to her father's house, 55n
nšy bytn the slaves of our household, 133 n5*
bayit house
beḇēṯ ʾabīhā binʿūrēhā (while still) in the house of her father, before attaining her majority, 55n
bikkēr to recognize as the major heir, 37n
bēn son
ben hāʾăhūḇāh the son of the beloved wife, 37n
bnh to build
bny wtb bgw build (the land) and settle on it, 24, 25n
lʾ bnyh unbuilt (land), 34n
br son; cf. index of personal names.
br wbrh son or daughter, 34n, 37
br ḥwryn free man, 40n
brh daughter, 34n, 37, 39, 135
bārīʾ healthy man
mattᵉnaṯ bārīʾ the gift of a healthy man, 36n
bᵉrīṯ covenant, 116n, 116 n3*

ǧbr (*aǧbara*) to coerce (Arabic)
lā muǧbar not coerced, 138n
gēṭ document
gēṭ mᵉquššār double document (lit. tied document), 191n
grh to litigate, contest; to sue in a suit), 5
lʾ (ʾkhl) ʾgrnk dyn wdbb I will not (be able) to sue you in a formal

and the heart of the priest was glad, i.e., he agreed, 140n

ṭōḇāh happiness, joy; willingness
  beṭōḇāṯō šellō' beṭōḇāṯō willingly or unwillingly (lit. with his joy or with his sadness), 136n, 136 n1*

ṭyb to be good
  ṭb lbby/k my/your heart is satisfied, 51
  ṭyb lbby my heart is satisfied, cf. table of contents.
  hwṭbt lbby you have satisfied my heart, 25, 30, 32, 36, 46 ff., 50, 53, 71, 83, 123, 151n, 153 f., 157 f., 161

ṭ'n to load; to obligate (someone to take an oath), 32n

ybl to deliver, 52, 56

yhb to give
  yhb dmwhy to pay its value, price, 34 f., 46 f., 48 ff.
  yhb ksp to pay silver, 33
  yhb mhr to pay the bride-price, 51
  yhb 'l yd to consign, 52, 56 f.
  yhb brḥmn/(b)rḥmt/brḥmh to give in affection/as a gift, 25 f., 36, 38 f., 40 ff., 43, 128, 133-35, 185
  l' yhbt lk I did not give (it) to you, 23n
  lmn zy ṣbyt hbhy give it to whomever you want, 41
  zbn wyhb to sell and transfer, 34 f., 49, 152

ywm day; year(s)
  ywm 'ḥrn (tomorrow or) some other day, 23n, 31n, 59, 184, 183*
  mn ywm' znh (w)'d 'lm(n) from this day (and) forever, 30 f., 32, 34, 38, 31*

yōm day
  mēhayyōm ūl'aḥar mīṯāh from today and after death, 40n

yṭb: cf. *ṭyb*.

ykl: cf. *khl*.

yāḵōl to be able; to be allowed, 37n

ym' to take an oath, 32, 46, 61

yārad to go down
  hōrīḏ to exile, 119n (biblical and Canaanite)

yrt heir, 37n

yišraṯ lēḇāḇ honesty of mind, 134*

ytb to sit, dwell
  tb bgw settle on it (the land), 24 f.
  ytb bkrs'h (when the king) sat on his throne, 192

kibbēḏ to honor (a parent), 141*

kdb lying; forged, 182

khl to be able; to be allowed, 37n, 36 n2*
  l' 'khl 'grnk/'ršnk dyn I will not be able to sue you in a (formal) suit, 30, 32 f., 36, 38, 42, 49
  l' khl hwyt bydy I could not take care of myself, 39, 135

*kwh** window, 34n

kwt thus, so, 43n

kzy since, 43; when, 192

kzt like this, 43n (read: *kwt*)

kl everything
  kl šbw everything in it, 20n

kslw month of Kislew, 192

ksp silver; money, 33, 56, 61, 184, 187, 189
  zbn bksp to sell, 41n
  ntn bksp to sell, 42

k'n now (I want to take it back), 43

krh (*akraha*) to force (Arabic)
  lā mukrah not forced, 138n

kurhānā sickness (Syriac), 136 n1*

koraḥ unwillingness (lit. sickness, sadness), 136 n1*

ktb to write, 43, 188 f.

lb heart, mind
  blb' slym' with full (control of) mind, 138n

lbwš clothing, 61

lh'n to where ever, 55n

lāšōn language
  lešōn hedyōṭ the layman's formulary, 193

m'h military company of one hundred, 52

md'm anything; something, 76

mhr bride-price, 51, 59, 181

mohar bride-price, 51-57, 60n, 86, 163, 168

mwm'h oath, 32, 50, 61, 83

mw'h šmš east, 34n

mwt death, 25, 36, 40, 128, 135

mezummānīm ready cash, 51n

mḥr tomorrow
  mḥr 'w ywm 'ḥrn (if) tomorrow or another day, 23n, 31n, 59, 184, 183*

ʿdh congregation (?)
qwm bʿdh to stand up in the congregation (?), 59
ʿdh to pass away; to be removed
lhʿdyh to (illegally) remove (from someone's possession), 37
ʿdw
šṭr ʿdw deed of expropriation, seizure (?) (Nabatean), 37n
ʿṭyq old (document), 182
ʿṭr to remove, 126n, 126 n2* (Targum)
ʿiṭṭūr sōfᵉrīm scribal removal (of extra *waws*), 126 n2*
ʿṭrʾ Talmudic deed of slave-sale (lit. removal), 126n
ʿylʾ above; and up
lʿlʾ (from a penny's worth) and up, 76, 181
ʿl on; (outstanding) against; owed by, 36n, 184, 188n; (owed) to the account of, 35, 36n, 47, 53n, 76, 181, 188n
ʿldbr concerning, 38
ʿl yd (consigned) to, 52, 56 f.
ʿlyh upper part; north
l ʿlyh lh north of it, 34n
ʿll to enter
ʿl ʿlyk/y you/I have received (the *mohar*), 51 ff., 75, 173n
hnʿlt she brought in (her dowry), 58 f., 60n
ʿlm eternity; world
ʿd ʿlm(n) for ever, 30, 32, 34, 38
bʿlmʾ in the world, 76
ʿmd to stand, 116n
ʿpp to be doubled, 184
ʿṣ tree(s), 20n
ʿaqlu mind (Arabic)
fī ṣiḥḥah min ʿaqlihī being of sound mind, 138n
ʿqp to be doubled, 184 f.
yʿqp kspk wmrbyth your money and its interest shall be doubled, 184
ʿrr (*ʿrʿr*) to contest; to go to court; to stirr up a litigation, 182n, 188n
lqblh dyn ʿwry go to court against him, 182n
ʿšt to think about (kindly), 25, 36, 39, 39 n1*
ʿštt lk (*bḥyy*) I have turned my thoughts to you (during my lifetime), 25, 36, 39 f., 128, 134 f., 185
hiṯʿaššeṯ to think about (kindly), 39n

pṭr to set free, 40n
plg half (of a house), 38
plgn division, assignment (of a slave), 188
plny PN, 76
prwṭh penny, 76, 181
przl iron, 61
prs wages, 56
pāraq to unload; to solve a problem, 32n
prtrk Persian official, 5
pittaḥ to be open, 118n

ṣōn barzel a type of property, 193n
ṣbh to wish, want
lmn zy ṣbyt (give it) to whomever you want, 24, 41
thk lhʾn zy ṣbyt she shall go wherever she wants, 55n
ṣbw wish, volition
bṣbw npšy by my own volition, 138n
ṣdq to win (a suit)
yhk bdyn wlʾ yṣdq though he go to court, he will not win, 6, 185
ṣiḥḥah health (Arabic)
fī ṣiḥḥah min ʿaqlihī being of sound mind, 138n
ṣᵉmīṯūṯ sale beyond redemption, 20n

qbl to lodge a complaint
qbl ʿl PN lsgn wmrʾ to lodge a complaint against someone before prefect or lord, 37
(*l*)*qbl* because, 39, 135; at the disposal of (creditor), 37n; against, 182n, 188n
qdm before; (to secure property) in the possession of, 37n; (to remove property) from the possession of (*mn qdm*), 37; due to, owed to, 37n
qwm to stand up, to rise up, 116n
qwm bʿdh to stand up in the congregation (?), 59
qayyēm property *qdm* PN (to clear property of claims and) secure it in someone's possession, 37n
qām to stand up, rise up, 116n
*qām lᵉ*PN *lᵉmiqneh* to pass to

blbʾ šlymʾ wbdʿt šlmtʾ with sound heart and mind, 138n
šālōm (moral) integrity, 134*
šilšōm the day before yesterday, 184n
šm name
bšm concerning, in the matter of, 31n, 49, 182
šmʿ to listen to
lʾ yštmʿ lh he shall not be listened to; no heed shall be paid to him (in court), 43, 185
šnh year, 192
šrw/šrtʾ mealtime, 133n
tʾnym fig trees, 20n
tḥtyh lower part; south
tḥtyh lh south of it, 34n
tkwnh dowry, 51, 60n, 171
tom perfection, integrity, 134*
t^e^nai condition
t^e^nai māmōn monetary (secular) condition (in a rabbinic deed), 193n
tqp valid document (Nabatean), 193 n3*
trbṣ courtyard, 34n
try Egyptian building term, 38

II. CUNEIFORM TERMS

(*asterisk indicates addendum*)

batāqu to divide (inheritance property), 59n, 182
bâ'u to pass
kišāduma ana līti abāḫ I passed from neck to cheek (symbolic gestus at Khafajah), 100n
bēlu owner, 55n, 183n
bēl dēqti companion, 134, 134*
bēlu to own; to take possession of, 21*
eqlu ša-mu ba-a-lu the field is sold (and) taken into possession, 21*
biblu
ina bibil libbiya by my own resolve, 134 f.
biltu products, 87
bukānu (*bukannu*) pestle, 64*
bukānam (*šūtuq*) the pestle (was passed, i.e., the sale was concluded), 21n, 64-67, 74 f., 79, 96n, 101n
būnū face, countenance, gaze, 130f.
ina būnīšu namrūti with his bright gaze, shining countenance, 130, 135, 131 n1*

dabābu litigation, suit, proceedings; appeal
dēnu dabābu itti PN *gerû* to institute a formal suit against someone, 31n, 182, 31 n2*
tuāru u dabābu laššu there shall be no appeal for reversal, 19
dabābu to bring an action; to plead; to raise/lay a claim, 6, 38n, 185
šudbubu to instigate someone to raise a claim, 38n
damqu good, 33n*; sparkling, shining (eyes), 130, 135
damiq ana yāši it would be good for me (Amarna), 33n*
dannatu (*dannitu*) valid document, (19), 187, 189, 19 n3*, 187*, 188*
dapāru to sate the thirst (?), 117n
dārītu eternity
ana dārīti for eternity, 20, 31n
dayānu judge
dayānī kašādu to go before/approach the judges, 125
šarram u dayānam ul imaḫḫar he shall not approach king or judge, 37n
dēnšu dayānu lā išammû the judge will not listen (to his claim), 43n, 185
dīnu lawsuit, case, proceedings, claim; decree
dēnu dabābu itti PN *gerû* to institute a formal suit against someone, 31n, 182, 31 n2*
dīnam nummušu to stirr up a litigation; to institute proceedings, 188n
ina dēnišu idabbubma lā ilaqqi though he plead in his suit, he will not receive (anything), 6, 185
dēnšu dayānu lā išammû the judge will not listen to his claim/suit, 43n, 185
dīn ālim the decree of the 'city,' 121
duppur to remove oneself; to absent oneself (from service, 118-120; to relinquish (ownership rights), 21n, 117-120, 128, 158 f., 177; to be deprived of rights; disinherited, 118n, 119n
nasiḫ duppur he is disinherited, removed, 118n, 119n
zīzū mesû duppurū they have finished dividing; they have removed themselves, i.e., they are quit, 117 f., 117*
dūru continuation
ana dūr u pala for continuation or change, i.e., for all time, 183n, 183 n7*

ebēbu to be pure; to be free (from claims)
eb pure; free from claims, 127
ubbubu to purify; to free (from claims), 110, 124 f., 127
é . d ù . a built land, 18
egertu document, 187n
ekallu palace, 134, 134*
ekurru temple, 134*
elēlu to be pure; to be free (of claims)
el free (of claims), 127
eqlu e-el ša-mu ba-a-lu the field is clear, bought, and taken into possession, 21*
ullulu to purify, 110, 127
pūt PN *ullulu* to purify someone's forehead; to manumit, 110n
ellān from

hepû to break (a tablet); to cancel
ana ḫepî nadi/ana ḫīpi nadāt (the document) is to be broken/cancelled, 187n

ḫūdu joy; willingness
ina ḫūd libbišu in the joy of his heart, willingly, 41, 128 f., 131, 136, 139 f., 148 f.

ḫurāṣu gold
ištu pê adi hurāṣim zīzū gamrū they have finished dividing from straw to gold, 59n, 64, 182

huṣābu splinter, 59n, 182

id wages, 87

igāru wall
qadi igārātišu (a house) together with its walls, 34n
igār birītim a common wall, 84

ilu god
asak ilim akālum to eat the taboo of the god, 45n
ina awāt ili u šarri waṣû/elû to forfeit the protection of god and king, 183n

inanna now
u inanna ᶠPN *tirtaṣip bīta ann[â]* and now, let her rebuild this estate, 33 n3*

inim.bi al.til its transaction is completed, 67, 74, 75n, 79 f., 96n, 101n, 108n

īnu eye
īnā našû to lift up one's eyes; to consider, 134, 185
ina damqāti īnāšu naplusu to look at with his sparkling eyes; to consider favorably, 130, 135

iškinū supplementary payment in archaic sale, 106 f., 108n, 114n

išû to have
mīnâm elīya tīšû do you have any claim (outstanding) against me?, 176

kabātu
kubbutu to honor (a parent) (RS), 141*

kanāku to seal off (a port), 191

kānu to be firm
kunnu to confirm (someone's rights), 134
igārum ša gušūru kunnu a wall with beams in place, 34n

karānu vineyard, 20

kāru (*karru*) port; trading-station
karri māt Muṣur kan-gu aptēma I opened the sealed port of Egypt, 191, 191 n2*

kāru plate (?)
kāram akālum to eat (from the same) plate (?), 137, 137*

kaspu silver; money; price
kaspam (*gamram*) *šīm bītišu* the (complete) money/silver, the price of his house, 72 ff., 76, 122, 176
kaspu ana 4-tu-šu irabbi the money will bear interest at ¼ its value, 185
kaspu eṣip nadānu to pay back the money in double (as a fine), 184 f.
kaspu gammur complete money; full price, 20, 181
kaspu lā gammur the money was not complete, 31n
kaspu leqi the money has been received, 21*
kaspu ul nadin the money was not paid, 125
ana kaspi ul inamdin he shall not sell it for money, 41n, 134
qāssu/ina kasapšu illi he forfeits his money, 181
ākil kaspim the eater of the silver (the seller), 111 f.

kāsu cup
kāsam šatû to drink (from the same) cup (sale gestus at Mari), 137

kašādu to go before, to approach (the judges), 125

kīma equivalent to; in exchange for
bītam kīma bītim a house in exchange for (my) house, 176

kīnātu faithfulness
ina maḫar PN *ina kīnāti uzzuzu* to serve someone faithfully, 134, 134*

kīniš faithfully; steadfastly; kindly
kīniš naplusu to look at faithfully, steadfastly; to consider kindly, 132n; 131 n1*, 183*

kišādu neck
kišāduma ana līti abāḫ I passed from neck to cheek (sale gestus at Khafajah), 100n

ana maškāni ul išakkan he shall not give it as a pledge, 134
matēma when(ever); at some time
ina urkiš ina matēma (if) sometime in the future, 183
matmatma for all times, 183n
maṭû to be small
muṭṭû to diminish (the flock), 87
memēni something
memēni lā rēḫe nothing (of the price) is outstanding, 76 ff., 182
mesû to terminate (a transaction); to purify (?)
zīzū mesû duppurū they have finished dividing; they have removed themselves, i.e., they are quit, 117 f., 117*
dīnam mussû to determine a law suit; to clarify a law suit, 117*
*mḫṣ/*mḫš* to smash, 15n, 116n
migru agreement
ina migir libbišu with the agreement of his heart, 128, 129n
ina migir ramnišu with the agreement of his self/person, 129n
mīnummē whoever, 60n
(*ina*) *muḫḫi* (to raise a claim) against, 38n; (to come near) to the person of, 178; above, in addition to, 76
muṭīb libbi Marduk the one who makes the heart of Marduk glad; or—he who serves Marduk to his satisfaction, 141, 141*

nadānu to give; to donate; to sell
ana kaspi/rēmūti ul inamdin he shall not sell/give as a gift, 41n, 134
ana maṣṣartim nadānum to intrust, 78
ana šīmim nadānum to sell, 100n, 107n, 107 n4*
ina ḫūd libbišu nadānu to give willingly, 41, 128 f., 131, 136, 139 f., 148 f.
ina nar'amātišu nadānu to give voluntarily, 43, 64, 132 f., 139 ff.
batāqu nadānu to give as a division portion, 59n, (182)
nadānu u šuppû to transfer permanently, 19, 34n, 71
eqlu lā nadin the field was not sold/given, 23n
kaspu ul nadin the money was not paid, 125
nadītu *nadītu*-woman, 141*
nadû to throw; to place (a mark on a slave), 129; to be lax (in work), 119n
naḫālu to to assign a share of ancestral property (Mari), 137
nakāru
nukkuru to alienate, sell (RS), 60n, 61*
namāru to shine; to be bright
immerū zīmūšu his countenance became bright, 130
ina būnīšu namrūti with his bright gaze, 130, 135, 130*
napāšu to run far away (from service), 119n
nar'amātu affection; free will
ina nar'amātišu nadānu to give voluntarily, 43, 64, 132n, 133n, 139 ff., 139 n2*
nasāḫu to uproot; to transfer, deport, 118n; to cancel (claims), 118n; to disinherit, 119n; to absent oneself (from service), to depart, 119n; to pass (time), 119n
naṣ/zrat 3n
našû to lift, carry; to have, 104; to provide for, 39n, 39 n4*
našû nadānu to transfer (ownership/property) (RS), 20n
īnā našû to lift one's eyes; to consider (favorably), 134 f., 185
nekelmû to look at
ezziš nekelmû to look at with anger (a god), 132n
nesû to be/go far away, 118n
nibzu deed, receipt, 186
níg.ba an extra payment in archaic sale, 108, 111, 114
níg.diri an extra payment in archaic sale, 114n
níg.gar an extra payment in archaic sale, 114n
níg.šám sale-price, 108
nisḫātu a type of tax (Kültepe), 122n, 122 n1*
nišū personnel, slaves, 134
nišē bīti slaves, 133 n5*
nubazu deed, receipt, 186
nullānu deceipt
ul nullānu (this transaction took place) without deceipt (Mari), 138, 146

râmu to love, like; to want, wish, 43, 129, 132n
ana ša irammu inaddin he may give (it) to whomever he wants, 43, 132n, 133n, 137, 139
raṣāpu to build, 33 n3*
raṣāpu šūšubu to build and settle, 24n, 25n
rāšû creditor
rāšâ (ul) uzakki he has (not) satisfied the creditor, 83, (105), 125, 127n
rašû to acquire, 33n, 33 n3*; to institute a formal suit (?), 31n, 31 n2*
ša ta-ar-te-ši ᶠPN *ittiya* (all the goods) which she shall acquire with me (RS), 33n, 33 n3*
rēḫu to remain; to be outstanding
1½ *siqlu lā rēḫe* one shekel, one half shekel is not outstanding, 76, 173n, 182
memēne lā rēḫe nothing is outstanding, 76, 173n, 182
rêmu to be merciful; to bestow a gift, 41n, 43n, 132 f., 132n, 133n, 134 f.
šurêmu to cause (a god) to be merciful, 133n
rēmūtu beneficence; gift, 41n, 43n, 132 f., 132n, 133n, 134 f.
ana rēmūti ul irêm he shall not give it as a gift, 41n, 133n, 134 f.
rêqu to go far away; to remove oneself, 110; to absent oneself (from service), 118 ff.; to relinquish to relinquish/forfeit (rights), 118 ff., 128, 177 f., 181; to defect (from the cause of), 178*
lā iqerribū ullān eqlētišunu irtêqū they shall not approach (their property); they have removed themselves from their fields (Nuzi), 178.
rēšu head
rab rēši general, 134
rēš šarrūti period between the death of the old king and the coronation of the new one, 192
reʾû to tend (sheep), 87
riʾītu tending (of sheep), 129
riksātu contract, 87
ruāqu to go far away; to be lost (investments) (Kültepe), 118n, 181
rugummû claims, 82, 119n
rugummê maḫārum to receive one's claims (from the court), 82
rugummê nasāḫum to remove (reject) claims, 119n
ruššû ruddy; bright, shining
ina zīmūšu ruššûti with his features bright/ruddy, 130, 130*

saḫāru to turn towards
pān DN *saḫāru* to turn towards a god; to seek his presence (in order to petition), 132n
pānam suḫḫuru to turn one's face towards; to consider (favorably), 133n
sar measure of land, 18
sarāru to be false, forged, invalid
ṭuppu ša eliam sar the deed which appears is invalid, 182, 187n
serdu olive tree, 20
siba shepherd, 87
sikiltu goods belonging to the wife, nest-egg, 184n
sipirru scribe (West-Semitic loanword), 188*
sum to give, 109n

ṣamād/tu to become final property (RS),
eqlu ṣamid/t qadu serdīšu . . . qadu gabbu mimmūšu ana PN *ana dārīti* the field, together with its olive trees . . . and together with everything in it whatsoever, has become the final property of PN for all generations, 20
ṣarāpu to buy, acquire (?), 20, 23n, 71, 21*
ṣarip laqi (the property) is permanently transferred, 20, 71
ṣeḫēru to be small
ṣuḫḫuru to diminish (the flock), 87
ṣillu shade; protection, aegis
ša ina ṣilliya iqnû that which he acquired under my aegis, 20n, 134
ṣiptu interest, 71, 122
ṣītu the rising (of the sun)
ana ṣīt šamši pān PN *šakānum* to set someone's face in the direction of the rising sun (OB gestus of manumission), 110n

šēru 'dawn/morrow' or of *šerru* 'progeny')
ana dūr u pala ana šēršer(r)i for continuation or change; for all time/generations, 183n, 183 n7*
šērtu dawn; tomorrow
ina šērtu ina lidiš (if) tomorrow or the day after, 183, 186n, 183*
šēru dawn; morning after
urram šēram (if) tomorrow or the morning after, 31n, 45n, 183, 186n
še'û to turn towards (a deity in prayer), 132n
šīmātu salable property
šīmātim ša išāmu . . . ana gamertim išām the salable property he bought, he bought completely, 101n
šīmu sale transaction; sale-price; salable property, 76*, 107 n4*
šīmā išāmu šīmam gamram the buying he bought was a complete buying; the property he bought (was bought) as a final sale (Khafajah), 101n
šīmam gamram išām he bought a complete buying/as a final sale (Khafajah), 101n
ana šīmim gamrim kaspam išqul he weighed out the money as/at the full price (Khafajah), (100n), 101n
ana šīmišu gamrim kaspam išqul he weighed out the money as/at its full price (OB), 72, 100n, 101n
ana šīm gamir išām he bought at full price (Alalakh), 75, 123
ana šīm gamir iddin he sold at full price (MA), 19
ana šīmim nadānum to sell, 100n (Khafajah), 107n, 107 n4* (Old Akkadian Susa)
ana šīmim maḫārum to receive at a price; to sell, 107n (Old Akkadian)
ana sīmim gamrim šu.ti.a he received at full price, 100n (Khafajah), 107n (Old Akkadian Susa)
šipru message, 188*
šiqlu shekel, 76, 78, 121, 173n, 182 neither a shekel or a half shekel is outstanding, 76, 173n, 182
šu ba.ti he received, 100n, 107 ff. 111, 114
šub.lugal a soldier of low rank, 96n
šumma if, 183n
šuppû to purify (?); to effect a final sale; to transfer permanently, 19, 34n, 71 f.

tabālu to take away; to seize (property)
šutbulu to instigate (someone) to seize (property), 38n
taḫanātu benefaction, 133n
taḫḫu a type of soldier, 138
talittu offspring; increase (of the flock), 87
tamû to take an oath, 60n
tappūtu partnership, 59n, 124
tarāṣu to extend, turn
itruṣa būnīšu (the king) turned his face, 130 f.
tāru to return (in order to contest), 78
tuāru u dabābu laššu there shall be no appeal for reversal, 19
qāt PN *turru* to remove the hand of the seller; to cause a seller to relinquish ownership by tendering him full payment, 126
tayāru compassionate, forgiving (a god), 132n
tazkītu purification; liquidation (of common holdings); settlement, 124 f.
tēbibtu purification; liquidation (of common holdings); settlement, 124, 125n
terḫatu bride-price, 55n, 84 ff., 97n

ṭābu to be good, sweet, 136n; to be happy, 136
ašar ṭābušim (*elīšu ṭābu*) *inaddin* he may give to whomever he pleases, 136 f., 176, 141*
cf. *libbašu ṭāb/ṭūb/uṭīb.*
ṭūbātu joy, gladness; free will
ina ṭūbātišu ina nar'amātišu of his own free will and voluntarily (lit. in his joy and in his affection), 64, 137-139
ṭūbu joy, gladness; willingness
annûm ṭūbu ul nullānu this (transaction took place) willingly, without deceipt, 138, 146

III. OTHER

EGYPTIAN TERMS

GREEK TERMS

SOURCES

I. WEST-SEMITIC

(*asterisk indicates addendum*)

II. CUNEIFORM

III. EGYPTIAN

INDICES

I. SUBJECT INDEX

(*asterisk indicates addendum*)

II. INDEX OF PERSONAL NAMES

(*asterisk indicates addendum*)

III. INDEX OF MODERN SCHOLARS

(*asterisk indicates addendum*)

HANDBOOK OF ORIENTAL STUDIES
(HANDBUCH DER ORIENTALISTIK)

Section I: NEAR AND MIDDLE EAST
Abt. I: DER NAHE UND MITTLERE OSTEN

ISSN 0169-9423

Band 6. Geschichte der islamischen Länder

5/1. *Regierung und Verwaltung des Vorderen Orients in islamischer Zeit.* Mit Beiträgen von H. R. Idris und K. Röhrborn. 1979. ISBN 90 04 05915 6

5/2. *Regierung und Verwaltung des Vorderen Orients in islamischer Zeit.* 2. Mit Beiträgen von D. Sourdel und J. Bosch Vilá. 1988. ISBN 90 04 08550 5

6/1. *Wirtschaftsgeschichte des Vorderen Orients in islamischer Zeit.* Mit Beiträgen von B. Lewis, M. Rodinson, G. Baer, H. Müller, A. S. Ehrenkreutz, E. Ashtor, B. Spuler, A. K. S. Lambton, R. C. Cooper, B. Rosenberger, R. Arié, L. Bolens, T. Fahd. 1977. ISBN 90 04 04802 2

Band 7

Armenisch und *Kaukasische Sprachen.* Mit Beiträgen von G. Deeters, G. R. Solta, V. Inglisian. 1963. ISBN 90 04 00862 4

Band 8. Religion

1/1. *Religionsgeschichte des alten Orients.* Mit Beiträgen von E. Otto, O. Eissfeldt, H. Otten, J. Hempel. 1964. ISBN 90 04 00863 2

1/2/2/1. Boyce, M. *A History of Zoroastrianism. The Early Period.* Rev. ed. 1989. ISBN 90 04 08847 4

1/2/2/2. Boyce, M. *A History of Zoroastrianism. Under the Achaemenians.* 1982. ISBN 90 04 06506 7

1/2/2/3. Boyce, M. and Grenet, F. *A History of Zoroastrianism. Zoroastrianism under Macedonian and Roman Rule.* With a Contribution by R. Beck. 1991. ISBN 90 04 09271 4

2. *Religionsgeschichte des Orients in der Zeit der Weltreligionen.* Mit Beiträgen von A. Adam, A. J. Arberry, E. L. Dietrich, J. W. Fück, A. von Gabain, J. Leipoldt, B. Spuler, R. Strothman, G. Widengren. 1961. ISBN 90 04 00864 0

Ergänzungsband 1

1. Hinz, W. *Islamische Maße und Gewichte umgerechnet ins metrische System.* Nachdruck der Erstausgabe (1955) mit Zusätzen und Berichtigungen. 1970. ISBN 90 04 00865 9

Ergänzungsband 2

1. Grohmann, A. *Arabische Chronologie* und *Arabische Papyruskunde.* Mit Beiträgen von J. Mayr und W. C. Till. 1966. ISBN 90 04 00866 7
2. Khoury, R. G. *Chrestomathie de papyrologie arabe.* Documents relatifs à la vie privée, sociale et administrative dans les premiers siècles islamiques. 1992. ISBN 90 04 09551 9

Ergänzungsband 3

Orientalisches Recht. Mit Beiträgen von E. Seidl, V. Korosc, E. Pritsch, O. Spies, E. Tyan, J. Baz, Ch. Chehata, Ch. Samaran, J. Roussier, J. Lapanne-Joinville, S. Ş. Ansay. 1964. ISBN 90 04 00867 5

Ergänzungsband 5

1/1. Borger, R. *Einleitung in die assyrischen Königsinschriften.* 1. Das zweite Jahrtausend vor Chr. Mit Verbesserungen und Zusätzen. Nachdruck der Erstausgabe (1961). 1964. ISBN 90 04 00869 1

1/2. Schramm, W. *Einleitung in die assyrischen Königsinschriften.* 2. 934-722 v. Chr. 1973. ISBN 90 04 03783 7

Ergänzungsband 6

1. Ullmann, M. *Die Medizin im Islam.* 1970. ISBN 90 04 00870 5
2. Ullmann, M. *Die Natur- und Geheimwissenschaften im Islam.* 1972. ISBN 90 04 03423 4

Ergänzungsband 7

Gomaa, I. *A Historical Chart of the Muslim World.* 1972. ISBN 90 04 03333 5

Ergänzungsband 8

Kornrumpf, H.-J. *Osmanische Bibliographie mit besonderer Berücksichtigung der Türkei in Europa.* Unter Mitarbeit von J. Kornrumpf. 1973. ISBN 90 04 03549 4

Ergänzungsband 9

Firro, K. M. *A History of the Druzes.* 1992. ISBN 90 04 09437 7

Band 10

Strijp, R. *Cultural Anthropology of the Middle East. A Bibliography.* Vol. 1: 1965-1987. 1992. ISBN 90 04 09604 3

Band 11

Endress, G. & Gutas, D. (eds.). *A Greek and Arabic Lexicon.* (*GALex*). Materials for a Dictionary of the Mediæval Translations from Greek into Arabic.

Fascicle 1. Introduction—Sources—ʿ – ʿ-kh-r. Compiled by G. Endress & D. Gutas, with the assistance of K. Alshut, R. Arnzen, Chr. Hein, St. Pohl, M. Schmeink. 1992. ISBN 90 04 09494 6

Fascicle 2. ʿ-kh-r – ʿ-ṣ-l. Compiled by G. Endress & D. Gutas, with the assistance of K. Alshut, R. Arnzen, Chr. Hein, St. Pohl, M. Schmeink. 1993. ISBN 90 04 09893 3

Fascicle 3. ʿ-ṣ-l – ʿ-l-y. Compiled by G. Endress, D. Gutas & R. Arnzen, with the assistance of Chr. Hein, St. Pohl. 1995. ISBN 90 04 10216 7

Fascicle 4. Ilā – inna. Compiled by R. Arnzen, G. Endress & D. Gutas, with the assistance of Chr. Hein & J. Thielmann. 1997. ISBN 90 04 10489 5.

Band 12

Jayyusi, S. K. (ed.). *The Legacy of Muslim Spain.* Chief consultant to the editor, M. Marín. 2nd ed. 1994. ISBN 90 04 09599 3

Band 13

Hunwick, J. O. and O'Fahey, R. S. (eds.). *Arabic Literature of Africa.* Editorial Consultant: Albrecht Hofheinz.

Volume I. *The Writings of Eastern Sudanic Africa to c. 1900.* Compiled by R. S. O'Fahey, with the assistance of M. I. Abu Salim, A. Hofheinz, Y. M. Ibrahim, B. Radtke and K. S. Vikør. 1994. ISBN 90 04 09450 4

Volume II. *The Writings of Central Sudanic Africa.* Compiled by John O. Hunwick, with the assistance of Razaq Abubakre, Hamidu Bobboyi, Roman Loimeier, Stefan Reichmuth and Muhammad Sani Umar. 1995. ISBN 90 04 10494 1

Band 14

Decker, W. und Herb, M. *Bildatlas zum Sport im alten Ägypten. Corpus der bildlichen Quellen zu Leibesübungen, Spiel, Jagd, Tanz und verwandten Themen.* Bd.1: Text. Bd. 2: Ab-bildungen. 1994. ISBN 90 04 09974 3 *(Set)*

Band 15

Haas, V. *Geschichte der hethitischen Religion.* 1994. ISBN 90 04 09799 6

Band 16

Neusner, J. (ed.). *Judaism in Late Antiquity.* Part One: The Literary and Archaeological Sources. 1994. ISBN 90 04 10129 2

Band 17

Neusner, J. (ed.). *Judaism in Late Antiquity.* Part Two: Historical Syntheses. 1994. ISBN 90 04 09799 6

Band 18

Orel, V. E. and Stolbova, O. V. (eds.). *Hamito-Semitic Etymological Dictionary.* Materials for a Reconstruction. 1994. ISBN 90 04 10051 2

Band 19

al-Zwaini, L. and Peters, R. *A Bibliography of Islamic Law, 1980-1993.* 1994. ISBN 90 04 10009 1

Band 20

Krings, V. (éd.). *La civilisation phénicienne et punique.* Manuel de recherche. 1995. ISBN 90 04 10068 7

Band 21

Hoftijzer, J. and Jongeling, K. *Dictionary of the North-West Semitic Inscriptions.* With appendices by R.C. Steiner, A. Mosak Moshavi and B. Porten. 1995. 2 Parts.
ISBN *Set (2 Parts)* 90 04 09821 6 Part One: ʿ - L. ISBN 90 04 09817 8 Part Two: M - T. ISBN 90 04 9820 8.

Band 22

Lagarde, M. *Index du Grand Commentaire de Faḫr al-Dīn al-Rāzī.* 1996. ISBN 90 04 10362 7

Band 23

Kinberg, N. *A Lexicon of al-Farrā''s Terminology in his Qur'ān Commentary.* With Full Definitions, English Summaries and Extensive Citations. 1996. ISBN 90 04 10421 6

Band 24

Fähnrich, H. und Sardshweladse, S. *Etymologisches Wörterbuch der Kartwel-Sprachen.* 1995. ISBN 90 04 10444 5

Band 25
Rainey, A.F. *Canaanite in the Amarna Tablets.* A Linguistic Analysis of the Mixed Dialect used by Scribes from Canaan. 1996. ISBN *Set (4 Volumes)* 90 04 10503 4
Volume I. Orthography, Phonology. Morphosyntactic Analysis of the Pronouns, Nouns, Numerals. ISBN 90 04 10521 2 Volume II. Morphosyntactic Analysis of the Verbal System. ISBN 90 04 10522 0 Volume III. Morphosyntactic Analysis of the Particles and Adverbs. ISBN 90 04 10523 9 Volume IV. References and Index of Texts Cited. ISBN 90 04 10524 7
Band 26
Halm, H. *The Empire of the Mahdi.* The Rise of the Fatimids. Translated from the German by M. Bonner. 1996. ISBN 90 04 10056 3
Band 27
Strijp, R. *Cultural Anthropology of the Middle East.* A Bibliography. Vol. 2: 1988-1992. 1997. ISBN 90 04 010745 2
Band 28
Sivan, D. *A Grammar of the Ugaritic Language.* 1997. ISBN 90 04 10614 6
Band 29
Corriente, F. *A Dictionary of Andalusi Arabic.* 1997. ISBN 90 04 09846 1
Band 30
Sharon, M. *Corpus Inscriptionum Arabicarum Palaestinae (CIAP).* Vol. 1: A. 1997. ISBN 90 04 010745 2 Vol.1: B. 1999. ISBN 90 04 110836
Band 31
Török, L. *The Kingdom of Kush.* Handbook of the Napatan-Meroitic Civilization. 1997. ISBN 90 04 010448 8
Band 32
Muraoka, T. and Porten, B. *A Grammar of Egyptian Aramaic.* 1998. ISBN 90 04 10499 2
Band 33
Gessel, B.H.L. van. *Onomasticon of the Hittite Pantheon.* 1998. ISBN *Set (2 parts)* 90 04 10809 2
Band 34
Klengel, H. *Geschichte des hethitischen Reiches* 1998. ISBN 90 04 10201 9
Band 35
Hachlili, R. *Ancient Jewish Art and Archaeology in the Diaspora* 1998. ISBN 90 04 10878 5
Band 36
Westendorf, W. *Handbuch der altägyptischen Medizin.* 1999. ISBN *Set (2 Bände)* 90 04 10319 8
Band 37
Civil, M. *Mesopotamian Lexicography.* 1999. ISBN 90 04 11007 0
Band 38
Siegelová, J. and Souček, V. *Systematische Bibliographie der Hethitologie.* 1999. ISBN *Set (3 Bände)* 90 04 11205 7
Band 39
Watson, W.G.E. and Wyatt, N. *Handbook of Ugaritic Studies.* 1999. ISBN 90 04 10988 9
Band 40
Neusner, J. *Judaism in Late Antiquity, III,1.* 1999. ISBN 90 04 11186 7
Band 41
Neusner, J. *Judaism in Late Antiquity, III,2.* 1999. ISBN 90 04 11282 0
Band 42
Drijvers, H.J.W. and Healey, J.F. *The Old Syriac Inscriptions of Edessa and Osrhoene.* 1999. ISBN 90 04 11284 7
Band 43
Daiber, H. *Bibliography of Philosophical Thought in Islam.* 2 Volumes. ISBN *Set (2 Volumes)* 90 04 11347 9
Volume I. Alphabetical List of Publications 1999. ISBN 90 04 09648 5
Volume II. Index of Names, Terms and Topics. 1999. ISBN 90 04 11348 7
Band 44
Hunger, H. and Pingree, D. *Astral Sciences in Mesopotamia.* 1999. ISBN 90 04 10127 6
Band 45
Neusner, J. *The Mishnah.* Religious Perspectives 1999. ISBN 90 04 11492 0

Band 46
Neusner, J. *The Mishnah.* Social Perspectives 1999. ISBN 90 04 11491 2
Band 47
Khan, G. *A Grammar of Neo-Aramaic.* 1999. ISBN 90 04 11510 2
Band 48
Takács, G. *Etymological Dictionary of Egyptian.* Vol. 1. 1999. ISBN 90 04 11538 2
Takács, G. *Etymological Dictionary of Egyptian.* Vol. 2. 2001. ISBN 90 04 12121 8
Band 49
Avery-Peck, A.J. and Neusner, J. *Judaism in Late Antiquity IV.* 2000. ISBN 90 04 11262 6
Band 50
Tal, A. *A Dictionary of Samaritan Aramaic.* (2 Volumes) 2000. ISBN 90 04 11858 6 (dl. 1) ISBN 90 04 11859 4 (dl. 2) ISBN 90 04 11645 1 (set)
Band 51
Holes, C. *Dialect, Culture, and Society in Eastern Arabia.* Vol. 1 : Glossary 2001. ISBN 90 04 10763 0
Band 52
Jong, R.E. de. *A Grammar of the Bedouin Dialects of the Northern Sinai Littoral.* Bridging the Linguistic Gap between the Eastern and Western Arab World. 2000. ISBN 90 04 11868 3
Band 53
Avery-Peck, A.J. and Neusner, J. *Judaism in Late Antiquity III,3.* Where we stand: Issues and Debates in Ancient Judaism. 2000. ISBN 90 04 11892 6
Band 54
Krahmalkov, Ch. R. *A Phoenician-Punic Grammar.* 2001. ISBN 90 04 11771 7
Band 55
Avery-Peck, A.J. and Neusner, J. *Judaism in Late Antiquity III,4.* Where we stand: Issues and Debates in Ancient Judaism.. *The Special Problem of the Synagogue.* 2001. ISBN 90 04 12000 9.
Band 56
Avery-Peck, A.J., Neusner, J., and Chilton, B. *Judaism in Late Antiquity V,1.* The Judaism of Qumran: A Systemic Reading of the Dead Sea Scrolls. *Theory of Israel.* 2001. ISBN 90 04 12001 7
Band 57
Avery-Peck, A.J., Neusner, J., and Chilton, B. *Judaism in Late Antiquity V,2.* The Judaism of Qumran: A Systemic Reading of the Dead Sea Scrolls. *World View, Comparing Judaisms.* 2001. ISBN 90 04 12003 3
Band 58
Gacek, A. *The Arabic manuscript tradition.* A Glossary of Technical Terms and Bibliography. 2001. ISBN 90 04 12061 0
Band 60
Marzolph, U. *Narrative illustration in Persian lithographed books.* 2001. ISBN 90 04 12100 5
Band 61
Zammit, M.R. *A Comparative Lexical Study of Qur'ānic Arabic.* 2002. ISBN 90 04 11801 2
Band 62
Grossmann, P. *Christliche Architektur in Ägypten.* 2002. ISBN 90 04 12128 5
Band 63
Weipert, R. *Classical Arabic Philology and Poetry.* A Bibliographical Handbook of Important Editions from 1960 to 2000. 2002 ISBN 90 04 12342 3
Band 64
Collins, B.J. *A History of the Animal World in the Ancient Near East.* 2002. ISBN 90 09 12126 9
Band 65
Avery-Peck, A.J. and Neusner, J. *The Mishnah in Contemporary Perspective.* Part I. 2002. ISBN 90 09 12515 9
Band 66
Muffs, Y. *Studies in the Aramaic Legal Papyri from Elephantine.* 2003. ISBN 90 04 12868 9